INTERNATIONAL BANKING
in the 19th and 20th Centuries

INTERNATIONAL BANKING
in the 19th and 20th Centuries

KARL ERICH BORN

Translated by Volker R. Berghahn

St. Martin's Press
New York

Born, Karl Erich
    International banking in the 19th and 20th centuries.
    1. Finance — History.
    2. Money — History.
    3. Banks and banking — History.
    4. Banks and banking, International — History.
    I. Title.
    HG171.B6713 1983   332'.09   82—42715

ISBN 0—312—41975—9

Printed in Great Britain
First published in the United States of America in 1983

Contents

Introduction

This book is designed to present an historical synthesis of the basic problems and developments of the monetary and credit system during the 19th and 20th centuries. It covers the national characteristics and the international relations of banking in the most important industrial and commercial countries. It is not the intention to discuss every bank in every country, as this is not a reference book in the strict sense.

The first of the questions which this book addresses and seeks to answer concerns the development and significance of monetary systems and monetary policy in modern national economies and in the world economy. Secondly, we shall have to describe the emergence and structures of various types of banks (private bankers, public banks, state-owned banks, joint-stock banks, savings banks, credit co-operatives and others). What were the decisive economic, social and political influences behind their development? This will be followed by an examination of the financing of railway construction in the 19th century and of industrialization. In the closing years of the 19th century, the period of rapid industrialization was paralleled by a concentration movement. There occurred the formation of cartels, syndicates, concerns and trusts. What role did the major banks play as intermediaries and initiators in this process? There was also a strong merger movement and a great accumulation of power within the banking sector itself. Accordingly the emergence of banking empires, banking concerns and banking groups and their spheres of influence will be traced within the relevant periods of the 19th and 20th centuries. The dramatic events in the history of the credit system are, of course, the great banking crises. Their causes, courses and consequences will also be discussed. International capital relations are a key problem of the world economy, and we shall have to describe the direction and volume of international capital movements against the background of their economic and political causes and repercussions. In the course of this, the relationship between banks and foreign policy will be examined in greater detail in certain typical cases, such as the Suez Canal and the Baghdad Railway projects. Finally, this book explores the special development and structure of banking systems in several major industrial and commercial countries. Thus, on the whole, our historical synthesis focuses on the economic and political aspects of banking, with questions of industrial management and the credit economy taking second place.

There is a further limitation. Our analysis relates only to those highly industrialized countries which have a market economy and play a special role in the world economy. The second largest industrial power in the world today, the Soviet Union, is not considered here because, given her centrally administered economy, her financial institutions are no more than money collection centres and counting houses for the large state-controlled economy. To be sure, financing problems arise in Russia as well; but they belong to the field of governmental planning and fiscal policy and not to the functioning of banks which act and operate independently. Consequently, the history of money institutions in states with a centrally administered economy belongs less to a history of banking than to a history of fiscal administration and state-economic planning. This explains why this analysis comprises only the banking systems of capitalist countries like Britain, France, Germany, the United States and Japan.

I Currency and Monetary History in the 19th Century

1. From Silver and Bimetal Currency to the Gold Standard

At the beginning of the 19th century three different types of currency systems existed side-by-side. Most countries still maintained the old silver currency and only a few, but significantly the economically strongest, had replaced the silver standard with another currency system: the double currency or the gold currency.

Britain was the first country to adopt the gold standard and the change-over took almost a century. At first gold coins (guineas), struck since 1663, replaced silver coins in business transactions. The fact that gold coins had become predominant was recognised by law in 1774, when they were declared an unrestricted legal tender, whereas silver coins could be accepted in payments to a limit of £25. The transition to a legal gold currency was completed in 1816. Thenceforth silver money was admitted only in small coin, not exceeding 40 shillings.

The United States (since 1792) and France (since 1803) had a double currency standard. In both countries gold and silver coins were legal tender and the exchange ratios between the gold and silver dollar and the gold and silver franc were laid down by law and made inflexible. In 1865 Italy, Belgium and Switzerland joined this system, having reached agreement with France, in the Latin Coinage Convention, on a monetary standard and the reciprocal acceptance of coins. This standard specified how many monetary units were to be minted from a given amount of gold and silver. Greece joined the Latin Coinage Convention in 1868, whereas Spain and Rumania adopted the French monetary standard and the double currency standard without formal agreement.

All other countries, on the other hand, maintained a silver currency, and did so with greatly differing monetary standards. Within the German Confederation, which was founded in 1815, there were nine different standards in existence. The *Zollverein* provided the impetus for this multiplicity of currencies to be simplified, and the *Zollverein* Treaty of 22 March 1833 stipulated that all coins, weights and measures be standardized in the member states. Eventually, under the terms of the Dresden Coinage Agreement of 1838, two currency areas were formed within the *Zollverein*: the North-German thaler area and the South-German gulden area. At the same time a fixed ratio between the thaler and the gulden standards was established. It provided for 14 Prussian thalers or 24.5 gulden to be coined from one *Kölnische Mark* of silver, the *Mark* being an ancient unit of weight equalling 233.8555 grams.

Until the middle of the 19th century gold reserves were rather limited and would have been totally insufficient for a general gold currency had not large gold fields been discovered in Australia in 1848 and in California in 1852. At first the increased amount of gold available threatened its role as a currency metal, as its price fell in the wake of greatly increased supply. In France Michel Chevalier, one of the leading theoreticians of the French Free Trade Movement, was demanding a return to a pure silver currency as late as 1859. However, actual developments took the opposite course. Silver lost out against gold.

In the countries with a double currency standard a discrepancy arose between the market value and the legally fixed coinage value of gold and silver. Silver became more expensive in relation to gold as its market value remained stable, whereas the market value of gold declined on account of the increased supply. But the official exchange ratio between gold and silver coins remained unchanged. It was more profitable therefore for those making payments to do so with gold coins — i.e. with coins of the metal whose value was declining. Silver coins, on the other hand, were being hoarded because their value was rising in relation to gold. Thus, by the 1860s, the countries with a double currency standard — the United States, France and the member states of the Latin Coinage Convention — had, in practice, generally accepted a gold currency. In this way other countries, and the German states in particular, were given an incentive to change over to gold as well.

In Germany the initiative to introduce a gold currency was taken by the *Kongress deutscher Volkswirte* (Congress of German Economists), the *Vereinigung der Freihändler* (Union of Free Traders), the *Deutscher Handelstag* (German Commercial Assembly) and the *Vereinigung der deutschen Handelskammern* (Association of German Chambers of Commerce). Of the parliamentarians, it was Ludwig Bamberger who became the foremost advocate of the gold standard. The transition to the gold currency was facilitated by Germany's victorious war against France in 1870; for France settled the war indemnity of five milliard francs, imposed on her by the Treaty of Frankfurt (10 May 1871), by paying 220 million marks in gold coins and about 500 million marks in bills of exchange, which were made out in pounds sterling and thus convertible into gold. On the strength of the Coinage Act of 9 July 1873, the mark was declared the currency unit for the new German Reich and the gold standard was introduced at the same time. However, the German gold standard was to remain a 'limping gold currency' for over 30 years, since the existing silver coins maintained their full value until 1907.

At about the same time, France and her partners in the Latin Coinage Convention, which had already given preference to gold coins in business transactions, also introduced the gold standard by law (between 1874 and 1878). Like Germany, the member countries of the Latin Coinage Convention had a 'limping gold standard' at first, since silver coins kept their full value until the turn of the century.

In the United States just as in other double currency standard countries, the gold currency had become generally accepted in practice, and the minting of silver coins was therefore suspended in 1873. But pressure from the silver producers and dealers forced the United States to return to bimetallism once again. In 1878, the agitation of the bimetallist lobby met with success, and the American Congress made it a legal requirement for the Treasury Department to buy four million dollars worth of silver each month and mint coins or issue silver certificates, i.e. to write out orders for a certain amount in silver coins. The parties with a vested interest in silver even succeeded in pushing through the Sherman Silver Purchase Act of 1890, which allowed silver certificates to be exchanged for gold at the Treasury Department. Meanwhile the price of gold had stabilized once again, whereas that of silver had fallen sharply after 1877, enabling the owners of silver certificates to make handsome profits by exchanging the nominal amount of their certificates for gold. This caused the Treasury Department's gold reserves to dwindle so rapidly that, in order to maintain U.S. monetary gold reserves, the Sherman Silver Purchase Act had to be repealed in 1893. But it was not until after 1900 that the opposition by those with an interest in silver was finally overcome, so that the gold currency could be legally introduced in the United States with the passage of the Gold Standard Act. During the last decade of the 19th century, the Netherlands, Austria-Hungary, Russia and Japan also adopted the gold standard.

Thus, around 1900, all the countries of commercial significance were on the gold standard. This gold standard was a gold currency circulation standard until 1914, which meant that the gold currency metal circulated in the form of gold coins as a means of payment. In so far as bank notes were in circulation, the banks which issued them had to convert them on demand into gold coins or into the corresponding amount of bullion. The general gold standard facilitated the emergence of the modern world market economy and the intensification of international trade, as did the new technological developments in transport and communications, such as railways, steamship navigation and telegraphy. The gold parities of monetary units remained unchanged until 1914; the exchange rates were free, but remained quite stable between the currencies.

2. The Development of the Bank Note into Legal Tender

In the monetary history of the 19th century, another course of events was of equal significance to the introduction of the gold standard and, indeed, much more far-reaching in its long-term consequences: the development of the bank note into legal tender, into ready money. Unlike gold and silver coins, bank notes were not regarded as ready money right up to the late 19th century and in Germany, Switzerland and the United States not even to the beginning of our own. But bank notes did not constitute paper money; only cash vouchers put into circulation by the state were considered as such, as for example, the *assignats* during the French Revolution, the

Austrian 'Viennese Currency' or the 'greenbacks' issued by the American Treasury Department during the War of Sucession. Bank Notes were neither ready money nor paper money. They simply represented a promise by the issuing bank to pay.

Bank Notes and Issuing Banks in England until the Mid-19th Century

The bank note came into use in England in the course of the 17th century. At that time wealthy individuals began to leave their money and gold in safe deposit with a money-changer or a goldsmith. Certificates were issued for the money or gold deposited. These notes — they were called a 'goldsmith's note' or a 'banker's note' — represented an instantly realizable claim, and so were used as a convenient means of payment which could easily be carried around. Naturally, they could only be used within a limited area; for the individual accepting such notes in payment wished to be able to convert them at any time into money or gold at the money-changer or goldsmith who had issued them.

Since the deposit certificates, i.e. the notes, were never all presented for payment at the same time, the money-changers and goldsmiths were able to issue more notes than they had money or gold in their deposit. The money-changers and goldsmiths obtained credit in this way, but this also enabled them to grant their customers more credit than they had available in cash; for they gave the credits in bank notes. Thus arose the business of 'bankers'; they were the people who financed their credit operations by accepting deposits (in coin or gold) and by issuing notes.

The Bank of England — founded in 1694 by subscribers to the state loan which was to finance the war against France and established by law as a joint-stock company — likewise issued notes. The Bank's capital stock amounted to £1.2 million, which represented the amount of the state loan which its founders had subscribed. Thus its total joint-stock capital had been lent to the State, which paid an annual 8% interest on it. The Bank of England was the second public issuing bank to be founded after the Sveriges Riksbank in 1668, and the first issuing bank to be constituted as a joint-stock company. When the Bank of England increased its lending to the State by £400,000 in 1707, during the War of the Spanish Succession, and, at the same time, reduced its interest rate to 6%, it obtained an important privilege at the time of the renewal of its Charter which paved the way for its later development into a central issuing bank: except for the Bank of England, no other bank in England and Wales with more than six partners was allowed to issue bank notes. As a consequence, the numerous private issuing banks in England remained small private banking houses. The Bank of England's privilege did not apply in Scotland which was tied to England until 1707 only by a dynastic union. In Scotland the issue of notes was in the hands of a few joint-stock companies: the Bank of Scotland, founded in 1695, the Royal Bank of Scotland of 1727 and the British Linen Company of 1746.

The issuing banks only served British domestic payment and credit transactions, and their role was rather provincial when compared with the financial power and volume of international business of the big merchant bankers — i.e. of those private bankers who financed their credit dealings predominantly with their own capital. The Bank of England alone was more prominent amongst the issuing banks, because it was the biggest public creditor and held the funds of the largest number of public authorities.

In the first half of the 19th century the issuing banks, the Bank of England included, were considerably more susceptible to crises than the private banking houses of merchant bankers. During the economic crisis which followed upon the Napoleonic Wars, almost 90 private issuing banks went bankrupt between 1816 and 1817. Ten years later, during the crisis of 1825-6, 70 private issuing banks had to suspend payments when the holders of bank notes tried to convert their notes into gold. In the two years prior to the crisis, the private issuing banks had more than doubled their note circulation and were unable to cope with the run. The public was finally pacified by the Bank of England which, by drawing on its own gold funds, underwrote all credit claims. Although this crisis did not discredit the note as a means of payment, it revealed a dilemma in which many private issuing banks had been placed. They were unable to satisfy business needs, if they pursued a cautious policy in issuing notes; on the other hand, they jeopardized their capacity to convert the notes into ready money, if they issued large quantities of them. For this reason the Prime Minister, Lord Liverpool, considered it necessary to found issuing banks which were well-equipped with capital: joint-stock issuing banks.

On his initiative, the government obtained legal powers in 1826 to authorize more joint-stock banks to issue notes in England and Wales alongside the Bank of England, excluding London and a 65-mile radius around the capital. This clause continued to safeguard the Bank of England's privileged position. When its issuing privilege was renewed in 1833, the new Bank Charter Act laid down 'that from and after the First Day of August One thousand eight hundred and thirty-four, unless and until Parliament shall otherwise direct, a Tender of a Note or Notes of the Governor and Company of the Bank of England, expressed to be payable to Bearer on Demand, shall be a *legal Tender*, to the Amount expressed in such Note or Notes, and shall be taken to be valid as a Tender to such Amount for all Sums above Five Pounds on all Occasions on which any Tender of Money may be legally made, so long as the Bank of England shall continue to pay on Demand their said Notes in legal Coin'. Consequently bank notes — in so far as they stemmed from the Bank of England — became legal tender in England, the country where they first originated. In Scotland, Bank of England notes became legal tender in 1845.

Peel's Bank Charter Act

The system did not function as yet however. In 1839, the Bank of England, after having converted notes to gold for many months, found that in order to fulfill its obligations it had to take credit from the Banque de France and from Hamburg, mediated by the merchant banker Thomas

Baring. This crisis prompted the British Government, when the Bank of England's note privilege next came up for renewal in 1844, to safeguard the Bank's ability to convert its notes at any time by introducing precise regulations on the proportion between coin and gold reserves and notes in circulation.

According to the currency theory of Ricardo and Lord Overstone which considered bank notes to be money, two-thirds of the notes in circulation were to be covered in gold. In contrast, the banking theory of Tooke and Fullarton which designated bank notes as 'paper credit', required only one-third cover for note circulation. In formulating the new banking law, the Prime Minister, Sir Robert Peel, was guided by the former theory. The fundamental and trend-setting significance of Peel's Bank Charter Act, which has since been frequently criticised for its faulty theoretical basis, lay in the fact that it paved the way for a central issuing bank in England, when there were still about 300 private issuing banks in operation. The Charter laid down that no concessions for new issuing banks were to be granted in England and Wales in future. (The Act did not yet apply to Scotland). Those issuing banks already in existence were not permitted to expand their note circulation any further. In this way private issuing banks had fixed quotas for the amount of notes they could issue. Should an issuing bank abandon its note-issue or forfeit its right of issue — for example through merger with a non-issuing bank — its quota was 'inherited' by the Bank of England. In the end it took decades before English private issuing banks suspended or lost their right of issue. In 1881, about 150 private issuing banks continued in business and there were still 60 of them in 1901. It was only in 1921 that the last English private issuing bank, Fox Fowler & Co., lost its right of issue, when it was taken over by Lloyds Bank. As regards the notes in circulation, however, the purpose of a central issuing bank was achieved more quickly. In 1850, the ratio of the Bank of England's notes in circulation to those of private issuing banks was 3:1, in 1880 it was 9:1, until it reached 27:1 in 1901.

Although Peel's Bank Charter Act aimed at establishing a central issuing bank, it did not consider nationalizing the issue of notes. For over 100 years the Bank of England remained a private joint-stock company, enjoying legal privileges, until the Bank of England Act of 1946. It was bound by the rules of law but was not subject to any government directives. The Bank's shareholders also appointed the management team: the Governor, the Deputy Governor and the 24 further members who made up the Court of Directors. They had to abide by certain rules. The Governor and Deputy Governor were, except in special cases, appointed for a two-year term of office. Prominent members of the London business world were elected to the Court of Directors, but this on principle never included a chairman of a large bank.

In so far as the Bank of England's Charter was to secure its future role as a central issuing bank, it met with the approval of both the Currency and the Banking Schools; for, notwithstanding their opposing views on the nature of the bank note, both schools of thought agreed that a central bank had to have a concentration of metal reserves for the country's coinage and had to regulate the proper ratio between note circulation and metal supply. Only the stipulations which regulated that ratio remained controversial.

The Bank of England was divided by law into two independent and separate departments: the Banking Department for actual banking operations and the Issue Department for the issue of notes. The Issue Department received an allocation from the Bank of England's gold reserve — about £28 million — and a further £14 million in securities, which included £11 million of state bonds of indebtedness as cover reserve. In its note-issue, the Issue Department was allowed to exceed the existing gold cover by the full amount represented by these easily realizable holdings of securities. This meant that it was permitted to issue a total of up to £42 million in bank notes and that two-thirds of the Bank of England notes in circulation were covered by gold. Soon after the passage of the Bank Charter Act, Tooke and Fullarton, taking the standpoint of the Banking School, criticised the cover regulations as too narrow and rigid. Their criticism was confirmed by subsequent developments; for the inflexible cover regulations have, indeed, proved to be a failure.

During the economic crises of 1847, 1857 and 1866 the Bank of England's gold reserve became so badly depleted each time that, had it observed the cover regulations closely, it would have had to deny the British economy credit when it was most needed. This would have deepened the economic crises even further. The government only prevented this negative consequence of the Bank Charter Act by temporarily suspending the cover regulations in each of the three crisis years and by authorizing the Bank to exceed the quota of notes not covered by gold. Hence the cover regulations in Peel's Bank Charter Act remained in force, unaltered, until 1914, only because the Act was not applied in emergencies. In the long run, the Act's terms meant that Britain's note circulation increased only slightly compared to the other large industrial and commercial countries of the 19th century. However, Britain compensated for the shortage of bank notes by making wide-spread use of cheques and other means of transfer.

The Banque de France in the 19th Century

The first attempt to establish an issuing bank in France was made by the unfortunate John Law in 1716. His bank was converted into a state bank in 1718, at which point the issue of notes, having hitherto been sound and solid, became excessively inflated, until their convertibility was finally discontinued in 1720. At the same time their value was fixed at a compulsory rate. Thus the notes produced by what was originally a private issuing bank had become inflationary state paper-money. This happened when the note printing press was used to repay the enormous state debt, which had been run up during the wars of Louis XIV. The second French issuing bank, the Caisse d'Escompte, which was founded in 1776 by Isaac Panchaud with the support of the then General Controller of Finances, Turgot, also foundered because it was linked too closely to the state debt. In return for the large credits it had been giving to the State, the Bank had been receiving *assignats* which rapidly lost their value. Because its debtor, the French state, had become insolvent, the Caisse d'Escompte became illiquid and had to be closed in 1793.

It was only after Bonaparte's *coup d'état* of 18th Brumaire (9 November 1799) that it became possible to reconsolidate French public finances and to safeguard the currency. In the event, it was particularly important to steer clear of unwelcome deflationary effects during the stabilization of the currency and the efforts to balance the budget. French trade and industry were underemployed at the time and in need of credit. Therefore, at the beginning of 1800, Bonaparte ordered the foundation of an issuing bank limited by shares, the Banque de France, on the recommendation of Jean Frederic Perrégaux and several other private bankers. Perrégaux became the Bank's first Governor. In 1803 it obtained its Statutes, which were to remain in force until 1936. It was a public bank in the form of a joint-stock company; its shares were in private hands. The Governor was appointed by the Head of State. The Bank was permitted to issue notes, but had no legal monopoly in this respect. Its first task was to provide the economy with credit. Since the notes were to be a means of credit only, and were not to be used in everyday business, the bank was at first only allowed to issue bank notes worth a minimum of 500 francs. The State did not draw on more than a portion of the Bank's capital for its credit needs, and some of its capital in gold and silver was placed at the government's disposal in the form of a loan. On the whole, the attitude of the Banque de France to public finances was, until the beginning of the Third Republic, determined above all by the memory of the close and unhappy connection which its two unsuccessful predecessors had had with the state debt. Up to the time of the Third Republic, it supplied the French state with credit only on a modest scale.

Apart from the Banque de France, several other issuing banks emerged in a number of *Départements* between 1837 and 1838; but by 1848 they had all been amalgamated with the Banque de France. From that time on, the latter was *de facto* the central issuing bank in France, even though it did not become the central issuing bank *de jure* until 1936. Remembering the fate of its predecessors, the Banque de France took care throughout the 19th century to hold large gold and silver reserves; even today the bank strives to maintain substantial gold reserves. Its notes had by far the highest cover, and as the Statutes did not contain any precise cover regulations, it varied, in general, between 75% and 90%. The Banque de France has lived up to the highest expectations of the Currency School. The French Government had to suspend the Bank's obligation to convert its bank notes on only two occasions throughout the entire 19th century: in the revolutionary year of 1848 and during the Franco-Prussian War in 1870-71.

In both cases, however, an upper limit for note issue was laid down at the same time. Quotas were fixed in order to reassure the public, which was quick to remember John Law and the *assignats*. When the convertibility requirement was suspended for the second time in 1870, the notes of the Banque de France were declared legal tender. This policy remained in force after convertibility was re-established in 1873 and so did the system of fixing quotas on issues of bank notes. In order to satisfy the increasing demand for means of payment, the quota was increased by law at regular intervals. During the Third Republic, the Banque de France became more closely linked to the State and also supplied it with direct loans, although the Bank's management remained faithful to its previous issuing policy. It was basically thanks to the Banque de France — to its independent and sound issuing policy — that bank notes inspired general confidence, when elsewhere on the Continent they were viewed with suspicion as being worthless paper money well into the second half of the 19th century. If they were ultimately accepted, it was not because the principles of the Currency or Banking Schools had established themselves, but because the issuing banks had won the public's confidence all over Europe.

Overcoming the Federal System of German Issuing Banks

In Germany, the development of bank notes and issuing banks started with a state-owned issuing bank. Subsequently there emerged numerous private and public issuing banks until the Reichsbank became the central issuing bank. The oldest German issuing bank and, at the same time, the immediate predecessor of the Reichsbank, was the Preussische Bank. Frederick the Great founded it in 1765 as a state institute under the name of Königliche Giro- und Lehnbanco (Royal Giro and Loan Bank) and granted it the privilege of note-issue. However, the Bank could scarcely take advantage of its privilege because it had too little precious metal and too few coins to cover larger issues of notes. Yet as a state bank the Königliche Bank could have had plentiful silver- and coinage reserves, had the Prussian Treasury deposited the state chest with the Bank which amounted to 23.6 million thalers in 1775: this was more than the total national income for that year and by 1786 it had increased to 55.2 million thalers. But it was withdrawn from circulation in the economy, since it was stored in barrels in the cellar of the Royal Castle and Spandau fortress. Frederick the Great could have boosted the Prussian economy to a much greater extent and undertaken bigger public investments, particularly in the badly neglected area of road construction, had he not let the Treasury funds accumulate in line with cameralistic doctrine, but deposited them instead in the Königliche Bank as cover for bank note circulation which he favoured in principle.

The Königliche Bank's small issue of notes was suspended in 1806. Thereafter, state paper-money was brought into circulation instead of bank notes. However, the Prussian state was cautious in the issue of paper-money and was hence able to avoid an inflation of its currency. When the building of railways began around 1840, which also accelerated the pace of German industrialization, the demand for money and credit rose sharply. An efficient issuing bank was needed in order to meet this demand, and England provided the object lesson demonstrating the importance of bank notes and issuing banks. In 1846 the state-owned Königliche Bank was changed into the Preussische Bank when the new Prussian bank regulations came into force. It had the legal structure of a joint-stock company, with the State taking one-sixth of its joint-stock capital; the remaining shares were in private hands. However, since the State did not acquire any further shares on the occasion of later capital increases, the proportion of shares owned by it diminished to one-eleventh. As regards the management of its banking operations, this issuing bank was indistinguishable from a state bank; it was managed by state officials. From 1851, the Prussian Prime Minister was also the head of the Preussische Bank. His permanent representative was the 'President', who functioned as the general manager and was likewise a state official. Thus, this issuing bank differed considerably from the Bank of England or the Banque de France as far as its relation to the State was concerned.

The Preussische Bank had the right to issue notes; however, this was at first restricted to a maximum quota of 21 million thalers. When, in 1856, the Bank took over all state paper-money still in circulation for conversion into bank notes, the fixing of quotas which restricted note-issues was discontinued. From then on, it was laid down that one-third of the bank notes in circulation had to be covered by precious metal or coins. The Preussische Bank was hence the first issuing bank whose legal cover regulations were based on Banking School principles. Its bank notes did not become legal tender, however; national and municipal money institutes were merely obliged to accept them as means of payment. Once the quota system had been abolished, the Preussische Bank's note-issue increased rapidly. In 1855, when still subject to quotas, the Bank had issued bank notes worth 20 million thalers. By 1866 its note circulation had risen to 125 million thalers. Since price levels had remained basically unchanged during this decade, the growth in the circulation of bank notes reflects the pace of industrialization and of economic development in this first stage of advanced industrialization in Germany.

When the Prussian banking regulations were enacted, there were five issuing banks in those German states which later came to form the German Reich. The most significant was the Bayerische Hypotheken- und Wechselbank (Bavarian Mortgage and Exchange Bank) although its significance was not based on its rather small note-issue, but on its activity in the field of mortgages. The Prussian banking law caused a great number of issuing banks to be founded, particularly outside Prussia. Between 1847 and 1857, 25 private and public issuing banks were established in the German states, 18 of them being outside Prussia. The large number of issuing banks was in part the result of Germany's political fragmentation, and there were no uniform regulations on note-issue and note-cover.

That the German system of issuing bank notes did not find itself in utter confusion by virtue of its many divergent bank statutes and practices was merely due to the fact that most issuing banks were engaged in a fairly small volume of business and were geographically restricted in their sphere of operation. In 1866, only the Frankfurter Bank and the Preussische Bank had a note circulation of more than 10 million thalers. In fact, Prussian influence had to a large extent already unified German issuing policy before the military conflict between Prussia and Austria broke out in 1866. The Preussische Bank had begun to establish branches outside Prussia in 1865. By 1866, of the total of 179 million thalers in bank notes circulating in Germany, i.e. in the member states of the German Confederation with the exception of Austria, 125 million thalers were Preussische Bank notes.

At the time when the Reich was being established, further issuing banks were set up, though on this occasion rather more for political than economic reasons. The liberal parties which, through their domination of Parliament, strongly influenced the shaping of Reich institutions during this period demanded that the German monetary and note-issuing systems be standardized as a logical consequence of political unification. The National Liberals and Free Conservatives also called for the foundation of a German central bank: a Reichsbank. In order to prepare the ground for the planned reform, the North German Confederation promulgated a law on 27 March 1870 which forbade the founding of new issuing banks and the extension of existing note privileges; and the renewal of privileges was possible only if a clause was added to the effect that they could be withdrawn at a year's notice. Once the Reich was founded, this law was extended to the South German states even if it did not come into force there until 1 January 1872.

In contrast to North and Central Germany, the foundation of issuing banks made very slow progress in South Germany: Baden and Württemberg did not have an issuing bank of their own until 1870. The development in the North German Confederation prompted the governments of these two states to forge ahead with the establishment of their own issuing banks (which they had long contemplated, but repeatedly postponed) in order to head off the introduction of centralized regulations. Baden founded the Badische Bank in 1870, and Württemberg established the Württembergische Bank in the autumn of 1871. In Bavaria, the Bayerische Hypotheken-und Wechselbank abandoned its note privilege in 1875. Its right of issue was transferred to the newly founded public Bayerische Notenbank. In 1875, Germany had a total of 34 issuing banks, with two-thirds of the circulating bank notes being issued by the Preussische Bank.

The South German states were not the only opponents of a central issuing bank. In 1874, the Reich Chancellor drafted a law designed to introduce uniform regulations for issuing banks within the Reich's institutional framework. However, the Prussian Finance Minister, Otto Camphausen, saw to it that there was no mention of a Reichsbank in the draft. Subsequently, Prussian and South German particularism joined forces in the Federal Council, which was dominated by the Federal Princes, and ensured that the Bank Act was passed without a Reichsbank being established. It was only when the majority in the Parliament *(Reichstag)* — influenced by Ludwig Bamberger and Eduard Lasker — refused to consent to a Bank Act which did not provide for the establishment of a Reichsbank that the Federal

Council withdrew its particularist reservations. Thus the Reichsbank was founded at the same time as uniform regulations on bank notes and issuing banks were passed in the Bank Act of 1875. The Reichsbank emerged from the Preussische Bank which Prussia sold to the Reich. In this process, private shareholders in the Preussische Bank received Reichsbank shares at par in exchange.

The Bank Act's cover regulations, which applied to the Reichsbank and all other issuing banks, followed the Banking Principle and stipulated that one-third of the bank notes in circulation had to be covered in gold or in negotiable coin, the remainder in first-class trade bills. The authors of the Bank Act, Bamberger and Rudolf Delbrück, the 'President' of the Reich Chancellery, had been hoping to establish the Reichsbank as the central issuing bank. But note privileges could not simply be withdrawn from private issuing banks, whose concessions in many cases still had several decades to run, and even less from the public issuing banks of the Federal German states. Therefore the Bank Act pursued the setting-up of a central issuing-bank as a longer-term objective and by means of indirect coercion. It was with this aim in mind that it was laid down that powers of note-issue could be granted or extended only through Reich legislation; rights of issue, which had been abandoned or had expired, were to be transferred to the Reichsbank. In addition, the Reichsbank also obtained two important privileges which other banks did not possess: it was the only issuing bank permitted to establish branches throughout the Reich; the others were allowed to set up branches only within the Federal state in which they had their head office. Secondly, the Reichsbank was given privileges in respect of the taxation of bank notes. A certain quota of bank notes with no gold cover was tax-free up to a maximum of 385 million marks for the whole of the Reich. Almost two-thirds (250 million marks) of this tax-free quota were allocated to the Reichsbank. These regulations, which were to open the way for a central issuing bank, were modelled on Peel's Bank Charter Act. Within a year of the Reichsbank's opening, 16 issuing banks had suspended their note issue. After 1910 only the Bayerische Notenbank, the Sächsische Bank, the Badische Bank and the Württembergische Notenbank continued to issue notes alongside the Reichsbank.

State officials managed the Reichsbank as they had the Preussische Bank. The Reich Chancellor was at the top of the hierarchy; his permanent deputy had the title of President of the Reichsbank — a life-long appointment made by the Emperor on the recommendation of the Reich Chancellor.

Reichsbank notes were accepted everywhere, but they were not recognised as legal tender until the international situation deteriorated in the wake of the First Moroccan Crisis of 1905. Because of the dangerous developments in foreign relations before the First World War, the Reichsbank began to hoard gold and sought to expand the circulation of bank notes rather than of gold coins. In order to support this policy, Reichsbank notes were declared legal tender when its note privilege was renewed in 1909. At the same time, the Reichsbank prompted state authorities and private enterprise to pay salaries and wages in notes, except for the small change.

The United States' Arduous Journey towards the Federal Reserve System

The United States took the longest of all the major countries to centralize its bank note system, even though the Americans were almost entirely dependent on bank notes as a means of payment, particularly in the first 25 years of independence. At the time of the Declaration of Independence, the 13 New England states did not have their own currency; nor, because of their unfavourable balance of trade, did they have more than very few foreign coins. In order to finance the War of Independence, the Continental Congress of Philadelphia, the first joint political organization of the New England states, issued bank notes called 'continentals' in 1775. They were made out in dollars, the new monetary unit. Thus the dollar began its history, unlike the other traditional currencies, not as a coin but as a bank note, as a promise to pay; for the notes bore the inscription that they would be converted later into 'Spanish dollars', i.e. into Spanish gold or silver pesos. The Spanish peso was known and valued in North America on account of the trade relations with neighbouring Spanish colonies. At first, only two million 'continentals' were issued. Of course, this was not enough; hence further notes were constantly brought into circulation. Some of the 13 States also issued notes. By the end of the War of Independence, about 240 million dollars' worth of 'continentals' and approximately 250 million dollars in notes issued by individual States were in circulation. It was, however, impossible to procure the equivalent amount in coins in order to exchange them. Thus they became mere paper money, whose purchasing power progressively declined. It was not until 1792 that the United States began to mint their own coins, the gold and silver dollar, in accordance with the Coinage Act.

The large unfunded state debt and the deterioration of the currency prompted the Secretary of the Treasury, Alexander Hamilton, one of George Washington's closest collaborators, to draw up a basic programme of American commercial, fiscal and monetary policy, which he presented to Congress in his 'Report on Public Credit, Commerce and Finance' in 1790. This plan also provided for the creation of a national issuing bank; for Hamilton had clearly perceived that, with its lack of coinage, the young Republic would not be able to manage without bank notes as a means of payment. He also wanted to centralize note circulation and control it through a national bank. Thomas Jefferson and the Democrats, who still called themselves 'Republicans' at that time — the present Republican Party only came into being after 1850 — rejected Hamilton's plan, since the Constitution did not include powers to establish a bank. Jefferson regarded a national bank as an unwelcome and unconstitutional strengthening of the Government of the Union.

Hamilton repudiated Jefferson's objections. In his view, the Union Government had the right under the Constitution, both to incur and repay debts, and a national bank would be extremely useful for this purpose. In the end, President Washington and the majority of Congress supported Hamilton's plan and the First Bank of the United States was founded in 1791. It was a public bank and structured as a joint-stock company. A quarter of the joint-stock capital had to be paid in gold or silver coins, three-quarters in Government bonds. Almost three-quarters of the shares were held by the English, although foreign shareholders had no voting rights. The First Bank of the United States was not only a central issuing bank but a universal bank as well. It undertook all banking operations and also acted as a tax collector and customs office. Its main seat was in Philadelphia, and it built up a branch network which stretched from New Hampshire to Georgia. Its notes circulated in the whole of North America as a means of payment. Yet the Bank did not last for long. Its concession expired in 1811 and was not renewed; at that time, the former opponents of Hamilton and of the Bank he had founded, of whom President James Madison was one, had a majority in Congress.

After the costly and wholly successful war which the United States had waged against Britain in 1812-14, the state debt had increased enormously. The currency was again under threat and business was crippled. The Democrats now copied Hamilton's fiscal and monetary policy which they had fiercely criticized 20 years earlier. In 1816, the Second Bank of the United States was founded on the model of the First National Bank. However, the Bank was ill-fated from the start. To begin with, it proved very difficult to place its shares amongst the public. Only two million of the 35 million dollars of joint-stock capital were paid up in gold or silver coins. Like its predecessor, the Second Bank of the United States was both a central issuing and a universal bank. It soon ran into financial difficulties as a consequence of speculative transactions, which credit from Europe, amounting to 2.5 million dollars, helped overcome. After the Bank had successfully engaged in note-issue and in the bill discount business for several years and been closely associated with the private English banking house of Baring Brothers & Co., it began to decline after 1829. The new American President, Andrew Jackson, had constitutional doubts as to whether the Union Government was authorised to grant bank concessions. He therefore ordered that the Government's assets held in the Second Bank of the United States be withdrawn and placed with other banks which had received concessions from individual States. In 1836, the Union's concession was no longer renewed. The Bank continued to exist as a private bank until 1841, with a concession granted by the State of Pennsylvania; it then went bankrupt, after having been involved in speculative deals which resulted in heavy losses. The ill-starred history of the Second Bank of the United States constituted the second big obstacle, next to strong federalist reservations, to the centralization of the note-issuing system in the United States.

The two short-lived national banks were not the only institutes in North America to issue notes. On the contrary, more and more banks were granted concessions by the individual Federal states, obtaining the right of issue at the same time. In 1800, 28 private issuing banks operated in the United States, and by 1815, their number had increased to 208. In 1845, 707 banks issued notes; and by 1860, bank notes from 1562 different issuing banks were in circulation. All these banks were primarily commercial banks and undertook note-issue to create credit. There were no regulations concerning gold and silver cover for issuing banks and the legal requirement governing the activity of issuing banks differed from one Federal state to another. There were also very different kinds of bank notes, and of course they were not recognised as legal tender. Nevertheless, they could be used as a means of payment not only within the restricted radius of the bank which had issued them, but also throughout the whole area of the Union; for, in 1818 the private issuing banks had founded the Suffolk Bank in Boston as a central clearing and conversion office. The participating issuing banks paid a certain amount in gold or silver coins into this bank, and the Suffolk Bank used these deposits to convert bank notes presented to it. The note issuing banks then had to repurchase these converted notes from the Suffolk Bank by handing over the corresponding amount in gold or silver coins. About 500 issuing banks were involved in this system and their notes were accepted throughout the Union. The notes of banks not participating in this system were accepted by other banks only at a discount.

During the Civil War, the United States again found themselves in a monetary crisis. Most issuing banks suspended the conversion of their notes to gold and silver. The Treasury Department issued cash vouchers which were not convertible into silver or gold either. Because of their green reverse side, they were called 'greenbacks' and since they were not convertible, they became state paper-money. These too met with the same fate that state paper-money had so far always suffered: the public soon lost confidence in them and they were devalued. By the end of the Civil War, more than one-third of the total means of payment in the United States were 'greenbacks'. The disruption of currency and of public and private credit that the war had caused, led Treasury Secretary Salmon P. Chase to submit proposals for a reform of the credit and bank note system which Congress passed in the form of the National Banking Act in 1863. This bill gave the Union full powers to introduce legal regulations for banks and to grant them concessions. The legal division of the American banking system into State Banks and National Banks, which obtains to this day, is based on this Act. Both kinds of institutions are private banks, their designation nothwithstanding. State Banks merely comply with their Federal state laws and are licensed by their State. National Banks, on the other hand, comply with Federal law and have their charter from the Federal government. We shall look in more detail at this reform of American banking in another context.

The new National Banks, founded on the basis of a Federal Charter, were allowed to issue notes just like the State banks. The creation of these new banks — in 1864 over 500 National Banks were granted licenses — facilitated the placing of state loans; before starting business, the National Banks had to buy bonds from the Federal government amounting to a minimum of 30,000 dollars and to deposit them with the Treasury Department. The

National Banks issued notes in accordance with uniform regulations and with standardized bank notes printed by the Federal government. These notes had to be covered to one-third in gold or silver by the issuing banks and were to be accepted as means of payment by the Federal government and by the other National Banks. The State Banks were also permitted by law to continue their issue of notes, though their issuing activity was brought to a standstill in 1865 when taxation became too heavy. They had to pay a note tax amounting to 10% of the total value of their circulating notes, whilst the National Banks paid a tax of only 1% of their note-issue. As a consequence, the State Banks either suspended their note issue or acquired the status of a National Bank. In 1880, over 2,000 National Banks issued notes; by 1905, they numbered 5,668! Note-issue at the time took place in accordance with uniform legal regulations and standard technical conditions.

The American banking system's supply of notes and coins as means of payment was vulnerable, however. The crisis of 1907-8 revealed this vulnerability when a not particularly big run on financial institutes forced 243 banks, including 31 National Banks, to suspend their payments for several months, many others were able to meet their clients' demand only in part.

The American system's vulnerability has been attributed in the main to the lack of elasticity in the money supply and to insufficient opportunities for refinancing. Since central issuing banks had been established in all economically important countries outside America, the United States founded a central issuing bank for the third time, following the failures of the First and the Second Bank of the United States. On the strength of the Aldrich-Vreeland Act — named after its two main sponsors, Senator Aldrich and Congressman Vreeland — a National Currency Commission was set up to study the statutes of European central issuing banks and then to draft and submit a bill for an American central issuing bank. The Aldrich-Vreeland Act stipulated that, until such a bank was established, a certain number of National Banks would be permitted, in cases of emergency, to extend their note circulation beyond the cover limit during the transitional period through an additional issue of treasury notes for a restricted period of time. This option was used only once, at the outbreak of the First World War, when the banks found themselves temporarily exposed to a greatly increased demand for money from their customers.

In 1913, the Federal Reserve Act finally provided the United States with a central issuing bank, or rather a central bank system: the Federal Reserve System. The Act divided the United States into 12 Federal Reserve Districts, each of which obtained a Federal Reserve Bank as a note issuing bank. This decentralization into 12 districts and 12 issuing banks took place for organizational and technical reasons only and did not constitute a concession to federalism. As central management for the 12 districts and the 12 Federal Reserve Banks, a Board of Governors was set up, whose members were appointed by the President of the United States. This Board in effect carried out the duties which the President of a central issuing bank would perform. Once the Federal Reserve Banks had been obliged by law to hold a gold cover of at least 25% and, furthermore, to convert their notes into gold, their bank notes were valid as legal tender.

The establishment of the Federal Reserve System confirmed the existing division of State Banks and National Banks. All National Banks had to become member banks of the Federal Reserve System. They had to keep a credit balance in their account with the Federal Reserve Bank of their district, with the precise amount depending on the size of their total deposits. In return, they gained adequate refinancing opportunities from the issuing bank. The State Banks could become members on a voluntary basis, but they were not compelled to do so. Thus from 1913, there were some commercial banks in America which were able to refinance themselves from within the central banking system, and others that were debarred from doing so.

II Banks and Banking from the Early Phase of Industrialization to the Middle of the 19th Century

1. Bank Types at the Beginning of the 19th Century

During the first phase of industrialization and railway construction until about 1850, the credit system was still dominated by banks which had been established in the pre-industrial period: private bankers, public banks and state banks. The great joint-stock and universal banks did not begin to operate until after the mid-century.

Private Bankers

Before the rise of the great joint-stock banks, private bankers were the most powerful and most important pillars of the whole credit system. The term 'private banker' applies to all individual entrepreneurs and managing partners who engage in banking operations, using their own capital, and whose liability is unlimited (i.e. it includes all their assets not invested in the banking business) and with exclusive powers of decision-making (i.e. without an authority, such as a board of directors, above them). It was also the practice in the 19th century that a private banker had no branches of his own but had his business conducted through banks elsewhere with which he had friendly links.

The older private banking firms had often grown out of another business which subsequently continued for some time alongside the banking business. Such 'forerunner' enterprises were particularly those in which high profit margins made strong capital formation possible and in which a knowledge of the market and a far-reaching network of customers could be acquired. These included the shipping and forwarding business, wholesale trade, money exchange, and the goldsmith and jewellery trade. In Germany, it also included the function of court factor at one of the many courts. In England, private bankers were initially known, depending on the origin of their banking enterprise in the goldsmith's business or in wholesale trade, as 'goldsmith bankers' or 'merchant bankers'. Banking operations were at first usually pursued as an occasional supplementary business. Banking then became a regular additional occupation alongside the established main business; finally only banking remained.

At the beginning of the industrial era at the turn of the 19th century, England had the largest number of private banking houses. Her private banks also had the greatest financial power and the most extensive business network. Banks were differentiated according to their place of business as either 'city banks' (or 'London bankers') and 'country banks'. Their location either within or outside the capital made for considerable differences in their business operations. Thus London banks suspended their own issue of notes as early as the 18th century because the Bank of England had far outstripped them, thanks to its note-issuing privileges; outside London, on the other hand, an increasing number of private note-issuing banks were established from the final third of the 18th century onwards. The city banks, instead of issuing their own notes, engaged in a lively business using the notes of the Bank of England; the country banks functioned, in a way, as exchange offices for numerous private note-issuing banks and the Bank of England. Moreover, almost every city bank acted as a 'correspondent' for several country banks, i.e. they attended to all business to be transacted in London, and in particular looked after the clearing with the Bank of England. This enabled the city banks to acquire a key position, and it also explains why some country banks transferred their headquarters to London. However, the main activity of both the city banks and the country banks was to provide short-term commercial credit.

Shortly after the middle of the 18th century there were no more than about 30 private bankers in London, with hardly more than a dozen in the rest of England and in Wales. However, this number grew quickly, when commercial firms began to penetrate the banking business and the merchant banks emerged. By 1776, the number of banks in England and Wales had risen to about 150, one third of which were city banks. In 1803-4 there existed 70 private banks operating in London and a further 473 country banks in England and Wales. In Scotland, by contrast, credit business was chiefly in the hands of the privileged joint-stock banks and their branches.

The oldest private banks in England were those which had grown out of the goldsmith's trade or had been founded as private note-issuing banks. The firm of C. Hoare & Co., to the present day owned by the founding family, held special place in this respect. In 1672 the goldsmith Richard Hoare took over his master's business and combined his work as goldsmith with that of banking. Very soon the Hoares were among the most influential bankers and became part of the English Establishment. The firm's founder was knighted by Queen Anne in 1702 and became Lord Mayor of London in 1712. The rise of merchants in banking began after the Seven Years' War when Britain had won the struggle for naval supremacy, for India and America. The oldest and largest merchant bank in the City of London was the House of Baring. The Barings were of German origin, the founder of the English family, Johann Baring, being the son of a Bremen parson. He came to England in the first half of the 18th century and founded a drapery business in Exeter. His sons, John and Francis, founded the firm of John and Francis Baring & Co. in London in 1763, which engaged in the import and export business and, from 1770, was also active as a credit institution. The Barings rapidly acquired wealth and influence, with Francis becoming a member of the East India Company's board and a baronet in 1793. The Barings' main sphere of activity was trade with America and, in the wake of this, credit business with American firms and the American government. In 1803 the Baring company, together with the Dutch banking house of Hope, placed

an 11 million dollar loan which the U.S. government had issued in order to
pay France for the Louisiana Purchase. In the first third of the 19th century,
the Barings were the greatest financial power in the world, later to be
replaced by the Rothschilds.

  With a few exceptions, the country banks could not, in general, compete
with city banks in significance and in capital formation. These exceptions
included the bank of Taylors & Lloyds in Birmingham, whose partners
participated in the banking house of Taylor Lloyd Bowman & Co. in London
in 1785; the firm of Leyland Bullins & Co. in Liverpool, and the Gurney
banking house of Norwich, whose owner was a partner in numerous private
banks in eastern England.

  The most significant private bankers in France at the turn of the 18th
to the 19th century were mostly Protestants of French and Swiss descent.
They were therefore simply known as *banque protestante*. This predominance of a Protestant minority in banking is, in part, due to the fact that a
great many of the merchants whose enterprises produced banks were
Protestants from French coastal and commercial towns. In spite of the
oppression of Protestants in France in the period between the abolition of
the Edict of Nantes (1685) and the Toleration Edict of Louis XVI (1787)
and despite the mass emigration of Huguenots from the country of His Most
Christian Majesty, these factors did not interfere with the existence and
growth of the French *banque protestante*. Since the Swiss and Dutch
Calvinists as well as the Huguenot *réfugiés*, who settled as merchants or
bankers in Amsterdam, Geneva and Genoa, maintained business relations
with their co-religionists in France, the international connections of the
French *banque protestane* were in fact furthered. Their opponents in France
actually used the expression *la banque protestante cosmopolite* in approximately the same sense in which 'international Jewish high finance' was
spoken of in our century. Many foreign bankers, most of them Swiss, were
also drawn to France during the 18th century by the great financial transactions which arose, during the *ancien régime*, from the State's continuing
need for loans and the leasing of indirect tax collection privileges to financially powerful companies.

  The oldest of the private Huguenot banking firms, which were still
active in the 19th century, was founded by Isaac Mallet. Mallet came from
a Huguenot family which had moved from Rouen to Geneva in 1557. He
returned to France and set himself up as a private banker in Paris in 1711.
He soon joined the Geneva banker, Barthélemy De la Rive, to establish the
firm of De la Rive & Mallet. After it had been renamed several times, the
name of Mallet Frères & Cie. was finally adopted. Mallet Frères & Cie. was
one of the most distinguished of France's private banks and lives on today
in de Neuflize Schlumberger Mallet & Cie., the product of a merger. The de
Neuflize branch of this banking house also came from the old *banque
protestante*. In the 17th century the Huguenot, David André, migrated to
Genoa and began a trading enterprise in silk, tobacco and goods from the
colonies. His successors added a banking business. Having gone bankrupt in

the confusion of the War of the First Coalition in 1797, Dominique André opened a new banking house in Paris in 1799, which came to the de Neuflize family through inheritance at the end of the 19th century.

Another banking house which was very influential during the *ancien régime* had to transfer its business to England during the French Revolution and was reopened in Paris only after Napoleon's downfall, never to recover its former significance. This bank began as Tourton & Guiger in about 1700; it was taken over by Isaac Thellusson in 1715 and had extensive business ties with Geneva, Genoa and Amsterdam. In 1756, Jacques Necker, who came from Geneva, became Thellusson's partner, and, with Necker's entry, the bank established closer relations with the French state as a supplier of loans. When Necker was entrusted with the management of French public finances for the first time in 1776, his appointment came about not only because he had attacked his deposed predecessor, Turgot, in his writings, but primarily because he was one of the largest creditors of the French state. When Necker entered public service he gave up his partnership in the bank. Later the Greffulhe family, which had operated a banking house in Amsterdam from the middle of the 18th century, joined the bank. During the Jacobin dictatorship in 1793, they fled to London and continued to manage the bank from there. From 1819 onwards, the bank operated from Paris under the name of Sartoris & Cie.

Two important French banking houses were founded by immigrants from Switzerland shortly before the Revolution. In 1781, when Jean Frédéric Perrégaux from Neuchâtel, the son of an officer in a Swiss regiment of the French army, opened a bank in Paris, he was also engaged in significant enterprises in the *ancien régime*, including the Caisse d'Escompte. During the Revolution he granted the Utopian socialist Claude Henri de Saint-Simon a loan for the latter's speculative deals with former church property. He later became a promoter of General Bonaparte. Perrégaux was one of the co-founders and first governors of the Banque de France; the management of the bank was carried on by his colleague and later partner, Jacques Laffitte, who was to play a major political role in the July Revolution of 1830. A few years after Perrégaux, in 1785, Hans Konrad Hottinger (from 1798, Hottinguer), who came from a Zurich family of scholars, established himself as a banker in Paris. At the time of the Revolution and during the Napoleonic period, the Hottinguer & Cie. banking house played but a minor role; however, after the Restoration of the Bourbons it became one of the most important banks to the French cotton industry.

All these banking houses belonged to the *banque protestante*. A Jewish banking house of significance prior to the founding of the Rothschild Bank in Paris was Worms & Cie. The Worms family began as army suppliers to the *ancien régime* at Saarlouis. In 1787, they moved to Paris and founded a bank there which remained in the family's possession beyond the Second World War.

In Germany, just as in England, many of the old private banking houses developed from forwarding agencies and trading enterprises. The commercial undertakings which expanded their occasional credit transactions to regular banking business were primarily the wine and cloth trade and trade in colonial goods, in particular dye-stuffs like indigo and cochineal. Alongside these merchant bankers, the Jewish court factors to the numerous German courts were very significant as early private bankers. However, it was only around 1800 that enterprises were founded which were, from the outset, exclusively concerned with banking. Frankfurt was the greatest German banking centre until approximately 1860. Here were based not only the largest number of banks, but also those which were the strongest financially. Next to Frankfurt, Cologne was the most important banking city in Central Europe.

Among the Frankfurt merchant bankers, Bethmann Brothers and the House of B. Metzler seel. Sohn & Co. had the most wide-ranging business connections around 1800. From the middle of the 18th century both firms began to provide credit side-by-side with their trading in commodities. Since 1754, the Bethmanns had been issuing, or negotiating, loans to the Viennese Court. When Austrian interest and amortization payments came to a standstill at the end of the century, the Bethmanns were, nevertheless, able to 'unfreeze' their claims. They issued bonds in denominations of 1,000 guldens on the Austrian loan and, with these 'Bethmann bonds', made the financial resources of the middle classes available for state loans. It was during the dispute over the Bavarian succession in 1778-79 that the Metzler banking house moved into large-scale banking which the state loans business offered until the financing of railway construction and heavy industry came along. Metzler raised a loan of 200,000 guldens, to help Prince Karl Theodor of the Palatinate, who inherited the throne of Wittelsbachs, with the first instalment of a compensation payment to the Elector of Saxony, who had also laid claims to the Bavarian succession. When Prussia, with her public finances exhausted, withdrew prematurely from the War of the First Coalition against revolutionary France, the Metzler house, together with the Frankfurt banker, Johann Jakob von Willemer (whose future wife, Marianne, is immortalized as Suleika in Goethe's *West-Östlicher Diwan*) procured a loan of over one million guldens.

In Cologne, three commercial houses took up the credit business at the turn of the 19th century. The oldest of them was the silk weaving mill and silk trading firm founded by Johann David Herstatt in 1727. From 1792 he was officially referred to as a banker. Abraham Schaaffhausen and Johann Heinrich Stein also founded commercial firms in Cologne at the same time. Schaaffhausen traded in wine, skins and cotton and from the outset also engaged in banking. Stein pursued the forwarding business, traded in leather, wine and hardware and became involved in the credit business after the turn of the century.

Berlin, which was to become the central German capital market after the founding of the Reich in 1871, had, until the beginning of the 19th century, only one private enterprise able to carry out important credit transactions.

This enterprise was founded in 1712 by the merchant, David Splitgerber, and a former non-commissioned officer, Gottfried Daum. The firm of Splitgerber and Daum first traded in iron and artillery ammunition. As King Frederick William I of Prussia had no great liking for pure traders, Splitgerber and Daum acquired the lease of four state metal factories and set up a rifle factory at Spandau in 1722. From the 1720s they also granted loans and bore the designation *banquiers*. During the Seven Years' War, they were both suppliers of arms and ammunition, and financiers to Frederick the Great. From 1796, the firm, in which the bank was henceforth the most important branch of the business, was managed by Splitgerber's grandchildren under the name of Schickler Brothers.

Many private banking houses in Germany in the early 19th century originated from the work of Jewish court factors. These court Jews were suppliers and financiers to the German courts during the Age of Absolutism. They granted or procured credit for the court and the state, provided the armies' requirements and supplied courts with jewellery, ornaments and precious metal. As 'coin factors', they stamped small coins from copper and nickel. In addition to their profits from business, they also received a fixed salary. Since they were absolutely indispensable to the courts, they could obtain privileges for their families, such as exemption from special taxes levied on Jews; in many cases, they were even ennobled. Approximately 150 Jewish court factors' families, mostly in the Southern German states and in Austria, were raised to the nobility in the period before the emancipation of the Jews at the beginning of the 19th century. But the emancipation process in general was also accelerated by the court factors. Four of these court factors' families were to play an important role in the world of high finance in the 19th century: Rothschild, Oppenheim, Seligmann and Kaulla.

Meyer Amschel Rothschild, the founder of the Rothschild 'dynasty' and banking house, began his business activity in Frankfurt as a dealer in antiques, medals, coins, textiles and also in bills of exchange. From 1764 he maintained business relations with the Court of the Landgrave of Hesse-Kassel, becoming one of the court factors there in 1769. The Landgraves (Electors since 1803) of Hesse-Kassel were among the wealthiest of Germany's princes. The Court of Kassel derived a large income from the sale of Hesse regiments to Britain during the American War of Independence (1776-1783), earning 19 million thalers all told from this trade in human beings. The British payments were transferred annually in bulk, partly in cash and partly in bills of exchange, and this transfer was handled by several court factors, Rothschild among them. Since the transfer took a lengthy period of time to complete, the factors were able to use the money and make a profit for themselves. The Landgrave wanted to invest his large capital assets profitably and loans to other German princes seemed to offer the best deal. So he gave his factors large amounts of money for them to invest. He thereby avoided appearing as a money lender which would have been incompatible with his social rank. The business was also profitable for the factors; they could gain interest as intermediaries. From 1802, Rothschild collaborated with Buderus, Privy Councillor in Hesse and a nephew of the founder of the future *Buderus Eisenwerke* (Buderus Iron Works). With Buderus's help, Rothschild successfully eliminated other court factors and became the sole factor to the Court of Hesse-Kassel. Even though he retained his trading business, banking was increasingly becoming his main activity. After taking his sons into partnership, he converted his business into the firm of M.A. Rothschild & Söhne in 1810. An account of the establishment of the individual banks by the five Rothschild sons, and of the rise of the Rothschild House to the position of greatest financial power of the 19th century, will be given below (see pp. 52-58).

Salomon Herz Oppenheim also came from Frankfurt and was court factor to the Elector of Cologne in Bonn, the Elector's residence since 1740. Oppenheim's grandson, Salomon the Younger, founded a banking house in 1789. In 1794, during the War of the First Coalition, the last Elector of Cologne, Maximilian Franz of Habsburg, left his residence and the Electoral Court was never to return. Under the terms of the Peace of Lunéville of 1801, Bonn became French with other parts of Germany on the left bank of the Rhine, and after losing its residential status, the town declined as a commercial centre. But fresh opportunities opened up for Oppenheim at Cologne, once this old imperial town had become French and was obliged to abolish the still extant discrimination of Jews and Protestants. Thus Salomon Oppenheim could move with his banking house to the commercial centre of Cologne in 1801.

The family of Seligmann lived in the Palatinate. The Seligmanns had worked as court factors both to the Elector of the Palatinate at Mannheim and the Duke of Württemberg since the mid-18th century. Aron Elias Seligmann led his family into the Bavarian nobility. From 1773 he was factor to the Württemberg Court and from 1779 factor to the Elector of the Palatinate. He also had extensive trading interests in Reichenhall salt and in tobacco. When Karl Theodor, the Elector of the Palatinate, inherited Bavaria, Aron Elias Seligmann became Bavarian court factor, too. During the War of the First Coalition (1792-1797), he procured loans for Bavaria and Austria. He accepted Bavarian loans during the Napoleonic era. He was appointed Bavarian court banker for his services in 1805 and, in 1814, was ennobled. He took the name of Leonhard Baron von Eichthal; five years later, he converted from Judaism to Catholicism.

The Kaulla family, which came from Hechingen in Württemberg, served as factors first to the Bavarian and then to Württembergian Courts. More importantly, they acted as suppliers of the army. In the autumn of 1802, Duke Frederick of Württemberg signed a contract with the heads of the family, Karoline Kaulla and her brother Jakob, which cleared the path for the founding of a banking house. The Duke and the Kaulla family each contributed half of the original capital of 300,000 guldens. At first the bank adopted the company name of M. & J. Kaulla (Madame & Jakob Kaulla), with no mention of the Duke as their partner. Several years later — probably in 1805, at the Peace of Pressburg, when Württemberg merged with the Austrian parts of Upper Swabia to become a Kingdom — the banking house was renamed Königlich-Württembergische Hofbank. In 1817, it was given a new constitution by royal decree. It remained a private commercial bank, however; the king simply held one half of the capital. Control of the bank was shared between a director, appointed by the king, and an authorized representative of the Kaulla family; he was usually a family member. The bank was supervised by a curatorium, which consisted of three higher officials whom the king nominated. This peculiar semi-public organization of a private banking house was a consequence of the king's large share in it, notwithstanding the fact that he was a private investor and was involved, not as sovereign, but as an ordinary businessman.

Public Banks

The public and semi-public banks which existed at the turn of the 19th century had three roots: they arose partly from the need for order in the field of monetary policy and were to facilitate payment transactions; they originated partly from amalgamations of public creditors or they were the result of the mercantilistic economic policy of the 18th century. In order to regulate the monetary system, and in particular the exchange of one type of coin into another, and to stimulate the giro transfer business, the city of Amsterdam established the Amsterdamsche Wisselbank in 1606. It was a financial institution under municipal supervision. The scope of the Bank's activities, originally limited to the exchange of money, safe custody of securities and valuables, and payment transactions, was extended in the course of the 17th century to include the credit business. Its principal borrower was the Dutch East India Company. During the Napoleonic era it had to reduce its activity to a minimum, but once the independence of the Netherlands had been restored, the Amsterdamsche Wisselbank had to give way to the Nederlandsche Bank which had been founded in 1814 as an issuing bank on the model of the Banque de France; the Wisselbank was finally liquidated in 1819. Following Amsterdam's example, Hamburg also founded a public bank, the Hamburger Bank, in 1619. It carried out the same tasks as the Amsterdamsche Wisselbank and came into its own during the French Revolution; for, after French troops had conquered the Netherlands in the War of the First Coalition and the country became a satellite state of the revolutionary France known as Batavian Republic, a large part of the Amsterdam's trade and money business transferred to Hamburg. The Hamburger Bank flourished between 1795 and 1805, in the very decade during which its Amsterdam model decayed under the impact of England's naval war against France and her satellites. In 1795, the Peace of Basle between Prussia and France, in which the whole of Northern Germany was neutralized, created the political conditions which enabled Hamburg to rise as a commodity and credit centre in this period of war and unrest.

The Banco di San Giorgio, founded in Genoa in 1408, the Bank of England and the Bank of Scotland emerged from a union of creditors of the state. The Banco di San Giorgio, deeply involved in the state credit business as it was, collapsed in 1797 when the heavily indebted city-state of Genoa defaulted on its payments. The development of the Bank of England and the Bank of Scotland as issuing banks has already been mentioned.

State Banks

Mercantilist economic policy led several German states to establish state banks, i.e. credit institutions wholly or largely owned, administered and run by the state. Large sums were needed to finance the recovery following the Seven Years' War and this prompted the founding of the Herzogliches Leyhaus at Brunswick (now Braunschweigische Staatsbank) and of the Königliche Giro-und Lehnbanco in Prussia. Both these state banks accepted interest-bearing deposits and gave credit on bills of exchange and mortgages. The Leyhaus also accepted very small deposits and granted small credits against pledges. In this respect, it fulfilled a function which was later taken over by savings banks. The Prussian Giro- und Lehnbanco, on the other hand, later developed into a central issuing bank, as has already been mentioned.

Prussia owned two more state banks at the beginning of the 19th century. One of them, the Königliche Seehandlung, was something like a state merchant bank. Frederick the Great founded it in 1722 as a trading and shipping company to promote Prussian overseas trade. It was constructed as a joint-stock company, and at its foundation the king owned seven-eights of its capital. But in the course of the next ten years, over half the shares passed into private hands. In order to give the undertaking a secure footing, it was granted two monopolies: one for salt imports to Prussian ports and the other for the export of wax which was shipped abroad from the south of the Vistula. From 1790, the Seehandlung also got involved in the credit business, granting acceptance credits and issuing state loans. The first 40 years of the Seehandlung's history were a series of failures and severe setbacks. After barely 10 years of activity, it had lost two-thirds of its capital due to careless management and embezzlement by Christopher von Goerne, its head. Goerne was sentenced to life imprisonment; his property was confiscated. Most of the losses were recovered when it was sold. When its principal debtor, the Prussian state, became insolvent during the war against France in 1806-7, the Seehandlung had to suspend its payments. In 1809 it resumed business, henceforth purely as a state institution, following the conversion of its shares into state bonds. Between the end of the German Wars of Liberation and the Revolution of 1848, the Seehandlung was to become the most powerful financial and credit institution in Prussia.

Prussia had inherited its third state bank when the last Margrave of Ansbach-Bayreuth, Karl Alexander, a nephew of Frederick the Great, renounced his position in favour of the King of Prussia in 1791. The Hochfürstlich Brandenburg-Anspach-Bayreuthische Hofbanco was established on the model of the Prussian Giro-und Lehnbanco. Like the latter, it was to improve the credit supply in the country. However, it was also supposed to render court factors superfluous and hence enable the sovereign to retain the profits. Anspach-Bayreuth was engaged in remittances of money on a relatively large scale; since 1777, the Margrave had been receiving subsidies from the English after he, like the Landgrave of Hesse-Kassel, had sold them soldiers for the war in America. Furthermore, he frequently travelled abroad and money had to be forwarded to him on these occasions. Such remittances were usually managed by private bankers and particularly by the court factors. By running its own transfer business, the Ansbach-Bayreuth Bank was able to make savings on the commissions. And by taking the remittances into its own hands, the Margrave's Treasury could also expect to pocket the profits to be made from short-term credit operations in various places. The Bank developed well, surviving the loss of some of its assets during the French revolutionary wars without losing its liquidity. It maintained an extensive remittance service for private persons as well as bill brokerage. Prussia kept the flourishing bank for just under 15 years; in 1805 she was forced to cede Anspach-Bayreuth to France in the Treaty of Schönbrunn, receiving Hannover in return. Napoleon gave the Franconian areas to Bavaria in exchange for the Wittelsbach lands on the Lower Rhine. Thereafter, the Ansbach-Bayreuth Bank adopted the company name of Königlich-Bayerische Bank and became the most important credit institution in Bavaria in the first third of the 19th century.

Prussian 'Landschaften'

The Prussian *Landschaften* occupied a special position among credit institutions, particularly at the beginning and more generally throughout the 19th century. They were founded after the Seven Years' War in order to provide the landed nobility with credit to help them rebuild their manors. All Prussian provinces had been the theatre of fighting during this war, though Silesia had suffered most. The *Schlesische Landschaft* was therefore the first to be founded in 1771, followed by the *Märkische Landschaft* in 1777, the *Pommersche Landschaft* in 1781, the *Westpreussische Landschaft* in 1787 and the *Ostpreussische Landschaft* a year later.

The term *Landschaft* originally denoted all the estates (the clergy, nobility, town councillors) and their assembly. The credit institutes which came to be called *Landschaften* were institutions of these estates. Every manor within a province belonged to a *Landschaft* and assumed corporate general liability for every single credit granted to any individual landowner. In the *Märkische Landschaft*, all mortgaged manors were corporately liable for an individual credit, after the nobility of the Brandenburg March had rejected both compulsory membership of the *Landschaft* and corporate general liability, which would have included their unmortgaged landed properties. This is interesting because it shows that the estates, even under an absolute monarchy, had not lost all political power.

Except for the *Märkische Landschaft*, the *Landschaften* hence constituted compulsory credit co-operatives under public law; every single unit had been created by special legislation. Members of the *Landschaften* received mortgage bonds issued by the *Landschaft*, rather than cash loans. The liability was certified on these bonds and it was then left to the persons in receipt of these credits to sell the mortgate bonds to investors with enough capital to buy them. The manors belonging to a particular *Landschaft* were valued and mortgages between one half and two-thirds of the assessed value could be raised on them. This system was occasionally misused by members who, by taking up credit, were able to acquire several manors. At the same time it contributed to the increased mobility of manorial property.

2. The State Loan Business and the Political Role of Private Bankers

In the first two-thirds of the 19th century, the big financial operations of the private bankers consisted of state loans. States had two possibilities: they offered the loan directly for general subscription or they issued it indirectly through the mediation of a banking house or a consortium of banks. The first alternative, direct issue, was open only to states enjoying a good financial reputation. Less credit-worthy states required the mediation and guarantee of a banking house. Credit-worthy states often left the technical work of bond issue to one or several banking houses for greater convenience. When a banking house or a consortium of banks issued a loan — until the mid-19th century it was usual for only one bank to be involved in issuing a state loan — it accepted the total sum at a certain rate of its own account, or it guaranteed the borrowing state at least a minimum of the issue's expected result. The issuing house or the consortium put the loans in bonds of various denominations on the market, either privately or on the stock exchange.

In this operation the bankers' profit was made up, firstly, of the commission, i.e. the remuneration for the technical execution of bond issues, and secondly, of gains made on the rate of exchange. These gains arose from the difference between the rate at which they accepted the loan and the rate at which they placed it among the public. All state bonds were issued at a discount, for the nominal payment of interest was relatively low (2.5% up to 5% at the most), and hardly anybody would have bought at par. Issuing at a discount meant a higher interest yield for buyers: the borrowing state had not only to pay interest on the full nominal value of the loan, but also to redeem it in full, rather than merely the sum which it actually received as a loan on the basis of the rate of issue. Those states which were already heavily indebted, and thus less credit-worthy, had to accept particularly low issue prices. These states included Spain, the Italian states, the Austrian Monarchy (until the 1860s), the Ottoman Empire and later the Balkan states. As regards these countries, a very low rate of issue (about 70%-80%) already contained a risk premium for creditors. For this reason, state loan transactions with heavily indebted states were speculative. They contained a high risk, but at the same time the prospect of high profits.

In the 19th century there were also, in addition to redeemable state loans, 'perpetual' state loans under the terms of which a state undertook to make regular payments at a fixed rate of interest (annuity), but was not committed to amortization. An example of this kind of state loan was the French *rente perpetuelle*. Its holders obtained an inheritable claim to an annuity from the State, amounting to the nominal interest. This *rente perpetuelle* could be cancelled neither by the creditor nor by the State. The French state could reduce the annuity charge only by repurchasing the annuities *(rachat)*. After the First World War, inflation cut the ground from under this type of state loan. As long as state loans were floated without formal law or parliamentary control, the banking houses which purchased the issue could occasionally acquire real collateral, either through a mortgage on a sovereign's real estate, or a pledge for a demesne or certain public revenues. Clearly, it was not possible to demand such securities from the Great Powers; but they could be obtained from smaller states or from those in decline, such as the Ottoman Empire in the second half of the 19th century.

Until shortly after the German Wars of Liberation, the London banking house of Baring Brothers & Co., in close co-operation with the Amsterdam house of Hope & Co., was the greatest financier and money-broker to the European powers. They were ousted from their position as the leading financier to princes and governments on the European Continent by the Rothschilds from 1819-20. As far as Britain and the United States were concerned, the Barings remained their most important lender until the middle of the century. In issuing her state loans, France collaborated with the Rothschild Bank in Paris and with other firms of the Paris *haute banque*, where either the Rothschilds or one of their rivals were dominant, depending on the domestic situation. The main financier to the Austrian Monarchy, until the end of the Wars of Liberation, was the Frankfurt banking house of Bethmann; its place was subsequently taken by the Viennese Rothschild Bank, which had been founded in 1816. Prussia chiefly used the services of three Frankfurt banking houses, namely Bethmann, Metzler, and M.A. Rothschild & Söhne. Russian loans were mediated by Hope, Baring and later by the bankers in Berlin.

Expectation of profit was the main incentive for private bankers to accept state loans, but it was not the only motive. Many state loans were bad business for bankers from the outset, promising only minimal returns or no profit at all, but they would accommodate such a situation in order to establish contacts with important statesmen or monarchs. These business relationships were useful publicity, as they demonstrated solidity and financial strength; furthermore they could help launch other profitable business deals. The Jewish bankers, and the Rothschilds in particular, also used the political contacts which they had made as creditors to improve the position of the Jews. Thus Karl Meyer Rothschild, the founder of the Rothschild Bank in Naples, mediated several loans for the Papal States. In return for his services he was awarded the Order of the Redeemer by Pope

Gregor XVI and successfully persuaded Pope Pius IX to release the Jews in
the Papal States from the requirement to attend a weekly Christian sermon.
In 1835, Salomon Meyer Rothschild, the founder of the Viennese Rothschild
Bank, induced his patron, Metternich, to allow Jews in Austria to acquire
real estate. However, such successful interventions can hardly be taken as
proof that the Rothschilds had a significant political influence; for whereas
improvements in their social position were of great importance to the Jews,
the small concessions made by the non-Jewish elites were barely commen-
surate with the advantages they received from their Jewish financiers.

What political influence or leverage did the bankers have? The fact that
they were members of parliaments does not signify very much; members of
other professions and social groups were much more strongly represented
here. Since banking families belonged to the upper class, and had, in many
cases, already been raised to the nobility, the sons, grandsons and nephews
of bankers were holders of high political and administrative office just like
the sons of other rich and respected families. Thus Francis Thornbill Baring
of the Baring family repeatedly held the office of Secretary to the Treasury
and was made First Lord of the Admiralty in John Russell's Liberal cabinet
(1849-1852). His son, Thomas George, occupied several government positions under Palmerston; between 1872 and 1876 he was Viceroy of India
and finally First Lord of the Admiralty under Gladstone. The best known of
the Barings in politics was Evelyn Baring, later Earl of Cromer, who, as the
British Consul-General in Cairo from 1883-1907, was the actual ruler of
Egypt.

Jean Casimir Périer came from the French banking family and was the
French Prime Minister in 1893-4 and President of the Republic in 1894-5;
he resigned for constitutional reasons after only one year in office. Even so,
the political and administrative careers of the offsprings of banking families
do not provide circumstantial evidence that bankers had any special political
influence. They merely testify to their social position. It is possible to speak
of their political influence only when they themselves held high political
office, or participated in political events and developments because they
were financing them.

During the 19th century, we find bankers in high political positions
where, as supporters of a moderate liberalism, they joined the struggle for
the establishment of a constitutional monarchy in their country. In the city
republics of Frankfurt and Hamburg, they formed the ruling patriciate
alongside the great merchants and 'jurists'. In France and Prussia, bankers
were prominent among the leaders of political Liberalism. In France, the
haute banque initially welcomed the Restoration of the Bourbon Monarchy
in 1814-15, because it meant the end of the Napoleonic Wars; but the
authoritarian style of the royal government soon pushed the bankers into
opposition. They got themselves elected in large numbers to the Chamber
as Liberal deputies. Laffitte, the head of Perrégaux Laffitte & Cie., and
Casimir Périer were rival spokesmen for the liberal opposition. Bankers
also helped to finance the political press. Laffitte had a share in several

newspapers, such as *Le Courrier Français* and *Le National.* In the July Revolution of 1830, Laffitte's house became the centre of activity, with Laffitte and the one-time Napoleonic general, Etienne Gérard, heading the movement.

There were three bankers on the Committee of Eight which functioned as a provisional government; Laffitte, Odier and Casimir Périer. It was basically due to Laffitte that Louis Philippe, the Duke of Orléans, was proclaimed the new King and not appointed merely as Imperial Vice-Regent for the young grandson of Charles X who had been toppled. Political and banking connections had already existed between Laffitte and Louis Philippe for several years, and a few months after the Revolution Laffitte became Prime Minister and Minister of Finance. However, he soon lost the new King's favour and in March 1831 had to hand over the office of Prime Minister to his political and business rival, Casimir Périer, who, at the same time, also assumed the office of Minister of the Interior. Périer revealed himself a very energetic head of government who stabilized the new regime against Bourbon and republican revolts. He created the policy of *juste milieu*, which was as far removed from extreme liberalism as it was from extreme conservatism. During the July Monarchy, from 1830 to 1848, the upper bourgeoisie, and in particular its elite, the *haute banque*, held political power in its hands.

The Second Napoleonic Empire also had a private banker among its leading politicians: Achille Fould. He was partner in the banking house of Fould-Oppenheim, which had been founded in Paris by his father and his father's friend, Salomon Oppenheim, the Cologne banker. After the Revolution of February 1848, Fould emerged as fellow party-member and financier to Prince Louis Napoleon. When the latter was elected President of the Republic, he appointed Fould Minister of Finance in 1849. In the 1850s, Fould functioned as Minister of State to the then Emperor Napoleon III. But it was only in his second term of office as Minister of Finance that Fould could influence the financial and commercial orientation of the Second Empire more decisively.

In Germany, the Revolution of 1848 propelled certain private bankers into high government office as liberal politicians, among them the Rhenish bankers Gustav Mevissen and Ludolf Camphausen from Cologne and August von der Heydt from Elberfeld. Melvissen was one of the founders of the first German joint-stock banks which will be discussed below. His political activity began when he partcipated in the founding of the *Rheinische Zeitung,* a paper in whose editorial office the young Karl Marx worked until 1843. In 1848, Mevissen was a member of the German National Assembly, which met in the Frankfurt *Paulskirche* for a few months; he also worked as Undersecretary of State in the Ministry of Commerce of the Imperial Ministry, which was formed at Frankfurt, although he was unable to develop an effective programme. Camphausen, his colleague from Cologne, took charge of the Prussian Ministry of State after the uprising in Berlin in March 1848. His moderate Liberal position on the constitutional question very quickly clashed with the radical-liberal demands of the majority of the Prussian National Assembly, and he resigned in June 1848. He continued to work as a Prussian representative in the National Assembly at Frankfurt and endeavoured to obtain — without success — a *'kleindeutsch'* solution to the German question (i.e. a united Germany without Austria).

The political activity of the Elberfeld banker August von der Heydt had a much more lasting effect. It was not until December 1848, when the policy of reaction was launched in Prussia under the Brandenburg-Manteuffel Ministry, that he joined the government as Minister of Commerce. He retained this office for 14 years until 1862. For the first nine years he, the liberal banker, served as Minister in a strictly conservative government. This was typical of Prussia between 1815 and 1878 when a conservative domestic policy went hand-in-hand with a liberal economic policy. Von der Heydt transformed the Preussische Bank into a modern central bank with a monopoly of note-issue (1856) and initiated the liberalization of Prussian mining law by abolishing state-direction; he did away with the managerial authority of the State Mining Inspectorate over the private mining enterprises. In 1862, von der Heydt took over the Ministry of Finance, but left when Bismarck became Minister President. He rejoined the government again as Finance Minister on the eve of the Prusso-Austrian war of 1866 and financed the mobilization of the Prussian Army, not by taking up a loan but by selling state-owned railway shares to the Bleichröder banking house for 11 million thalers. Apart from these three bankers who held high political office, David Hansemann must be mentioned, although his career took a different course. He started off as a businessman before becoming a politician in 1848-49. He left his ministerial position to take over the management of the Preussische Bank and moved into private banking only towards the end of his career.

This survey of bankers occupying high political positions during the 19th century still does not answer the question of private bankers in politics. To find it, we have to examine which political ventures they participated in as financiers. It is also important to ask what role their financing played. As a general conclusion, it may be said that banking interests were not a driving force behind the outbreak of any European war. On the contrary, the bankers had — and have — a great interest in the maintenance of peace because they tend to have more to lose than to gain from wars; judging from the historical evidence, wars lead, if not to national bankruptcy, to a depreciation of money. Such experience is not confined to a specific political, social and economic system. Parliamentary democracies suffered it in the same way as absolute monarchies and dictatorships. Following the Second World War, even the Soviet Union was hit by inflation! In order to spread the risk which was always — and still is — connected with state loans, private bankers do not restrict their lending activities to one state; they were invariably involved with several governments. They set great store by the prosperity and solvency of their debtors. What mattered to them was not so much to press for certain political actions, but rather to maintain an equilibrium among the powers and peace in Europe. This was the situation they stood most to profit from. After all, the banks did not particularly like fierce competition between their customers within the private economy either. The same considerations which caused them to support the balance of power policy in Europe at state level induced the major banks to promote cartelization and the formation of industrial combines in the private economy in the closing years of the 19th century and in the 20th century (see below p. 89f.).

Until the end of the 18th century, Amsterdam was the greatest international market for state loans, but it lost this position when French troops occupied the Netherlands in the War of the First Coalition (1795). A considerable part of Amsterdam's movement of goods and capital shifted to Hamburg, whereas London assumed the role of the leading money and capital market. The greatest private Dutch banking house of Hope & Co. transferred to London for the duration of French rule and intensified its earlier co-operation with the Baring Brothers. The long European fight against revolutionary France and Napoleon had to be financed from London by English merchant bankers. The important Continental banking centres were excluded from this task as they lay in the French sphere of influence. However, the merchant bankers were in many cases not prepared to accept the issue of loans for states on the Continent; their expectation of low profits did not seem to justify the high risks involved. The British government therefore had to help out and pay subsidies to its allies. Britain was the only country to be continuously at war with France, with the exception of a short interval following the Peace of Amiens of March 1802 until the renewal of hostilities on 18 March 1803. The costs of these wars and the additional subsidies to her temporary allies burdened the British national budget so heavily that the Government had to run up an enormous state debt. Between 1793 and 1816, it placed loans totalling £911 million with the help of various consortia of merchant bankers. The actual amount obtained by the Government was a mere £590 million, however. Some £321 million were pocketed as discounts and commissions by the merchant bankers. The long war, the growing state debt and the depreciation of money — from 1798 until 1819 Britain had paper money as the Bank of England's obligation to convert it to gold was suspended — all diminished the British government's credit-worthiness with the banks. On the other hand, the Government was in such urgent need of money that it could not but accept their conditions. Thus, in 1800, in accepting a loan of £20.5 million negotiated through the Baring Brothers and two smaller banks, the Government issued bonds for over £157, bearing 3% interest, for each £100 it received.

During the long years of war from 1793 to 1815, the English bankers made loans available not only to their Government and its allies, but also carried out credit transactions with neutral countries; occasionally they even accepted loans where the proceeds were destined as payment to the French enemy, with the British government raising no objection. The Baring banking house was appointed universal plenipotentiary by the American government in 1803 for the financial operations of the United States (loans and international remittances), which it carried out until 1835. In 1803 the Barings were to execute a large financial deal for the Americans which had the following background: in the May of 1801, President Jefferson had learned that Spain and France had agreed, in the secret Treaty of San Ildefonso of October 1800, to effect an exchange of territories by which France was to obtain Louisiana to the West of the Mississippi river, which belonged to Spain; Spain was to get the Toscana for King Charles IV's son-in-law. Before this contract was implemented, which would have enabled the French to re-establish themselves in North America, Jefferson made an offer for the United States to buy Louisiana from France. A contract was signed in 1803; under its terms the United States bought Louisiana for the sum of $15 million. Claims made by American citizens against French citizens, amounting to £3.75 million, were deducted from the purchase price, which left the sum of $11.25 million. The Baring and Hope banks undertook the placing of the loan which was issued to raise the sum; they also arranged the transfer of the monies to France. Francis Baring and a partner of the Hope banking house stayed in Paris, the enemy capital, for several months to make preparations for the transactions. With the British government's consent the Barings also advanced the money which Portugal and Spain had to pay to France, in 1802 and 1805-6 respectively and they also took care of the remittances.

The financial power, the credit and the international experience of the Barings and the Hopes were also called upon when it came to raising money for the reparations which had been imposed upon the defeated France by the Powers of the Anti-Napoleonic Coalition in the Second Peace of Paris of 1815. However, this large loan brokerage saw the end of the Barings' leading role in financing international politics. France had to pay 700 million gold francs in reparations and to cover the costs of keeping 150,000 allied occupation forces in Northern France. The French Treasury was depleted after the long wars and government credit was exhausted. An internal French loan was out of the question. The tax screw could not be tightened any further without crippling the already stagnant French economy and destroying the popularity of the restored Bourbon Monarchy again. However, the French government had compelling reasons for paying the reparations as soon as possible; for once this question was settled, the country's credit-worthiness would be boosted, the rate of French government securities — the *rentes* — would rise and lead to the withdrawal of the occupation forces. These developments would in turn strengthen the new Government's prestige and also contribute to a revitalisation of the economy.

However, these objectives could not be achieved without a foreign loan. There was a great deal of liquid capital available in Britain owing to the economic boom at the end of the war and the lifting of the Continental Blockade. In February 1817, the Barings, together with their Dutch business friends, Hope, took on a French government loan of over 100 million francs, at an interest of 5% and an issuing price of 55%. Four French banking houses — Greffulhe & Cie., Hottinguer & Cie., Baguenault & Cie and Perrégaux Laffitte & Cie. — participated with a one-third share in the issue of the loan. The fact that distinguished banking houses had accepted the loan without any fuss, dramatically increased the standing of French government securities and stimulated demand for them. It enabled the next government loan to be issued within five months, again at 5% interest and an issuing price of 64%. Baring and Hope accepted the loan, this time in association with the Paris banking houses of Perrégaux Laffitte & Cie. and Delessert & Cie. A month later, the bonds *(rentes)* were traded at 68.5%. These loans helped France pay the upkeep of the occupation forces, though not her reparations. Britain, as the biggest creditor power among the victors, saw to it that the reparations were sufficiently reduced in order to get them paid and cleared up quickly. The United States, finding itself in a similar position as creditor after 1918, came to the same conclusion only after Germany, the country owing reparations, had become insolvent.

France's reparations debt, of which nothing had as yet been paid, was reduced from 700 million to 265 million francs at the Congress of Aachen in 1818. Some 165 million of this was to be paid in bills of exchange drawn on the Houses of Baring and Hope, as stipulated by Article VI of the Aachen Convention, signed by France, Britain, Russia, Austria and Prussia on 9 October 1818. The remaining 100 million were to be settled by the issue of new *rentes*. Baring and Hope accepted this new loan at 74% and sold the *rentes* at 75.5%. Those who bought the *rentes* also included statesmen from other European countries, among them Metternich and Gentz. But the price of these highly valued *rentes* fell shortly afterwards. A great deal of gold was flowing from Britain and France into Central Europe because of the reparation payments and the raising of loans by Central European countries. This resulted in a shortage of credit in Britain and particularly in France, so that many buyers sold their *rentes* to other purchasers in order to regain their liquidity. There had also been some speculation: some had bought *rentes* at the time of the Aachen Congress in expectation of a further rise in the rate and began to sell when it rose to 80%. This glut of *rentes* was a prelude to the sudden collapse of their price, which had fallen to 60% by December 1818. Criticism was now also directed against the issuing banks of Baring and Hope. Not only had they not suffered any losses from the *rentes* business, they had actually emerged with profits — the amount of which is not known. But the criticism had the effect that in future the Continental powers entrusted their financial dealings primarily to the new rising power of the Rothschilds.

In the century between the fall of Napoleon and the outbreak of the First World War, there were few wars between the Great Powers, and those conflicts that did occur were of short duration and geographically confined. That this century, in comparison to others, was relatively peaceful and knew only limited conflict was due to the fact that the European Balance of

Power worked well. International relations were determined by 'realistic' power calculations. The political unification of Germany was brought about, within such a constellation, not by a popular movement but by Prussian *Realpolitik*. Among the technical conditions allowing this Balance-of-Power system to operate were factors such as contemporary diplomacy, which drew its recruits from the aristocracy with its supranational family connections, and the *haute banque*, which played the role of international public creditor. The European system began to decline only with the rise of nationalist movements and the formation of a system of world powers in the age of imperialism from the end of the 19th century. The European Balance of Power and the safety mechanisms for the maintenance of peace, which had been negotiated at the Congress of Vienna, functioned best from 1815 until the Crimean War (1853-1856). These 40 years were also the great era of the Rothschilds. All European powers owed them money in this period. This is not to say that the equilibrium between the powers and peace in Europe was dependent on the Rothschilds and the scale of their influence. What matters is that the two factors were mutually interdependent: on the one hand, the balance between the European states was a pre-condition for the international scope of the Rothschild's business; on the other, their financial power was in itself a weighty factor within the European system during these decades. Their financial power was just as vital as the state bureaucracies and the standing armies. Whoever wishes to understand the functioning of the European Balance-of-Power system in this period must not overlook the role of the Rothschilds within it.

After the final defeat of Napoleon, the European powers turned their attention to preventing the repetition of a revolution like that of 1789 with its international consequences. This international counter-revolutionary policy was institutionalized in the Holy Alliance and the Quadruple Alliance. The Holy Alliance, concluded on 26 September 1815, was conceived by Tsar Alexander I as a Christian brotherhood of nations to oppose the return of the revolutionary fraternity. Metternich brought it down to earth by treating it as a brotherhood of monarchs whose partners regarded themselves as *membres d'une même nation chrétienne* and promised mutual support with all the means at their disposal, *en toute occasion et en tout lieu*. All European rulers except the Pope, the Sultan and the King of England joined the Holy Alliance. The first two were not called upon to join, the Pope because of his exclusive position within the Catholic Church, and the Sultan because he was not a Christian. The King of England could not enter into a purely royal treaty for constitutional reasons. The Quadruple Alliance between Austria, Russia, Britain and Prussia, of November 1815, extended the Anti-Napoleonic Coalition into the post-war period.

Both alliances ushered in an era of congresses and interventions. The first Congress, held at Aachen in 1818, reduced French reparations and put an end to the occupation of France by the allies of the Wars of Liberation. The next congresses — Troppau in 1820, Laibach in 1821 and Verona in 1823 — were prompted by revolutionary movements springing up in the

Mediterranean countries (in Spain, Portugal and Italy in 1820, in Greece in 1821). Austria was given authority to intervene in the Kingdoms of Naples and Sardinia; at the Verona Congress France was given authority to move against Spain. The British government protested against these interventions. Military costs and the economic consequences of these operations, as well as Britain's rejection of interventionism meant that large-scale financial transactions had to be undertaken. A loan from the Rothschilds financed the mobilization of Austria's troops. Later they granted a loan to the Kingdom of Naples, but they took care that the Kingdom was put in a position to pay for the upkeep of the Austrian occupying army.

The first loan to Austria was insufficient to cover her financial requirements, and another loan became necessary in 1822. Apart from the Viennese banking houses and the Rothschilds, Laffitte tried to float the loan through a consortium of Paris banking houses which he had organised. Yet Laffitte was not acceptable as a financier; Metternich thought his views too liberal. After long negotiations, in which the Austrian government took advantage of the competition between the bankers to increase the loan of 30 million guldens from 67% to 82%, Rothschild and three Viennese banking houses accepted. At this point, the British government stepped in. It claimed repayment of two loans, totalling £6.2 million, which it had granted Austria in 1795 and 1797. Subsequently, it reduced its demand to £4 million or 40 million guldens, but insisted on immediate payment in full. In this way Austria, already suffering a budget deficit, ran into danger of financial ruin, which could have been prevented only through the quick withdrawal of her troops from Italy, amounting to a renunciation of her interventionist policy. This had been the intention behind the British government's move. Metternich was saved from retreat and humiliation by the Rothschilds. Salomon and Nathan Rothschild contacted the British government through Alexander Baring and succeeded in getting the sum owed by the Austrian government reduced to £2.5 million. The Rothschilds and Barings advanced the money and accepted in its place Austrian bonds at 82.7%. This was good business. By 1825, these bonds had risen to 94%.

In the Spanish case, the interaction between politics and finance was such that the Rothschilds, together with the Paris *haute banque*, assumed a position almost equalling that of one of the great powers. Spain's constitutional government, installed by the Revolution of 1820, issued two loans with the consent of the *Cortes*, which were accepted by banks in Paris and London. The Rothschilds were prepared to participate, but desisted when pressured by the Austrian government. Metternich found it intolerable that financiers with whom he collaborated should support a 'rebel government'. The situation changed, once the absolutist party was again in power in Spain, following the intervention of the French army in 1823. The new reactionary Spanish government urgently needed money. It had to pay for the 95,000 French troops which were stationed in Spain until 1828. It also wanted to restart the war against the former Spanish colonies in South and Central America, which had seceded from their mother country in 1810. On the other hand, the reactionary Spanish government did not want to pay interest and amortization on those loans which had been issued by the liberal *Cortes* government. It regarded these loans, which had been issued by the 'rebels' in the name of King Ferdinand VII, as illegal and criminal.

The Spanish problem was complicated by the divergent interests of three groups of countries and banks. Austria, Russia and France were keenly interested in supporting the reactionary Spanish government; their ministers and diplomats favoured Spain's request for loans from the Paris *haute banque* and, in particular, from the five Rothschild brothers. Prussia, whose government was as conservative as those of Austria and Russia, did not play an independent role in European politics in the years between 1815 and 1862 and hence had no part in the Spanish Question. The second group consisted of British exporters, merchant bankers in London and finally the conservative British government. It was of great importance to this group to maintain the independence of the young Latin-American states; British export trade to South America had gained a large additional market with the end of Spanish colonial rule, and the merchant bankers had also taken on South American loans. The third group was made up of the Rothschild House and the Paris *haute banque*. Basically, they were prepared to grant the conservative Spanish government a loan, but only on certain conditions: the Spanish administration appeared so unreliable to them that they demanded sound guarantees for interest and amortization payments. They saw two possible ways of arranging such guarantees: either the French government could exercise control over Spain's financial administration or else the Spanish clergy would sequester part of the public revenue and administer the servicing of the loan. Secondly, they demanded that the loans which the *Cortes* government had taken out be recognized and repurchased by the new government at least at the current price at which they were still being quoted on the stock exchange. Finally, they requested that Spain take British mercantile interests in South America into consideration. What was meant by this was that the British would be given free access to the South American market, if Spain reestablished her colonial empire there. The Rothschilds had no desire to risk upsetting the London merchant bankers and the British government because of South America.

The Spanish government sent a special envoy to negotiate with the five Rothschilds. The Spanish Minister of Finance took the trouble to go to James Rothschild's country-seat. The Russian and American ambassadors also exerted pressure on the Rothschilds. However, the Spanish government was only prepared to accept the intervention of the Spanish clergy in servicing the government debt and refused to meet the remaining demands; so two years of negotiation ended without result. Neither the Russian nor the Austrian government met with success, however much they pressed the Rothschilds in Spain's favour. This caused a Spanish minister to remark angrily: 'A handful of rebels ... inspired the bankers with more confidence than four great powers which joined forces on behalf of a monarch who had been unlawfully deprived of power'. Spanish domestic affairs remained unstable, and in the 1830s the country plunged into civil war, known as the 'Carlist War'.

Following the French Revolution of July 1830 and after Belgium had seceded from the Netherlands, the threat of war hung over Europe. Tsar Nicholas I and Metternich were prepared for military intervention against the massive support which France proffered to the Belgians in their fight against the Dutch. At that time James Rothschild in Paris and Salomon Rothschild in Vienna feverishly tried to preserve peace. James Rothschild had suffered great losses through the July Revolution, and war between the European powers would increase these losses and seriously disrupt the Rothschilds' international business. They therefore supported Louis Philippe's efforts to come to an agreement with Austria.

In parallel with the official government contact between Paris and Vienna, there existed an unofficial exchange of views and information between Louis Philippe and Metternich via James Rothschild and Salomon Rothschild. In order to put pressure on the Austrian government to preserve the peace, the Rothschilds finally exploited Austria's financial crisis. In March 1831, the Rothschild Bank in Vienna, together with three other Viennese banks, subscribed an Austrian loan to the nominal amount of 57.1 million guldens at 84%. It was to be a long-term loan, but it was recallable and would have to be repaid, should war break out within the following three months. Metternich could not therefore use the money for the purpose for which he wanted it. In order to get hold of at least some money for a possible war, Metternich entered into a convention with Prussia, under the terms of which some 20 million francs of French reparation money was divided between Prussia and Austria. This money had been earmarked for the military programme of the German Confederation and, more precisely, for the construction of a fortress, but had not yet been claimed. Yet both parties were allowed to use the money only in an extreme emergency. The pressure which the Rothschilds exerted on Austria over the loan did not settle the situation at the time; international tension lasted for almost another year, but it is nonetheless a symptom of the vital interest bankers had in maintaining the Balance of Power and peace in Europe.

3. The Financing of Railway Construction

State loans apart, private bankers specialized in another area of large financial dealings at that time, namely in providing credit to members of the nobility who owned latifundia. The biggest transaction of this kind was a credit of over 6.4 million guldens which the Frankfurt Rothschild Bank gave to Prince Esterhazy in 1844 at 4% interest and with an amortization period of 55 years. From 1830 onwards, railway construction became another field of large-scale financial operations.

Up to the second half of the 19th century, private companies had mostly undertaken the construction and operation of railways. Few countries had a policy of public railway building and service, in addition to their private railways. Among them were Belgium, where the railway network was expanded very quickly and systematically, the Netherlands, Bavaria, Württemberg and Baden. In France, railway construction made sluggish progress at first, though from 1842 state participation in railway construction was regulated by law; thereafter the State bought up the required land and built the embankments. Private companies were then expected to provide tracks, buildings and rolling stock and to maintain the railway services. To recompense the State for its preliminary construction work, the railways were to be transferred into public ownership after 99 years. The French state also guaranteed railway companies a minimum-interest rate on their joint-stock capital, and should this yield not be achieved, the shareholders were to be paid the difference. Several French towns gave those railway companies to whose networks they wished to be linked interest guarantees for part of their joint-stock capital. Other countries such as Prussia, Austria and the Federal States of the North American Union also gave such guarantees. In North America the railway companies obtained, moreover, large donations of land in areas which could only be opened up through the building of railways. Prussia, on the other hand, took shares in those railways in which it had a special political, and above all, military-strategic interest. Both railway construction and railway services were wholly private in Britain; they received no state aid.

According to German calculations, about 85 milliard marks were invested in railways in all countries up to 1880, of which 25.5 milliard was invested in the United States, 14.9 milliard in Britain, 8.9 milliard in Germany and 8.5 milliard in France. Thus 68% of the total capital invested in railway construction was concentrated in the four largest industrial countries of the 19th century, before the building of railways in the colonies and countries rich in raw materials outside Europe and North America became an interesting field for investment during the era of imperialism from about 1880.

The huge funds required for railway construction could not be raised by private bankers alone; nor could state railway construction be financed from recurrent state revenue. The capital of medium and small property owners had to be mobilized through the formation of joint-stock companies. Following the bad experiences with limited liability companies such as John Law's Mississippi Company in the 18th century, the South Sea Bubble and the decline of most overseas trading companies, the early 19th century viewed joint-stock companies with a scepticism similar to that with which bank notes were regarded in many places. In Britain, the foundation of private limited liability companies was forbidden until 1825, after which they could be established by royal charter. It was only from 1865 that joint-stock companies could be formed without restrictions. In both France and the German states, private joint-stock companies required a state concession during the first two-thirds of the 19th century. Thus until railway building began, several important public joint-stock companies were founded, such as the Bank of England, the Royal Bank of Scotland, the Banque de France, the Preussische Bank or the British East India Company, but hardly any private joint-stock companies. Only canal- and road-building companies existed as such. Consequently, there was also no significant speculation in equities on stock exchanges before then. Only a few securities were traded and they were almost exclusively state bonds. Stock exchange business underwent an enormous expansion with the issue of railway shares and bonds, and railway construction also heralded a period of massive speculation on the stock exchange, with many speculation crises.

What role did private bankers play in the railway business? They participated in the promotion of railway companies by taking over a considerable part of the share capital themselves. This is particularly true of the first 45 years as far as the European Continent is concerned. It was only after 1860 that large numbers of railway shares were placed among the public outside England. Private bankers also granted railway companies credit by accepting their bonds. There thus developed interlocking capital arrangements and personal ties between banking houses and railway companies similar to those which emerged between joint-stock banks and industry in Central Europe at the close of the 19th century.

The first railways were built in Britain, where there was also a plentiful supply of capital looking for investment. As the first, and only, London banking house, the firm of Glyn Mills & Co. had participated in the early promotion of the railways and kept a leading role in financing British railway construction later on. In Britain, however, the greater part of the railway capital was collected in comparatively small shares, ranging from £100 to £2,000, from the savings of the provincial middle classes. The railway companies raised these sums by inviting subscriptions to their issues.

Unlike in Britain, private bankers played a dominant role during the first 45 years of railway construction on the Continent. The Rothschilds were again the most pre-eminent. In the course of 30 years, a virtual network of railway lines emerged between Paris and Madrid in the West, Liège and Magdeburg in the North, Lemberg and Kronstadt in the East, and Marseille and Bari in the South, of which the Rothschild banks were the principal shareholders. At the beginning there were only two short lines running from Paris to Saint-Germain and to Versailles, which were built between 1835 and 1837. Before 1840, longer routes were not yet considered profitable by many bankers. After 1842, the large junction lines from Paris to the Belgian border in the North and to the South via Lyon and Avignon to Marseille were built with heavy investment from the Paris Rothschild Bank. By 1848, Rothschild held 10% of the total capital of France's railway companies. In Austria, Salomon Rothschild took over the management of the company which, from 1836 onwards, built the *Nordbahn* from Vienna via Pressburg, Oderberg and Cracow to Bochnia. The Viennese Rothschild Bank later also participated in financing the *Südbahn* from Vienna to Laibach and the large East-West connection in the southern part of the Austrian Monarchy, from Laibach via Agram to Kronstadt in Transylvania. From 1850 onwards, Germany saw the construction of several railways to

the north of the river Main; the Frankfurt Rothschild Bank, together with
some of the newly founded joint-stock banks (Darmstädter Bank für Handel
und Industrie, Disconto-Gesellschaft, Schaaffhausenscher Bankverein), took
over the financing of the following railways: the *Hessische Ludwigsbahn*,
the *Thüringische Eisenbahn*, the *Bergisch-Märkische Eisenbahn* and the
Oberschlesische Eisenbahn. By comparison the London Rothschild House,
under Nathan Rothschild and his son, Lionel, was very cautious about the
railways business.

In Germany, the first larger railway routes were built on the initiative of
private bankers in Cologne who also invested heavily in them. After several
years of deliberation, the *Rheinische Eisenbahngesellschaft* was founded in
1837. The original purpose of the company was to set up a rail link between
Cologne and Antwerp to eliminate the Dutch middle-man. In the course of
the next decades, the company built a network of railway lines between the
Western border of Prussia, the Rhine and the Saar. In addition to the
Rothschild banks in Frankfurt and Paris, four Cologne banking houses —
J.H. Stein, A. Schaaffhausen, J.D. Herstatt and Sal. Oppenheim Jr. & Cie.
— participated decisively in promoting these projects. Of the original capital
of 325,000 thalers, the Paris Rothschild Bank subscribed 50,000 thalers,
and the Oppenheim bank 35,000 thalers. The Schaaffhausen, Oppenheim
and Prussian Seehandlung banks contributed heavily to later successive
capital increases. The capital of the *Köln-Mindener Eisenbahn-Gesellschaft*
was incomparably larger than that of other companies when it was first
founded in 1843. Its original capital amounted to 13 million thalers of
which the Prussian state took over one-seventh. The Cologne banking houses
of Camphausen, Herstatt, Stein, Oppenheim, Schaaffhausen and Seydlitz &
Merkens also participated in raising the capital. The Oppenheim bank
participated, mainly in co-operation with the Rothschild Bank in Frankfurt,
in financing railways outside western Germany and even outside Prussia so
that its railways business eventually stretched as far as Russia and Italy. In
Russia they were part of the consortium, led by the Barings, the Paris House
of Fould-Oppenheim and the Berlin banking house of Mendelssohn, which
placed the Petersburg-Moscow railway shares on the market. Following in
the wake of the Rothschilds, Abraham Oppenheim, the then head of the
Oppenheim banking house, who led it to great prosperity, also participated
in the financing of the *Südbahn* in Austria.

Towards the end of the first stage of railway development on the Continent, dominated as it was by private bankers, railway construction also
began on the Balkan Peninsula which for the most part still belonged to the
Ottoman Empire. For twenty years, the financing of railways in European
Turkey, the 'Oriental Railways' as they were then called, was dominated by
the Brussels banker, Baron Moritz von Hirsch, known as '*Türkenhirsch*'.
He came from a court factor's family in Munich which ran a banking house
in the Bavarian capital. Hirsch had already made a fortune in the credit-
and commodity trade when, in 1869, he asked the Ottoman government for
the concession to build railways in European Turkey. Because of resistance

in Constantinople, Hirsch was at first unable to construct more than a few sections of the railway, with no connections between them. In order to finance these building projects, Hirsch issued premium bonds, called *'Türkenlose'* ('Turkish lottery tickets') because they carried, apart from fixed interest, a bi-monthly chance of winning a lottery prize of 600,000 francs. Some 15 years later, in 1883, the first 'Orient Express' was able to run from Paris to Bucharest, and in 1888 the railway link to Constantinople was finally completed. Around that time, however, the great joint-stock banks began to appear on the scene and in 1890 *'Türkenhirsch'* sold his shares in the *Betriebsgesellschaft der Orientalischen Eisenbahnen* to the Deutsche Bank and the Wiener Bankverein. The deal involved no less than 88,000 out of a total of 100,000 shares. This figure gives an idea of the dominant role which Hirsch had played in Turkish railway construction and of the wealth he had acquired in the process.

In the United States, railway building was at first financed by firms of brokers which simultaneously functioned as banking houses. Boston was the most important banking centre for American railways up to the middle of the 19th century. Boston brokers and bankers, such as J.E. Thayer & Brother, sold railway company shares to the public, acquired shares themselves and also gave credit to companies. From the middle of the century, New York and Philadelphia also became important centres for financing railway construction. In New York, the banking house of Winslow Lanier & Co., founded in 1849, became the largest railway stockbroker in the United States. It had strong financial backing through its connection with the Rothschild banks and Hope & Co. Winslow Lanier & Co. financed above all the building of the railway to the West across the Alleghenies. In Philadelphia, a broker's firm which had been founded in 1838 by the Austrian immigrant, Franz Drexel, was soon also involved in the railways business, mainly in the issuing of railway shares. However, this company enjoyed its period of greatness only after John Pierpont Morgan had become a partner in the banking house in 1871; it changed its name to Drexel Morgan & Co. and its head office was transferred to New York.

The banking house of Cooke & Co., which was founded in Philadelphia in 1861, became the main pillar of speculation in railway bonds. It mobilized small savings for state loans and for railway shares. Cooke & Co. expanded their business steadily. In 1870 they acquired the total joint-stock capital of the Northern Pacific Railroad as payment for the delivery of goods which they had credit-financed. They wanted to sell a large part of these shares at a profit on the exchange rate on the American capital market and in Europe; but the plan misfired. Consequently, the bank suffered from liquidity problems as the bulk of its capital was tied up. When the Northern Pacific Railroad became insolvent in 1873 as a result of mismanagement and underhand manipulation, Cooke & Co. had to suspend their payments, too. Cooke's bankruptcy dragged other American railway companies and banks down with them. This American railway crisis also spread to Germany, since a great deal of German capital had been invested in American railways. It was ultimately one of the causes triggering off the *Gründerkrise* in the Reich in the early 1870s.

In financing railway construction, the private bankers had made a fundamental contribution to the economic and social development of the 19th century; for, next to the rapid development of science and technology, the building of the railways was the main driving force behind economic growth and industrialization in this period. It made possible the transport, on land, of bulk goods; it opened up new markets and brought existing markets closer together; it reduced overland transport costs. Finally, railway construction gave the decisive impetus to the rise of heavy industries which ushered in the second phase of industrialization. And in North America the opening up of the West was dependent on the construction of the transcontinental railways.

4. The Financing of Early Industry

Whilst private bankers were primarily the ones who dealt with and negotiated the financing of the railways from the outset, banks were only one of several sources providing the initial capital of industry, and not even the most significant at that. It was only after the mid-19th century that joint-stock and universal banks in particular began to participate prominently in the long-term financing of industry. Until a few years ago, it was assumed that this development explained why industrialization outside England progressed rather slowly in the early 19th century and accelerated only after 1850. The slow pace of industrialization in the first half of the century was thus attributed chiefly to lack of capital or, at least, to the insufficient mobilization of capital for industry. This explanation seemed very convincing in view of the parallel course of both stages of development — slow industrialization and the inadequate financing of industry by the banks before 1850; rapid industrialization and strong involvement of the joint-stock banks in the financing of industry after the middle of the century. However, recent research both in the field of credit history and the history of technology has shown that this explanation is misleading.

It was not the banks' capacity to mobilize capital that determined the pace of industrialization in the 19th century, but technology. In the early 19th century technology was basically empirical. Its innovations and inventions were introduced into the production process mainly through experimentation and often through the accidental discoveries by industrial practitioners. Usually they lacked the will and the ability to evaluate and transmit their inventions in a systematic and theoretical fashion. It was only after 1850 that technology began to be science-based, which meant that it could be systematically taught and that technological innovation and the diffusion of technological discoveries were tremendously accelerated. These were the technological prerequisites of the era of high industrialization and large-scale industry after 1850.

It is true that a capital market in the modern sense did not yet exist in the first half of the 19th century, and the formation of joint-stock companies was still legally hampered in most countries. Nevertheless, in the early phase of industrialization, there was no lack of capital in any of those countries where industrialization had set in. Factories certainly succeeded in raising the required investment capital during this period. Indeed, it was frequently more difficult to find opportunities for investment than to meet the demand for capital. Complaints could be heard to this effect in Stuttgart in 1826 and in Munich and Basle at the end of the 1830s. The generally low interest rates also point to a plentiful capital supply.

In comparison to the capital which was mobilized for railway construction, the capital requirements of early industry were quite small. Around 1820, approximately 15,000 thalers were needed to set up a smaller spinning mill; the original capital outlay for a medium-sized spinning mill was about 50,000 thalers; and it cost about 100,000 thalers to establish a larger spinning mill or dye-works with 100 workers. A steam engine of 100-200 HP cost about 15,000 thalers at that time. In 1837, Borsig founded his machine factory with a capital of 67,000 thalers, only 8,000 of which were from the firm's own funds.

What were the sources of the money which financed plant installation and the extensions to factories, mines and ironworks in the early phase of industrialization? And how large was the relative share of each of the various sources in the financing of industry? As Francois Crouzet has aptly remarked, the capital which made the development of modern industry possible came in good part from industry itself. To begin with, the capital which had already accumulated in the branch which was being industrialized was of great importance. In the textile industry, wealthy entrepreneurs who, in proto-industrial times, had put out cloth to be produced by cottagers, were able to raise sufficient capital to establish a factory with mechanized equipment. For some time they often maintained the cottage industry with its workers alongside the factory. The capital of artisans and smaller tradesmen also played a significant role in financing new factories. An artisan, it is true, could not as a rule finance a new installation on his own, but he could join forces with other artisans, tradesmen or with financially strong merchants to form a partnership, a *société en nom collectif,* or an *offene Handelsgesellschaft.* If his share was small, he could upvalue his contribution by means of his technical expertise. The management of business in such a partnership was usually taken over by the person contributing the technical know-how, not by the financially stronger partner.

The second source of finance for industry can be traced to the collaboration between artisans and technicians, on the one hand, and merchants, on the other. Here the supply of capital originated from other sectors of the economy, particularly from trade. Wealthy wholesale merchants used their capital, acquired in trading, to establish industrial enterprises and often in order to produce precisely those goods in which they traded. Thus we find many great merchants in iron and hardware among the founders of

ironworks. However significant the equity capital put up by industrial
pioneers and factory founders may have been, it was sufficient in only a
few cases to furnish the total financial requirements of a factory promotion.
The capital which was additionally required had to be raised through —
long-term — credit. Many industrialists collected these investment loans
from members of their extended families, from their circle of friends and
acquaintances and from wealthy private persons to whom they were recommended. Among these persons we find *rentiers,* notaries, lawyers, physicians,
merchants and other well-to-do people. Thus Borsig received the investment
loan of 59,000 thalers, which he needed in addition to his 8,000 thalers
equity capital, from friends and from a master tailor who had become
wealthy on account of his skill as a craftsman and his thrift. Apart from the
land on which the factory was to be built, Borsig had no securities to offer.
Nevertheless, he received the credits at a very favourable low interest rate of
3.33%. In a few cases the governments in France and several German states
(such as Württemberg and Baden) granted advances. Bank credit played only
a small role in raising initial capital investment, except in the case of the
mining industry.

For enterprises which were already in existence, there were better
sources of credit supply. Short-term working credits were given by banks,
above all by the provincial banks which were well-acquainted with local
conditions. To finance expansion programmes, larger enterprises, from
the 1830s onwards, mobilized capital by issuing bonds on the model of
government securities. At the same time, a further possibility of long-term
industrial finance emerged in the form of credits secured by mortgages — on
the model of agricultural credit systems. France was among the leaders using
this form of long-term credit at the time. The banks also participated quite
frequently in financing the expansion of existing industrial enterprises; the
argument that banks played only a subordinate role in financing industry
before 1850 basically applies merely to the financing of new enterprises.
Beyond these general, supranational structures and developments, there were
a number of characteristic national features in the relationship between
banks and early industry which must be mentioned here.

In Britain a special relationship between banks and industry developed
due to the fact that many of the country banks which had been founded as
partnerships in the late 18th and early 19th centuries, had one or more
manufacturers among their founders and partners. Thus the iron manufacturers S.N. & C. Lloyd were partners in the Taylors & Lloyds banking
house in Birmingham. They enjoyed overdraft facilities, and one of the
largest credits was made available to them on current account. In the late
18th and early 19th centuries, the ironworks at Coalbrookdale, which had
become famous thanks to the Darby family's achievements in developing
blast-furnaces, founded several banks which merged to become the Shrop-
shire Banking Company in 1836. There were particularly close relationships
between the partners of ironworks, breweries and textile factories, on the
one hand, and the partners of banks, on the other. However, the question of

the extent to which English banks made long-term credit available for industrial investment remains debatable. It was rare for credit to be given on a long-term basis from the start, like the £20,000 credit which Parr's Bank granted the Crown Glassworks at St. Helens; nor was it important to the financing of industry in general. More frequently, what were formally short-term loans became, in fact, long-term credits; they were repeatedly prolonged so long as the bank regarded its clients as 'very respectable and a very good man of business'.

Lloyds Bank and some country banks in Lancashire practised this form of credit extension in relation to the local textile industry, but on the whole, British industry raised its investments by self-financing and by long-term credit other than from banks. Between 1855-57 the requirement for joint-stock companies to obtain a licence was lifted in England, and thereafter a trend began to promote companies limited by shares. But whereas the issue and administration of shares became an important part of banking business on the Continent and in the United States, English banks left this activity to finance companies and trust companies founded for that sole purpose. These companies did not and still do not count as banks.

In the United States, the development of industry and of financially powerful banks took place up to the 1880s predominantly in the old commercial centres of the North-East. The plantation economy was dominant in the South, and the West had to be opened up through the building of railways. Modern banking developed in the Southern and Western parts only from the last quarter of the 19th century. As in Europe, the long-term capital required by American industry was provided, during the first decades of industrial development, by a multitude of investors from very different backgrounds, mainly from outside the banking community. The particularity of the American development lies in the fact that, in the early phase of industrialization, the savings banks played a leading role in granting investment credit. Savings of immigrants also contributed to the early financing of industry. They preferred to deposit their money with the savings banks, many having brought their savings with them from Europe. Between 1839 and 1859, about 40% of credit (on 12-monthly terms) was given by the savings banks, not quite 30% by trust companies and just over 20% by individuals. By comparison the share of banks in a narrower sense, i.e. the commercial banks, in investment credits was only 3-4%. The savings banks were not replaced in this field until after the Civil War when the expansion of trust companies and the development of many banks into universal banks set in.

In France the *haute banque* had become engaged more strongly and much earlier than in other industrial countries in the long-term financing of industry either by direct participation or by providing long-term credits. It was in this connection that France developed, in addition to limited companies, the partnership limited by shares as a new type of joint-stock company which other countries adopted from the middle of the century. For a long time the promotion of joint-stock companies in France was complicated and difficult. Until 1867, it required a licence from the Head of State, and between 1819 and 1867 a mere 599 joint-stock companies were granted such a licence, half of which were railway, shipping or insurance companies. In the industrial sector, joint-stock companies were established mainly in coal and iron-ore mining and in ironworks, although these represented but a small fraction of the total number of industrial enterprises. Since the opportunity to invest in industry by establishing joint-stock companies was restricted, entrepreneurs at first chose to participate on a limited scale as partners, the advantage being that in France the limited partnership required notarization only. The limited partnership was not, however, very suitable for accumulating large funds from a variety of investors. In view of this investors obtained a court decision in 1832 which allowed limited partnership shares to be treated as negotiable securities. From now on, the partnership limited by shares evolved side-by-side with the traditional form of limited partnership which had existed since the Middle Ages. It possessed the benefits of a joint-stock company, i.e. the opportunity to mobilize capital by issuing shares; on the other hand, it avoided the handicap of a joint-stock company, i.e. the requirement to obtain a licence.

French bankers concentrated their direct participations in mining and in the iron and steel industry as the branches of industry requiring very large capital investments. The *haute banque* participated in the long-term financing of other industries only in exceptional cases, the engineering industry not excluded. This was because the demand for capital was very small in those branches; self-financing was the predominant mode of capital mobilization. The French private bankers, in Paris as well as the provinces, began to finance industry sporadically in the mid-1820s and more vigorously from 1835. In order to mobilize the funds of small capital owners for this purpose, Laffitte, one of the leaders of the July Revolution of 1830, founded the Caisse Générale de Crédit pour le Commerce et l'Industrie. It was constructed as a partnership limited by shares. In addition to the traditional banking business of short-term bills of exchange and government loans, it was to undertake share brokerage. By issuing bank-note-type bonds, Laffitte endeavoured to expand his institute's credit base. Although the Banque de France prevented him from realizing this plan, the bank developed quite well until it collapsed in the economic crisis of 1848. Laffitte and Rothschild also invested in mining companies in the Artois. The most important coal mining region in France at this time was the Basin of the Upper Loire near Saint-Etienne and it was here that some of the Paris banks, particularly Odier, participated in enterprises, as did banking houses from the locality and from Lyon and Geneva. In 1845, at the instigation of the bankers the individual mining companies were merged into the large Compagnie Générale des Mines de la Loire. Nine years earlier, the Paris Rothschild Bank had supported the large ironworks of the Compagnie des Mines de la Grande-Combe which had run into financial difficulties, by giving a credit of 16 million francs. It was not only these millions, but also the Rothschilds' name, which improved the company's solvency and credit-worthiness.

The bankers' experience with industry was not always favourable. In 1825 Soult, who had been a marshall under Napoleon and minister under the July Monarchy, founded a mining and metallurgical enterprise with the help of the Paris bankers Bérard and Vassal. But the hoped-for ore was never found, and, having spent a lot of money on a fruitless development, the enterprise went bankrupt. Both bankers became insolvent as a result of this unsuccessful involvement with industry. The Paris banking houses of André & Cottier, Pillet-Will, Milleret, Paravey and Goupy fared little better when in 1826 they supported another former minister, the Duc de Decazes, in the promotion of a mining and metallurgical enterprise in the Valley of Aveyron. Because of technical difficulties, the capital had to be doubled, and profits failed to materialize for many years. The ironworks in Le Creusot, which put the first French coke blast-furnace into operation in 1785, were also unprofitable for decades. After its former owners had closed the works down in 1828 through lack of capital, the firm was re-established as a joint-stock company with capital of four million francs. Its major shareholders included the Paris banker, Benoît Fould, who was to be one of the important co-founders of the Crédit Mobilier. The company went bankrupt after five years in 1833. In 1836 the Sellière banking house in Paris bought up the industrial plants at Le Creusot. The Sellières had started their business as army suppliers. With the profits which they had thus obtained they acquired textile mills. From 1815, they expanded their industrial investments and also went into banking. They sold the works in Le Creusot to the Schneider Brothers, the founders of the Schneider-Creusot industrial dynasty.

The growing capital requirements of large-scale industry, a series of disappointments and the numerous bankruptcies during the crisis of 1848 dampened the *haute banque's* interest in financing industry and prompted efforts to establish joint-stock banks.

Unlike the French *haute banque*, private bankers in Germany and partic-ularly the old Frankfurt banking houses approached early industry generally with great caution. The Cologne banking houses and the Württembergische Hofbank were the exceptions. Until 1820, the largest share of the Cologne banks' credit business went to commercial companies. In the 1820s, credit to industry became and remained their main business during the heyday of railway construction, in the financing of which the Cologne banking houses also had a major share. The most widespread form of industrial credit consisted of advances on current account. Around 1840, the Cologne banking houses began the long-term financing of industry with issues and acceptances of bonds and shares of the existing joint-stock companies and by providing long-term credit. The early connection between the Cologne private bankers and industry was fostered by their close proximity to the industrial regions in the Eifel, on the lower Rhine, on the Ruhr, the Wupper and the Sieg rivers as well as in the Bergisches Land. There also existed friendly, occasionally even familial, ties with the industrialists of the area.

Gradually the banking houses built up geographical centres for their activity in industrial credit. Schaaffhausen maintained close links with mining and the iron and steel industries in the Ruhr district; Oppenheim was involved with the iron and hardware industries in the Eifel, on the Saar and in the Luxembourg industrial region.

During the economic crisis of 1848, the Schaaffhausen banking house plunged into a liquidity crisis. It had liabilities totalling 5.75 million thalers, with six million thalers in claims against it, assets worth 0.75 million thalers, land worth 700,000 thalers, but only about 300,000 thalers in ready cash. Of the total amount due from its debtors, 573,000 thalers had to be written off. The value of assets had to be reduced by 128,000 thalers. Even now, the bank had more assets than liabilities, but the assets could not be converted into cash within a sufficiently short time. On 29 March 1848, the bank had to suspend its payments. On the same day, David Hansemann, former president of the *Rheinische Eisenbahngesellschaft,* and very well acquainted with Rhenish conditions, assumed office as the Prussian Minister of Trade in Berlin. He was aware of Schaaffhausen's importance for Rhenish industry and saw how disastrous the consequences of a compulsory liquidation of this banking house would be. Following a proposal by Hansemann, the Prussian Cabinet agreed to the conversion of the banking house into a joint-stock company; the creditors were to be given shares. The State agreed to guarantee dividend payments for part of the shares. Of the share capital of 5.187 million thalers, the creditors received 4.3 millions. The Government undertook to guarantee half of the creditors' shares at a fixed dividend of 4.5% as well as the repayment of 10% of these shares per annum until 1858. The other half of the creditors' shares, which was not guaranteed in this way, was to yield a dividend of not more than 4% until 1858 when the first half had been repaid; the shares remaining with the bank's former partners amounting to 887,000 thalers could not attract more than 2% for the duration of the state guarantee. Beyond this, the Minister of Trade had the right to appoint one of the three directors of the bank whilst the state guarantee was in force. Hansemann installed as director his successor to the executive committee of the *Rheinische Eisenbahngesellschaft,* Gustav Mevissen. Thus the first large German joint-stock bank emerged in 1848 from the reorganization of an illiquid banking institution. Unlike Hansemann, however, the other Prussian ministers regarded the reorganization as an emergency measure only and certainly not as the beginning of a new type of bank.

5. The International Financial Power of the Rothschilds

Until the mid-19th century, which saw the promotion and development of the big joint-stock banks and universal banks, the credit system was dominated by private bankers. Since 1818-20, the greatest financial power of all these private banking houses lay with the House of Rothschild. The Rothschilds were an international financial power in two ways: they had extended their credit business to many countries and dealt with the governments of all the great powers and several smaller states and they were also represented in several countries through their own firms, which was quite exceptional at that time.

We have already followed the economic rise of the founder of the Rothschild 'dynasty', which had been greatly enhanced by his position as court factor in Hesse. When in 1810 old Meyer Amschel Rothschild took his five sons into partnership and thenceforth used the company name of M.A. Rothschild & Söhne, there was another Rothschild Bank already in existence in London. Meyer Amschel's third son, Nathan, had gone to England in 1798 and started a trading business in Manchester. After profitable transactions in raw materials and finished textile goods, he moved to London in 1803 and founded the N.M. Rothschild banking house a year later. Because of the war, which had restarted between England and France in May 1803 and lasted until Napoleon I's fall in 1814, no contact between the two Rothschild firms was possible. James, the youngest of the Rothschild sons, went to Paris in 1812 as a representative of the Rothschild Bank in Frankfurt. Old Meyer Amschel died in the same year.

After the Congress of Vienna had restored and consolidated the European state system, the five Rothschild brothers restructured the business organization of the House in 1815. They concluded a partnership agreement under the terms of which the House of Rothschild consisted of three firms, each connected with the other and situated in Frankfurt, London and Paris. Thus the branch established in Paris in 1812 became a banking firm in its own right. Amschel, the eldest of the brothers, took over the management of the parent firm in Frankfurt, together with his brother Karl. Nathan retained the management of the London firm, James and Salomon managed the firm in Paris. When the capital was distributed between the brothers, Nathan, who had contributed most to their common property through his trade and credit transactions, received five-eighths; Salomon and Amschel got one-eighth each and Karl and James one-sixteenth each. The three firms' joint capital amounted to 3.3 million francs at the time the agreement was concluded. The London branch remained pre-eminent within the House of Rothschild until Nathan's death in 1836; he had not only the largest volume of business but also the greatest flair. The partnership agreement had a three-year life and was renewed every three years either tacitly or with the addition of new clauses. When it was renewed in 1818 the terms were tightened up. In the intervening three years their capital had increased twelve-fold to 42.5 million francs.

To the present day, research has failed to explain this astonishing growth within such a short period of time, even after the studies undertaken by Bertrand Gille in the Rothschild Archives at Paris. When the capital was distributed among the five brothers in 1818, Nathan maintained the first place although the shares of his brothers increased substantially. Nathan's share of the joint capital was fixed at 12 million francs; Amschel and Salomon, the two eldest brothers, received 7.75 million each and Karl and

James, the two youngest, were allotted 7.5 million francs each. The capital was divided between the three branches in such a way that the London bank received 17.8 million, the Frankfurt house 16.3 million and the Paris house 8.4 million francs. Their profits and losses were distributed among the brothers according to the following scheme: Nathan participated in both the profits and losses to the extent of 50% in the London firm and 25% in each of the Paris and Frankfurt branches. The corresponding shares of the remaining four brothers came to one-eighth each in the London operation and three-sixteenth each in the Paris and Frankfurt businesses. Nobody was allowed to withdraw his profit, either in whole or in part, before the agreement expired and none of the five was allowed to pursue other business activities. They were obliged to exchange information every week, even when they were travelling, on the balance of assets and liabilities and on the progress of business. Once a year, the balances of the three Rothschild firms were to be put together at Frankfurt, to show the overall balance of the Rothschild family. Internally, the three firms were regarded as branches of one single enterprise. Hence it might be called the first large multinational company. Outwardly, they had to operate as legally independent companies, conforming to the statutory requirements of the countries in which they were domiciled.

Side-by-side with the three firms, Salomon Rothschild set up branch offices at Vienna in 1816. Carl Rothschild did the same in 1820 at Naples, the capital of the Kingdom of the Two Sicilies. These two establishments functioned as branches of the Frankfurt firm until 1844. When the agreement was renewed in 1825, a significant change in the distribution of the capital was effected between the three firms — though not between the five brothers. Of the total capital which had meanwhile increased to 102 million francs, 37.25 million were allotted to the Paris branch, 36.25 million to Frankfurt and 28.5 million to London. The Frankfurt house received such a large share because it had to provide funds for the branches in Vienna and Naples. The share of the Paris firm had risen at the expense of the London firm because better investment possibilities presented themselves on the Continent, particularly within the Paris branch's scope of business.

When the partnership agreement was renewed in August 1844, the branches in Vienna and Naples also became independent firms with their own capital. From then on there were five Rothschild banks: M.A. von Rothschild & Söhne at Frankfurt, N.M. Rothschild & Sons at London, de Rothschild Frères at Paris, S.M. von Rothschild at Vienna and C.M. de Rothschild at Naples. The London firm occupied a special position in the sense that, following the death of Nathan in 1836, his four sons were the exclusive partners, whereas each of the European Rothschild branches participated in the firms on the Continent, with the London branch having no direct share in them at all.

The bond uniting all Rothschilds was preserved after the deaths of Carl, Salomon and Amschel within nine months of each other in 1855. As Amschel had no heirs, Carl's sons, Meyer Carl and Wilhelm Carl assumed the management of the Frankfurt house. When Naples lost its position as the capital of a kingdom, and thus its significance as a banking centre following the political unification of Italy in 1860 — for Naples was not an important commercial centre — the Rothschilds, after some hesitations, gave up their firm there in 1863. A new partnership agreement was drawn up between the remaining four Rothschild firms in the same year and the joint capital, which had meanwhile reached 558 million francs, was distributed among the four branches of the family — not the firms — in such a way that each of them received one quarter of the total capital. The ties between the Rothschilds were maintained not only by means of the partnership agreement, but also through intermarriage between the separate branches of the family. In important commercial centres outside their head offices, the Rothschilds had their business interests looked after by other private bankers acting as their agents. Thus the Mendelssohn banking house was at first a Rothschild agent in Berlin. In 1828, this position was given to the Bleichröder banking house. The reason for this sudden change of agent is not known, although it may be connected with the fact that the majority of the Mendelssohn family had converted to Lutheranism. The Rothschilds wanted complete social and political integration into their native countries, but they did not abandon the Jewish faith.

In places where they pursued larger business activities, the Rothschilds set up their own agencies rather than entrusting the representation of their interests to other bankers. In 1830 the Paris house set up an office in Brussels; London and Paris established agencies in Madrid (1833-4), New York (1835-6), New Orleans (1843), Havanna (1843) and Mexico (1843). The Vienna and the Paris firms also established agencies in Rome (1843), Turin (1850) and Trieste (around 1870). The management of these agencies was assigned, not to local people familiar with the area, but invariably to their own employees who were familiar with the Rothschilds' business practices. Some of these agencies were provided with their own capital and later developed into separate banking houses, albeit closely connected with the Rothschilds. Thus the Brussels office, whose manager, Baron Léon Lambert, married James Rothschild's granddaughter, became the Lambert banking house.

Once the above-mentioned four agencies had been set up in North and Central America, Alphonse Rothschild, James's son, undertook an exploratory trip to North America in 1848-9. What had prompted his trip was not only an interest in the New World, but also the political turmoil in Europe during the 1848 Revolution, which was accompanied by a serious economic crisis. Alphonse Rothschild saw the tremendous potential for economic development in the United States, in particular in the West, which had not yet been opened up; he also appreciated the future potential of the East Asian trade and therefore proposed that a Rothschild bank be set up in the United States. The older Rothschild generation did not share his enthusiasm for America, however. James had no confidence in the American economy, finding it overly dominated by speculators. Ten years later, Salomon James,

Alphonse's brother, was sent on another investigative mission to the United
States. The American economy was still suffering from the effects of the
1857-9 crisis; the visitor did not gain a favourable impression, and the
Rothschilds abandoned the plan to establish their own bank in America.

The large-scale banking operations of the Rothschilds have already been
described elsewhere. This leaves the further development of the House and
its firms to be outlined briefly here. The Rothschilds remained a significant
financial power in the second half of the 19th century, even if the big joint-
stock banks had begun to assume a leading role. The first joint-stock and
universal bank, the Crédit Mobilier, had been founded quite simply as an
anti-Rothschild venture which tried to undermine the Rothschilds' position
in France, Austria and Italy. In the prolonged competitive struggle, the
Rothschilds emerged victorious by setting up joint-stock banks to rival the
Crédit Mobilier. They established the Österreichische Creditanstalt in
Vienna in 1855 and the Société Générale pour favoriser le développement
du Commerce et de l'industrie en France in Paris in 1864, both under their
control. The Crédit Mobilier collapsed in 1867; the two rival joint-stock
banks which the Rothschilds set up exist to this day.

When the London house celebrated its centenary in 1904, it published a
catalogue of public loans the Rothschilds had accepted in the course of that
century. It showed that during those 100 years they had granted loans
amounting to £1,300 million to European countries, a sum equal to the
total expenditure of the Kingdom of Prussia in the years 1884-1899. The
most significant Rothschild loans in the late 19th century were the floating
of five milliard francs within two years which enabled France to pay the war
indemnity imposed by Germany in 1871; there were also those £4 million
which Lionel Rothschild, Nathan's successor as manager of the London
house, remitted to the British Prime Minister within a matter of hours in
1875 to enable him to make a swift surprise purchase for the Crown of the
majority block of shares in the Suez Canal Company (see below pp. 138f.).
Russia did not receive any Rothschild loans on principle, because of the
anti-Jewish policies of the Tsars. However, the London Rothschild Bank
subscribed one million roubles of a 'freedom loan' which Kerenski issued
after the Revolution of February 1917. The Rothschilds did not see their
money again. In general, however, they did excellent business with state
loans as they managed to sell acceptances at the most favourable dates,
when the difference between the acceptance price and the stock exchange
quotation was particularly large.

At the time of the London centenary celebrations, only three Rothschild
Banks were still in existence. The Frankfurt branch, which had been carried
on by Meyer Carl and Wilhelm Carl, the sons of the 'Neapolitan' Carl, died
out in 1901, when Wilhelm Carl passed away without leaving a male heir.
Long before this date, business in Frankfurt had been conducted much
less energetically than in Paris, London and Vienna. Although Emperor
Wilhelm II repeatedly expressed the wish that the German Rothschild Bank
should continue its business, and should do so from Berlin, the Rothschilds

liquidated the Frankfurt firm and transferred its commitments to the Disconto-Gesellschaft. Only the name survived in Frankfurt for a time: Wilhelm Carl's son-in-law, the private banker Max Goldsmith, called himself Goldsmith-Rothschild from 1903. The Viennese firm, together with the Österreichische Creditanstalt which it had founded and controlled, played a leading role in the capital market of the Dual Monarchy for decades, but had to be liquidated in March 1938, after the absorption of Austria into Nazi Germany.

The English and French branches continued to flourish after the Second World War. The English Rothschilds had to fight for their complete integration into a tradition-conscious English society for a particularly long time, notwithstanding the fact that they had long been among the leading bankers in the City. In 1846, Lionel stood as a Liberal candidate and was elected to Parliament; he was prevented from joining his seat in the House of Commons because he could not take the Christian oath required of every Member of Parliament at the beginning of each session. There were two repeat performances of this drama: Lionel was duly elected but could not take his seat. It was only in 1858 that, having been elected for the third time, he was allowed to take the Jewish oath on the Old Testament. Eleven years later Gladstone, the Prime Minister, proposed offering Lionel Rothschild a peerage, thus admitting him to the House of Lords; but Queen Victoria rejected the proposal. She believed it would make a bad impression and harm the Government, if a Jew became a peer. After Lionel had rendered the British government a signal service in connection with the Suez Canal deal and after Nathaniel ('Nattie'), his successor on board, had started a number of ventures which were not only profitable for the Rothschilds, but also beneficial to British colonial policy, Nathaniel was raised to the peerage in 1885 and admitted to the House of Lords. He also invested large sums of money in Indian mines and financed the development of the diamond mining district which Cecil Rhodes had taken over in South Africa. In the 20th century, the English Rothschilds retreated almost completely from politically sensitive credit deals and acquired large direct stakes in various investment schemes, particularly in overseas mines. After the Second World War, their interest was primarily directed towards Canada, where they acquired large holdings in uranium, copper and tin mining.

The Paris firm, which had been the most successful in the 19th century, took a similar development, and shifted towards industrial investment as its main activity. Its business began to stagnate after the First World War, however, and ultimately it confined itself to the administration of its enormous assets. The business links which had been maintained between the Rothschild banks into the early 20th century almost disappeared. It was only after 1945, under the cousins Guy, Alain and Elie Rothschild, that the banking interests of the French branch were reactivated, at first as an investment bank. In 1967, the bank reopened its deposit banking and short-term credit business. This time, credit and investments were organizationally separate: the bank was transformed into a joint-stock company under the name of Banque Rothschild, and its direct participations in banks, insurance, shipping and mining as well as in the iron- and steel industry were put into several investment trusts.

When Britain drew closer to the European Economic Community in 1962, the business links between the French and the English Rothschild, were re-established when the Paris Rothschilds took a 60% stake in a holding company which their English relations had founded to manage their large mining interests in Canada. The former Rothschild agency in Brussels, the Banque Lambert, has also a share in this holding company. The company's name, 'Five Arrows', recalls the five Frankfurt brothers with whom the rise of the House of Rothschild began and from whom an international enterprise combining banks, insurance, mining and shipping interests has developed.

III Joint-stock Banks, Big Banks and Concentration up to the First World War

1. Economic, Ideological and Legal Preconditions

Until the mid-19th century, the textile industry and particularly the cotton industry had been the leading sector in the industrialization process. In these industries the most significant technological innovations had been introduced, and they also achieved the highest growth rates. In England this period was called 'the age of cotton'. As we have seen, the textile industry only required relatively small amounts of capital in order to start production. The capital requirements of contemporary mining and metallurgical enterprises were comparatively much larger; yet, as there were so few of them, both their needs and those of the textile industry could be satisfied with the help of the credit institutions and practices of capital mobilization which existed in the early 19th century. Changes began to occur in the two decades between 1850 and 1870. The mining industry and the iron producing and metal-working industries assumed the leading role in technological-industrial development.

The construction of the railways and scientific-technological progress provided the strongest impulse for this shift. The more railway routes were opened, the greater the demand for coal and iron, and rising demand was complemented by technological change. In the mining industry improved technology — such as winding ropes made from braided iron wires, more efficient pumps and the use of nitro-cellulose and nitro-glycerine — meant that shafts could be driven deeper to thicker and richer seams. It was only after such improvements that coal mining became possible in the heart of the Ruhr district, to the North of the Emscher river near Gelsenkirchen, Herne, Bocholt and Recklinghausen; there the rich coal seams, so important for the iron foundries, were deposited under a layer of marl, 300-500 metres thick. From 1850 to 1870, German coal output increased sixfold from seven million tons to 42 million tons. With the construction of the Bessemer converter in 1855, the English had succeeded in achieving an epoch-making technological breakthrough which improved and rationalized the conversion of crude iron into iron which could be forged and moulded. The Bessemer converter dramatically shortened this process.

The period of advanced industrialization was initiated by these technological-industrial developments; the introduction of the new technologies and the expansion of the mining, iron, steel and metal-working industries taxed the capital resources and the existing framework for the mobilization of capital tremendously. The traditional credit system, which was almost wholly based on private bankers, could no longer meet these needs. Private bankers succeeded in mobilizing no more than a fraction of the money capital available in a particular national economy. It would have been much too costly and unprofitable for them to set up branches in a large number of places to attract medium-sized and small cash deposits. The tapping of this wealth for credit purposes was not the only problem, however. To provide the long-term loans which industry required, the banks needed capital which would be available to them for at least the same length of time as they lent it to industry.

In the middle of the 19th century, many businessmen in central Europe and in North America believed that private issuing banks were the appropriate financial institutions for credit expansion and the mobilization of large amounts of capital. For this reason, twenty new issuing banks were founded in Germany between 1848 and 1856 and well over 800 in the United States between 1845 and 1860. The issue of bank notes could not solve the problem of long-term credit, though; for apart from the fact that the notes of many of the issuing banks were accepted only in a very limited geographical area, the issuing banks also had to exchange their notes for gold coin upon demand. Consequently bank notes were not suitable as a means of financing long-term credits. If the banks wanted to mobilize larger amounts of capital and, moreover, if they wanted to have it at their disposal on a long-term basis, they could only do so by establishing joint-stock banks. By issuing shares, it became possible to concentrate funds for large-scale business activities which would otherwise have become dissipated as small loans to friends in the locality. Joint-stock banks could channel credit more effectively and adapt their capital stocks to accommodate the growing volume of business.

Long before the middle of the century when joint-stock banks were created for the long-term financing of industry, the French banker Jacques Laffitte had pondered how funds might be mobilized for industrial credit needs. In 1818, he published proposals for a reform of the French banking system in which he defined the nature of credit as follows: 'Funds do not always belong to those who work with them. Those who own them, and who are described as being rich, do not intend to spend these funds themselves, but to lend them to those who are forced to work; they do so on condition that they get a share of the profit on which they can live a life of leisure: this is what is called credit'. And he added: 'The whole work of society is entirely dependent on credit'. In order to mobilize and organize industrial credit, Laffitte thought of founding an industrial share-holding company constituted as a joint-stock company; what he was hoping to promote with the help of this construction were enterprises which had either started as a new branch of industry or had introduced new production processes in an already existing industry. Laffitte's views on the nature, significance and organization of credit have a certain affinity with the concepts of Saint-Simonians who adopted them. Conversely, Laffitte and other bankers such as André, Bethmann, Mendelssohn and Odier showed, temporarily at least, an interest in the political and social ideas of the Saint-Simonians.

Saint-Simon, who can be described as a socialist thinker only in a qualified sense, had criticized the lack of congruity between the contribution made by different members to society and their social status within the existing social order. He wanted to replace the aristocracy by an 'industrial class' which he considered to be the most important class of all. By 'industrial class' he meant *all* men who accomplished useful work, whether in industry, agriculture, trade, banking or science; he applied the term to entrepreneurs as well as workers. His concept of class, therefore, has nothing in common with that of Marxian socialism. Saint-Simon also wanted to preserve property, provided it had been acquired through honest work and was used in the interest of the commonweal. However, he was rather an eclectic thinker. It was his disciples — Prosper Enfantin, a banker, and Saint-Amand Bazard, who systematized his ideas and thought them through in their political consequences.

The problem they faced was how to supply those, who showed technical and industrial skills, with the capital they needed to deploy their expertise creatively. It was here that Laffitte's ideas on credit and credit organization offered a solution. The money owned by rich idlers was to be put at the disposal of the 'industrial class' with the assistance of banks. Under Laffitte's influence Enfantin and Bazard came to believe that joint-stock banks could fulfil this task. Bazard went even further than Enfantin. He thought of setting up a big central credit bank together with special banks for every branch of industry; the central bank was to be given the primary task of directing production. Bazard also argued that inheritance laws should be abolished: the property of the deceased person was to be added to the banks' capital. Enfantin and Bazard did not have the backing of a coherent group of supporters. Nevertheless their ideas were taken up by some. The most important of these were two brothers, Isaac and Emile Péreire. They came from Bordeaux and were active at first as bill brokers at Paris. For a while they were employed by the Rothschild Bank in Paris dealing in railways until they joined up with Rothschild's rival and opponent, Benoît Fould, probably for political reasons: James Rothschild supported the old monarchy; they did not. The Péreire brothers were Saint-Simonians of Enfantin's moderate orientation. Like him, they visualized a big, financially powerful joint-stock bank to provide the driving force behind industrial development and the reorganization of society from a feudal to an industrial state. This at least was the ideological component which came to bear on the creation, in 1852, of the first big joint-stock and investment bank, the Crédit Mobilier.

The impact of Saint-Simonian ideas remained confined to France. In Germany, the protagonists of the joint-stock bank justified it by reference to the idea of association, of voluntary combination to pursue common interests and to solve common problems. This idea provided the intellectual impetus behind the co-operative movement, numerous societies for the promotion of trade and transport, the *Arbeiterverbrüderung* of 1848 and trade unions. Hansemann, Mevissen and other advocates of joint-stock banks used it against their opponents to justify their 'capital associations'. This justification was indispensable at a time when the creation of every single joint-stock company required a government licence which it was very difficult to obtain.

The call for the establishment of joint-stock banks first appeared in England. During the banking crises of 1816-17 and 1825-6, many private bankers who issued notes had become insolvent and had to suspend the convertibility of their bank notes into gold coins. The public joint-stock issuing banks in Scotland, on the other hand, weathered the crises well. Many English businessmen therefore came to believe that joint-stock banks were more crisis-proof than private banks and demanded the abolition of the law applicable to England and Wales, with the exception of the Bank of England, forbidding banks to have more than six partners. Parliament met this demand half-way in 1826 by legalizing private joint-stock banks in England and Wales, outside a 65-mile radius of the capital. When the Bank of England's right to print bank notes was renewed in 1833, private joint-stock banks were admitted to the capital and its vicinity on condition that they refrained from issuing bank notes.

This did not mean that joint-stock banks in the modern sense had been introduced; the liability of these banks was not limited to company assets, but extended to the total assets of all shareholders. Furthermore, the joint-stock banks did not have the right to litigate; only individual shareholders could start a law suit. And finally, under the Acts of 1826 and 1833, registration of every single joint-stock bank continued to be by Royal Charter. Several bills reformed British company law between 1855 and 1862; joint-stock companies were freed from the obligation to obtain a concession and their liability was limited to company assets. In the following years, company law was also liberalized in France and Germany. The new French law of 1867 on limited companies, and amendment to the laws of the North German Confederation, ratified in the summer of 1870 and relating to joint-stock companies, no longer stipulated that joint-stock companies required a special permission. Switzerland obtained a uniform law relating to joint-stock companies in 1881. Until then, the regulations of individual Cantons were in force, which, generally speaking, tied the creation of a joint-stock company to the approval of the cantonal authority. The requirement to obtain this permission lapsed in 1881. In the United States, legislation on joint-stock companies remained within the authority of individual states. Capital companies could develop earlier here than elsewhere. The shares of the first American joint-stock banks were being quoted on the New York Stock Exchange as early as the beginning of the 19th century.

Until the liberalization of company law in France and Prussia, alternative forms of 'capital association' were adopted which were not subject to a permit. The Crédit Lyonnais was founded as a limited liability company in 1863 and converted into a joint-stock company five years after the liberalization of French company law. In Prussia two major joint-stock banks, the Disconto-Gesellschaft and the Berliner Handels-Gesellschaft, were founded as limited partnerships in 1856; such partnerships were not subject to the law on limited companies under which a licence was required.

2. General Trends

Following the passage of the English Bank Acts of 1826 and 1833, the first private joint-stock banks emerged in Europe, at first in the north of England and from 1833 in London. These credit institutions differed from private bankers and merchant bankers only in the greater number of partners involved and their larger equity capital, rather than in the type of business. It was only with the establishment of the Crédit Mobilier in 1852 that a new kind of commercial bank came into existence which was also engaged in the long-term credit business, issued shares and invested directly in industry. In the 20 years that followed, many 'Crédit Mobilier banks' came into being on the Continent. Only a few of these, such as the Banque de Paris et des Pays Bas, were specialized investment banks *(banques d'affaires)*, involved in the issuing and related business. Most of the Crédit Mobilier banks became universal banks, covering all aspects of banking. Universal banks did not survive in France for long, however; after the bank crisis which followed upon the collapse of the Union Generale (see below p. 81), most French universal banks began to liquidate their long-term business and switched to deposit banking in the British tradition.

The great significance of the Crédit Mobilier banks derived from the fact that when joint-stock companies were founded, or increased their capital, they helped these industrial enterprises to place their shares. Sometimes their involvement was limited to simple services such as advertising the issue of shares and settling the accounts. It was greater when the bank took shares on commission; in this case it distributed the shares, in its own name, but for the account of the joint-stock company. In other words, the bank placed its name and reputation at the disposal of the joint-stock company, whilst the risk of a successful issue remained with the joint-stock company. This type of business obviously gave the bank a higher commission than mere servicing. The most far-reaching role a bank could play in the issue of shares was to buy all or part of the shares at a fixed rate, thereby assuming the sole or partial responsibility for the issue's success or failure. In return, it could retain the eventual profit on stock prices which, of course, it expected to gain in such a transaction entirely for itself. The advantage of this practice from the viewpoint of the joint-stock company was that it obtained from the share issue a guaranteed capital sum which was at its immediate disposal. The bank, on the other hand, stood to make a large profit or to suffer considerable losses. The commission was much higher under this arrangement by which the risk was assumed by the bank. Another possibility was for several banks to form a consortium in order to distribute the risk. Members of the consortium jointly accepted the total amount of the issue and divided it amongst themselves; with each individual member's share in the profits or losses corresponding to their share in the issue.

Usually only one bank would represent the syndicate *vis-à-vis* the public. The banks had various ways of placing the shares. Sometimes they would use advertisements in daily newspapers, calling for subscriptions to shares at a fixed rate. This rate was, of course, higher than the rate at which the banks had accepted the shares. Once they had been subscribed, they would be allotted to the subscribers. If an issue was oversubscribed, which occurred quite often during an economic upturn such as those at the beginning of the 1860s and 1870s, investors were simply allotted fewer shares than they had subscribed. This method required considerable publicity whose costs the banks were expected to bear themselves. They could place shares among the public at lesser cost to themselves by introducing them on the stock exchange. In this case the shares' sale price would fluctuate in response to public demand; it also tended to take longer for the whole issue to be placed. Finally, the banks could sell privately to interested clients without publicity. This was, without doubt, rather a time-consuming method, but it enabled the banks to vary their offer according to changing demand; sluggish sales did not become public and were hence not immediately liable to depress share prices.

However, the banks did not just act as intermediaries and brokers between joint-stock companies and investors; they also became shareholders themselves. Occasionally this occurred against their will when they failed to place more than a part of the shares they had accepted at a fixed rate. On other occasions, the banks happily acquired shares in order to gain an influence in the firm in question. These issuing practices, which continue to this day, were developed in the second third of the 19th century when the universal banks, which were themselves mostly joint-stock companies, began their long-term financing of industry on a large scale.

With the creation of private joint-stock banks, a concentration movement began to affect the credit system after 1880, which has not yet run its course. The number of credit institutions declined; a few banks developed into major banks, whose capital strength and volume of business was many times larger than that of other institutions, including the long-established private bankers. Which banks became the major banks? Outside Japan, where a unique development took place under wholly different historical conditions, and with the exception of the American Morgan Bank, only joint-stock banks grew into major banks. But later the big Japanese banks and J.P. Morgan & Co. were also converted into joint-stock companies.

Almost all institutions which were to rise to the rank of major banks had a large initial capital, some even five or ten times larger than the equity capital of private bankers or provincial joint-stock banks. The most significant factor behind the rise of the big bank was the establishment of a large nationwide network of branches, whereby business opportunities could be seized and customers could be reached across the whole country. A bank with such a network was in a position to attract many more deposits than a local bank. By expanding their networks, banks also acquired a greater and more precise knowledge of individual industries and concerns in various parts of the country. By 1914 the densest networks had been developed by French and English banks. The French Société Générale had some 668 branches by the time of the First World War. In 1914, the Crédit du Nord in Lille also completed its transition from a regional to a major bank by extending its branch network to the South of France. By 1910, each of the big English joint-stock banks operated several hundred branches; the Midland Bank, for instance, had some 689. In Germany, the big joint-stock banks also created branch networks covering the whole country; however, before 1914 they established branches only in the important industrial and commercial cities. In 1911, the six biggest German banks had no more than 98 branches throughout the country between them. In the United States banks were not allowed until 1927 to set up branches outside the area in which they had their head office. To the present day they cannot establish branches beyond the Federal State in which they are registered. However, it was easy for an expanding bank to bypass this rule. Some Federal States took a very liberal line on this. California permitted branches to be estab lished throughout its territory as early as 1909. As for the rest of the United States, the ban could be circumvented quite legally: instead of opening branch offices, a bank could set up subsidiary companies in import- ant business centres outside the area of its registered office. Where it did not seem profitable to establish a joint-stock bank, an expanding bank could gain a foothold by acquiring a sufficiently large number of shares in an existing local bank to enable it to put its own man on the management.

Big banks came into existence not only through the creation of extensive branch networks, but also through mergers. Every major bank took over other credit institutions in the course of its expansion. The most intensive merger movement occurred within the English and German banking systems before the First World War. Between 1865 and 1914 Lloyds Bank took over some 50 banks; another major bank — Barclays Bank Ltd. — was established after the merger of some 20 private bankers' firms. Of Germany's major banks, both the Dresdner Bank and the Bank für Handel und Industrie at Darmstadt developed largely through mergers. By 1911, the Dresdner Bank had absorbed some 25 banks and the Darmstadt Bank für Handel und Industrie had taken over some 19 institutions. Of course, the banks also pursued mergers in order to acquire new customers and business con- nections. This tended to be the strategy particularly when a bank wished to move into another important banking centre; in this case it would try to take over a long-established bank and its clientele. Obviously, this policy provided a considerably better start than to establish a branch alongside locally entrenched competition. Thus Lloyds Bank, established in 1881 and the Midland Bank, established in 1891, in setting out from Birmingham, gained a foothold in the capital by taking over London banking houses. In Frankfurt, the Deutsche Bank established a branch alongside the traditionally wealthy private bankers in 1886 by buying up the Frankfurter Bankverein. The Disconto-Gesellschaft acquired a branch in the banking centre of Frankfurt by taking on the business of the liquidated banking house of

M.A. Rothschild & Söhne. The Dresdner Bank was able to open its Frankfurt
branch office in 1904 after a successful take-over bid of the Erlanger &
Söhne. Although these were mergers involving provincial banks, they were
mainly undertaken by the big joint-stock banks, with the result that the
concentration process strengthened their dominant position.

3. The English 'Big Five'

Within seven years of the 1826 law permitting the establishment of
joint-stock banks in England and Wales outside London and its '65-mile
Zone', almost 50 joint-stock banks had been founded in central and northern England, with a total of about 10,000 shareholders. These joint-stock
banks accepted deposits, issued notes and provided short-term commercial
credits. They continued to be private issuing banks and, as their range of
business was limited, they were not regarded as competitors by the London
banking world or the Bank of England. However, the directors of the
Bank of England and the London private bankers opposed, albeit unsuccessfully, the admission of joint-stock banks to London in 1833. It was the
landed gentry and the merchant class who introduced a bill in Parliament
which changed existing statutes. The argument with which they convinced a
majority of M.P.s was that the law concerning the Bank of England merely
barred issuing banks with more than six partners from access to London,
but did not forbid commercial banks with a larger number. To effect
a change, they added, was just a matter of adding this in the form of a
'declaratory clause' to the law on the Bank of England's note privilege.

The same group of 'many noblemen, gentlemen, merchants and tradesmen', as they called themselves, which was trying to get joint-stock banks admitted to London, also founded the first joint-stock bank in London. The
man who initiated the project was William R.K. Douglas of a Scottish
trading firm based in London. Next to this Scottish businessman, there were
two Scottish aristocrats, the Marquess of Bute and Lord Stuart de Rothesay,
on the founding committee. The response of the Bank of England, the
London private bankers and the financial press to their plan ranged from
opposition to scepticism. Samuel Lloyd, the later Lord Overstone, and
theoretician of the Currency School, took the view that joint-stock banks
would lack the reliability, adaptability and discretion of private bankers, as
their business would be conducted by mere employees and not by the owner
himself. He also feared that joint-stock banks would reduce the number of
private bankers in London, and, worst of all, the more conscientious ones.
Could it be that he foresaw the fate which was to befall his own private
bank? Some 32 years later, and still within his own lifetime, his firm was
taken over by the London & Westminster Bank, the very joint-stock bank
whose creation he had fought against in 1833! The *Circular to Bankers* had
sharper things to say in its issue of October 1833. It described the founding
committee as 'a conspicuous display of the names of men high in station,
though altogether inexperienced in banking affairs' and concluded its

criticisms with the curt statement: None of the men of sagacity and experience in banking and money affairs can be induced to unite with the projectors of Joint-Stock Banks in the metropolis.'

In their own publications, the members of the founding committee stressed the advantages of the joint-stock bank: its large capital, which could not be reduced by the death or retirement of a partner; the control of the management by the owners who were personally liable; its restriction to 'legitimate banking operations' — i.e. to the acceptance of deposits, provision of short-term credits and interest payments on deposits. Despite the opposition from the London banking community, the equity capital found enough subscribers and the London & Westminster Bank was able to start business in February 1834. On the other hand, those who had campaigned against the creation of the first London joint-stock bank did have a measure of success in opposing it. The bank had to content itself with a launching capital of £182,000 instead of the originally planned equity capital of £10 million which was to be increased step by step to £5 million. The Bank of England and the metropolitan private bankers continued to fight their new competitor even after the London & Westminster Bank had been founded. They refused to admit it to the London Bankers' Clearing House. It was thus debarred not only from clearings with the London credit institutions, but also from opening an account with the Bank of England. Because of these restrictions on its dealings, the bank could not yet take on the profitable business of acting as a banking agent for one or more of the country banks which were obliged to settle their accounts in London through one of the member banks of the Clearing House. After a long struggle, the London & Westminster Bank finally gained admission to the Clearing House in 1854. The new bank prospered steadily until the economic crisis in 1875, having suffered no more than temporary setbacks in the crises of 1857 and 1866. In 1874, on the eve of the great depression of the late 19th century, it had a capital and reserves of £3 million, with deposits worth £30 million. During the crisis of the 1870s it lost well over a quarter of its deposits. The bank reacted to these withdrawals by increasing its cash holdings from £4 million to £8 million and by substantially reducing its debit account. It was not until 1908 that its balance sheet total once again reached the 1874 figure of £34 million. Nevertheless, by the turn of the century, the London & Westminster Bank was one of the 11 major English banks.

A further four joint-stock banks (London Joint Stock Bank, Union Bank, London & County Bank and the Commercial Bank) were founded in London on the model of the London & Westminster Bank in the period up to 1840. They, too, suffered from the obstructive attitude of the Bank of England and the member banks of the Clearing House; until 1854 they were excluded from the Clearing House; nor were they allowed to open an account with the Bank of England. The latter also refused to discount bills drawn on one of the London joint-stock banks. Until 1844, the directors of London joint-stock banks were also barred from dealing with the legal aspects of the business. Thus a contract could not be signed without obtaining express prior approval of every single one of the several hundred shareholders. Such obstacles notwithstanding, the joint-stock banks stood up well to the long-established private bankers' firms and even succeeded in outstripping them in the volume of their business. They granted their customers fixed rates of interest on deposits, unlike the private bankers who paid no interest and thought it sufficient to offer as their service the safekeeping of the money deposited with them. The private bankers believed that in order to pay interest on deposits they would have had to work with all the money they accepted and to engage in credit business where the interest rates exceeded the interest paid on deposits. This, they felt, would push them into risky credit transactions. Meanwhile, the joint-stock banks attracted a steadily growing body of regular customers, and did so because they paid interest. Also they accepted small deposits, whereas private bankers were only interested in wealthy customers.

The law was considerably more favourable for joint-stock banks in the provinces than it was in the capital; the special restrictions to which the London joint-stock banks were subject did not apply to them. Until the ratification of Peel's Bank Act in 1844, joint-stock banks with the right to issue notes could be established quite easily outside the 65-mile limit from London. Out of more than 2,000 joint-stock banks founded in England and Wales during the 18 years between the lifting of the general ban on joint-stock banks in 1826 and the Peel's Bank Act, some 72 banks issued notes and thus created the means for expanding their credit business. Most of these joint-stock banks differed from private banking houses in their legal structure, rather than in their capital basis and turnover. In the industrial centres of Manchester, Liverpool and Birmingham, there was a good deal of wealth which was eagerly deposited for the interest it would bring. This greatly strengthened the joint-stock banks and facilitated the emergence of a group of major English banks: the Manchester & Liverpool District Banking Company in Manchester in 1829; the Bank of Liverpool in Liverpool in 1831 and the National Provincial Bank of England (the present National Westminster Bank) in Birmingham in 1833 and the Birmingham and Midland Bank (the present Midland Bank) in Birmingham in 1836.

The provincial joint-stock banks began to set up and expand their branch networks both earlier and more intensively than their London counterparts. Whereas the London banks found their customers and their deposits in the capital with its international and commercial connections, the provincial banks enlarged their operations by establishing branches in rural districts which had hitherto not been tapped by banks at all. By 1884, the London joint-stock banks — which had meanwhile grown to 21 — had opened some 52 branches; the provincial joint-stock banks had some 1,052.

A new phase in the history of English joint-stock banks began in 1862, when the shareholders' full liability was reduced to one covering their share capital in the company. Now a share could be made a negotiable security which was no longer obliged to bear the owner's name. Once the risk of shareholders had been restricted to their stake in the company limited by shares, a great many more investors were prepared to buy shares; this, in turn, enabled existing joint-stock banks greatly to increase their share capital in subsequent years. The London & Westminster Bank doubled it from £1 million to £2 million within seven years after the 1862 amendment to the law on joint-stock companies. The London & County Bank was able to increase its share capital from £600,000 to £1 million during the same period. As the incentive to buy shares had become so much greater, new joint-stock banks were established and private banking houses converted into joint-stock companies. In 1865, the private bank of Parr Lyon & Co. at Warrington was transformed into a joint-stock company and re-named Parr's Banking Company (Parr's Bank Ltd. from 1896) and the old Taylors & Lloyds bank in Birmingham became the Lloyds Banking Company Ltd. (Lloyds Bank Ltd. from 1889). Both were major banks at the turn of the century.

The steady growth and increasing dominance of the joint-stock banks at the close of the 19th century prompted many English private bankers to convert their banking houses into joint-stock companies or to give up their independence by allowing a joint-stock bank take them over. The director of the *Journal of the Institute of Bankers* explained the causes of this development as follows:

> Competition has now developed in a manner hitherto unknown. With some notable exceptions that will, I trust, long continue, the Private Banker has the feeling that his day is past. His great Joint Stock neighbour overshadows and disturbs him. . . . and lastly the desire created in the public mind for large reserves and public balance sheets will drive some to adopt the habits of Joint Stock Banking and others with less courage into the haven of amalgamation.

When this statement was made, the transformation of private banking firms into joint-stock companies was already well underway. In 1885, the banking house of Glyn Mills & Co., which had held a leading position in financing British railways, became a joint-stock Company. Following the Baring crisis (see below pp. 118f.), Baring Brothers were forced to opt for the legal structure of a joint-stock company in a way similar to that of the Schaaffhausen banking house at Cologne in 1848. At the same time as the Barings, the banking house of Williams Deacon & Co. took the plunge and became a joint-stock bank. They were followed in 1891 by Alexander & Co. which had played a leading role in discounting trade bills. In the following year, even the private banker's firm of Coutts & Co., which was 200 years old and was keeping the accounts of members of the aristocracy and the Royal Family, were reconstituted as a joint-stock company. The most significant transformation took place in 1896 when 20 private banks controlled by the London bank of Barclay Bevan Tritton & Co. amalgamated to become Barclays Bank Ltd. This new joint-stock bank was provided with an initial capital of £3 million and was thus a major bank from the start.

The growth of the joint-stock banks brought about an unparalleled process of concentration in Britain's banking system during the final third of the 19th century which far surpassed similar developments in other countries. Lloyds Bank achieved the record number of amalgamations by taking over no less than 50 banks between 1865 and 1914, many of which had themselves already incorporated several other banks. When these are added to the final total, more than 100 credit institutions merged with Lloyds. Parr's Bank took over some 21 institutions during the same period. The banks that had been taken over continued to function as branches of the absorbing bank. Mergers not only engulfed the private bankers, but the larger banks swallowed up scores of smaller joint-stock banks, together with their branch networks. As a consequence, by 1913 only some 43 independent institutions remained out of the more than 2,000 joint-stock banks which had been in existence in 1844. This figure also includes those private banking houses which had been converted into companies limited by shares.

Until 1920, the merger movement in the English banking system stood out from that of other countries, not only in respect of the number of mergers which took place, but also in respect of the size of the companies involved. Not only were the medium- and smaller-sized banks taken over by larger banks, or they merged themselves; from the start, the large banks also fused with each other. The first and, in this respect, epoch-making large-scale merger, was that between the London & Westminster Bank and the London & County Bank, which produced the London County & Westminster Bank in 1909. These two institutions had occupied the second and third rank among English banks in the mid-1890s; but other credit institutions like Lloyds and Barclays which had been deeply involved in the merger movement had outgrown them. And so, in 1909, the two other major banks which had been left behind merged in order to join the struggle for the top positions in the English credit system.

Their decision to pool their resources had been encouraged by the fact that they complemented each other well from the point of view of their business interests. The London & Westminster Bank's main field of business was in the capital; the London & County Bank's, on the other hand, operated mainly in the provinces. Moreover, the management of the London & Westminster regarded its institution as overcapitalized, having a share capital of £2.8 million with deposits amounting to £26.7 million in 1908; the London & County Bank had £2 million in share capital and £44.4 million in deposits. At the time of merger the share capital was raised to £3.5 million, with deposits totalling £70 million. During the same period, the Deutsche Bank in Germany had slightly less than 500 million marks in deposits with a share capital of 200 million marks. The London & Westminster Bank was therefore not at all overcapitalized by contemporary international standards, but merely in the British view. This point remains valid, even if one considers that the major English banks were exclusively deposit banks, with nothing but short-term credit commitments; the central European and the then major American banks, on the other hand, were universal banks, which used a greater proportion of their own share capital for long-term lending.

What the directors of the London & Westminster Bank called 'over-capitalized' in fact reflected falling profitability as a consequence of rising costs. The large branch networks forced costs of English banks up much more steeply than those of German or even American credit institutions, which had few branches or none at all. Even prior to 1914, the English banks therefore tried to keep the ratio of borrowed capital to their own capital as favourable as possible, in order to be able to pay high dividends on paid-up capital, irrespective of declining gross profits. There were hence two considerations behind the first merger of two major banks: rivalry with their rapidly expanding competitors, and the desire for higher returns on the firm's share capital. The amalgamation movement in the English credit system culminated, towards the end of the First World War, in a series of mergers between major banks. It resulted in the formation of the 'Big Five' and their subsequent domination of the English banking system. The wave of mergers during 1917-18 was stimulated by the rivalry between the major English banks themselves and preparations for the stiffer international competition which they anticipated after the end of the war. Competition led them to expand their business networks over the whole of England and Wales with the aim of having a presence in all industrial areas, the big ports and commercial cities. It would have been too costly for them to establish competing branches everywhere. In these circumstances it was expedient to amalgamate with other major banks whose business interests and branch networks complemented their own. Hence the new groupings which resulted from the merger wave of 1917-18.

To begin with, the London & Provincial Bank merged with the London & South Western Bank in 1917. The former had its main business in the vicinity of London, the latter in the Welsh coal-mining districts. The London Provincial & South Western Bank was absorbed by Barclays Bank at the beginning of 1918 to complement the latter's activities. After this, every-thing went with clockwork precision. Within the same year, the following banks merged: the National Provincial Bank of England and the Union of London & Smiths Bank to become the National Provincial & Union Bank of England (from 1924, National Provincial Bank); the London City & Midland Bank and the London Joint Stock Bank to form the London Joint City and Midland Bank (from 1923, Midland Bank); the London County & Westminster Bank and Parr's Bank to become the London County Westminster & Parr's Bank (from 1923, Westminster Bank). Finally, Lloyds Bank and the Capital & Counties Bank combined into the Lloyds Bank.

In this way the 'Big Five' emerged from what had previously been 11 major banks. This powerful concentration aroused deep concern in the City of London. It appeared that the credit system threatened to become a monopoly and that diminished competition would lead to a poorer service to the public. As early as 1918, the British government had set up a com-mission of inquiry which concluded its findings with the statement that further mergers between 'big banking institutions' would mean an intolerable reduction in competition and that the branch network had become too dense. Legislation was subsequently drafted which was to put a ban on further mergers involving the major banks. The 'Big Five' defeated this bill before it was even debated in Parliament by promising to undertake any future mergers, capital participation and co-operation agreements only with the approval of the Treasury and the Department of Trade.

The 'Big Five' justified the number of mergers in public by pointing to the expected competition from German industry after the end of the war. In order to be able to counter this competition, it was allegedly necessary to form trusts, the bigger and more powerful banks were needed to finance such trusts. The three biggest German banks (Deutsche Bank, Dresdner Bank, Disconto-Gesellschaft) with their 200 million marks each, certainly had considerably larger share capitals in 1914 than the major English banks. However, they never became Britain's rivals at an international level. During the war, then, they lost most of their international connections, and Germany's impending defeat was bound to aggravate further the international position of the German banks and the German economy. On the other hand, America had become Britain's all-powerful competitor. It was also during those years that the creditor-debtor relationship between Britain and the United States was reversed to Britain's disadvantage. But this could not be mentioned in public during the war so long as America was Britain's military ally. Hence when one talked of 'German competition' it was in fact 'American competition' which one had in mind.

After the major mergers of 1918, the 'Big Five' continued to grow, a concentration movement which was essentially completed by 1923. The mergers of the early 1920s involved take-overs of local and regional banks outside London. The major banks also participated in, or absorbed, the Northern Irish and Scottish joint-stock banks. Ultimately, the 'Big Five' handled about 85% of England's total banking business, deposits as well as credits.

4. The 'Crédit Mobilier' and the Big French Banks

Although they were the first to develop, the English joint-stock banks did not set the pattern for joint-stock banks and big banks on the Continent. The Crédit Mobilier, which had been founded in 1852, was the epoch-making model in Europe, even though neither the Saint-Simonian nor the Bonapartist ideals of its founders were adopted; nor was its striking failure an example to be emulated. Nevertheless, it became the prototype of the new joint-stock banks which had been developing since the middle of the century. They were even called 'Crédit Mobilier banks' for a long time afterwards, with no hint of criticism being intended by this designation.

There were many and often quite divergent reasons which led to the founding of Crédit Mobilier banks. After the economic and political crisis of 1848, the French economy continued to stagnate during the early 1850s.

Bearishness prevailed on the stock exchange, and the construction of the railways was in danger of running into difficulties owing to the reduction in the supply of capital. Moreover, a large part of the *haute banque*, including James de Rothschild, continued to support the House of Orléans and showed little inclination to co-operate with Prince Louis Napoléon, who had been elected President of the Second French Republic on 10 December 1848 and was preparing to establish his plebiscitary regime. After the *coup d'état* of 2 December 1851, he got himself elected as president for 10 years, and in the following year he elevated himself to the position of Emperor of the French. In order to further his political ambitions, he wished to stimulate investment in railway construction and industry. So he was looking for a financial institution which would make him independent of the *haute banque*. Persigny, his Minister of the Interior, who played a substantial part in the promotion of the Crédit Mobilier, later openly admitted this to have been the political motive behind the establishment of the Crédit Mobilier. In a conversation with the banker Jules Mirès he said, 'I wanted an instrument which would free the new regime from the hold which financiers usually have over governments; a hold which was all the more dangerous when I sensed the animosity which the great, influential financiers harboured towards the new regime. Without the support of the Crédit Mobilier, which has swept the financiers along with it and forced them to move forward, the Emperor's policy could not have been so boldly and freely implemented as when he had been forced to take the *haute banque* into account'.

It remains a controversial point as to who gave the initial stimulus for establishing the Crédit Mobilier. What can be determined with certainty are the identities of those who first discussed the project. They were Persigny, the Minister of the Interior; Achille Fould, the Minister of State, and his brother Benoît Fould, the banker; Mirès, the banker and journalist; finally, Napoleon III's stepbrother, the Duke of Morny. Mirès and the Fould brothers were the only professed supporters of Napoleon III from within the *haute banque*. The financial institution they envisaged was a joint-stock bank so that it could be endowed with sufficient capital. They took the structure and functions of the Société Générale de Belgique as their model. In various articles, the brothers Isaac and Emile Péreire had long been making a strong case that France's economy needed a joint-stock bank. Accordingly they were also drawn into the consultation.

Saint-Simonian ideas were introduced into the project by the Péreire brothers. They did not merely wish to set up a joint-stock bank which would be able to compete with the *haute banque*. For them this new bank was to usher in a new era and to become the heart of a wholly new economic and credit system. The joint-stock bank was to take on and centralize the long-term financing of the entire transport system and of heavy industry. On the strength of its dominant financial position, it would systematically control industrial development and, above all, eliminate competition which Isaac Péreire considered to be the root of nearly all evil.

The Péreire brothers intended to provide smaller industrial and commercial enterprises with credit channelled through co-operative credit banks. These banks were in turn to be directed by a head office, attached to the central joint-stock bank. The result of these arrangements would be an economy which was centrally directed via the credit system. Nor was it to be limited to France. Similar central joint-stock banks were to be founded in the commercial centres of other European countries. The Péreire brothers hoped to export their ideas to other countries by participating in railway construction in Russia, Spain and the Austrian Monarchy; this they expected would enable them to promote their concept of joint-stock banks there, alongside the newly established railway companies. These banks would all function on the same principle and were to issue internationally valid, convertible credit notes covered by industrial and railway shares in the banks' possession. The credit notes would also be an international means of payment. It was a programme by which the ideas of Enfantin and Bazard were to be realized.

The Péreire brothers made no secret of their far-reaching ambitions and publicized them in pamphlets and articles. It may occasion surprise that, in Napoleon III's Empire, the professed supporters of a 'socialist' sect were allowed to participate in the creation of what was generally considered to be a very important bank; what is more: they were entrusted with its management. Yet the Saint-Simonians had no political party or movement of their own, and the Péreire brothers, their Saint-Simonian ideals notwithstanding, belonged to the *corps législativ* as zealous Bonapartists.

In the autumn of 1852, the project was presented to the appropriate ministers. They demanded a few changes, which the founders carried out, as permission was conditional upon these amendments. One such change concerned the name. The founders wanted to establish the bank under the name of 'Banque des Travaux Public'. The Minister of Finance, however, wanted to reserve the designation 'Banque' for institutions with the right to issue notes, i.e. in fact exclusively for the Banque de France. In the end, the designation 'Société Générale de Crédit Mobilier' was chosen. The bank also had to submit to control by the Ministry of Finance. The Crédit Mobilier was finally founded on 20 November 1852. The Péreire brothers and the Fould brothers acquired over half of the 20 million francs launching capital, which was soon increased to 60 million francs. Two firms of the *haute banque*, Mallet and d'Eichthal, participated in the promotion out of rivalry towards the Rothschilds. Foreign banking houses also took part in the promotion: Heine from Hamburg and in particular the Cologne banking house of Oppenheim, which had connections with the Fould bank through the common Fould-Oppenheim bank, owned by Abraham Oppenheim, Benoît Fould's brother-in-law.

The Péreire brothers assumed the management of the Crédit Mobilier; Benoît Fould became chairman of the supervisory board. Its statutes permitted the bank to accept deposits, to advance credits against securities, to undertake investment transactions (the issue, purchase and sale of shares) and to finance railways and industrial enterprises. The bank was also allowed to issue bonds with a minimum duration of 45 days and up to ten times the amount of its joint-stock capital. Gilt-edged securities and railway and industrial shares were to be purchased with the receipts from bond issues. The bonds were to be covered by these securities. Although they knew that the value of securities fluctuated, they believed that fluctuations in the quotations of various types of securities would — given their total volume — balance themselves out. The designation Crédit Mobilier derived from these bonds and their collateral; the mobile assets (shares, annuities) were to make up collateral in the same way as the mortgage bonds issued by the Crédit Foncier (see below, p. 104) were secured by mortgaged property, i.e. fixed assets. However, the extensive issue of bonds which the bank anticipated making in fact hardly materialised. The Crédit Mobilier secured a plentiful supply of money by selling its own shares at prices which occasionally amounted to four times, and, on average, to more than double the nominal value. The bank participated in the promotion of new railway companies in France, Spain, Northern Italy, Austria, Russia and Switzerland. By 1860, the Crédit Mobilier had financed the construction of approximately 10,000 kilometres of railways outside France in this way. Its involvement in industry was no less strong and included the French coal and steel industry and the Silesian zinc industry. The Bank also participated in the promotion of Crédit Mobilier banks abroad by large-scale acquisitions of shares. Thus, in 1853, it gained a stake in the Darmstädter Bank, one of whose founders was Abraham Oppenheim, Benoît Fould's brother-in-law. It also participated in the Crédit Mobilier Espagnol; the Crédit Mobilier Italien and in the Banque Ottomane based in Paris. In many areas, and particularly in railway construction, the Crédit Mobilier appeared in the path of the Rothschilds and this was certainly not unintentional.

James de Rothschild had been hostile to the Crédit Mobilier from its creation. The fact that the Crédit Mobilier had been founded to compete with the *haute banque* and especially the House of Rothschild could not be ignored. Just before the new bank's statutes were approved, Rothschild, on 15 November 1852, submitted a petition to Louis Napoléon in which he pointed out that, in view of its aims, the bank would, in times of crisis, be immediately threatened with illiquidity. He also argued that it would gain control over commercial and industrial enterprises and that such control could easily be misused. Given the political position of the founders and the critic, his petition met with no success. After these manoeuvres to prevent the founding of the Crédit Mobilier had failed and the Crédit Mobilier had successfully initiated a very aggressive, expansionist business policy, the Rothschilds began a sweeping counter-offensive. In the spring of 1856, a group of private bankers in Paris were joined by Cahen of Antwerp and the Swiss Hentsch to form a syndicate called the Réunion Financière; the syndicate was under the control of the Paris Rothschilds and designed to counter the Crédit Mobilier. It possessed excellent connections abroad and started its battle with the Crédit Mobilier on the foreign credit markets,

as the Péreire and Fould brothers had a very strong influence within France
at that time.

The Rothschilds' counter-offensive was successful. Within the same year,
it had prevented the establishment of a Crédit-Mobilier bank in Austria, by
founding the Österreichische Creditanstalt as a joint- stock bank with the
help of the Viennese Rothschild Bank. The Rothschilds' influence also
blocked the foundation of Crédit-Mobilier banks in Belgium and Russia. In
Spain and Italy, the Rothschilds set up rival banks to the subsidiaries of
the Paris Crédit Mobilier there. The Péreire brothers were able to prevent
the Rothschilds from setting up a rival joint-stock bank in France thanks
to their political connections up to 1864. But by 1864, the Rothschilds
and the private bankers allied with them had won such strong support
from public opinion that the Government gave in and granted them permission to found a joint-stock bank, both for regular banking business and
for the issue of shares. Thus, under the leadership of the Paris Rothschilds,
the Société Générale pour favoriser le développement du commerce et de
l'industrie en France was founded as a competitor of the Crédit Mobilier
and was managed by the Rothschild bank in Paris. By that time, the Crédit
Mobilier was encountering its first difficulties. In 1866, in order to restore
its liquidity, it had to increase its capital from 60 to 120 million francs. A
year later, however, the bank was again in trouble. To obtain new liquid
assets, bonds were issued totalling 75 million francs. But the Bank's critical
situation could not be concealed from potential investors, and it was unable
to place all bonds. The Banque de France had to step in to support the
Crédit Mobilier, but did so only on condition that the Péreire brothers
withdraw from the management. As a consequence of the economic crisis
of 1866-67, the market value of a large part of its assets had gone into a
steep decline and some were no longer realizeable. The bank had to be
reconstructed and shareholders received two new shares for five old ones.
Although the Crédit Mobilier had been saved from bankruptcy, its business
had suffered a severe blow; in effect, it only continued to exist to honour
existing business commitments until it was quietly liquidated in 1902. A
smaller bank, the Crédit Mobilier de France, was founded in 1902 to take its
place. It operated successfully until its merger with the Banque de l'Union
Parisienne in 1932.

Nevertheless, it was not its enemies who had caused the decline of the
Crédit Mobilier; the counter-offensive launched by the Rothschilds and the
Réunion Financière had not been intended to ruin it, but to put a damper
on its excessive expansion. In the final analysis, the failure of the Crédit
Mobilier was the result of the way in which its business had been conducted. The regular deposit business with the individual customers had been
neglected. It accepted only large deposits from capital companies; nor had
it paid much attention to the short-term credit business. As a result, the
Crédit Mobilier missed out on information about its customers which it
would otherwise have acquired. Another mistake was that it paid dividends
which at first were far too generous. Thus, it distributed a dividend of 40%

in 1855 and of 23% in 1856. However, the Crédit Mobilier's most glaring weakness lay in its extraordinary immobilization of capital. Almost everything was invested in shares and in bonds of its subsidiaries. Individual commitments were also too high. Thus when the Compagnie Immobilière collapsed in 1867, the bank lost claims of almost 80 million francs which could not be recovered. It was this loss which prompted the unsuccessful bonds issue of 75 million francs of that year.

The reasons for its creation (which can be understood only if seen in a contemporary context) and its miserable failure notwithstanding, the Crédit Mobilier became, by virtue of its structure and original aims, the prototype of the new big commercial bank in France's neighbouring countries. It was a joint-stock bank designed to combine regular banking business — accepting deposits and granting short-term credits — with the issue of shares and with investment banking.

When the Crédit Mobilier ran into difficulties in 1867, there were four other big joint-stock banks in existence in France. Two of them were deposit banks on the model of English joint-stock banks; the other two, the Comptoir d'Escompte de Paris and the Crédit Industriel et Commercial, engaged both in regular banking and in investment. The former was founded as a temporary joint-stock company in 1848 by a decree of the French Minister of Finance. As a result of the economic crisis of the late 1840s, many industrial and commercial enterprises were unable to sell their goods and so had no ready cash to meet their commitments or to buy new stock. In order to deal with these problems, the Finance Minister established discount offices in Paris and 65 other towns for a limited period at the end of March 1848. Their joint-stock capital was divided up among three groups — private shareholders, municipalities and central government — and allocated in equal portions. However, a mere fraction of it was paid up and later topped up by income from interest. These offices granted traders and industrial enterprises credit through bills of exchange against the pledge of goods or, where the debtors had stored their goods in one of the established public warehouses, against their warehouse receipts. At first, there was a lively interest in the new system. The discount branch office at Paris granted credit totalling 80 million francs in bills of exchange within the first five months of operation alone. Once the crisis had subsided, the demand for credit from the discount offices slackened and some were dissolved; others were transformed into private joint-stock companies or limited partnerships.

The discount office at Paris was converted into such a private joint-stock company, the Comptoir d'Escompte de Paris in 1854, with a capital of 20 million francs. Increasingly it became involved in credit-financing French foreign trade and in particular in promoting French import firms with the help of acceptance credits similar to those granted by English discount houses. The company made credit available to the importer who was now able to draw a bill on the Comptoir. The latter accepted the bill and passed it on to the foreign supplier, who was then able to cash the bill without delay at his own bank because it was endorsed by a reputable French bank.

The supplier now despatched the goods to the French importer and gave his bank the title documents establishing the ownership of the goods. The Comptoir d'Escompte de Paris then had 90 days in which to honour the bill at the supplier's bank, whereupon the title documents were handed over to the Comptoir. As soon as the French importer had honoured his bills of exchange with the Comptoir d'Escompte de Paris — having 90 or 180 days to do so — he received the title documents. It was only at this point that the goods which had been delivered to him became property over which he could dispose. The importer benefited by this system in that he obtained instant delivery of his goods on credit terms of 90 or 180 days. He was unlikely to obtain such credit terms from a foreign and, in most cases, overseas supplier, had a reputable bank not assumed liability with its bill of acceptance. The supplier enjoyed the advantage of immediate payment as soon as the goods had been despatched. The risk for both the lending banks, the Comptoir in Paris and the supplier's bank, was quite small, because they held the title documents. It was a form of reimbursement credit which had been developed by the London discount houses during the 19th century. The Comptoir d'Escompte de Paris undertook this business on a large scale, and from 1860 onwards established branches in Shanghai, Bombay, Hong Kong, Yokohama and London in order to expand the range of this business.

From the end of the 1860s, the Comptoir also participated in issues of foreign government loans. In 1876 it was entrusted with the consolidation of the Egyptian government debt. After 1880, the Comptoir was less successful. Its reputation suffered when it sold Argentinian, Greek, Portuguese and Mexican state bonds to the French public whose rates failed to live up to expectations. Moreover, the Comptoir suffered an enormous loss in another deal. It had granted the Société des Métaux a very large advance for speculative purchases of copper. The price of copper had fallen and the company bought enormous quantities (some 120,000 long tons) of the metal in the expectation that the price would soon rise again. It continued to drop, however, and remained at a very low level for some time. The director of the Comptoir had guaranteed several of the Société's contracts without informing the supervisory board, and so the Comptoir had to pay out large sums of money. A few major customers suspected that the situation was precarious and began to withdraw their deposits. When, on top of this, the director of the Comptoir panicked and committed suicide on 5 March 1889, the run on the bank could not be stopped.

Within a few days, the share price had fallen from 200% to 40%. Because there was danger of a general banking crisis — when a major bank finds itself in difficulties most of the customers of all the banks become anxious — the Banque de France, at the insistence of Finance Minister Rouvier granted the Comptoir a credit of 140 million francs, which was guaranteed by the joint-stock banks and the *haute banque* firms of Paris. The Comptoir was liquidated and most of its creditors were paid off. Had it not been for the panic reaction of the director and the subsequent alarm of the customers the Comptoir could have survived the crisis which the Société des Métaux had unleashed, as was revealed by the favourable outcome of its liquidation. Since it had played an important role in the commercial credit business, a successor, the Comptoir National d'Escompte de Paris, was founded in the summer of 1889, with a joint-stock capital of 40 million francs, soon to be increased to 60 million and to 185 million francs by 1909. The new Comptoir functioned as a deposit bank and, for several years, was also very active in the issuing business. However, it accumulated extensive holdings of industrial shares in the process which reduced its liquidity. Faced with the problem, it gradually scaled back both its issuing activity and its share-holdings. Like the Comptoir and its successor, the Crédit Industriel et Commercial was founded in 1859 as a deposit bank. Its structure and business activity was modelled on the major English deposit banks.

Whereas the first two major French deposit banks emerged during the heyday of the Crédit Mobilier, the first big universal banks were only founded when the venture of the Péreire brothers had begun to stagnate. The first of them, the Crédit Lyonnais, started business in Lyon in 1863. It was founded as a 'société à responsabilité limitée' since a joint-stock company still required a licence from the Head of State. After this regulation had been lifted, the Crédit Lyonnais was converted into a 'société anonyme' (joint-stock company) in 1872. The founder and director for many years was Henri Germain. He came from a silk manufacturing family in Lyon, taught philosophy in a grammar-school for a while and then worked in a bill-broker's office. He raised the foundation capital of 20 million francs with the help of Lyon manufacturers and Geneva bankers. In the history of the major French banks he was the really significant trend-setter. The Péreire brothers were imaginative planners but wretched bankers because of their inability to restrain their imagination and misguided in their reckless competitive struggle with the Rothschilds.

By taking the English joint-stock bank as his model, Germain demonstrated how a well-managed institution could expand into a major bank and how the business of a major bank could be managed rationally. That, despite their shortcomings, the Péreire brothers and their Crédit Mobilier became more famous than Germain is to be attributed to their journalistic activities. There is also the fact that their bank experienced a very dramatic development and that it was the prototype of the universal bank. The latter statement is only partly correct; for the first universal joint-stock bank was undoubtedly the Société Générale de Belgique, except that it was not consciously founded as a new type of bank, nor was it recognised as such at the time.

Unlike the Péreire brothers, Germain regarded the deposit bank as a means of collecting and mobilizing, for commercial purposes, the many small deposits of money which, had they not been aggregated, would have remained unused. After one and a half years, the Crédit Lyonnais had more than 10,000 depositors. Germain saw the main threat to a bank in the immobilization of its capital; for this reason he preferred to acquire liquid investments and attached great importance to a high cash liquidity, even if this meant lower profits, because money kept in the vault could not earn any interest. Since Germain was averse to speculation, he also sought sound background information when he assessed potential projects. For this purpose, he set up an investigation department with 50 employees in his Bank, called the Bureau des Etudes Financières. Germain also became a pioneer in the field of welfare provision by establishing the first pension fund for bank employees in France.

At first the Crédit Lyonnais was no more than a regional bank. Within 15 years it had become a major bank by building up a large network of branches throughout France. In Britain the growth of joint-stock banks to the large size which some of them achieved was primarily a consequence of mergers. In France, on the other hand, mergers played but a subordinate role in the development of major banks until the First World War. In France the growth of a bank into a big bank depended on its ability to establish a large network of branches. The Crédit Lyonnais set an example in this field too.

In 1864, a year after the foundation of the Crédit Lyonnais, James Rothschild and the *haute banque* firms in alliance with him in the Réunion Financière established the Société Générale pour favoriser le développement du commerce et de l'industrie en France as a counterweight to the Crédit Mobilier. In the meantime the relationship between Achille Fould and the Péreire brothers had seriously deteriorated and so the Fould and Oppenheim banks also acquired shares in the Société Générale. The new bank engaged in similar business transactions as its competitor, but did so much more cautiously. It strove to acquire deposits on fixed terms so that it could deal with borrowed funds in greater certainty. The bank succeeded in obtaining about half of its deposits on fixed terms. It accepted securities and direct participating investments in line with the amount of these long-term deposits, which corresponded to about five-sixths of the joint-stock capital; the short-term deposits were used only in liquid investments. The Société Générale's business developed as favourably as that of the Crédit Lyonnais. The success of both institutions encouraged the creation of two more issuing banks after 1870.

In 1870, several members of the *haute banque* founded the Banque de Paris, but it was unable to begin its work because of the Franco-Prussian War. After the end of that War, it merged with a similar credit institution in Amsterdam, the Banque de Crédit et de Dépôts des Pays Bas, founded in 1863 with the assistance of the Brussels Bischoffsheim Bank. The bank to emerge from this fusion was the Banque de Paris et des Pays Bas, 'Paribas' for short. The character of 'Paribas' was strongly determined by its Dutch partners; it had a joint-stock capital of 62.5 million francs and no more than a few shareholders. Its customers were exclusively domestic and foreign banks and a very few very wealthy individuals. It worked only with its own funds and the long-term deposits of well-endowed companies and wealthy private persons. Following the example of the Crédit Lyonnais, the bank also set up a Bureau des Etudes Financières, where economists and engineers examined the economic and technical prospects of companies under consideration for issuing transactions and investments. The 'Paribas' participated in the issue of French and foreign state loans, for example, to Austria-Hungary, Russia, Rumania, Greece, Netherlands, Belgium, and the Ottoman Empire; it helped to establish railway companies in Argentina and China and to finance a few selected large French and foreign industrial enterprises. It took part in the foundation of several foreign banks and acted as their agent in Paris.

The Société de l'Union Générale, founded in Paris in 1878, was completely different from the 'Paribas' which, because of its many contacts with foreign banks, was something like a 'permanent syndicate of major finance houses' (E. Kaufmann). As in the case of Crédit Mobilier, there were political and ideological motives behind the creation of the Union Générale and, like the former, it was designed to counteract the power of the Jewish and Protestant *haute banque*. However, the driving force behind the bank was not the Bonapartists and Saint-Simonians, but rather the clerics and supporters of the Bourbons. The Union Générale was conceived as a major Catholic bank and accordingly its joint-stock capital was raised above all from among the Catholic and legitimist-minded aristocracy. By 1880, its starting capital of 25 million francs had been increased to 100 million francs. The leading personality in the Union Générale was Eugène Bontoux, a man without prior experience in banking. A railway engineer, he had been employed by the Austrian state railways. For several years he had been director-general of the *Österreichische Südbahn* whose major shareholder was the Viennese bank of Rothschild. Bontoux had used his position and his good connections with the Rothschild bank to engage in extensive speculation during the period of rapid industrial expansion in Austria between 1869 and 1873, known as *Gründerjahre,* and had acquired participations in railways, mines and factories. During the crisis of 1873, he lost a large part of his speculative gains and subsequently fell out with the House of Rothschild.

On returning to France, he established close contact with Henri Comte de Chambord, the pretender to the Bourbon throne. When Bontoux took over the directorship of the Union Générale, he was able to do some profitable business in the Dual Monarchy, thanks to his previous connections with the Austrian government. *Inter alia* he participated in the creation of the Österreichische Länderbank in 1880. Bontoux was seduced by his early, large profits into engaging in a number of risky speculative ventures. He bought shares in the Union Générale in order to push up their price. At the same time he began a bearish attack on the joint-stock companies controlled by the Rothschilds, the Société Générale among them. These moves miscarried disastrously when his competitors took counter-measures. When a major subsidiary of the Union Générale became insolvent in 1882, the latter had to suspend payments and went bankrupt. Bontoux was brought to trial for misusing his customers' money for speculative purposes and was sentenced to five years' imprisonment. The collapse of the

legitimist-clerical and government-supported bank and the criminal con-
viction of its president furnished the republicans and anti-clericals with
excellent ammunition in their fight against the legitimists and the renewed
struggle between Church and State in France.

The bankruptcy of the Union Générale was followed by a panic on the
stock exchange and a general banking crisis, from which the Crédit Lyonnais
and the Société Générale were both to suffer for several years, whereas the
'Paribas' was hardly affected. As a result of the crisis, France abandoned this
type of universal bank, the major banks becoming either institutions comparable to the English deposit banks, or investment banks, though to be
more precise they should be referred to as *predominantly* deposit banks
and *predominantly* investment banks, for in practice they never wholly
represented the one type or the other. The Crédit Lyonnais and the Société
Générale cautiously reduced their long-term engagements and, together with
the Comptoir National d'Escompte de Paris and the Crédit Industriel et
Commercial, became a group of major deposit banks. Only the 'Paribas'
continued to function primarily as a larger bank until other investment
banks were founded after the turn of the century. The Banque de l'Union
Parisienne was the most significant of these, even if it lagged far behind the
'Paribas' in size. Whereas the latter had been founded by members of the
predominantly Jewish *haute banque*, the establishment of the Banque de
l'Union Parisienne in 1904 brought together the members of the old *banque
protestante:* the banks of Hottinguer, Mallet, de Neuflize, Vernes and
Mirabaud. They took over the failing Banque Parisienne and converted it
into the Banque de l'Union Parisienne. Since they could not keep pace
with the 'Paribas' in the issuing business, they founded a new joint-stock
bank in order to secure a larger share in the issue of state loans. The Banque
de l'Union Parisienne also established close contact with industry. Its
most important industrial customer became the armaments manufacturers
Schneider-Creusot.

5. Universal Banks in Central Europe

The Universal bank of the Crédit Mobilier type was to become the most
wide-spread in Central Europe. The Bank für Handel und Industrie was
founded at Darmstadt in 1853 as the first credit institution on the model of
the Crédit Mobilier. The Cologne bankers Gustav Mevissen, Abraham
Oppenheim, Wilhelm Ludwig Deichmann and Viktor Wendelstadt seized
the initiative to set it up. With the exception of Oppenheim, they all belonged to the directorium of the Schaaffhausenscher Bankverein which had
become a joint-stock bank after the crisis of 1848. They realized that, in
view of the strong industrial upswing which had begun to affect Prussia
after 1850, the supply of capital through private bankers was no longer
sufficient. Indeed, in order to finance industry it was necessary to mobilize
medium-sized and small savings through the device of a joint-stock company.
Apart from this primary reason, the Cologne bankers were guided by a

further motive which had also contributed to establishing the Crédit Mobilier: according to Mevissen, a counterbalance was to be created against 'the autocratic rule of the private financial power' of the Rothschilds. Yet, the Prussian government was not inclined to licence further joint-stock banks after the Schaaffhausenscher Bankverein. The ministers feared that industry would be supplied through the joint-stock banks with funds which would otherwise have been made available to agriculture. Although Prussia was the most industrialized German state, its ministers stuck firmly to the view that industrial development should not be at the cost of agriculture.

If they were not to be permitted to establish the proposed joint-stock bank in their own state, Frankfurt, the leading banking centre in Germany was the obvious alternative. However, the Cologne bankers also ran into insuperable difficulties there; most of Frankfurt's private bankers, under the leadership of Amschel Rothschild, exerted all their influence to prevent the local authorities of the Free City of Frankfurt from granting a licence. In the end and rather by chance, Darmstadt became the seat of the new bank. The Mannheim banker Moritz von Haber whose own bank had collapsed in the Revolution of 1848 obtained a concession to establish a joint-stock bank in Darmstadt from the Grand Duke of Hesse, with whom he had previously had business connections both directly and on behalf of Oppenheim, a relation by marriage. Thus the Bank für Handel und Industrie was founded in the Grand Duke of Hesse's residence on 13 April 1853. Apart from Haber and the Cologne bankers, the two private banks of Bethmann and Goldschmidt — whose owners did not share the attitude of the other Frankfurt bankers — took part in setting it up. The greatest proportion of its first share issue, which amounted to a total of 10 million guldens, was acquired by the Crédit Mobilier. The German bankers did not particularly welcome this very substantial French involvement. When the capital was increased to 25 million guldens in 1856, they took care that the Crédit Mobilier obtained no additional shares.

The Prussian Envoy to the Assembly of the German Confederation at Frankfurt, Otto von Bismarck, recommended that his Government support the new bank, for it would weaken the influence of the Rothschilds and of Austria in Southern Germany to Prussia's advantage. However, King Frederick William IV considered the bank to be harmful both economically and politically. He ordered that it be prevented from proliferating into Prussia and that action be taken against it. In view of this, the Darmstädter Bank was unable to establish branches in Prussia — at least for the time being. It was also debarred from opening branches in Frankfurt itself; the private bankers there were, of course, not interested in a joint-stock bank (which they had rejected in the first place) gaining a foothold in the banking centre by the back-door. The Darmstädter Bank was allowed to set up an agency only. As a result, the bank expanded its business network in the first five decades of its existence not by creating branches but by forging partnerships with other banks in Berlin, Dresden, Leipzig, Halle, Mannheim, Vienna, Paris, Milan and New York.

In the first 25 years, the direction of the bank was in the hands of Gustav Mevissen as chairman of the supervisory board which was called *Verwaltungsrat* in Germany up to 1862. The most important business up to the end of 1873 consisted of railway financing, industrial investment and state loans. Their railway business began when the Darmstädter Bank acquired shares in the *Österreichische Staatsbahn* and the Hungarian *Theiss-Bahn* in 1854-55. In the 1860s, the bank bought shares in other railways, particularly the *Ludwigsbahn* in Hesse, the Austrian *Nordwestbahn* and several railway lines in Central and Western Germany. The bank also sold debentures of German, Austrian, Hungarian and Russian railways to the public. In the course of promoting industrial companies, the Darmstädter Bank in many cases acquired a part of the shares it issued. This was done not out of necessity but as a matter of deliberate policy so that the bank would gain control of the industrial joint-stock companies it was helping to found. Thus, in 1856 alone, it raised a total of 1.6 million guldens for the establishment of such joint-stock companies and acquired shares to the tune of 813,000 guldens in them.

From 1860, the Darmstädter Bank also participated more prominently in the issue of state loans. For this reason, it became a member of the Prussian Consortium. This was a group of banks which had combined in 1859 in order to place a large Prussian loan and which had acted since then as a permanent issuing consortium for Prussian state loans. Like both the Crédit Mobilier and the Schaaffhausenscher Bankverein, the Darmstädter Bank did not at first attach much importance to deposit banking. If by 1870 the bank nevertheless held deposits of about 11 million guldens, surpassing those of the Schaaffhausenscher Bankverein and the Disconto-Gesellschaft many times over, it was due to the fact that a few major customers, such as railway companies, had deposited their liquid assets with the Darmstädter Bank.

Like the Crédit Mobilier, the Darmstädter Bank concentrated on several major commitments. Although these business links had been very carefully chosen, it suffered considerable losses in the great economic crisis of 1857-59. It was able to maintain liquidity only by reducing its current account credits from 4.5 million guldens in 1857 to 360,000 guldens by the end of 1859 and also by drastically restricting its credit business.

With the establishment of the Bank für Handel und Industrie only one half of Mevissen's and Oppenheim's banking plan had been realized. From the very beginning they had wanted to found two banks, a Crédit-Mobilier bank for investment business and an issuing bank for short-term credit as well as for the issue of bank notes. They were able to realize the second part of this banking project in 1856 when they obtained the licence to set up the Bank für Süddeutschland at Darmstadt. It issued bank notes although it always remained in the shadow of the Frankfurter Bank which had been founded for the same purpose two years earlier.

At the same time as Mevissen and Oppenheim, David Hansemann tried to establish a joint-stock bank in Prussia. Yet, whereas the former had evaded the Prussian government's strict refusal to licence another joint-stock company in the credit system in addition to the Schaaffhausen 'emergency case' by moving to the neighbouring Hesse-Darmstadt, Hansemann chose a different legal structure as a way-out. After retiring from the management of the Preussische Bank he founded the Direction der Disconto-Gesellschaft in 1851 as a co-operative credit association. Within a few years, he had re-organized the Disconto-Gesellschaft, converting the company to a partnership limited by shares in the process, with a capital of 10 million thalers. Thus the bank became the largest in Prussia in respect of capital, and next to the Darmstädter Bank für Handel und Industrie, it was the second biggest inside the *Zollverein* (German Customs Union). It participated in the issue of shares and debentures of Russian and Prussian railway companies. When Prussia mobilized its army during the Italian war in 1859, the Disconto-Gesellschaft assumed control of the banking syndicate which accepted the Prussian mobilization loan. This remained the bank's only involvement in the public loan business until 1866. Between 1866 and 1869, partly on its own and partly in co-operation with the Preussische Seehandlung and the banks of Ladenburg & Söhne at Mannheim and Erlanger & Söhne at Frankfurt, it accepted loans for Bavaria, Baden, Prussia, Brunswick and the cities of Mannheim and Danzig. In the industrial sphere, the Disconto-Gesellschaft founded the *Heinrichshütte* mining and iron works in 1863, which, having suffered considerable losses, it turned into an independent company. Thenceforth the bank participated in the company as a limited partner only. Unlike the Crédit Mobilier, but even more strongly than the Darmstädter Bank, the Disconto-Gesellschaft moved into the business of credits on current accounts.

Following David Hansemann's death in 1864, his son became the bank's moving spirit for almost four decades. In 1869 he took a prominent politician into the group of owners: Johannes Miquel, the future Prussian Finance Minister. Miquel was at that time the lord mayor of Osnabrück and also member of the Prussian Chamber of Deputies and of the North German Imperial Diet. As a student in 1848, he had belonged to the Radical Democrats and until 1857 had kept up a correspondence with Marx; but in the 1860s he became one of the leading men in the National Liberal Party which grew into the strongest political party in Germany and Bismarck's most important ally in Parliament in the decade between 1867 and 1877. This was, of course, the period in which the German Empire was founded and consolidated. On the strength of his political activity and connections, Miquel was extremely useful to Hansemann and the Disconto-Gesellschaft in several large projects. These included the creation of the Preussische Central-Bodencredit-Aktiengesellschaft in 1870, direct investment in the *Gotthardbahn,* and finally the acquisition, in 1871, of shares owned by Henry Strousberg, the bankrupt 'railway king' and speculator in Rumanian railways. Just before Miquel ceased to be an active member of the bank in 1873, the Disconto-Gesellschaft acquired a newspaper, the *Post,* from Strousberg. Two years later, in 1874, the bank sold the paper to a group of industrialists, among them the Neunkirchen manufacturer Stumm who subsequently turned it into the party organ of the Free Conservatives.

A few months after the Disconto-Gesellschaft's transformation into a partnership limited by shares, several private bankers in Berlin — Mendelssohn, Gelpcke, Magnus, Bleichröder and Warschauer — founded a rival institution, the Berliner Handels-Gesellschaft, with Oppenheim's and Mevissen's direct participation. This company was also organized as a partnership limited by shares; but with a joint-stock capital of 3.75 million thalers, it was substantially less well equipped with capital than Hansemann's enterprise. Like the Disconto-Gesellschaft, the Berliner Handels-Gesellschaft pursued its main-line business in financing railways and the issue of public loans in Prussia, in the Austrian Monarchy and in Russia. Apart from these two credit institutions in Berlin, there were two bigger joint-stock banks which were founded outside Prussia in 1856: the Norddeutsche Bank in Hamburg and the Allgemeine Deutsche Credit-Anstalt (ADCA) in Leipzig.

The *Gründer* years in Germany began with the liberalization of company law through the amendment of the law on joint-stock companies in June 1870 and not, as is often assumed, with the French reparations payments from the following year onwards. After 1867, there had been a strong upturn in the German economy, and joint-stock companies were founded in large numbers when the licensing requirement was lifted in the middle of this economic boom. The influx of French reparations money gave this development a further boost. The general fever of starting up joint-stock companies also seized the credit system and the traditionally cautious bankers. Thus between 1870 and 1872, 107 joint-stock banks, with capital totalling 740 million marks, were founded in Germany. Most of them did not survive for long, however, and as early as the end of 1879 some 73 out of 108 newly created companies had gone into liquidation.

Three credit institutions grew rapidly into major banks of paramount importance: the Deutsche Bank in Berlin, the Commerz-und Disconto-Bank in Hamburg and the Dresdner Bank. The Commerz-und Disconto-Bank and the Deutsche Bank had been founded in March 1870, still under the old restrictive company law. However, as the amendment of the law on joint-stock companies was already under discussion in the Diet of the North German Confederation, they also benefited from the liberalization of the law to the extent that they speedily obtained a concession. The Dresdner Bank emerged from the conversion of the old Dresden private bank of Michael Kaskel into a joint-stock company in 1872. The joint-stock capital of these banks differed greatly at the time of their foundation. The Deutsche Bank was established with a joint-stock capital of five million thalers and, in the following year, it was increased to 10 million. After the currency reform of 1871, when the thaler was converted into the mark, it rose to 30 million marks. In 1872, the Deutsche Bank increased its capital to 45 million marks. On the strength of its capital, the bank occupied the third rank after the Disconto-Gesellschaft and the Schaaffhausenscher Bankverein. The Commerz-und Disconto-Bank was at first provided with capital of four million bancomarks. The bancomark was the clearing unit of the Hamburg currency. It had a coin value of 8.3 grams of silver and, following the reform, it equalled 1.50 marks. After this reform and a capital increase, its joint-stock capital amounted to 21 million marks at the end of 1872. The Dresdner Bank was to have a joint-stock capital of 24 million marks. Some 9.6 million of this was to be paid up when it was established; but following the *Gründer* crisis of 1873 it was decided to leave the joint-stock capital at 9.6 million marks.

The Darmstädter Bank für Handel und Industrie, the Disconto-Gesell-schaft, the Berliner Handels-Gesellschaft, the ADCA and the Dresdner Bank were all modelled on the type of investment bank represented by the Crédit Mobilier. The founders of the Commerz- und Disconto Bank and of the Deutsche Bank, on the other hand, looked to the example of the English joint-stock banks. Both these major banks, founded in 1870, were designed to finance foreign trade in particular. This objective was very clearly reflected in the composition of the founding committee of the Commerz-und Disconto-Bank. It was made up of representatives of private banks and major trading companies. Banking was represented by the Hamburg firms of M.N. Warburg & Co., Lieben Königswarter, Conrad Hinrich Donner and Hesse Newman & Co., the Frankfurt house of B.H. Goldschmidt and Mendelssohn & Co. from Berlin. Commerce was represented by the shipping company of Woermann and the firms of Theodor Wille, Wm. O'Swald and L.E. Amsinck (New York) among others. The new institution sought business links with foreign banks, at first particularly in Scandinavian countries. It acquired a 50% participation in the London & Hanseatic Bank of London. During the first 20 years, its most important line of business was provision of credit on current account. As far as its stocks and share business was concerned, the Commerz-und Disconto-Bank acted for Hamburg enterprises like the HAPAG (Hamburg-America-Packet Company), the Woermann Line and the German East Africa Line. The economic crisis of the mid-1870s and the subsequent depression hit business so hard that the bank's capital had to be reduced to 16.5 million marks in 1875. However, five years later, it was once again increased to its original amount. In order to gain a foothold in Berlin, the Commerz- und Disconto-Bank directly participated in the founding of a new big joint-stock bank in the Reich capital, the Nationalbank für Deutschland.

The founders of the Deutsche Bank were all bankers, with one exception, who was referred to as a merchant. The driving force was the banker Adalbert Delbrück, partner of Delbrück Leo & Co. in Berlin. He had excellent political connections thanks to his cousin, Rudolf Delbrück, who, as President of the Federal Chancellery and, from 1871, of the Reich Chancellery, was one of Bismarck's closest collaborators. Apart from Adalbert Delbrück, the founding committee consisted of five other members. Two of them represented Berlin high finance: Hermann Zwicker, partner of Schickler Brothers, and Victor von Magnus whose father had been a co-founder of the Berliner Handels-Gesellschaft 14 years previously.

Two of the remaining committee members were less important in their own right than the firms they represented: Gustav Kutter of the Frankfurt bank of Sulzbach Brothers which acquired the largest parcel of shares and Gustav Müller acting on behalf of the Königlich-Württembergische Hofbank and the Württembergische Vereinsbank.

One of the founders, though not an actual member of the founding committee, was Ludwig Bamberger. He was not only one of the leading National Liberal politicians when the German Empire was created, but also the central and most prominent figure in the shaping of German monetary and banking policy. He made considerable contributions to the reform which unified the currencies and converted silver currency to the gold specie standard. He also helped to establish the Reichsbank as well as the commercial bank which was later to become the biggest in Germany. He brought to the venture his great experience in international banking which he had gained not only through his work for the Bischoffsheim banking group in London, Antwerp and Paris, but also by taking part in the foundation of one of the forerunners of the Banque de Paris et des Pays Bas. Since foreign trade was to become the Deutsche Bank's main business activity, Bamberger invited Hermann Wallich, an expert in overseas business, to join the board of directors. Wallich had worked for the Paris Comptoir d'Escompte for a long time and had until recently managed the bank's branch at Shanghai. Following the outbreak of the Franco-Prussian War, he was dismissed from his position because he was German. The actual brain behind the Deutsche Bank was a member of the board of directors with experience in foreign trade rather than banking: Georg Siemens.

The Deutsche Bank developed differently from what its founders had envisaged. Although actively involved in foreign business by setting-up branches in Shanghai and Yokohama in 1872 and in London in 1873 and also by direct investments in the German Bank of London and the Deutsch-Belgische La Plata Bank, it began to make losses as a result of the prolonged economic crisis of the 1870s. For this reason, both branches in the Far East were closed by 1875; the direct participation in the German Bank of London was disposed of in 1879, and the Deutsch-Belgische La Plata Bank was liquidated in 1885. It was only from the second half of the 1880s that its foreign business was successful and saw continued expansion, reaching its peak when it financed the construction of the Baghdad Railway and the exploitation of Rumanian oil (see below pp. 138-146). The initial unsatisfactory development of its foreign dealings, which the founders had intended to be its main business, induced Siemens to build up the bank's domestic interests and to make this the basis of its activity. Thus the emphasis shifted from the financing of foreign trade to the financing of German industry.

In the last quarter of the 19th century, the German joint-stock banks developed into universal banks. They were involved in all forms of credit business: short-term commercial loans, medium- and long-term industrial credit, overdrafts on current account and discounting business; they traded in equities, issued shares and debentures, floated loans for governments and municipalities at home and abroad and they also had a large number of deposit accounts. On the initiative of Georg Siemens, the Deutsche Bank was the first to start deposit banking on a really significant scale. After the crisis of 1873, a change took place in the methods of financing industry. Between the mid-century and the *Gründer* years, German joint-stock banks had themselves taken the initiative in founding industrial joint-stock companies and had directly participated in them. Thus the Schaaffhausenscher Bankverein had founded the Hörder Mining and Iron Company in 1851, followed by five other joint-stock companies in engineering, mining and cotton spinning in 1852. In 1856, the Darmstädter Bank had established seven joint-stock companies: a shipping company, two engineering firms, a mining joint-stock company, a wool- and calico factory, a weaving and a spinning mill. The Disconto-Gesellschaft, after establishing the barely prospering *Heinrichshütte* iron mill in 1857, became involved in the even more unprofitable *Dortmunder Union* in 1872. Following their bad experiences with industry in the aftermath of the *Gründer* crisis, the major banks left the founding of industrial enterprises by and large to others and restricted their collaboration to the issue of shares and debentures. Between 1870 and 1874, over five milliard marks' worth of shares in over 1,000 joint-stock companies were issued. There followed a new big wave of issues at the end of the Great Depression in Germany in the early 1890s, this time on a much sounder basis. From 1892 to 1910, shares worth 5.7 milliard marks and debentures worth 1.8 milliard marks were issued.

On the basis of this activity, and also of the banks' unlimited right to represent the votes of deposited shares, close and lasting links were forged between individual credit institutions and certain major industrial and transport enterprises. The banks stipulated in their general business conditions that they would exercise the voting right on deposited shares at the annual general meetings of the companies concerned. It was only in 1937 and 1965 that this right, which gave the banks a very powerful influence over a particular enterprise was drastically curtailed by law. The Deutsche Bank had lasting connections with *Siemens & Halske* (electrical engineering), the *Norddeutsche Lloyd* shipping concern, the *Huldschinskysche Werke*, and the *Deutsche Petroleum Aktiengesellschaft*. The Disconto-Gesellschaft was linked with enterprises in the mining - and steel industries: *Gelsenkirchener Bergwerks-Aktiengesellschaft, Schalker Verein, Bochumer Verein, Stummsche Eisenwerke* and other companies. The Dresdner Bank maintained close ties with the textile industry in Saxony, the cable works of *Felten & Guillaume* at Cologne and mining and iron works such as *Kattowitzer Bergwerks-Aktiengesellschaft, Aktiengesellschaft Lauchhammer* and *Laura-Hütte*. The Berliner Handels-Gesellschaft co-operated with companies in the electrotechnical and mining industries such as the *Allgemeine Elektrizitäts-Gesellschaft* (AEG), *Akkumulatorenfabrik Berlin*, Hibernia Mining, *Harpener Bergbau-Gesellschaft*. The Darmstädter Bank was closely involved with both chemicals and steel such as *Chemische Werke* (formerly

H. & E. Albert) and *Deutsch-Luxemburgische Bergwerks- und Hütten-AG.*
The banks took a particular interest in the markets of 'their' industrial
enterprises in areas in which they were already engaged with credits and
loans. Foreign railway loans above all presented a good lever with which
to improve the market positions of German business. The big banks also
persistently supported the move towards concentration in German industry
which had begun at the end of the 19th century. They were loath to have
their industrial customers competing too vigorously with each other, as
during the *Gründer* crisis when the competitive struggle had often assumed
ruinous proportions. For this reason, the major banks collaborated in the
formation of cartels and syndicates, in particular in the creation of the
Rheinisch-Westfälisches Kohlensyndikat in 1893, the Iron Syndicate of
1896 and the *Stahlwerksverband* cartel of 1904. In the same way, the
banks also helped create large concerns. Thus the Berliner Handels-Gesellschaft, the Deutsche Bank and Delbrück Leo & Co. participated in the
establishment of the AEG empire of Emil Rathenau, Walther Rathenau's
father. The second largest electrical engineering firm, *Siemens & Halske*,
came into being with the help of the Deutsche Bank, the Darmstädter Bank,
the Disconto-Gesellschaft and the Berliner Handels-Gesellschaft. In 1905,
the Darmstädter Bank and the Schaaffhausenscher Bankverein collaborated
to forge a link between the *Badische Anilin-und Soda-Fabrik*, the *Bayer-
Werke* and the AGFA, the preliminary step towards the future chemicals
giant of *I.G. Farbenindustrie Aktiengesellschaft.*

Contemporaneously with the concentration in industry began the process
of concentration in banking through mergers and the formation of banking
groups. In pre-1914 England, this process took the form of mergers, and
major banks did not evolve into bank groups until 1918. In France, two
bank groups were formed before 1914: a cartel of provincial banks in 1899
and a group of the Paris *haute banque* in 1904. In other words, French
banks organized themselves into groups of equals. In Germany, on the other
hand, groups under the control of big banks came into being before 1914.
The concentration that was taking place in industry provided the impetus
for this. In order to finance industrial concentration, it was usually
necessary for several banks to combine their financial power. Another
reason was the attempt to distribute risks and possible losses among several
banks. Bank groups were formed by contractual collaboration agreements,
by the exchange of shares between collaborating institutions or very often
by one major bank acquiring shares in regional joint-stock banks.

In the period up to 1911, the Deutsche Bank formed a bank group which
included such big regional banks as the Bergisch-Märkische Bank of Elberfeld with a joint-stock capital of 80 million marks, the Essener Creditanstalt with a joint-stock capital of 72 million marks and the Rheinische
Creditbank of Mannheim with a joint-stock capital of 95 million marks.
All told, the Deutsche Bank group represented a joint-stock capital of
691 million marks. Its reserves amounted to 238.5 million marks. The
Deutsche Bank itself had a 200-million stake and reserves of 107.8 million

marks in this group. For many of the regional banks, belonging to the Deutsche Bank group represented the first step towards merger. Accordingly, the Bergisch-Märkische Bank was incorporated into the Deutsche Bank in 1914, followed by the Schlesischer Bankverein in 1917 and the Essener Creditanstalt in 1925. When the Deutsche Bank increased its joint-stock capital to 250 million marks after absorbing the Bergisch-Märkische Bank, the *Frankfurter Zeitung* hailed the bank as the largest in the world. This was somewhat exaggerated; nevertheless, the bank was one of the five biggest banks in the world at that time. In 1976, it once again occupied sixth place in the world league.

Like the Deutsche Bank, the Disconto-Gesellschaft also had a joint-stock capital of 200 million marks in 1911. To the Disconto-Gesellschaft group there belonged, *inter alia*, the ADCA of Leipzig with a joint-stock capital of 90 million marks, the Norddeutsche Bank in Hamburg, and the Barmer Bankverein. The group was equipped with a total joint-stock capital of 504 million marks and reserves of 158 million marks. After the Deutsche Bank had taken over the Bergisch-Märkische Bank in the spring of 1914, the Disconto-Gesellschaft strengthened its position in western Germany by acquiring, in May 1914, the total joint-stock capital of the Schaaffhausenscher Bankverein, which had been stagnating for some time. The latter had entered into a collaborative agreement with the Dresdner Bank in 1904, but within a few months, they found themselves at loggerheads over the so-called Hibernia Dispute.

In 1904, the Dresdner Bank had bought shares in the Hibernia colliery in the Ruhr, on behalf of the Prussian government, which was then planning to acquire mining interests in the area, just as most coal-mines in Upper Silesia and the Saar were state-owned. Once it became known on whose behalf Eugen Gutmann of the Dresdner Bank had acquired Hibernia shares, the coal and steel industrialists in the Rhineland and in Westphalia got together. They combined to prevent the Prussian State, which they did not love as much as they claimed, from further penetrating the Ruhr mining industry. The other Hibernia shareholders formed a cartel in which they committed themselves not to sell any shares to the State. This countermove took place not in secret, but full public view, and ended in the defeat and a loss of prestige for the Prussian government. The opportunity to avenge this humiliation arose a few months later. In the spring of 1905, following a miners' strike in the Ruhr which had met with the embittered resistance of the mine owners, the government agreed to most of the miners' demands by amending the Prussian Mining Law. The Dresdner Bank had naturally taken the side of the Prussian government in the Hibernia Dispute. The Schaaffhausenscher Bankverein, on the other hand, as a consequence of its manifold links with Rhenish-Westphalian industry, had to make common cause with the industrialists. The community of interests between the two banks suffered a first severe blow. When the Schaaffhausenscher Bankverein proved to be much less successful than the Dresdner Bank, the agreement, which included a sharing of profits and losses, was terminated in 1908 on

the initiative of the latter. Thereafter, the Schaaffhausenscher Bankverein
went further downhill. When the Disconto-Gesellschaft acquired its joint-
stock capital in 1914, the amount had to be reduced from 145 to 100
million marks beforehand. In this way the first private Prussian joint-stock
bank, which had once upon a time been saved with David Hansemann's
assistance, became a subsidiary of the bank which he had founded.

The Dresdner Bank whose joint-stock capital in 1911 was 200 million
marks and the Darmstädter Bank für Handel und Industrie with a joint-
stock capital in 1911 of 160 million marks, had likewise built up bank
groups although their capital strength was only half of what the other two
groups could muster. The bank groups which have been reviewed up to this
point have been considered in the light of their links and interdependencies
within Germany. They have not been examined in terms of their direct
participation in credit institutions abroad.

By the beginning of the First World War, eight of the private German
joint-stock banks had become major banks. Five of them had their head
offices in Berlin: the Deutsche Bank, the Disconto-Gesellschaft, the Berliner
Handels-Gesellschaft, the Nationalbank für Deutschland and, from 1884,
the Dresdner Bank although its registered office remained in Dresden until
1950. The other three, the Commerz- und Disconto-Bank, Bank für Handel
und Industrie, Schaaffhausenscher Bankverein, had branches in Berlin.

6. Big Banks and Trusts in the United States

In the United States, private joint-stock banks were founded much
earlier than in Europe. The oldest were the Bank of New York and the Bank
of Boston (from 1864, The First National Bank of Boston). Both were
established in 1784, soon after the War of Independence. One of the
founders of the Bank of New York was Alexander Hamilton who had been
George Washington's adjutant during the War of Independence, and who
became Under Secretary in the Treasury Department in 1789. This bank
has always been distinguished for its cautious policy and so has never found
itself in difficulties. Towards the end of the 19th century, however, the
bank was overtaken by other credit institutions in terms of capital and
volume of business. Another bank, that of the Manhattan Company,
emerged from a public utility company. It was founded in 1799 as the
Manhattan Company, and at the beginning was charged with supplying New
York with fresh drinking water, a task which was vital from the viewpoint
of health and sanitation. As this was accomplished with less capital than
expected, a large part of the originally raised capital soon became available
for other purposes. And so a banking business was started. After several
mergers, the company which had once been concerned with the provision
of drinking water to Manhattan became the Chase Manhattan Bank, today
the third largest commercial bank in the world.

In the first half of the 19th century about 1,000 joint-stock banks
came into being, among them the City Bank of New York and the Chemical

Bank. The latter was originally a manufacturing enterprise which got involved in banking as a side-line. In 1844, the company became wholly a banking enterprise and in the process changed its old name of New York Manufacturing Company to the Chemical Bank.

Whereas the European joint-stock banks assumed the leading role in the credit- and issuing business soon after their introduction, the role of American joint-stock banks remained confined to local and regional business up to the Civil War. Since they were joint-stock companies which issued bank notes, they had to be given a charter by their Federal State government. The regulations governing the granting of such a charter varied from one Federal State to another. This meant that joint-stock banks had to restrict their business to their home state. Private bankers, on the other hand, were not subject to any special banking regulations, for they were 'unincorporated banks' and did not issue bank notes; hence they did not require a charter and had greater freedom of movement. For many decades, therefore, they were the institutions to conduct the large transactions connected with the financing of railways and industry.

It was on the strength of the banking and currency legislation of the mid-1860s that the legal basis was created which enabled the joint-stock banks in some cities, and New York in particular, to experience a great expansion of their business and to develop into big banks, far surpassing the rest in terms of their capital resources and volume of business. In 1863, the National Banking Act, covering the whole territory of the Union, created the legal framework for the operations of issuing banks. The Act also divided American banks, with the exception of private bankers, into National Banks and State Banks, depending on whether they decided to apply for a charter to be granted by the Federal government or whether they retained the charter given by their Federal State government. In the following year, the National Currency Act promulgated further regulations relating to the liquidity reserves which had to be maintained by National Banks. These regulations stipulated that the National Banks in New York had to keep liquidity reserves in the form of legal tender — gold or silver coins and gold or silver bars at the time — equalling 25% of their deposits and of their notes in circulation. New York was made the 'Central Reserve City'. A further 18 cities, among them Chicago, Boston and St. Louis, were also proclaimed 'Reserve Cities'. The National Banks in those cities also had to maintain liquidity reserves amounting to 25% of their deposits and notes in circulation, but they were only obliged to keep half their liquidity reserves in legal tender and allowed to deposit the remaining half with National Banks in the Central Reserve City, New York. National Banks outside these cities were required to maintain liquidity reserves amounting to 15% of their deposits and circulating notes. They had to keep 40% of this reserve in coin in their vaults; the remaining 60% — i.e. a reserve equalling 9% of their deposits and notes — could be deposited in National Banks in one of the Reserve Cities or in New York. Later on, Chicago and St. Louis also became Central Reserve Cities.

As a consequence of the National Currency Act regulations, a large volume of deposits which had come from National Banks in other banking centres accumulated in the National Banks in Reserve Cities, and particularly in the New York National Banks. The banks took full advantage of the opportunity to keep part of their liquidity reserves as deposits in the banks of Reserve Cities, as interest was paid on these deposits, whilst reserves kept in their own vaults fetched nothing. Indeed, National Banks in those cities which were not privileged as Reserve Cities kept even higher reserves than prescribed by law; and these excess reserves were naturally deposited in interest-bearing accounts in New York or in one of the other Reserve Cities. Country banks may have regarded the maintenance of reserves at a moderate interest less lucrative; but it was less risky than granting credit to trade and industry in their own region. The tendency to maintain additional liquidity reserves intensified after the economic crises and bank failures in 1873 and in the 1890s.

The money flowing in from the country went predominantly to New York, the Central Reserve City, and fostered a massive and continuing growth of banking and of individual National Banks there. The older New York joint-stock banks acquired the status of National Banks. New joint-stock banks, which obtained their charter from the Federal government, were founded: the First National Bank in New York in 1863, the Hanover Bank in 1871 and the Chase National Bank of the City of New York in 1877. The latter added the name of the author of the National Act to its own. Despite the booming development of the New York joint-stock banks, by virtue of which they far outstripped other credit institutions in the country, they were by no means in control of the money- and capital market in America's commercial metropolis. There were three other types of financial institutions of considerable importance besides them: the trust companies, the life insurance companies and the large private bankers.

The trust companies were primarily trustees for the administration of property, and their work often included the investment of capital, depending on the powers which owners decided to transfer to the trust companies managing their property. Because they invested the funds which they administered, the trust companies gradually took on the role of investment banks. Later they were permitted by law to accept deposits and to grant short-term commercial credits. In terms of their foundation and activity, these companies were subject to generally very generous legal regulations which existed in individual States. Three of them became major banks: the Guarantee Trust Company of New York (1864), the Bankers Trust Company (1903) and the Manufacturers Trust Company (1905). All three had their head offices in New York. From 1880, life insurance companies also participated directly in big financial operations on a considerable scale. They were particularly involved with railway finance, often collaborating with big banks. Occasionally there was even a personal link between the boards of directors of life insurance companies and banks.

It is a very astonishing phenomenon in the history of banking that in the United States a few big private bankers were able to uphold their position among the greatest financial powers in the country; what is more: well into our own century, the most influential money- and credit institution in America was a private banker! This is remarkable because the large private banks in Europe were already financially powerful and influential undertakings with many international ties at the time when joint-stock banks were first promoted; and yet they were relatively quickly overtaken by the most successful joint-stock banks. In America, the private bankers who had played a significant role at the turn of the century, had won their pre-eminence only in the last quarter of the 19th century while competing with big joint-stock banks. What probably explains their success is that they had collaborated in the formation of big trusts at the end of the 19th and the beginning of the 20th century, thereby not only gaining opportunities for control and influence in industry and transport, but also making considerable profits.

The big private banking houses which began to flourish in America as the great era of private bankers was already drawing to a close in Europe, were those of Kuhn Loeb & Co. and J.P. Morgan & Co. The former was founded by two Jewish immigrants from Germany, who arrived with very little money. Their success corresponded quite accurately to the stereotypical ideas and hopes with which many an immigrant from Europe stepped onto the soil of 'the land of unlimited opportunities'. Abraham Kuhn earned his first money in America as a peddler in 1849. The next stage on his way up was a small textile shop in Cincinnati. Soon afterwards he was able to start a small textile factory. He took Salomon Loeb in as a partner who organized the sales side and also established a branch in New York. In 1867, the two of them were able to open a private banking house in New York with an initial capital of 500,000 dollars. Although they were not trained bankers, their firm flourished. Loeb was the driving force behind the firm, whilst Abraham Kuhn retired to Germany after a few years. Over the years, the circle of partners grew larger and included Abraham Wolff (1875), Jakob Schiff (1885), Otto Kahn, Felix Warburg (1897) and Paul Warburg (1902). All partners came from Jewish families in Germany. The partners' own families inter-married so that Kuhn Loeb & Co. ultimately formed a big family clan.

The Warburg brothers, Felix and Paul, were both partners in their father's banking house, M.M. Warburg & Co., in Hamburg at the same time. Paul Warburg became one of the creators of the Federal Reserve System. In 1914, he was appointed to the Federal Reserve Board by President Wilson. Jakob Schiff was the head of Kuhn Loeb & Co. His best known undertaking, which laid the foundations of his fame and status in American high finance, was the reorganization of the almost bankrupt Union Pacific Railroad, which he undertook together with Edward H. Harriman who took over its management. With the exception of these two men, hardly anybody expected the rescue operation to succeed. In the course of 15 years, between

1897 and 1912, Kuhn Loeb & Co., together with other banks, accepted securities to the value of more than two milliard dollars, the bank itself issuing over half a milliard of this in the final six years.

The banking house of J.P. Morgan & Co. was founded by an Austrian immigrant in Philadelphia in 1838 as a brokerage firm (later the banking house of Drexel & Co.). John Pierpont Morgan entered the firm as a partner in 1871, and thereafter the firm was carried on under the name of Drexel Morgan & Co. Morgan had originally studied mathematics in Göttingen and was then apprenticed to the London banking house of George Peabody & Co. where his father, Junius Spencer Morgan, was a partner. The new partner soon controlled the management of Drexel Morgan & Co. and transferred its head office to New York. When the last member of the Drexel family died in 1895, Morgan changed the firm's name to J.P. Morgan & Co. By the end of his life, in 1913, he had transformed this private banking house into a financial empire of international significance, just as the Rothschild House had done between 1815 and 1875.

From the early 1890s, Morgan sought close collaboration with the First National Bank of New York. In 1892, he participated in the formation of the General Electric Trust, though the largest trust he created became the United States Steel Corporation. The first of the big trusts in the iron and steel industry was formed by the Scottish immigrant Andrew Carnegie. In 1892, Carnegie had united seven big enterprises to form the Carnegie Steel Corporation (from 1901, the Carnegie Steel Company of New Jersey). When Carnegie expanded his trust's production into new iron products, previously manufactured only by firms outside his trust, Morgan organized the amalgamation of Carnegie's rivals, whose business affairs he managed, into the Federal Steel Company (1898). The Morgan bank headed the consortium which handled the large financial transactions occasioned by the creation of the trust. Within three years, Morgan had effected the merger of the two rival steel trusts. He united the consortium under his control, directing it to undertake the exchange of shares and issue of new shares. Apart from J.P. Morgan & Co., the members of this consortium included another private banking house (Kidder Peabody & Co.), a joint-stock bank (The First National Bank of New York), a trust company (New York Security & Trust Company) and 22 industrialists, among them the financially powerful railway- and mine-owner, William K. Vanderbilt. From the fusion of the two trusts emerged the United States Steel Corporation (1901). Despite the Anti-Trust legislation, over 300 trusts of various sizes were founded in the United States shortly after the turn of the century. But the United States Steel Corporation created a sensation, even in a country accustomed to mergers: this was the first time a company had been created with a joint-stock capital of over a milliard dollars. U.S. Steel was producing around 70% of the iron and steel output of the United States. Actually, the trust was overcapitalized, for its effective value came to about 700 million dollars. Nevertheless, the level of joint-stock capital set by the consortium was an expression of its expectations. A further cause for sensation was the predominance of bankers on the board of directors of the big steel trust. Four of the seven board members were bankers, three of these being partners in J.P. Morgan & Co. The formation of the new trust brought the consortium a commission of 62.5 million dollars, almost one-fifth of which went to the Morgan Bank.

In the same year (1901), Morgan became involved in a big struggle on the stock exchange. In this battle, which passed into the history of the New York Stock Exchange as 'the battle of the giants', Morgan and his client, James Jerome Hill, a major shareholder in the Great Northern Railroad and the Northern Pacific Railroad, were on one side, with Jakob Schiff and his client, Edward Harriman of the Union Pacific Railroad, on the other. The subject of the dispute was the Chicago-Burlington Railway, regarded by both Hill and Harriman as a valuable addition to their railway networks; the Chicago-Burlington was a very profitable undertaking which extended into the mining area of Colorado and the agricultural areas of Illinois, Iowa and Nebraska. With Morgan's help, Hill pre-empted his rival Harriman and bought the shares in the Chicago Burlington. After Hill had refused to sell part of the Chicago-Burlington shares to Harriman and to cede him a place on the company's board of directors, Harriman began his counter-offensive with Schiff's assistance. He attempted to gain a majority in Hill's parent company, the Northern Pacific, and, with the aid of credits from Kuhn Loeb & Co., embarked on the systematic purchase of Northern Pacific shares. The price of these shares began to rise instantly. In order to mislead Hill and Morgan as to the cause of the rise in share prices — they were not supposed to find out too early who was buying up the shares — Schiff spread the rumour that the Northern Pacific shares had risen because the company's value had been enhanced by the acquisition of the Chicago-Burlington. Thereupon Morgan and Hill began to sell part of their Northern Pacific shares in order to profit from the price rise. It was only after Schiff had acquired the majority of non-voting preference shares, though not yet the majority of ordinary shares, that Morgan and Hill found out who had bought their shares. This changed the situation. Schiff suspended further purchases of shares, whilst Morgan immediately began to repurchase them on a large scale.

This struggle for the majority of shares in one of the largest railway companies had devastating repercussions on the stock exchange. At the beginning of 'the battle of the giants', the rate for Northern Pacific shares was 110 dollars per share. When Morgan began to repurchase shares, they rose to 1,000 dollars. Many speculators joined in to buy these shares. They sold others in order to obtain liquid funds, and prices of other companies tumbled. When it became known that Schiff had suspended the purchase of shares, the 'bears' stepped in in anticipation of a sharp fall. They expected Northern Pacific shares to drop and tried to manipulate the price. However, this speculation failed; Morgan, who had forced prices up when he repurchased the shares, had no intention of selling them again. After all, he wanted to uphold his majority in Northern Pacific. Many 'bears' were on the brink of ruin and panic broke out. General confusion reigned and panic-selling set in. The capital market was temporarily crippled and without direction.

After this Morgan, Hill, Schiff and Harriman concluded a compromise. There was a less dramatic, but longer-lasting, struggle which Morgan and his ally, George Baker, President of the First National Bank of New York, conducted against Rockefeller and Stillman, President of the National City Bank of New York. As before, the bone of contention was the control of railway companies. It ended in 1907 when Morgan acquired a large parcel of shares in the National City Bank. At the same time Jakob Schiff also obtained a large stake in this bank.

When John Pierpont Morgan died in 1913, his bank which was carried on by his son, John P. Morgan Jr., was represented on the supervisory boards of 112 companies. The bank had a controlling position in the United States Steel Corporation, the American Telephone and Telegraph Company, the Western Union, the General Electric Company, International Harvester, the Bankers Trust Company and in the Guaranty Trust Company of New York. Morgan had acquired the majority of shares in the latter two trust companies in 1912. The J.P. Morgan bank was principal shareholder in the National City Bank of New York, the New York Central Railroad, the Northern Pacific Railroad, the Great Northern Railroad and the Baltimore and Ohio Railroad.

Both Republicans and Democrats had been critical of the great concentration of power in the hands of the major banks for some considerable time, and so, prompted by the Democrats, the House of Representatives set up the Pujo Committee to examine this 'concentration of money and credit'. A majority of the Committee accused six banks of being the driving force in the concentration movement: J.P. Morgan & Co., the First National Bank of New York, the National City Bank of New York, and the banking houses of Lee Higginson & Co., Kidder Peabody & Co., and Kuhn Loeb & Co. But the Committee was unable to prove the existence of a bank trust, and its findings had no judicial or legislative consequences. Only the Morgan banking house considered it advisable, for tactical reasons, to withdraw from 30 of the 112 boards on which it was represented. Although the existence of a bank trust could not be established, there can be no question that the major banks had a decisive hand in the concentration process in American industry as large industrial trusts could only come into being with the help of large financial institutions.

During the period when leading New York banks were competing with one another for major industrial customers and for influence in the managements of big corporations and trusts on the Atlantic Coast, the Pacific Coast saw the emergence, in the Italian quarter of San Francisco, of a bank with very modest initial capital. Regarded, up to the end of the First World War, as an outsider in the banking business because of its customers and its deposit policy, it was to become the greatest commercial bank in the world after the Second World War. The Bank of Italy was founded in San Francisco in 1904 by several businessmen of Italian descent, with the modest capital of 150,000 dollars. Amadeo Giannini, who subsequently held the leading position in the bank for 30 years, was the most active and flexible of the bank's promoters and partners. What contributed to the rapid rise of the bank was that Giannini sought to attract his customers from among social groups which the more traditionally-minded banking houses had neglected or even completely overlooked: the lower entrepreneurial classes such as small retailers and artisans, in particular those from the immigrant and minority groups. Since the Bank of Italy did not have to compete for these customers in the same way as other banks were forced to in their dealings with big firms and corporations, the margins of interest on deposits and loans were relatively large and this meant relatively high bank profits. Small borrowers were also included in the Bank of Italy's credit business. They were granted hire-purchase credits at high interest rates of up to 13%. If it was to expand its business with this circle of customers and increase its working capital, the bank had to attract as many small customers as possible. This meant that it had to spread its wings more widely. In building up the requisite branch network, the bank benefited from California's generous legislation on the opening of branches. When in 1909 California permitted branches to be established throughout the State, the Bank of Italy immediately created a branch network which extended all over California. Thus, the Bank of Italy began to develop into a major bank.

7. The Japanese 'zaibatsu' Major Banks

From the end of the 1880s until 1945 the Japanese economy was moulded by a specific form of economic concentration: the big 'zaibatsu'. These zaibatsu were family concerns which had preserved elements of a pre-industrial feudal society within their structure. Each zaibatsu belonged to a certain entrepreneurial family. This family owned the parent company to which all the other enterprises belonging to the family concern were strictly subordinated. The zaibatsu had a pyramid-like structure, and all leading positions were filled by members of the zaibatsu family. In the pre-industrial period, most of the zaibatsu families had been wealthy merchants. Some of them had started their economic rise as early as the 17th century by establishing business links with the *Shogun* of the House of Tokugawa and the Daimyo, the feudal princes. When the power of the *Shogun* declined in the course of the 19th century, the families, who were later to become the founders and rulers of the zaibatsu, made timely contact with the imperial family which, after 600 years of political impotence, was beginning to recover its power. Consequently, these families retained their leading economic position, and this did not change after the so-called Meiji Restoration of 1868 when the Emperor regained full powers. Although the zaibatsu families were not members of the old feudal aristocracy, they nevertheless adopted the feudal model with regard to the

internal organization of their families and their firms. Each zaibatsu family
formed a large dynasty which was subdivided into several main and subordinate branches. The hierarchy within the family, and the rights and duties
of its members, were laid down in special codes. In 1901, the Statute of
Mitsui family comprised no less than 111 chapters. Loyal employees could
be rewarded for their services by being accepted as a member of a distant
branch of the zaibatsu family. The greatest zaibatsu were dominated by
banking houses, among them the Mitsui, Mitsubishi, Sumitomo, Yasuda.

At the time of the Meiji Restoration all these banking houses, except for
Mitsubishi, existed as exchange bureaus. But it seemed at first that, with
the beginning of industrialization, the money and credit system would be
patterned on foreign models and without being linked with the traditional
exchange bureaus. In 1872, the National Bank Regulations were promulgated, following the example of the American National Banking Act. Under
this law, 153 'National Banks' were established, with the Government's
permission, in the period up to 1879. They were joint-stock banks — most
of them, of course, with little capital. These National Banks were to issue
bank notes which were to replace the national paper currency brought into
circulation towards the end of the *Shogun* era. The notes were convertible.
Apart from issuing notes, the National Banks were to engage in the credit
business. The system proved to be a failure, however. The notes of the
National Banks inspired little confidence in the public. The banks put only
a few notes into circulation, and were hence unable to fulfil their task of
supplying the economy with credit. Finally, in 1882, a central note bank,
the Bank of Japan (Nihon Ginko), was founded on the initiative of the Finance Minister Matsukata who, during a trip to Europe, had sought the advice
of Leon Say, his French counterpart and a nephew of the famous economist. In 1884, the bank obtained the note issuing monopoly, and by 1899
all National Banks had to suspend their issue of notes and become commercial banks. Such banks had been in existence as private banks alongside the
National Banks since 1876. The Mitsui banking house became the first
purely commercial bank in 1876 after the conversion of the Mitsui exchange
bureau.

In the early 17th century the Mitsui family had been *sake* distillers. In
1673, they began to trade in textiles in Edo (now Tokyo), and in 1863
they also opened an exchange bureau. They supplied money to the *Shogun*
and the Imperial Court and also maintained business ties with several
Daimyo. They successfully survived the political upheaval of 1868, thanks
to their old contacts with the Imperial House. They were entrusted with
the administration of government funds and also participated in the establishment of the first National Bank, the Dai-Ichi Bank of Tokyo in 1873.
However, since the Government had a strong influence in the bank, the
Mitsui withdrew from it and lobbied successfully for an amendment of
the National Bank Regulations. The result was that in 1876 they were able
to transform their exchange bureau into the Mitsui Bank. In the first ten
years their main activity was the administration of government funds and

the servicing of state loans. From the mid-1880s other banking business was taken on, and the end of the 1880s saw the emergence of the Mitsui zaibatsu. The group ultimately comprised textile factories, stores, docks, shipping companies and chemical factories. The Mitsui family represented the greatest concentration of economic power among the Japanese zaibatsu, with which they were able to wield great political influence. Max Warburg, the Hamburg banker, reports of the Mitsui family in his memoirs that in 1905 Baron Mitsui, the head of the House, asked him about a suitable structure for the family enterprise. Warburg writes that he suggested a sub-division of the enterprise into separate companies, in line with the various branches of the business, i.e. banking, shipping etc. And each of these companies should then be placed under the control of a branch of the Mitsui family, with their activities to be co-ordinated by a holding company. Of course, Warburg added, he did not know whether this would be permissible under Japanese law, whereupon Mitsui replied: 'Don't bother about the laws; I'll change them.' This was no empty boast. The political arm of the Mitsui was indeed very long. And more than once Japan's Finance Ministers came from their ranks. There was even a common saying in Japan: the Finance Ministry is domiciled in the Mitsui Bank. The House of Mitsui also had a powerful lobby among the political parties which emerged at the beginning of the 20th century. The party of the Mitsui was the conservative *Seiyukai*, founded in 1900 by Baron Ito, the leading politician in Japan's modernization process.

The House of Sumitomo has been in existence for about as long as the Mitsui. It owned a copper mine on the island of Shikoku, was engaged in the copper trade, and under the *Shogun*, ran one of the largest exchange bureaus in the country at Osaka. During the Meiji Restoration several Daimyo, the major borrowers of the Sumitomo, were deprived of their power. As a result the Sumitomos lost a large part of their assets and had to suspend their credit business. They resumed it in 1895 when they established the Sumitomo Bank at Osaka and built up an empire of enterprises in the metal, chemical and electrical industries. Zenjiro Yasuda, the founder of the Yasuda Bank, came from a relatively poor *Samurai* family which had risen to the military aristocracy only in the 19th century. Yasuda worked as an employee in an exchange bureau before opening his own independent office in Tokyo in 1864. Having participated in the founding of the Third National Bank, he converted his exchange bureau into a joint-stock bank in 1880, whose capital was wholly owned by the Yasuda family. Unlike other banking houses, Yasuda built up a large banking empire into which he had absorbed some 17 banks by 1912. Moreover, the Yasuda zaibatsu owned several large insurance companies.

The House of Mitsubishi was the only one of the big zaibatsu banks not involved in banking before the Meiji Restoration. The Mitsubishi zaibatsu was set up by Yataro Iwasaki. In 1870, he started up a shipping company and within a few years had gained a virtual monopoly of the Japanese coastal trade; these activities brought it into conflict with the Government which regarded the monopoly with suspicion. The Government now founded a rival enterprise. Nor was the House of Mitsubishi invited to participate in the Bank of Japan, established in 1882. The end of the 1880s saw the emergence of the Mitsubishi zaibatsu engaged in shipping, shipbuilding and mining, but the House of the Mitsubishi had yet to promote its own bank. Later it did attach a bank to the family concern and, in 1895, this bank became a department of the Mitsubishi holding company. Following the example of the Mitsui, the Mitsubishi also built up their own political interest representation within the nascent Japanese party system. The *Kenseikai*, founded in 1913, became the Mitsubishis' party. It was as conservative as the *Seiyukai*, the only difference being that it was sponsored by another zaibatsu.

The Yasuda Bank, which was not directly involved in industry, gave short-term credits, but also undertook the issue of industrial shares and debentures and long-term credits. The other zaibatsu banks, by contrast, confined themselves exclusively to short-term credit business. They only entered into long-term commitments where their own zaibatsu subsidiaries were concerned. Thus the zaibatsu banks operated at two different levels. Within their own sphere, they conducted themselves like the American or German banks; they acted like the big English deposit banks towards firms outside the family enterprise. It was for this reason that they played rather an insignificant role in mobilizing funds for industry before the First World War. Such funds came mostly from the private wealth accumulated by the founders of factories, or — as happened in England some 50 years earlier — the factories raised funds by selling shares to the public without the help of banks.

IV Agricultural Credit Institutions – Mortgage Banks – The Rise of Savings Banks – Credit Co-operatives

1. Agricultural Credit Institutions and Mortgage Banks

There was always a tremendous shortage of rural credit. Peasants in need of credit had to find a private creditor. If they were lucky, they found someone who would lend them money on a long-term basis, secured by mortgage. But only a small part of the required rural credit was made available in this way. Most peasants were dependent on usurers, people who usually engaged in money-lending as a sideline to the cattle trade. They burdened their debtors with enormously high commissions, and punitive interest rates. If their debtors were unable to repay on time, the usurers took cattle or land instead and, in the process, fixed the prices they paid at far below the market value of the animals. Equally they forced their debtors to buy inferior goods at greatly inflated prices on hire-purchase. When the debtors had been squeezed dry, their creditors would force them to send their property to auction. Many a peasant's livelihood was ruined by usurers and this aspect of the credit system became a genuine plague in the 19th century.

These problems could best be remedied by centralizing the funds of individual investors in credit institutions, as was happening in the case of commercial and industrial credit, and to establish them as centres of exchange and mediation between individuals with savings and the many farmers seeking credit. But credit institutions which were to grant long-term credit also had to have at their disposal correspondingly long-term means of financing, if they were to retain their liquidity; they had to have the right to issue long-term mortgage bonds and debentures. However, these mortgage bonds and debentures had to be negotiable to give their purchasers the opportunity to sell them at any time and thus procure liquid funds. This constituted the principle of a mortgage bank.

From the mid-19th century, rural landowners as well as bankers endeavoured to create the legal preconditions for such mortgage banks. The first German mortgage bank came into being with the founding of the Bayerische Hypotheken- und Wechselbank in 1835. Its privilege to issue notes was tied to an obligation to make three-fifths of its capital exclusively available to agriculture and private housing. In terms of its organizational structure, it was not yet a mortgage bank pure and simple; for it lacked the right to issue mortgage bonds. This right was granted only in 1864, after mortgage banks which held such privileges had been founded in other German states.

The first big specialized mortgage bank, which also became a model for neighbouring countries, was the Crédit Foncier de France. There was no institutional framework for mortgage credit in France until the mid-19th century. The Caisse Hypothécaire, established in 1820, had been a commercial failure and had to be liquidated in 1846. Thus long-term agricultural credit could only be obtained from private individuals. In order to meet the credit needs of agriculture, Louis Napoléon issued a decree in February 1852 — ten weeks after his election to the Presidency of the Republic for a ten-year term — which allowed agricultural credit institutions to be established, although concessions had to be obtained from the Government in every single case. In signing this decree, Napoléon was returning a favour to his supporters among the rural population. It was also the year in which he was elected Emperor by a plebiscite.

In accordance with the decree of February 1852, three *banques foncières* were founded as joint-stock companies in Paris, Marseille and Nevers. Emile Péreire, the co-founder of the Crédit Mobilier, participated in their establishment. During the same year, the Paris *banque foncière* was converted into the Crédit Foncier de France. In 1854 the new institution became a public mortgage bank, and merged with the other two *banques foncièrs.* The bank was permitted to issue long-term bearer debentures up to twenty times the amount of its joint-stock capital. It had to invest at least 25% of its funds in state bonds; another 50% were earmarked for municipal and mortgage credits and the remainder for property and for securities which could be mortgaged with the Banque de France. The Crédit Foncier did not do much to satisfy agricultural credit needs. It gave preference to mortgage credits for municipal housing and municipal loans; and both forms of credit were primarily of benefit to Paris. The great architectural transformation of the metropolis, which occurred during the Second Empire, was directed by George-Eugène Haussmann, and was primarily financed with long-term credits from the Crédit Foncier.

The example of the Crédit Foncier stimulated the development of mortgage banks in Germany; however, what emerged in Central Europe were private, not public, joint-stock mortgage banks. The first specialized mortgage bank in Germany was established in 1862 when a number of Frankfurt bankers founded the Frankfurter Hypothekenbank. In the same year, the Mitteldeutsche Creditbank in Meiningen, together with the Frankfurt banking houses of S. Sulzbach and W.F. Jäger, promoted the Deutsche Hypothekenbank (Meiningen). In the course of the next ten years, a further 17 mortgage banks were founded in Germany.

Until the turn of the century the German mortgage banks remained subject to separate legislation of the various States of the Reich. Stricter norms for mortgage banks came into force only after the Mortgage Banking Act of 1899 and the German Civil Code of January 1900 had reached the statute book. The Mortgage Banking Act laid down that the mortgage banks were to be joint-stock banks whose founding required a concession from the Federal Council. Concessions would only be granted once it had been established that there was a need for the proposed mortgage bank. The mortgage banks were to grant loans only to ventures which promised to yield lasting profits. They were permitted to accept a restricted volume of deposits not exceeding half of their joint-stock capital. They were allowed to issue mortgage bonds to a limit of fifteen times their joint-stock capital, provided their claims were secured by mortgages. Holders of mortgage bonds were granted the right to preferential repayment; if a mortgage bank went bankrupt, the claims of mortgage bond-holders had to be satisfied first. The Mortgage Banking Act was one of the very rare cases in which a bill was passed with the consent of all Reichstag parties, the Social Democrats included. The solution to this apparent paradox — i.e. that all parties voted for a piece of legislation irrespective of whether they represented upper middle-class industrial or working-class interests — is to be found in the fact that the Social Democrats had expectations of the law which were quite different from those of the middle-class parties. They believed that individual ownership of land could be gradually eliminated with the help of mortgage credits and through the protection of creditors, preparing the way for the socialization of land. As their spokesman put it: '...When a bill such as this contributes to, and encourages, the absorption of landed property through finance capital by granting mortgage creditors increased guarantees, my political friends cannot but fully agree with this . . . By adopting the Bill which has been presented, the bourgeois parties sacrifice their economic principles to ideas which are closer to socialism than they are to the present economic order.'

Originally, mortgage banks had been established in order to improve the credit situation of agriculture; but in the case of German mortgage banks, agricultural credit came to play a subordinate role, just as it had done for the Crédit Foncier de France. At the turn of the century rural mortgages amounted to just under 11% of the total of all mortgage credits granted by German mortgage banks. In 1912 they had dropped to a mere 6.6%. The financing of housing had become their business activity. The sharp increase in population and the rapid urbanization of Germany (the share of city-dwellers as a proportion of the total population increased from 4.8% in 1871 to 21.3% in 1910) generated an enormous demand for accommodation in the cities. Thus the building industry developed into an important branch of the national economy and became a profitable business proposition. And since the construction of houses also stimulated demand in other branches of the economy, it was one of the most important factors of economic growth in Germany. However, next to railway construction, house-building depended to a particularly large extent on borrowed money. Whereas railways were financed through the issue of shares and bonds or, in the case of state-owned railways, through state loans, the construction of houses was made possible through long-term credits secured by mortgages. Between 1870 and 1913, a quarter to a third of total German net investments was consistently put into urban housing. Although the mortgage banks took on the biggest share, the total volume of mortgage credits supplied by savings banks was not far behind. Insurance companies, too, had rather a large share in financing the urban building industry. In 1910, the mortgage banks

granted mortgage loans to the tune of over 10 milliard marks; loans by
savings banks reached a total of eight milliard marks and those of the
insurance companies 4.5 milliard marks.

Special agricultural credit institutions did not develop in Britain or the
United States until the First World War. The financing of housing by means
of mortgages had been undertaken by Britain's building societies since the
end of the 18th century; in the United States the loan and savings associations moved into this field from the middle of the 19th century.

2. The Rise of Savings Banks

The banks with which we have been concerned so far attended only to
the financial matters of individuals who were wealthy or at least fairly well
off. Members of the lower classes, such as wage-earners, journeymen, and
domestic servants, were denied access to these financial and credit institutions not by law, but by the business practices of the banks. The question
was: where could they invest whatever small savings they may have had to
give them some income from interest? Where could they borrow money in
an emergency apart from the usurious money-lenders? These problems were
frequently discussed long before the advent of industrialization, and not
only by philanthropic writers or clergymen but also by high ranking civil
servants and local authorities. Their motives for seeking out possible sources
of cheap credit and for helping the lowly-paid and poor save their money
were complex. Charity, the moral duty to help the weak and the poor, un-
deniably provided one impulse behind their reflections and attempts at
solving these problems. At the same time, however, we also find very
pragmatic considerations. It was argued that municipal funds for poor-
relief would be less strained, if the poor, by accumulating savings, were put
in the position to help themselves. The main spiritual driving force behind
the movement for savings banks derived ultimately from the overlapping
socio-political and educational ideas of Puritanism, the Enlightenment and
Liberalism. According to these ideas, if the poor were helped to accumulate
savings, they would improve their capacity to provide for, and to help,
themselves both materially and, above all, spiritually. They were to be given
the opportunity to set aside savings securely in an institution, not only to
have some money at their disposal in an emergency, but also to learn how to
keep their house in good order and to manage their economic affairs
systematically.

The Allgemeine Versorgungsanstalt, which was established in Hamburg in
1778 on the initiative of the *Patriotische Gesellschaft*, may be regarded as
the first savings bank. This institute acted in the first instance as an
insurance company and was divided into 10 different 'classes' each with a
different function and clientele; one of these sections was concerned with
'savings'. According to a decree by the Hamburg City Council, which had to
give its approval to the Versorgungsanstalt and laid down its statutes, it had
the following purpose: 'The savings section of this Versorgungsanstalt is set

up for the benefit of humbler, but industrious persons of both sexes, such as domestic servants, labourers, craftsmen and sailors, in order to give them the opportunity to save, even out of their small income, and to enable them to gain some interest on their hard-earned nest-egg or dowry. It is hoped thereby that this amenity provided for them will serve to encourage them to become useful and important to the State through diligence and thrift.' The savings section took in about one million marks in savings deposits until 1810. The savings were mostly invested in the Hamburg Treasury bonds. These deposits at first yielded 3% interest, and 2.083% later on.

Further savings banks were founded in other parts of northern Germany: at Oldenburg in 1786, at Kiel in 1796, at Altona and Göttingen in 1801. In 1818, the Städtische Sparkasse was set up in Berlin as the first Prussian savings bank; the first Württemberg savings bank was established in the same year; the first Saxon savings bank was founded at Königsbrück in 1819 and the first Bavarian savings bank at Nuremberg in 1821.

From the outset, German savings banks were communal savings banks, and at first were established only in municipalities. In general, individual German States contributed to the development of the savings bank only to the extent of granting permission for their foundation and approving their statutes. General regulations were issued in a few states only, such as in Prussia in 1838 and in Bavaria in 1843. Only the Grand Duchy of Baden passed a detailed Savings Bank Act in 1880.

Since the savings banks were to be institutions for the less well-off, most banks specified an upper limit for deposits in their statutes, varying between 50 and 300 thalers. During the early decades, depositors regarded them as investment institutions only, enabling them to save or withdraw smaller sums of money from their savings books; they could also withdraw all their money. However, they were unable to obtain credit from the savings bank to which they entrusted their money. This would have contradicted the purpose behind this type of bank. After all, the poorer people were to be encouraged to put their savings in these banks in small, and even very small sums, so as to enable them to live on these funds in their old age or in an emergency. Borrowing, on the other hand, was not to be made easy for them. To avoid losses, savings banks were obliged to invest the savings in absolutely safe securities, and their depositors could hardly be regarded as 'safe' debtors. Hence the savings banks invested in mortgage credits and gilt-edged securities.

Some 280 savings banks were founded in the German States until 1836, and by 1850 there were about 1,200 of them. The number of savings banks and savings books increased steeply when a new stage began in the process of industrialization from the 1860s onwards. The deposits of the Prussian savings banks increased threefold between 1870 and 1880. In 1876, the deposits of all German savings banks reached a total of two milliard marks; in 1902 they amounted to 10.3 milliard and in 1913 to about 19.7 milliard marks, held by some 3,133 savings banks. This figure should be compared with the eight biggest German joint-stock banks which, in 1913, had deposits totalling 5.15 milliard marks; and German capital investments abroad amounted to about 25-30 milliard marks in 1913.

With the introduction of health insurance in 1883 and old-age and disability insurance in 1889 in the Reich, the original socio-political task of savings banks, namely to lend wage-earners a helping hand in building up reserves for old-age and illness came to an end. This task was now assumed by social insurance institutions, and from the end of the 19th century the German savings banks became banks for middle-class depositors.

Following Germany and Switzerland, Britain was the third country to establish savings banks. Here the cities and local authorities had no hand in founding savings banks, however. On the contrary, the initiative to form such banks came exclusively from private individuals: clergymen and wealthy philanthropists. Britain's first savings bank was founded by one of William Penn's descendants, Priscilla Wakefield. She had begun by helping the poor women and children of Tottenham and found that many poor people, domestic servants in particular, would have liked to deposit their small savings, if only they had an opportunity and security to do so. Wakefield therefore thought it useful to found an institution where the poor of the immediate vicinity would be able to deposit their savings in complete safety. This institute would have to be guaranteed by 'a few respectable persons of property'. She put her plan into practice in 1804 when she founded the Tottenham Benefit Bank. Interest was paid on deposits at 5%. In its first years, the Tottenham Benefit Bank was a savings bank of a special kind, for it did not invest its deposits. On the contrary, the interest was paid out of the pockets of the 'respectable persons' who managed its business in an honorary capacity.

The actual founder of the British savings bank system was a Scottish clergyman, the Reverend Henry Duncan, who founded the Ruthwell Savings bank in his parish of Ruthwell in 1810. This institute was set up to be self-supporting from the start. Duncan also became an active propagandist of the savings bank movement when he published his 'Essay on the Nature and Advantages of Parish Banks for the Savings of the Industrious' in 1815. By 1816, 78 savings banks had been established in Britain. The British savings banks were private establishments, but they were bound by law to invest their money with the State. In 1858, an inquiry into savings banks revealed that investments in state bonds were making losses. In fact the bonds in which the funds of the savings banks had been invested had suffered such a sharp decline during the Crimean War and the ensuing economic crisis of 1857 that, if the State Debt certificates would have had to be made liquid, the loss would have been in the region of £4 million — with total deposits of £9 million. The bonds, moreover, yielded less interest than the State was paying to the savings banks.

In view of these flaws, an attempt was made in 1859 to change the legislation on savings banks and to reform the system. However, Government and Parliament could not agree on the objectives, and so the attempt ended in failure. At this point Charles William Sikes, a banker from

Huddersfield, took up a plan which had been outlined in a number of treatises in the 1850s. This was to enable the Post Office, which provided money order services, to accept deposits to be administered by its Money Order Office. Sikes canvassed support for this plan in the press, in Chambers of Commerce and with Members of Parliament. Gladstone took up Sikes's proposals and in the spring of 1861, in a *tour de force* which took the parliamentary advocates of the 'old' savings banks by surprise, got a bill passed which established the Post Office Savings Bank. In this way, Britain became the first country to have such a bank. It was established as a savings bank directly operated by the State. Compared to the private savings banks in Britain, it had several tangible advantages: the large number of post offices meant it had a dense branch network throughout the country. These branches were open daily, whereas private savings banks were open to their customers only once or twice a month. The Post Office Savings Bank paid only 2.5% interest on savings as compared with the 3.25% interest paid by private savings banks; but the latter deducted administrative costs from the interest so that they too actually paid their customers 2.5% interest on deposits.

The private savings banks continued alongside the Post Office Savings Bank, though many of them closed down sooner or later. Of the 638 private savings banks in existence in 1861, only 481 were still in existence by 1873. Hand in hand with the decline in the number of trustee savings banks, went the reduction in the number of their savers, albeit less sharply. In 1861, there were 1.6 million of them; by 1873, the figure had fallen to 1.4 million. On the other hand, the amount of deposits remained approximately the same. The Post Office Savings Bank was able to attract 1.5 million savers in the first 12 years of its existence, a figure somewhat higher than that of the trustee savings banks. But its deposits were only half of those held by private savings banks in 1873. This was partly because savings had not been deposited with the Post Office for long up to that point, partly because the state-owned Post Office banks were preferred by the small saver.

In France, savings banks began to develop after Napoleon's fall. In 1818 the directors and shareholders of the Royal Marine Insurance Company founded the Caisse d'Epargne de Paris. Over 350 savings banks based on its model were established up to 1845, mainly by private companies or by municipal authorities. French law required savings banks to place their deposits on current account with the state-owned Caisse des Dépôts et Consignations, a trustee savings bank which had been founded in 1816. If a saver's deposit reached 50 francs, it had to be converted into state annuities *(rente perpetuelle)* in the holder's name. Hence savings deposits were closely linked with the state debt, partly with the floating state debt, and partly with the 'perpetual annuity'. These legislative measures on savings banks greatly contributed to making the government annuity a widely popular security. On the other hand, locking up all savings of 50 francs and over created difficulties when it came to making larger amounts of the deposits liquid. In times of crisis, such as in 1848 and 1870-71, many savers would withdraw their deposits. Thus, at the time of the Franco-Prussian War and the Paris Commune, total deposits in French savings banks fell from 720 million to 540 million francs. Faced with such large-scale withdrawals, the banks had to sell part of their government annuities, and in times of political and economic crisis this caused them to suffer considerable losses on stock prices. By 1845 the average savings balance had reached about 575 francs, hardly representing the small savings of persons of moderate means for whom the banks were actually intended. In order to prevent the savings banks from becoming institutions for the prosperous middle classes, the maximum deposit for savings accounts was reduced several times until they reached the lower limit of 1,500 francs. This proved unsuccessful in practice, since the savings banks' network remained restricted to the cities and did not reach the rural population, which, after all, constituted two-thirds of the French population. In 1881, a Post Office Savings Bank was founded based on the British model.

In the United States, Mutual Savings Banks were formed as private savings banks from the beginning of the 19th century. Occasionally they were created by certain immigrant groups such as the German Savings and Loan Society, which was founded in San Francisco in 1868. Unlike the European savings banks, the American savings banks were heavily engaged in the long-term financing of industry. The institution of mutual savings banks remained, in general, confined to New England and the States of the eastern seaboard. Outside these areas mutual savings banks were founded in only four States, including California. In the other states in the West and Mid-West, only a few savings banks emerged in the form of joint-stock companies. Otherwise the savings banks system failed to gain a foothold in those areas; they became accessible only later, particularly when a Post Office savings network was established in 1910.

3. Credit Co-operatives

The German savings banks began to grant credit to small-scale manufacturers and artisans in many places, even in the early phase of their development. Yet the number and capital resources of savings banks were insufficient to satisfy the demand for credit from the lower middle-class strata of small-scale manufacturers, tradesmen and retailers. And the credit supply to peasants was even worse. This gap in the credit system was gradually closed with the formation of industrial and agricultural co-operatives after the middle of the century.

A few years after workers' co-operatives had begun to develop in Britain, the first middle-class co-operatives emerged in Germany and with them the first industrial credit co-operatives. Their founder was Hermann Schulze-Delitzsch who was a supporter not only of political, but also of economic liberalism. He was therefore strictly opposed to the idea of government aid to co-operatives. He wanted to enable small tradesmen to maintain a competitive position by joining the co-operative; but, of course, the idea of pure self-help could only work where those who joined to form co-operatives at least had some savings. Schulze-Delitzsch's idea of co-operatives was hence suitable for artisans and small tradesmen, but not for workers without means. This flaw was also the starting-point of Ferdinand Lassalle's criticism of the system.

The co-operatives which Schulze-Delitzsch founded, or instigated, were consumer co-operatives, co-operative raw material or buying associations, credit co-operatives or associations for the provision of credit to tradesmen (also known as people's banks). In 1849, two co-operative raw material associations of joiners and shoemakers emerged on Schulze's initiative in his home-town of Delitzsch, which bought raw materials for their members much more cheaply than they could have done as individuals. They were able to buy in bulk and to eliminate middlemen. The following year saw the founding of the first credit co-operatives. In the summer of 1850, Schulze established a credit association at Delitzsch. Several weeks later, another credit co-operative was formed in Eilenburg at the instigation of a physician, Dr. Bernhardi. Liability for the co-operative's obligations extended to the entire property of its members. It was only with the Prussian Co-operative Society Act of 1867, adopted by the North German Confederation in 1868, that liability was on principle restricted to the accumulated membership fees and full joint liability remained as a subsidiary safeguard. Thus the membership fees formed the equity capital of credit co-operatives, and it was on this basis that they took up bank credit from 1859 onwards.

The favourable development of the Eilenburger Vorschussverein (Eilenburg Credit Association) and of the Delitzscher Vorschussverein (Delitzsch Credit Association) after 1852, Schulze's own publicity work, the journalistic support of his political friends and, above all, the approval of the *Kongress deutscher Volkswirte* (founded in 1858) all contributed to the early creation of further credit co-operatives. In 1859, the German credit co-operatives set up a *Zentralkorrespondenzbüro* (Central Communication Office) to represent their joint interests, from which emerged the Allgemeine Verband der auf Selbsthilfe beruhenden Deutschen Erwerbs-und Wirtschaftsgenossenschaften (General Association of German Trading and Economic Co-operative Societies based on Self-Help) in 1864. There were some 80 credit co-operatives, with 18,676 members, which belonged to this group. With the help of the *Zentralkorrespondenzbüro* and, from 1864, of the Allgemeine Verband the co-operatives obtained credit for refinancing, notwithstanding the fact that their refinancing opportunities remained unsatisfactory. A guarantee association was therefore founded in 1863 whose guarantees were to raise the credit-worthiness of the co-operatives *vis-à-vis* the private commercial banks. This association was not very effective, however; and when the commercial banks restricted their credit during the German-Danish War, Schulze-Delitzsch pursued the idea of founding a central co-operative bank for the credit co-operatives which would assume the role of a refinancing institution.

In the late autumn of 1864, the new central co-operative bank was constituted in Berlin. It was a partnership limited by shares. Its legal form gave it access to the capital market and also obviated the need for a state licence. The Deutsche Genossenschaftsbank was to accept deposits from German co-operative societies and grant them credit on current account. It was also to look after the collecting business for the co-operative societies and the purchase and sale of securities. In the capital itself, it was to act directly as a credit co-operative for artisans and small tradesmen; in other words, the artisans and small tradesmen of Berlin were to receive credit from the Bank and were to participate through their deposits in its profits and losses.

The tasks for which the Deutsche Genossenschaftsbank was originally set up played only a subordinate role in its subsequent work. The Bank was insufficiently used by the credit co-operatives. Instead the credit co-operatives preferred to collaborate with a regional or with a major bank. Consequently, the Deutsche Genossenschaftsbank soon saw itself compelled to engage more and more in regular banking with non-members; ultimately the turnover with credit co-operatives came to no more than 15-20% of the total turnover. Its strong commitment to the investment and issuing business finally became the Bank's undoing. After big losses resulting from unprofitable participating investments in industry, its capital had to be reduced to 30 million marks at the same time as it was converted into a joint-stock company. But business prospects remained gloomy, and the Bank's management and shareholders finally consented to a merger with the expanding Dresdner Bank in 1904. The Dresdner Bank carried on its co-operative business and established a special co-operative department for this purpose.

Despite the success, and final failure, of the Deutsche Genossenschafts-bank, industrial credit co-operatives continued to develop. In 1870, 740 credit co-operatives with 314,656 members were in existence, and their number rose to almost 1,500 industrial credit co-operatives with over 800,000 members by 1913. Credits provided were in excess of 1.5 milliard marks.

In the same year in which the Deutsche Genossenschaftsbank von Soergel, Parrisius & Co. was founded, the first agricultural credit co-operative emerged in Germany. Friedrich Wilhelm Raiffeisen and Wilhelm Haas were the initiators. From 1845 to 1865 Raiffeisen was burgomaster of a number of rural communities in the Westerwald. Due to his family background he had an intimate knowledge of social and economic problems in the country areas.

In 1854, he founded the *Heddesdorfer Wohltätigkeitsverein* (Heddes-dorf Charitable Society) at Heddesdorf which, among its many other purposes, granted impoverished peasants loans at low interest rates in order to free them from the clutches of usurers. It raised the money for the loans by taking outside credit. The members of the Society were jointly liable for these monies; there was no liable capital. In the final analysis, it was based not on the co-operative idea of self-help, but of Christian charity and help for the poor, as the members of the Society were liable for the funds of which, as a rule, not they, but others were the recipients. This conformed completely to Raiffeisen's ideas, whose thoughts and actions were characterized by a passionate Lutheran religiosity. He regarded love of one's neighbour as the highest and universally applicable social law.

Raiffeisen clung to his Christian beliefs, even though he had to abandon the charitable principle and was compelled to adopt the idea of co-operative self-help. The *Heddesdorfer Wohltätigkeitsverein* began to flag after several years; it was a society which brought only risk and no returns and became a headache for its members. It was therefore dissolved in 1863, and thenceforth Raiffeisen, on the advice of Schulze-Delitzsch with whom he had corresponded on the matter, began to organize peasants into credit co-operatives. In 1864, he founded the Heddesdorfer Darlehnskassenverein (Heddesdorf Loan Bank Association), the first agricultural co-operative in Germany. Soon other co-operatives emerged, modelled on the Heddesdorfer Darlehnskassenverein, at first in the Coblence area, then throughout the Rhine Province.

The collaboration with Schulze-Delitzsch lasted for only a few years. At the beginning of the 1870s, the so-called 'System Dispute' broke out between the industrial and agricultural credit co-operatives, which resulted in the separation of the two co-operative branches in the mid-1870s. The 'System Dispute' was concerned with organizational and business issues. Raiffeisen aimed at a strict centralization of the co-operatives in a three-tier organization in order to level out the great differences between poor and wealthy agricultural credit co-operatives. Schulze-Delitzsch, on the other hand, maintained that every individual co-operative society should keep its full legal and economic independence.

A second point of controversy was the question of capital resource and joint liability. The industrial credit co-operatives formed an equity capital from the shares their members had to pay in. The equity capital was, in the first place, liable for the security of credit raised from outside sources, and the joint liability of individual members was merely a subsidiary one. Profits were distributed in the form of dividends according to the number of shares owned. The Raiffeisen co-operative societies, by contrast, did not create equity capital from participating shares and although their members owned assets which could be liable for the security of credit, they were not sufficiently liquid to buy participations in the share capital. Agricultural credit co-operatives therefore offered the joint liability of their members exclusively as security on credit borrowed from outside sources.

The 'System Dispute' led to the total separation of industrial and agricultural co-operative societies. The latter formed their own association in 1877. It represented the interests of the group *vis-à-vis* the outside world and took up counselling and revision of accounts on behalf of individual co-operative societies.

With the separation of the agricultural from the industrial co-operatives a simultaneous split in the rural co-operative movement began in 1877. The Hesse co-operatives did not join the association which Raiffeisen had founded; they formed their own associations in 1879 which at first comprised only the loan bank associations of Hesse, but soon also absorbed other agricultural co-operatives from Hesse and other parts of Germany. Thus, in 1883, alongside the association of agricultural co-operatives based in Neuwied, there emerged the Vereinigung deutscher landwirtschaftlicher Genossenschaften (Union of German Agricultural Co-operative Societies) based in Offenbach which, from 1903, called itself the Reichsverband der deutschen landwirtschaftlichen Genossenschaften (Reich Association of German Agricultural Co-operative Societies).

The split in the rural co-operative movement had its origins in the irreconcilable ideas of Raiffeisen and Wilhelm Haas, the Hesse organizer of co-operative societies, concerning the structure of co-operative societies and their field of activity. When Raiffeisen intensified his efforts to centralize the co-operative money- and credit-system, Haas opposed him by defending the independence of the individual co-operative societies. It was of utmost importance to him that individual co-operative societies were not merely cogs in a big organization but that, on the contrary, they maintained their business autonomy and joined together only for common tasks, such as the representation of common interests, counselling, and cash audits. Unlike Raiffeisen, Haas further demanded that co-operative societies should specialize — so that credit co-operatives would engage in credit business only. The Raiffeisen loan bank associations, however, often operated in other areas of business as well and acted, for example, as goods purchasing co-operatives.

The split in the rural co-operative movement did not hamper its development, however, and up to the First World War about 17,000 agricultural credit co-operatives were established in Germany. Yet it soon became apparent that the principle of a decentralized organization for rural co-operative societies, which Haas supported, harmonized more with agricultural interests than the centralism that Raiffeisen represented; about three-quarters of loan bank associations belonged to the Reichsverband der deutschen landwirtschaftlichen Genossenschaften founded by Haas.

In no other country were credit co-operatives of such great importance as in Germany. Agricultural credit co-operatives on Raiffeisen's model were founded, in small numbers, only in France, Japan and the Flemish parts of Belgium.

V Capital Export and Foreign Policy in the Age of Imperialism

1. Capital export by Britain, France and Germany, 1867-1914.

When demand for capital had been satisfied in the leading industrial countries and when, in consequence of the plentiful supply of capital, the level of interest rates showed a tangible decline, there began an extensive export of investment-seeking capital from these countries to other European countries and to overseas areas. This applied to Britain from 1867, to France from 1877 and to Germany from 1886. These three countries were to be the most important exporters of capital until 1914. They accounted for about four-fifths of foreign investments of all European countries. Apart from these three, the Netherlands, Switzerland and Belgium had significant foreign investments. From the turn of the century, the Americans also began to invest capital abroad on a larger scale, chiefly in Canada and Central and South America. Nevertheless, the United States remained a debtor country until the First World War, whilst Britain, France and, somewhat lagging behind them, Germany were the great creditor countries. Between 1870 and 1914, the stock exchanges in London, Paris and Berlin were the leading capital markets where the biggest international transactions were carried out. There were characteristic differences between the three countries in respect of the volume and direction of their capital exports and the type of foreign investment.

Britain

Britain was the first to export capital and emerged as the leader in terms of sheer volume. In 1870, British foreign investments had already reached £775 million. Britain's strong position as an international creditor was due to the favourable conditions under which she exchanged her finished goods for raw materials and foodstuffs, to the income from her merchant shipping and the profits from her banks and insurance companies. From the end of the 19th century onwards, Britain's balance of trade deteriorated, and her income from the merchant fleet declined as a consequence of stronger competition in shipping. And yet Britain's balance of payments remained favourable, thanks to the interest yields on her foreign investments.

London's leading role in the capital market also had an institutional basis: it was the place which had the most liberal regulations on the movement of capital. The London Stock Exchange was a private body and not subject to any government supervision. Its members elected a General Purposes Committee from the circle of stock-jobbers and stockbrokers to supervise stock exchange transactions. There was no official link between the Stock Exchange and the Government. There were, however, confidential contacts between the Treasury and the Foreign Office, on the one side, and the Stock Exchange, on the other. These contacts were often mediated by the Bank of England. But the Government's influence on the investment policies of investors was minimal in comparison with France and Germany. This will be shown in detail when the interaction between capital export and foreign policy is discussed later on (see below pp. 146ff.).

British loans were popular abroad because the borrower was very rarely obliged to buy British industrial products with them. The London City banks had such loose connections with industry in the country that they did not regard themselves as representing the interests of domestic industry. This was different in Germany and France where a closer connection existed between banks and industry. But wherever British companies built railways, gas works and electrical works abroad, British suppliers were given preference, even if they were sometimes more expensive than their foreign competitors.

In France and Germany, it was almost exclusively the banks which undertook foreign investment whereas Britain had a small section of very wealthy capital owners who not only did not entrust the banks with the investment of their capital, but also undertook foreign investments by themselves. Through the global expansion of the British Empire and its political, maritime and commercial interests, they had gained a wider experience than their Continental counterparts and were hence able to rely on their own knowledge of opportunities abroad when investing their capital. These investors, who were neither banks nor bankers, acquired their foreign investments through the London Stock Exchange. It is not possible to put a figure on the magnitude of their share in the total volume of British capital export, but it must have been very significant, for it was the presence of these non-bankers among foreign investors which accounts for the British government's virtual inability to influence capital exports.

Of the City banks, the Baring Brothers, C.J. Hambro & Son and the London Rothschild Bank (N.M. Rothschild & Sons) were predominantly involved in the international securities business. The Barings' main field of activity was in Russia, Italy, the United States, Argentina and Uruguay. They issued and bought state bonds of these countries as well as shares and debentures of railway companies and bank shares. The Hambros participated directly in the issue of Danish, Russian, Italian and Greek state loans. The London Rothschild Bank was involved in European state loans and railway business outside Russia (see above p. 56).

However, investment in overseas countries, and particularly in the territories of the British Empire, was primarily carried out by specialized banks, the Overseas Banks, which were founded for the sole purpose of banking in certain overseas regions. They were all represented in the banking centre of London, either by having their head offices there or by maintaining a branch. But their main field was, and still is, outside Britain. The first overseas banks came into being in the areas of white settlement in the colonies of Canada and Australia shortly after the end of the Napoleonic Wars. The Bank of Montreal and the Bank of New South Wales of Sydney were both established in 1817. Following the founding of two more over-seas banks in the 1830s, a further 68 were promoted between 1853 and 1913. The most important were the Hongkong and Shanghai Banking Corporation of 1864, which acquired a dominant position in the Chinese state loan business and in the financing of Chinese railways and mines; the Standard Bank of South Africa, which was established in 1862 and had investments in South African railway construction and gold and diamond mines, and the London & River Plate Bank, founded in the same year.

By 1870, British foreign investments already totalled £775 million. More than half of this, about £450 million, was invested in foreign state loans. About a quarter of these state bonds came from European countries, about a third from the United States of America and the remainder from South American countries and from British colonies, which, like all colonies, were constitutionally 'foreign countries'. The funds not invested in state loans were placed in railways, gas works and property companies. In the early 1870s, Britain's capital export rose rapidly and reached a first peak in 1872, with £93.9 million of new foreign investments. It declined sharply after the economic crisis of 1875. In 1877, a mere £19.4 million were newly invested abroad. After that, it began to recover, and in 1889 capital export from Britain reached £122.9 million. The Baring crisis in 1890 (see below pp   ) and the Boer War of 1899-1902, were more serious setbacks to Britain's capital export. From the end of the Boer War, however, British foreign investments showed a high annual growth rate. In 1913, no less than £207.5 million were newly invested abroad, and the total of British foreign invest-ments at that time amounted to just under £4 milliard. The interest yields from these foreign investments amounted to about one-tenth of Britain's national income.

Until the mid-19th century, most British foreign investments went to European countries. From 1850 onwards, North America became the main investment area, with South America emerging as the second most important region for British foreign investors from the beginning of the 1880s. Towards the end of the 1880s, more funds were going to South America than North America. This development was abruptly halted by the Baring crisis of 1890. New investment in South America recovered the level attained at the end of the 1880s only some 25 years later. Between 1895 and 1905, British foreign investors preferred the gold- and diamond mines in South America. Within the few years between 1895 and 1905, the new capital investments in South Africa surpassed even those in North America.

Capital export to independent states was subject to wild fluctuations, depending on the economic and political situation; meanwhile capital investment in the territories of the British Empire was increasing steadily. On the eve of the First World War, approximately 45% of British foreign capital had been invested within the Empire. More than a quarter of these investments (around £515 million) had gone to Canada; Australia and

New Zealand received over a fifth of the investments (£415 million); and one sixth each (£370-380 million) of the Empire investments had been placed in India and South Africa. Thus the bulk of capital invested in the Empire flowed into white colonial settlements which had been given Dominion status between 1867 (Canada) and 1909 (South Africa). Of the approximately £2 milliard of foreign investments that were made in sovereign states, more than three-quarters (£1.6 milliard) went to the United States and Latin America. The biggest share of British capital, around £750 million, was invested in the United States. Among the European countries, Russia received the largest amount of British capital export, namely £110 million. It was not only that the flow of British capital exports was increasingly directed towards America and the Empire between 1870 and 1914; there was also a fundamental change in the kind of investments made by Britain. In 1870, state loans still amounted to almost 60%; by 1914, their share in total British foreign investments had dropped to less than one-third. Because British investors developed a keen interest in railways in North America, Canada, China, South Africa and India, the share of railway securities had become the largest by 1914, amounting to about 37% in that year. The remaining foreign investment was spread among mines, public utility companies, plantations and industrial enterprises.

As has been mentioned above, the interest yields from foreign investments constituted a sizeable part of Britain's national income. However, this business also involved great risks and could become the source of big losses. The most spectacular setback in foreign investment was experienced by the big banking house of Baring Brothers in the so-called 'Baring Crisis' of 1890. The Barings had maintained buoyant business contacts with Argentina and were swept along with the boom which seized the Argentinian economy from 1886 onwards. Between 1886 and 1889 they undertook the issue of £17.5 million in Argentinian loans. However, they were unable to sell a large part of their Argentinian and Uruguayan securities to the public and were stuck with £7.75 million of these bonds. When the boom in Argentina and Uruguay ended in a slump and the interest payments from these countries dried up, the Barings ran into a dangerous liquidity crisis. They had short-term commitments amounting to £16 million. Although there were assets of £24.75 million to offset these liabilities, the above-mentioned South American bonds among them, they could not be mobilized quickly enough. Edward Charles Baring, the head of the House of Baring, and from 1885 the First Lord Revelstoke, informed the Governor of the Bank of England, William Lidderdale, of his bank's precarious position. The Governor immediately saw that for the Barings to suspend payments would constitute a grave danger to the British banking system and the Bank of England; such a step by an important bank would lead to a run on other English banks and to considerable withdrawals of gold from Britain. To prevent this from happening, Lidderdale hastily set up a guarantee consortium for the rescue of the Barings. All the big London City banks participated in the consortium since they saw the danger which was threatening them all should Baring Brothers collapse. Within 24 hours they subscribed to a £10 million guarantee fund which was ultimately increased to £17.5 million. The Bank of England also borrowed gold from the Banque de France in order to prepare itself against massive withdrawals of gold in the wake of an exchange of bank notes for gold. The public learned about the difficulties of Baring Brothers only when it could be disclosed that £10 million of the guarantee to cover the Barings' commitments had already been subscribed. Thus a panic was prevented. By 1894, Baring Brothers had reduced their liabilities so far that the guarantee fund could be dissolved. After the crisis, the Barings' private banking house was converted to a limited company, its capital being raised by members of the two Baring families and their friends.

France

Next to Britain, France was the second largest creditor country before 1914. The Paris capital market was much more exposed to government influence and more involved in political manoeuvres than London. Even prior to 1914, all securities to be traded on the French Stock Exchange required the official approval of an admissions board which was supervised by a government-appointed Stock Exchange Commissioner. Foreign investments were subjected to a special examination by the government before they could be quoted on the Paris Stock Exchange. The Finance Minister was to examine them from the fiscal point of view and the Foreign Minister looked into the political aspects. In case the Government deemed the admission of a foreign loan fiscally or politically undesirable it could, on the basis of one minister's verdict, forbid quotation on the Paris Stock Exchange. This regulation had been issued in an Order by King Louis XVIII in 1823. It was confirmed in 1873 during the Third Republic by a letter from the Finance Minister and finally by a governmental decree of 1880. Equipped with these powers, the Government, though unable to steer the foreign investments of French banks in any particular direction, could nevertheless block all foreign investment which it considered undesirable and thus obtained the possibility of controlling capital exports indirectly. Consequently, capital export could be used as the *'arme financière'* of French diplomacy.

The calculations which guided the Government in respect of the admission or non-admission of foreign loans were explained by the Finance Minister Caillaux in a letter which he sent to Foreign Minister Pichon on 23 December 1908: '. . . Indeed, we cannot, without being pushed into the role of dupes, provide a country which is hostile to us with funds; nor can we approve the placing of state loans which are primarily designed to procure orders for the industrial goods of one of our competitors. As a matter of principle we must endeavour to obtain certain advantages from foreign governments in exchange for the opening up of our capital market . . . But it is clear that conditions stand a serious chance of being met only to the extent that the governments themselves have a direct interest in the loans, for which they desire to attract French capital. Consequently, we can, in principle, demand and obtain compensation only for state loans or for loans guaranteed by a state. . . If the issue of a state loan puts us into a position in which we can demand from a foreign government political, commercial or industrial advantages in the sense of a settling of existing difficulties, of providing orders or jobs for our fellow countrymen or of obtaining tariff concessions favouring our exports, we must — as I have mentioned to you on an earlier occasion — beware of formulating exaggerated demands . . . Should we demand too much, the states will turn to English, German, Belgian, Dutch or Swiss banks in order to place their loans and these banks will then find the means to sell the loans in small denominations to French capitalists at a higher price, and to the detriment of our Treasury. Furthermore, and possibly even worse, we would ultimately supply the funds without being able to present the borrowers with a compulsory claim. . .' We shall see later how far the principles of capital export which Caillaux had formulated here were followed in practice.

The French banks began their foreign business when the Paris *haute banque,* headed by Rothschild, engaged in the issue of foreign loans, railway shares and bonds. In the last third of the 19th century, the major banks (Crédit Lyonnais, Société Générale, Comptoir Nationale d'Escompte de Paris, Banque de Paris et des Pays Bas and finally the Banque de l'Union Parisienne) became the most important intermediaries in the export of capital. As in Britain, colonial and overseas banks were also established in France, although with one exception, they remained rather insignificant. The colonial banks functioned as issuing banks in the colonies. Of these colonial and overseas banks, only the Banque de l'Indochine, which had been founded in 1875, acquired a large clientele and gained economic significance. This Bank was an institution under public law and subject to the supervision of the Minister for the Colonies. Unlike other colonial banks, it did not operate merely as an issuing bank for certain colonial areas (French Indochina and the French colonies in the Indian Ocean), but was permitted to conduct other banking business and to extend it beyond these colonies. The Bank's policy was directed by its major shareholders, and these were the major banks of Paris. The Banque de l'Indochine provided advances for the commodity trade from Indochina, issued colonial loans for Indochina and Madagaskar and participated in the financing of railway building in China.

One more bank must be included among the leading intermediaries in the export of French capital: the Banque Impériale Ottomane, a Turkish financial institute under public law which had its head office in Constantinople. It was founded in 1863 on the occasion of a large Turkish state loan, and its capital was raised by the Anglo-French consortium which had undertaken the issue of this loan. Frühling & Goschen, Stern and the Crédit Mobilier were members of this consortium and thus the major shareholders in the new bank. The statutes of the Banque Ottomane were issued by an edict *(firman)* of the Sultan. It was a universal bank in the full sense of the word, since it functioned as an issuing bank for the Ottoman Empire and also as a deposit and investment bank. It handled the servicing of the Ottoman state debt and collected revenues in Constantinople and those cities within the Ottoman Empire where it had branches. Whereas English capital was most influential at the time of its creation, French capital became dominant later on. Finally, the Banque de l'Union Parisienne held the largest parcel of shares in the Banque Ottomane. Several of the *haute banque* companies (Hottinguer & Cie., Mallet Frères & Cie., Mirabaud & Cie., de Neuflize & Cie. and Heine & Cie.) were also shareholders in the Banque Ottomane and were represented on its supervisory board. Of its two overseas branches in London and Paris, the latter was the more important, since it gave the Bank direct access to the Paris capital market, which was much more responsive to the financial needs of the Ottoman Empire than London's. The Banque Ottomane assumed control of the consortium for Turkish state loans, whilst the Paris banks transacted their financial operations in the Ottoman Empire through the Banque Ottomane while, at the same time, controlling Turkish public finances.

On the eve of the Franco-Prussian War of 1870-71, about 10 milliard francs of French capital had been invested in foreign securities. Up to 1890, foreign investments doubled, to about 20 milliard francs, and in 1913 they amounted to just under 45 milliard francs. The total of French foreign investments was just less than half the total on the British side. In the years between 1870 and 1914, foreign securities in British hands saw a shift from state bonds into railway securities. On the other hand, state loans continued to dominate the foreign business of French banks.

By 1900, almost two-thirds of all foreign assets in French portfolios were state bonds. Over half of the total of 30 milliard francs of foreign securities issued in France between 1900 and 1913 were state loans. It was only from the beginning of the 20th century that the French banks, under pressure from the *Comité des Forges*, the Government and the press, began to link the issue of foreign loans more insistently than hitherto with negotiations for overseas orders for French industry. However, the banks did not always yield to such pressures. On the occasion of the Argentinian state loan in 1908-9, the French government demanded that the Paris banks make the issue of the loan conditional upon an order from the Argentinian government to equip its army with modern artillery from Schneider-Creusot rather than Krupp. The banks did not meet the Government's demand because they would have lost the business. On 15 December 1908 the French envoy to Buenos Aires wrote an enraged letter to Paris in which he asked: 'Is the *haute banque* a State within the State? Does the Government of the Republic wish to protect French savings or not and use the all-powerful weapon which these savings represent in the national interest of France?'

Until the end of the 19th century, French banks confined their acquisition of shares in foreign enterprises almost exclusively to railway companies and banks. French capital participated directly in railways in Russia, Spain, Italy, South America and China. The most important among the foreign banks with strong French participation was the aforementioned Banque Impériale

Ottomane. The Banque de Paris et des Pays Bas and the Paris Société Générale also maintained close links with Austrian banks: the 'Paribas' owned a large parcel of shares of the Österreichische Bodenkreditbank, which had business ties with the Škoda Works and the *Steyr-Werke*. The Société Générale, on the other hand, was represented in 1912 on the supervisory board of the Wiener Bankverein by its president. The Foreign Ministries of Russia and Germany — respectively the allies of France and Austria-Hungary — observed with distrust the substantial involvement of French banks in the Dual Monarchy.

During the Witte era after 1892, the Russian government strongly encouraged industrialization, particularly by making a determined effort to attract foreign capital. The capital provided by the major Paris banks made a large contribution to this development. Some of the joint-stock banks in St. Petersburg, Moscow, Lodz, Kiev, Azov and Rostov operated with substantial participations of French capital. On the eve of the First World War, a good half of Russian bank shares held by foreigners was in French hands. The 'Paribas', the Paris Société Générale, the Banque de l'Union Parisienne and the Société Générale de Belgique had considerable direct participating investments in the coal-mines of the Donets Basin and in 13 of the 16 large iron and steel works in South Russia. Three-quarters of the foreign capital directly participating in the Russian ship-yards was French.

Although the Iberian Peninsula, the Ottoman Empire and Latin America had been the main areas for French capital export up to the end of the 1880s, Russia became the main recipient of French foreign investments thereafter. Until 1887, Germany was the principal creditor of the Tsarist Empire; but on 10 November 1887 Bismarck prohibited the Reichsbank from guaranteeing Russian securities, thus closing the German capital market to the country's eastern neighbour. The French banks willingly filled the gap. In 1914 a good 25% of the total of French foreign investments (11.3 milliard francs out of 45 milliard) were in Russian securities. Some six milliard francs, about half the amount tied up in Russian securities, constituted French capital investments in Latin America. In 1914, less than 10% of France's foreign investments (four milliard francs, to be precise) were invested in her own enormous colonial empire. The two Iberian states taken together received approximately the same amount, i.e. 3.9 milliard francs. Some 3.3 milliard francs were invested in the Ottoman Empire and in Egypt (Suez Canal). Having received 2.2 milliard francs in French capital exports, the Austro-Hungarian Monarchy had attracted a larger share of French investments than the United States and Canada in 1914. Both countries together obtained two milliard francs. On the whole, the French banks clearly preferred European countries, in which they had placed over 60% of their foreign investments by 1914. At the same time, only 6% of the total of Britain's foreign investments had been placed in Europe.

Germany and German banks also profited from the fact that the Paris banks preferred Europe. Between 1898 and 1911, the Paris banks invested a large volume of their liquid funds on short term in Germany because interest rates were considerably higher there than on the French and British money markets. On several occasions (in 1901, 1907 and 1909), the French also bought large amounts of German securities including Reich securities. The Paris bank of de Neuflize & Cie. collaborated with Hamburgian banks until 1911 and also granted them high acceptance credits. The Comptoir National d'Escompte de Paris, the 'Paribas' and the Société Générale co-operated with the Disconto-Gesellschaft and with the Bleichröder bank in the Rumanian state loans business, and the Berliner Handels-Gesellschaft belonged to an otherwise purely French consortium of banks for state loans to the Kingdom Serbia. This co-operation between German and French banks suffered severe restrictions when international relations deteriorated following the Second Moroccan Crisis of 1911.

Germany

German capital export was subject to government influence in the same way as that of France. However, it was not exerted directly through the control of stock exchanges, but indirectly through the policy of the Reichsbank. It was only in 1896, when the Stock Exchange Act came into force, that the admission of foreign and domestic securities to the stock exchange was made contingent upon the examination and consent of a committee consisting of representatives of banks and industry. The state commissioner for the stock exchange was allowed to take part in the committee's meetings, but had no voting rights, and a more precise definition of the powers of these admission committees which were attached to the various stock exchanges did not emerge until the 1908 amendment of the Stock Exchange Act and a decree issued by the Federal Council in 1910. Consequently, government control of, and influence on, the capital market, and particularly capital exports, by way of its supervision of the stock exchange was not very strict before 1914. It was able to exercise its influence much more effectively via the Reichsbank. Since the Reich Chancellor was also head of the Reichsbank, he was able to instruct the Reichsbank's board of directors. One way of driving or keeping undesirable foreign securities out of the German capital market was to deny them Reichsbank guarantees.

Bismarck used this device on 10 November 1887 when, the Reinsurance Treaty notwithstanding, Russo-German relations had begun to deteriorate. He instructed the Reichsbank president to forbid the Bank and all its branches to advance money against Russian securities, regardless of the fact that 60% of Russian state bonds were in German hands at that time. This ruling was not made public, but the banks naturally soon noticed that the Reichsbank was no longer advancing money against Russian securities. Thus Russian securities were discriminated against in Germany. They were no longer being purchased in Germany and many of those owning Russian securities before Bismarck's intervention decided to sell them. French banks were willing purchasers and were encouraged in this by their own Government. Soon Paris rather than Berlin became the main market for

Russian securities. After Bismarck's fall, several banks (the Disconto-Gesellschaft, the Berliner Handels-Gesellschaft, Bleichröder, Mendelssohn, Warschauer) all of which were interested in Russian business, tried to get the ban on guarantees lifted. However, the Foreign Ministry advised the new Reich Chancellor, Leo von Caprivi, not to comply with this request. The German government had just rejected the extension of the German-Russian Reinsurance Treaty and had begun to seek a rapid rapprochement with Britain, which was still Russia's rival in world politics at this time. Only after the German-Russian commercial treaty had been concluded in the spring of 1894, and on the Russian government's insistence, did Caprivi order the ban on guarantees to be lifted on 26 October 1894, the day of his own dismissal.

Alongside the major joint-stock banks, overseas banks which they had founded, and several important private banking firms were the agents of German capital exports. Among the latter were: Bleichröder, Mendelssohn, Warschauer, Oppenheim, Warburg, and Behrens & Söhne. Large consortia were formed for some particularly sizeable foreign transactions. Among them the 'Consortium for Italian Business' had a special role to play, since it gave participating German credit institutions a great and temporarily dominating influence on Italy's public loans and her credit system. The Consortium's history began in 1887, when the dealings with Russia were sharply curtailed by the ban on guarantees and when, at the same time, the Paris capital market was closed to Italian state bonds following the renewal of the Triple Alliance between Germany, Austria-Hungary and Italy. The Italians approached Berlin because Paris had turned a deaf ear to their requests for loans. The new Prime Minister, Francesco Crispi, was moreover of the opinion that a shift in Italian foreign policy from Paris to Berlin must lead to a similar shift of focus in financial relations, as it would be dangerous if diplomacy and financial relations were allowed to diverge. The Italians' need for loans suited the German banks which were looking for a new field of activity after their business with Russia had been drastically cut back. From 1887, the Bleichröder banking house, the Disconto-Gesellschaft and the Deutsche Bank collaborated with English and Swiss banks (Hambro, Baring, Rothschild, Schweizerische Kreditanstalt and the Basler Bankverein) in the issue of Italian securities.

In 1890 the 'Consortium for Italian Business' was promoted under the leadership of the Deutsche Bank and the Berliner Handels-Gesellschaft. Other banks belonging to the Consortium included the Dresdner Bank, the Disconto-Gesellschaft, the Bank für Handel und Industrie (Darmstädter Bank) and the banking houses of S. Bleichröder, Sal. Oppenheim & Cie. and L. Behrens & Söhne. Within the first 18 months of its existence, the Consortium raised four Italian state loans worth over 432 million lire all told. In subsequent years, the Consortium, together with an Italian group, handled the credit- and issuing operations of the Italian central government, the provinces, the municipalities and of railway companies, with two-thirds of the business falling to the German Consortium and one-third to the

Italian group. Germany's monopoly in the Italian state loan business lasted until the First Moroccan Crisis of 1905-6. Thereafter the French banks reappeared on the scene (see below, pp. 155f.). The Consortium's most important achievement was the establishment of a major Italian bank. In 1894 the major banks belonging to the Consortium, together with several Austrian and Swiss credit institutes (Schweizerische Kreditanstalt, Basler Bankverein, Union Financière de Genève, Österreichische Creditanstalt, Wiener Bankverein and the Anglo-Österreichische Bank), founded the Banca Commerciale Italiana in Milan which soon became Italy's biggest commerical bank. Some 20 million lire were brought together as the initial capital, and up to 1911 its joint-stock capital was increased to 130 million lire. The Banca Commerciale became the main institution to finance industry in Northern Italy as well as Italian shipping. German banks retained their participating investments in the Banca Commerciale Italiana until the First World War, and they were also each represented on its supervisory board. One of the big German banks, the Nationalbank für Deutschland, did not participate in this venture because it co-operated with a rival Italian enterprise. It helped the Banca di Genova, which wanted to extend its business to the whole of Italy, with arranging its conversion into the Credito Italiano (1895) by acquiring part of the new shares. The Credito Italiano developed into the second largest Italian bank before the First World War.

German financial dealings with overseas countries, with the exclusion of North America, were handled predominantly by special overseas banks which had been set up by the major banks. The first overseas experiences of the German banks were not encouraging. The Deutsche Bank itself was supposed to have been an overseas bank at first, but it shifted its main activity to domestic business after suffering setbacks and following the closure of its branches at Shanghai and Yokohama. A complete failure was the Deutsch-Belgische La Plata Bank, which was to promote trade between Belgium and Germany, on the one side, and Argentina and Uruguay, on the other. This Bank had been founded in 1872 by interested parties in Belgium, by the Oppenheim bank and the Disconto-Gesellschaft. Adolph von Hansemann, the head of the Disconto-Gesellschaft, soon came to realize what incalculable risks were involved in this business and was relieved when, in 1874, he managed to sell his shares and Oppenheim's — which together amounted to a third of the total joint-stock capital of three million thalers — to the Deutsche Bank which was keen to expand. The members of the Deutsche Bank board of directors might have asked themselves why Hansemann wished to get rid of these shares. And indeed, Hermann Wallich warned against the risks of financial dealings with the governments in Montevideo and Buenos Aires; but it was the optimistic Georg Siemens who gained the support of both the board of directors and the supervisory board.

Within a year it turned out that Wallich's warnings had been all too justified; for after a change of government in Uruguay, the new government suspended the servicing of the national debt for a year. As Uruguayan state bonds made up a considerable part of the Deutsch-Belgische La Plata Bank's assets, the Deutsche Bank had to set aside reserves to cover the expected losses. Fortunately, interest payments were resumed later on. In 1884, the Uruguayan government discharged its old debts by issuing fixed-interest bonds. Given its previous experiences, the Deutsche Bank saw to it that the bonds allotted to the La Plata Bank were quickly sold. A year later, in 1885, the Deutsch-Belgische La Plata Bank was liquidated. In view of the course which this affair had taken, it seems doubtful that the Deutsche Bank emerged from this abortive venture without losses, as reported by Fritz Seidenzahl in a volume published to celebrate the Bank's centenary. Nevertheless, two important lessons were learnt: firstly, that overseas business required larger capital resources than those with which the La Plata Bank had been equipped, and secondly, that banks participating in an overseas bank had to take a more active interest in its business operations.

These disillusioning experiences with the Deutsch-Belgische La Plata Bank notwithstanding, the South American investment business was not abandoned; in fact South America was becoming increasingly important for German foreign trade. Hides from Argentina, saltpeter from Chile and coffee from Brazil were imports which were greatly in demand in Germany. Only a year after the liquidation of the La Plata Bank, the Deutsche Bank founded the Deutsche Übersee-Bank in Berlin, with a joint-stock capital of 10 million marks. The new institute was kept on a tight rein, as three members of the Deutsche Bank's board of directors — Siemens, Wallich and Steinthal — were simultaneously board members of its subsidiary. The Deutsche Übersee-Bank established a branch in Buenos Aires and was involved in credit advances to finance the commodity trade between Argentina and Germany. Indeed, at first this constituted the Bank's main-line of business. In 1893 it was transformed into the Deutsche Überseeische Bank and provided with a capital of 20 million marks. From the late 1890's, the bank extended its activity over the whole of South America.

After the Deutsche Bank had regained a foothold in the La Plata region, the Disconto-Gesellschaft and the Norddeutsche Bank founded the Brasilianische Bank für Deutschland at Hamburg in 1887. With the establishment of the Bank für Chile und Deutschland in 1895, the two banks extended their South American business to the mining and trading of Chilean saltpeter. Each of the two overseas banks was provided with a joint-stock capital of 10 million marks. From 1895, they became the exclusive subsidiaries of the Disconto-Gesellschaft that had taken over the joint-stock capital of the Norddeutsche Bank. It was only in 1905 that other major banks followed the Deutsche Bank and the Disconto-Gesellschaft, when the Dresdner Bank, the Schaaffhausenscher Bankverein and the Nationalbank für Deutschland jointly founded the Deutsch-Südamerikanische Bank at Berlin.

In 1889 several major banks and private bankers got together to establish the Deutsch-Asiatische Bank at Berlin and Shanghai to promote German trade with the Far East. The venture was led by the Disconto-Gesellschaft and supported by the Preussische Seehandlung, Deutsche Bank, Darmstädter

Bank, Berliner Handels-Gesellschaft, Bayerische Hypotheken- und Wechsel-bank, Norddeutsche Bank and the banking houses of Bleichröder, Mendels-sohn, Warschauer, Oppenheim, Rothschild (Frankfurt) and Stern (Frankfurt). The Deutsch-Asiatische Bank also came to play an important role as an issuing house and an investment bank. Together with the English Hongkong & Shanghai Banking Corporation, the Bank issued Chinese state loans in 1896 and 1898 when China needed credit after losing the war against Japan of 1894-5. The activity of the Deutsch-Asiatische Bank was also influenced by the power-political aspirations of the Reich government in the coastal region of Northeast China which, in view of Germany's own geographical position, were no doubt quite ill-conceived. When, in 1897, the Reich occupied the Bay of Kiaochow with the port Tsingtao and took out a lease for 99 years, German economic interests concentrated on the Shantung Province which bordered on Kiaochow. In 1899, German investors obtained concessions to build the so-called Shantung Railway from Tsingtao to Tsinan, the capital of the Province, and to exploit coal deposits in Shantung. The Deutsch-Asiatische Bank took a lead in the establishment of the Shan-tung Railway Company as well as Shantung Mining Corporation. From 1895 onwards, the Dresdner Bank also acquired a direct stake in the Deutsch-Asiatische Bank.

When the Deutsche Bank became involved on a large scale in the financing of railway construction in the Ottoman Empire (see below pp. 129f.), and thus drew the eastern Mediterranean area closer to Germany, the Dresdner Bank joined hands with the Schaaffhausenscher Bankverein and the National bank für Deutschland in 1905 to found the Deutsche Orientbank. The latter participated directly in an Egyptian mortgage bank and a German cotton mill at Alexandria; it was also involved in an electricity generating trust in Constantinople. In 1906 the bank took over the small, but very active German banking house of Haessner-Joachimssohn at Tangier which granted commercial credits not only to German firms in Morocco, but also to Moroccan firms and, in addition, represented the interests of the Deutsche Bank, the Comptoir National d'Escompte de Paris, the Deutsche Überseeische Bank and the Anglo-Egyptian Bank in this North African city. At a relatively late date, in 1904-5, three colonial banks for the African colonies were also founded in Germany. Yet they did not play much of a role either in the German banking system or in the export of German capital, since the economic development of the German colonies remained just as insignifi-cant as the trade between the Reich and its colonies.

If one disregards the Deutsch-Asiatische Bank, the largest slice of foreign business was handled not by the overseas banks, but by the major banks and the private bankers themselves. Some private bankers, such as M.M. Warburg & Co. at Hamburg and the Houses of Mendelssohn & Co., Robert Warschauer & Co. and S. Bleichröder at Berlin, participated in the issue of Russian state loans, railway shares and railway debentures. The Russian government kept accounts with Bleichröder and Warschauer, whose extensive Russian business was hard hit by the above-mentioned ban on guarantees.

Although they maintained their links with Russia they were no longer able to raise substantial sums for the Russian government and the Russian railway companies as they had done before, because the German public did not purchase Russian securities during the period of the ban. Once the ban on guarantees had been lifted, they reactivated their business ties with Russia. Between 1894 and 1898, Bleichröder, Mendelssohn, Warschauer and Warburg, together with the Disconto-Gesellschaft and the Berliner Handels-Gesellschaft, issued Russian railway debentures amounting to 1.1 milliard francs. But at the same time Russian state bonds worth five times this amount were placed on the French capital market and, after the ban on guarantees had been lifted, German banks never again occupied more than second place in Russia.

Alongside the private bankers, two of the big German banks, the Berliner Handels-Gesellschaft and the Disconto-Gesellschaft, were also heavily engaged in Russian securities. From 1884, the Berliner Handels-Gesellschaft was moreover the leading financier to the new-established Kingdom of Serbia. It retained this role until 1914, even after the Serbian putsch and the change of dynasty of 1903, when Serbia gave up her previous association with the Triple Alliance (Germany, Austria-Hungary, Italy) and became a supporter of the Franco-Russian Dual Alliance. Business with Serbia was hard going for the first ten years. Only a year after a consortium for Serbian state loans had been formed in 1884, under the leadership of the Berliner Handels-Gesellschaft with the participation of Mendelssohn & Co. and Warschauer, Serbian public finances were in ruins following her unsuccessful war against Bulgaria. The Kingdom paid no more than two-thirds of the interest due. In order to prevent a slump in the price of Serbian state bonds, and more particularly in order not to destroy their reputation as issuing houses in the eyes of the public, the consortium banks chipped in the remaining third. The Serbian government had coolly expected this response when honouring no more than a part of their commitments. After this, the other members of the Consortium did not engage in any further financial dealings with the Serbian government.

The Berliner Handels-Gesellschaft, on the other hand, attempted, in a long tug-of-war, to persuade the Kingdom to reorganize its public finances to make regular interest payments and to repay its debts. For a number of years, punctual and complete payments of interest could be bought at the price of providing a further loan to Serbia. But it had to be issued by the Berliner Handels-Gesellschaft alone; the Consortium partners refused to co-operate after their negative experiences. Before long, the Bank was again compelled to provide Belgrade with funds to enable Serbia to meet its interest payments and, what is more, to defend the price of Serbian state bonds by supporting purchases. It was by such means that the despressing state of the Serbian national debt could be concealed until 1892-3. By then the problems had become so widely known that there was no point in launching further rescue operations. The Bank suspended its support and Carl Fürstenberg, the leading figure of the Berliner Handels-Gesellschaft, in negotiations which dragged on for two years, attempted to reach a reasonable compromise.

Since an indebted state is normally in a stronger position than its creditors, the result was a rather one-sided revision of the agreement in Serbia's favour. The Serbian government not only received a new loan of over 45 million francs, but the Berliner Handels-Gesellschaft also had to agree, by way of a compulsory conversion, to a reduction in the rate of interest on the old Serbian loan from 5% to 4%. At a time when it was not yet the custom for states to absolve themselves from *bona fide* obligations in financial matters, this compulsory conversion was a sensational, even scandalous event. It was found tolerable only because Fürstenberg got the Serbian government to pledge, as collateral for the interest payments and amortization of the new loan, the revenue from the administration of its financial monopolies, which was to be reconstituted. Thus it appeared that a firm guarantee against a future repetition of the earlier events had been obtained. As the Berliner Handels-Gesellschaft could no longer find any consortium partners for Serbian state loans among the German credit institutions, French banks took their place.

Outside Europe, the Berliner Handels-Gesellschaft participated in railway financing in the United States from 1884 and, from 1887, in Egypt and the Boer Republics in South Africa. The Bank also acquired a parcel of shares in the Dutch-South African Railway Company, which had obtained the concession to build and operate railways in the two Boer republics.

In addition to its leading role in the Deutsch-Asiatische Bank and the two Shantung companies and its participation in the 'Consortium for Italian Business', the Disconto-Gesellschaft had large financial commitments in Russia. Although the issue of Russian loans stopped after the 1887 ban on guarantees, the Bank continued to be involved in the financing of Russian railways, and invested in three Russian commercial banks in St. Petersburg and Warsaw. Owing to the financial ruin of Strousberg, the 'railway king', the Disconto-Gesellschaft was also brought into the financing of Rumanian railways. When the Rumanian railway company, which Strousberg had founded in 1871, became insolvent before all the planned sections had been completed, the Disconto-Gesellschaft, together with the Preussische Seehandlung and the Bleichröder banking house, stepped in to prevent it from going bankrupt. The 'rescue action' was good business for the banks since they acquired Strousberg's shares at a low price. Following this engagement, the Disconto-Gesellschaft and Bleichröder remained major financiers to the Rumanian railways until the First World War. In 1897, they also jointly established a bank in Bucharest, the Banca Generala Romana, which, with a capital of 12.5 million lei, was the second largest commercial bank in the country. Since Rumania had taken over the French monetary standard, 12.5 million lei corresponded to the same amount in French francs. In the financing of the construction of the Venezuela Railway from Caracas to Valencia, the Disconto-Gesellschaft experienced much greater difficulties. The concession for this railway had been acquired by Krupp. The

Disconto-Gesellschaft and the Norddeutsche Bank joined hands in financing the construction of the Venezuela Railway on the basis of a contract which was signed with Krupp in 1888. For many years it was only the German supply firms, on whose behalf the banks had secured the orders, which got any business out of this enterprise.

The Disconto-Gesellschaft was involved to a far greater extent than any of the other German banks in state loans to the Dual Monarchy and to the German colonies. Its participation in the issue of Austrian state loans began at the time of the German-Danish War in 1864. At that time Austria-Hungary had floated a loan of 70 million guldens. In competition with the Viennese Rothschild Bank and the Österreichische Creditanstalt which had so far exclusively managed the country's loan operations, the Disconto-Gesellschaft formed a consortium with the banking houses of Bleichröder, Oppenheim and Mendelssohn, which accepted one-third of this particular loan. Later, the rivals reconciled their differences and now formed the so-called 'Rothschild Consortium', which was subsequently joined by the Ungarische Allgemeine Creditbank, the Allgemeine Österreichische Boden-Credit-Anstalt, the Österreichische Länderbank, the Darmstädter Bank and, after 1900, the Österreichische Postsparkasse. The members of the Consortium jointly accepted Austrian and Hungarian loans and railway bonds. Until 1910, it was headed by the Viennese Rothschild Bank. Then a dispute arose over the redistribution of the Consortium shares, which ended with the Österreichische Postsparkasse assuming control of the Consortium, whilst the Rothschild Bank temporarily withdrew from it; it returned in 1913.

In the German colonies, the Disconto-Gesellschaft was the only German bank with larger capital investments. A number of bank directors and bankers joined the *Deutscher Kolonialverein* (German Colonial Association), founded in 1882 and renamed *Deutsche Kolonialgesellschaft* (German Colonial Society) in 1887. Among them were Siemens, Steinthal, Wallich, Fürstenberg, Schwabach (of the Bleichröder Bank), Franz Mendelssohn and Adolph von Hansemann. Yet most of them merely paid lip-service to the enthusiasm for colonies which was the political fashion of the day, without having the slightest intention of investing money in these territories. Only Hansemann, the chairman of the Disconto-Gesellschaft, was interested in colonial policy and considered the colonies as profitable areas for investment. Hansemann's economic activity in the colonies began in 1879 when the *Deutsche Handels- und Plantagen-Gesellschaft* (German Trade and Plantation Company), which belonged to the Hamburg firm of Godeffroy, had become insolvent through the mismanagement of what was in principle a very lucrative business in the South Pacific. Hansemann formed a consortium to reorganize the *Deutsche Handels- und Plantagen-Gesellschaft*. The reorganization was successful, even though a Reich guarantee for dividends, which Bismarck had granted on Hansemann's request did not materialize because the Reichstag did not consider the reorganization of a carelessly managed commercial enterprise a patriotic task and rejected the so-called 'Samoa Bill'.

After Hansemann had successfully reorganized the *Deutsche Handels-und Plantagen-Gesellschaft* he began to develop an interest in New Guinea as a trading base. With Bleichröder, he formed a New Guinea consortium and through Heinrich von Kusserow, his son-in-law, who worked as an official in the Foreign Ministry, he warmed Bismarck to the idea that the Reich should assume the protectorate over the North-East of New Guinea, whilst its administration, economic development and exploitation were to remain the business of a German commercial company. During the short phase of his active colonial policy (1884-5), Bismarck agreed to this programme. In January 1885, the North-Eastern part of New Guinea was placed under the protection of the Reich and its jurisdiction transferred to the *Neuguinea-Kompanie* which Hansemann and Bleichröder had founded. This imitation of British and Dutch colonial companies in the 17th century proved unsuccessful — and success could scarcely be expected, given the negative experience of the British and Dutch colonial companies in the 18th century. Administrative expenditure and investments were not counterbalanced by revenue to cover costs. The *Neuguinea-Kompanie* was therefore only too glad when in 1898 it finally succeeded in selling to the Reich the territorial rights which it held over North-East Guinea for a sum of four million marks. The Disconto-Gesellschaft also had direct investments in railway companies in the Reich's African colonies. These companies built and operated railways which extended inland from the ports.

Following the liquidation of the Deutsch-Belgische La Plata Bank, the Deutsche Bank continued to learn foreign business the hard way. In the United States its large stake in the American Northern Pacific Railroad Company also came to grief, but this time it got off unscathed. The episode evolved as follows: the Bank had participated in a consortium controlled by Drexel, Morgan & Co. to supply the illiquid Northern Pacific with fresh funds. To do this, the consortium banks issued bonds of over 20 million dollars. In subsequent years, the Deutsche Bank, together with the London Rothschild Bank, the New York firm of August Belmont & Co. and the Frankfurt house of Jacob S.H. Stern placed further bonds on behalf of the expanding Northern Pacific, the greater part of which was sold to German investors on the stock exchange. Whereas Drexel, Morgan & Co. withdrew in time from providing further financial support for the Northern Pacific, Siemens trusted the president of the railway company, Henry Villard, who was as active as he was dubious as a businessman for far too long. In 1893, the Northern Pacific had once more become illiquid and was placed under compulsory management. After much hesitation a consortium was formed in 1896 under the leadership of the Morgan bank and the Deutsche Bank, in order to change the terms of indebtedness and to reconstruct the capital of the Northern Pacific. In 1901, the 'battle of giants' between the groups of Morgan-Hill on the one hand, and Schiff-Harriman on the other (see above p. 97) forced the prices of the Northern Pacific shares to dizzy heights, and German shareholders took advantage of this rise in rates to sell their shares in a company which had caused them so much trouble.

At the same time as it was attempting to reorganize the Northern Pacific, the Deutsche Bank initiated what was to prove its greatest and most lucrative foreign business deal. The *Allgemeine Elektrizitätsgesellschaft (AEG)* had obtained a concession to build a power station in Buenos Aires, where British and French concerns had been building power stations before, and was looking for a financially potent partner in order to implement the project. Emil Rathenau, the AEG director, contacted a number of banks and a consortium was formed under the leadership of the Deutsche Bank which included the AEG, the Berliner Handels-Gesellschaft, the National-bank für Deutschland, the Schweizerische Kreditanstalt, the banking houses of Delbrück Leo & Co., Landau, Sulzbach Brothers, the Bank für elektrische Unternehmungen (Bank for Electrical Enterprises) in Zurich and the firm of Wernher Beit & Co. This Consortium promoted the *Deutsch-Überseeische Elektricitäts-Gesellschaft* (German Overseas Electricity Company) to construct and operate the projected power station with a joint-stock capital of 10 million marks. At the same time the Consortium members acquired debentures in the new company amounting to 10 million marks. The enterprise flourished from the start. It owned the power station with the largest capacity in the Argentinian metropolis. A few years later, it acquired, by purchase or by lease, the power stations belonging to its competitors in Buenos Aires. Up to 1905, the joint-stock capital had been increased three times to a total of 36 million marks. In 1901 the Disconto-Gesellschaft and the Dresdner Bank also joined the Consortium which issued shares and debentures, although the Deutsche Bank retained the controlling influence.

After the turn of the century the new oil industries became another field in which the Deutsche Bank had major foreign interests. Its first link with oil was established in 1901 during the initial stage of the Baghdad Railway project when the Anatolian Railway Company, in which the Deutsche Bank had participated prominently, obtained the concession to develop and exploit oil in Mesopotamia. In view of the high costs of developing, refining and transporting Mesopotamian oil, which made competition with oil products of Standard Oil and Royal Dutch hopeless, the use of the concession was not contemplated for the time being. Shortly before the First World War, the concession became the subject of a tit-for-tat between the Germans and the British. At about the same time when the concession for Mesopotamian oil was granted, the way was being paved for the Deutsche Bank to participate in the exploitation of oil wells which had already been developed. Apart from owning shares in an oil company in Galicia, the Bank acquired control of the Rumanian oil company Steaua Româna. When this company ran into financial difficulties in 1902, its principal creditor, the Hungarian Bank für Industrie und Handel at Budapest, became illiquid because its credits had been frozen. This in turn affected the Wiener Bankverein which had refinanced the Hungarian bank. In order to put both the Steaua Româna and the Bank für Industrie und Handel back on their feet, the Bankverein turned to the Deutsche Bank, with which it had maintained close contact. In 1903 the Deutsche Bank, together with the Bankverein, acquired the largest part of the Steaua Româna's joint-stock capital of 17 million lei.

Having refloated the oil company, it founded the *Deutsche Petroleum AG* in the spring of 1904 as a holding company for its oil interests. The Deutsche Bank held over 50% of the shares in this company; the Wiener Bankverein, which had brought Rumanian and Galician oil shares into the *Deutsche Petroleum AG*, received a 25% stake in the holding company. The remaining shares in the *Deutsche Petroleum AG* were taken over by the Darmstädter Bank, the Nationalbank für Deutschland, the Mitteldeutsche Creditbank and the banking house of Jacob S.H. Stern. Thus the Steaua Româna had become a subsidiary of the *Deutsche Petroleum AG*, which in turn was a subsidiary of the Deutsche Bank. The Bank also held the leading position in the oil business. Its 'oil specialist', Emil Georg Stauss, was on the board of Steaua Româna from 1905 and director-general of the *Deutsche Petroleum AG* from 1907. In 1914-5 he was the director-general of the Steaua Româna, before becoming a member of the Deutsche Bank's board in 1915. The oil business yielded no more than small profits during the first phase, and the Deutsche Bank therefore tried to sell its oil interests to Standard Oil. The deal failed when the American company refused to accept the conditions of sale. After negotiations with Standard Oil had fallen through in 1910, the Rumanian oil market took a very favourable turn owing to rising demand, and the Deutsche Bank no longer had any intention of selling. It finally lost its oil interests as a result of the First World War.

There are no precise data available on the total volume of German capital exports before 1914, nor on its distribution between different countries; there are only estimates based on fragmentary information. These estimates, relating to the years just prior to the First World War, vary between 23.5 milliard and 31 milliard marks. It is impossible to verify with any degree of reliability estimates which diverge so sharply. Nor is it to be expected that the discovery of further sources will yield more reliable figures. Hence the question remains as to which of the two estimates is the more plausible, if the pre-1914 situation is taken into consideration. One clue is provided by the registration of German-owned foreign securities during the second year of the War. Its overall balance was 16.5 milliard marks. It may be assumed that, compared with the situation before the outbreak of war, no significant changes occurred up to 1916, since free movement of money and capital was severely restricted during the War. It must also be remembered that capital investment abroad was mainly in securities; it seems therefore that the sum of 23.5 milliard marks which Herbert Feis quoted in his *Europe, the World's Banker, 1870-1914*, is more realistic than the figure of 31 milliard marks which Friedrich Lenz arrived at for the first time in 1922 and which Katja Nehls cited again in 1963. Another consideration supports the former figure: in 1914 the total of French foreign investments, for which there are rather more reliable estimates based on more abundant information, amounted to the equivalent of around 36 milliard marks. However, France had been exporting large amounts of capital for some 30 years before Germany arrived on the scene. In the years prior to 1914, low interest rates in France — which reached no more than between two-thirds to three-quarters of German rates — were a strong incentive for French capitalists to invest their money abroad in countries which offered higher interest rates. By contrast, the German capital market had been under great strain from 1906, when the naval arms race with Britain began in earnest. This is reflected in the sharp rise in the level of interest rates after 1906. Under these circumstances and considering the volume of capital exported from France, it is highly improbable that German capital exports of 31 milliard marks could have been achieved. In short, a comparison between Germany and France also reinforces Feis's estimate of 23.5 milliard marks.

By 1914 well over half of these exports had gone to other European countries. Just under a quarter of this (about three milliard marks) went to Austria-Hungary, whilst Russia and the Ottoman Empire each received approximately 1.8 milliard marks of German capital investment. Three-quarters of the overseas capital was exported to America. North and Latin America each imported some 3.75 milliard marks of German capital. Only 2% of the German total was invested in German colonies. Unlike both Britain and France, Germany had acquired a colonial empire, but did not know what to do with it.

Economic Effects of Capital Export

In relation to these international movements of capital in which Britain, France and Germany were the main creditors, Russia, Canada, China and the Ottoman Empire were the largest debtor countries. Their foreign debts amounted to 30 milliard, 26 millard, 16 milliard, 6.7 milliard and 3.4 milliard marks respectively.

There were great differences in the character of these countries and the causes of their heavy foreign indebtedness. The United States and Russia were world powers pursuing expansionist policies. China and the Ottoman Empire were former great powers which were politically impotent and economically underdeveloped at this time. Canada was a British Dominion. With the exception of the United States, all the debtor countries were either barely or at least much less industrialized than the creditor countries. Although from 1893 the United States was the greatest industrial producer in the world (by 1913, 38% of the world's industrial output originated in America) she was nevertheless in need of capital and offered profitable investment opportunities which American capitalists were not yet capable of meeting. This demand was created in the first instance by a rapid population growth caused by immigration: between 1870 and 1910 the population of the U.S. rose from 39 million to 92 million.

In several countries, and particularly in the Ottoman Empire and the Balkan states, it was no secret that part of the foreign debt was used to balance their budgets and to fulfil their international payment obligations. However, the debtor countries used most of the foreign capital for investments in transport, mining and other industries. It was in this way that the Americans financed the construction of their transcontinental railways and that Russia built the West Russian and Siberian railways. The United States and Canada also financed the further expansion of their industries with the help of foreign capital, whereas Russia used it to initiate the first phase of her industrialization.

However, as we have seen, capital export was not always followed by the export of goods to debtor countries or the purchase of cheap raw materials from debtor countries. The question as to whether the debtor countries also became politically dependent on the creditor nations will be examined below (see p. 146ff.).

2. Two Large International Business Projects: the Suez Canal and the Baghdad Railway.

Two projects which figured in international financial and diplomatic relations for a longer period than any of the other big international transactions during the last third of the 19th century and the beginning of the 20th must be described in some detail here: the construction of the Suez Canal and the building of the Baghdad Railway.

The Construction of the Suez Canal

A system of canals connecting the Mediterranean and the Red Sea had been created more than once in antiquity, but lack of maintenance and the effects of sand storms meant that the canals had deteriorated so completely that nothing remained of them. In the 17th and 18th centuries, the resumption of transport by ship between the Mediterranean and the Red Sea was discussed in France, in the Republic of Venice and in Austria, all of whom owned major Mediterranean ports. In Britain no-one took an interest in such plans, for the sea route round the Cape of Good Hope was more advantageous in their East Asian and Indian trade than for their Continental competitors. During his expedition to Egypt in 1798, Napoleon had the technology of a canal project examined by engineers, and one of them, Le Père, found that to construct a canal across Isthmus of Suez was technically perfectly feasible. Saint-Simon and his disciples also took up the project. They saw in it a possibility for improving the welfare of all mankind, just as they expected a similar result from railways and from joint-stock banks (see above, pp. 73f.). In 1846, the Saint-Simonian Prosper Enfantin, the French diplomat Vicomte de Lesseps, the Austrian railway engineer, Alois von Negrelli and a number of interested people from France and Austria founded a study group to work out plans and to draw up estimates of the costs of building a canal.

The territory through which the canal was to be built still formally belonged to the Ottoman Empire. However, after the Albanian officer

Mehmed Ali had become its governor in 1806, the country was an almost independent state with its own army and fleet. Only the intervention of the great powers had prevented the complete separation of Egypt from the Ottoman Empire. In 1841 Mehmed Ali was recognized as hereditary governor by the Sultan. From then on the government in Constantinople exercized its sovereignty over Egypt only in matters of foreign and fiscal policy. One of Turkey's remaining sovereign rights concerned concessions to be granted to foreigners. Abbas, Mehmed Ali's successor, was very cool towards the canal project. He was an Anglophile and knew of Britain's negative attitude. The British suggested to the governor that, instead of a canal, he should build a railway from Alexandria to Suez. This railway was built with the strong financial backing of British bankers in 1851-6.

It was only in 1854 that the tide turned in favour of the parties interested in the construction of a canal, when Muhamed Sa'id succeeded Abbas as governor. Sa'id had been on friendly terms with Lesseps since the latter's period of service as French Consul in Cairo. In 1854, Lesseps obtained from Sa'id a concession for constructing a canal in the name of the Compagnie Universelle du Canal Maritime de Suez which he had founded. This concession still required the approval of the Sultan as the nominal sovereign of Egypt. The British were successful in delaying his decision until 1866. When it was realized in Egypt that Constantinople's consent was not to be expected in the near future, construction work began illegally in 1859. The Suez Canal was completed after ten years in 1869.

The Compagnie Universelle du Canal Maritime de Suez financed the construction of the canal. The company was founded with a capital of 200 million francs divided into 400,000 shares, in denominations of 500 francs each. Lesseps wanted to distribute the shares between Britain, Austria, France, Russia and the United States. This proved impossible because of the Crimean War, which was followed by a world economic crisis. But most importantly, Britain showed a complete lack of interest. Over half the shares were sold in France. Sa'id bought some 64,000 shares. More than 85,000 shares, however, found no purchasers. Had they remained unsold, the canal project would have collapsed. To prevent this from happening, Lesseps induced the governor to take these shares as well, and in order to be able to buy them, Sa'id had to increase the Egyptian state debt, already very high due to his ambitious policies of independence and modernization. The consent of the Sultan was required for a state loan; but there was no hope of this being given since such a loan would have helped to finance a canal which had not yet been approved. Without Constantinople's consent the loan would have been illegal, and no bank would have accepted an illegal loan for issue. In view of this, Sa'id was able to obtain credit only by issuing short-term interest-bearing treasury bonds for which he did not need the Turkish government's consent. If these could not be redeemed on the due date, they had to be renewed at an interest of 14%, and later of 25%. And this became the norm. By 1861, Egypt's short-term indebtedness had risen to 222 million francs. In order to escape this vicious circle, it was imperative to procure a state loan and to convert the short-term, floating debt into a long-term, consolidated one. After extended negotiations, Egypt, with the Sultan's consent, was able to place a state loan with the London banking house of Frühling & Goschen in 1861. The nominal value of the loan amounted to £3.3 million, but the actual yield to Egypt was only £2.2 million. As collateral for interest payments and amortization, the governor had to pledge all revenues collected in the Nile Delta region. A year later, Egypt's short-term indebtedness began to rise again as the governor had to issue treasury bonds at 8-12% interest in order to service the long-term loans. It seemed impossible to escape this vicious circle.

The financial transactions which took place in connection with the construction of the Suez Canal enticed some European bankers to found banking houses in Alexandria: Edouard Dervieu & Cie. was established in 1860, followed by Hermann Oppenheim Nevieu & Cie. and the Anglo-Egyptian Bank in 1862. Sa'id's successor, Isma'il, increased the debts by handing out bribes in Constantinople and by doubling his annual tribute to the Sultan in an attempt to buy greater independence for Egypt, such as the right to deal with the succession on an independent basis, to bear the title of Khedive and finally to issue state loans entirely at his own discretion.

From 1864 until 1873, Isma'il took up four new loans which had been issued by Frühling & Goschen and H. Oppenheim Nevieu & Cie. In connection with the last big loan, the banks accepted the bonds at the rate of 63% and sold them to the public at the rate of between 70% and 84%. Thus Egypt received a mere £20 million out of a loan which had yielded £32 million. What is more, £8.7 million of this loan was paid out to Egypt in Egyptian treasury bonds which the banks had accumulated. As Egypt's short-term indebtedness had risen to £20 million by 1875 and the Egyptian State was increasingly threatened by bankruptcy, the French banks, which in previous years had bought not only Egyptian bonds, but also short-term treasury bonds on a large scale, conceived a plan to consolidate the finances of the Egyptian State with the help of a long-term loan. This loan was to be issued by a French consortium of banks headed by the Crédit Foncier de France. As collateral, the Consortium was to accept the Khedive's shares in the Suez Canal. However, Dervieu and the Société Générale wanted to take advantage of this favourable opportunity and purchase shares from the Khedive at a time when the share price was low due to the world economic crisis of 1873-75. Faced with the tough conditions which the Crédit Foncier wished to impose, Isma'il, who had not originally been wanting to sell his Canal shares, finally decided to sell.

The British government learned of the Khedive's intention to sell through two channels. The first was when the French inquired whether Britain would have any objection to the French banks acquiring Egyptian Suez shares. They also heard of the proposed deal through H. Oppenheim Nevieu & Cie. Disraeli, the British Prime Minister, now launched a surprise coup. He informed the French government that Britain wholly disapproved of French banks acquiring the Egyptian shares; then he bought Isma'il's parcel of shares in the Suez Canal for £4 million with the help of a credit which Lionel Rothschild procured for him within a matter of hours. Thus the British government came into possession of the largest parcel of shares — though not quite the majority, which remained with the French banks. Britain's gain from the purchase of these shares was purely financial. From the late 1870s, the Suez Canal Company paid sizeable dividends, but its statutes prevented control by a major shareholder. There were 32 members on the board of directors, of whom 16 had to be French, nine British and five Egyptian. Britain gained actual control of the Suez Canal only when she embarked upon the military occupation of Egypt following the Arabi Pasha Uprising of 1882. In the Anglo-Egyptian agreement of 1899, Britain was also granted military oversight over the Canal. Egypt had spent £11 million on the Suez Canal and received a mere £4 million for the sale of her shares, a consequence of her heavy indebtedness and the ruinous conditions of the loan which the creditor banks had forced on the country.

The Baghdad Railway

The building of the Baghdad Railway was the most spectacular enterprise undertaken abroad by German banks. Until 1888 German banking houses had not participated in any Ottoman loan issues. Loans were almost without exception provided by the Paris capital market via the Banque Impériale Ottomane and the Paris banks linked with it as share-holders. The Banque Ottomane also controlled Turkish state finances, because it supplied the top officials of the *Administration de la Dette Publique Ottomane*. Sultan Abdul Hamid II wished to escape from his exclusive financial link with France. This is why he aimed to finance the construction of a strategically important railway from the Bosphorus to Angora (since 1930, Ankara) and on to Baghdad with the help of British or German capital. The British Ambassador in Constantinople learned of this in the summer of 1887 and reported it to London. He pointed to the commercial, political and strategic advantages Britain would gain from railways in the Asiatic parts of Turkey. In April 1888, the British War Office also drew Salisbury's attention to the project which, constructed with British capital, would be of great commercial and political significance. Salisbury replied grumpily: 'What's the use of all this, unless we know where the money is coming from.' British banks and capital owners were not inclined to invest in the Ottoman Empire.

At first, the German banks showed no greater willingness to commit themselves in Turkey. In the spring of 1888 the Sultan sent a German engineer, Wilhelm Pressel, to take soundings in Berlin as to whether a German consortium of banks would be prepared to finance railway construction in Anatolia; the response was not friendly. The situation changed when, in the summer of 1888, the Ottoman government persuaded a German banker who had just established a tenuous business link with the Ottoman Empire to act as an intermediary. He was Albert von Kaulla, a great-grandson of 'Madame' Kaulla (see above pp. 26f.). He was a board member of the Württembergische Vereinsbank. His Bank had provided credit for the supply of Mauser rifles to the Turkish infantry and this had brought him into contact with Turkish government and Court officials. Unlike Kaulla, his colleagues on the board were not prepared to get involved in the railway business in Anatolia, although they allowed him to establish contacts between Turkey and the Deutsche Bank. In the end he went to Turkey as negotiator for the Deutsche Bank in which the Vereinsbank was a shareholder, with a representative on its board of directors. However, Siemens, one of the key figures on the board of the Deutsche Bank, began to show an interest in the Ottoman Empire only when the Government agreed to pledge certain state revenues as guarantee for interest payments on German capital.

Before the Deutsche Bank began more detailed negotiations, it made enquiries at the Foreign Ministry on 15 August 1888 as to whether the Reich government would have any political objections to a financial commitment and whether the German Ambassador in Constantinople would support it in its negotiations with the Turkish government. Bismarck personally replied on 2 September 1888 that he saw no political problems to the Deutsche Bank applying for a concession to construct railways in Asia Minor. He also agreed to authorize the German Ambassador to support Kaulla, the Bank's representative, in his negotiations. But he added a warning that the Reich could not provide insurance cover against business risks: 'No doubt [he wrote] German entrepreneurs are taking a risk by investing in the Anatolian railway project, a risk which arises, in the first place, from the difficulty of enforcing legal claims in the Orient and which could be exacerbated by wars and other complications. The dangers for German capital will be a charge solely on the entrepreneurs and the latter cannot rely on the Reich to insure their financial position against the vicissitudes of precarious commercial ventures abroad.'

Diplomatic protection of the project was ultimately provided by the ambassadors of Germany, Britain and Italy who came to an understanding among themselves that a company under the chairmanship of the Deutsche Bank was to build a railway line from Bosphorus to Angora. Up to now, only rather short branch-lines leading inland from the coast operated in Asiatic Turkey. Britain and Italy willingly gave their consent to the German plan, regarding it as a counterbalance to excessive French influence in the Ottoman Empire. Thus, in the autumn of 1888, the Deutsche Bank was granted a concession to build and operate a railway from Haidarpasha on the Asiatic bank of the Bosphorus, opposite Constantinople, to Angora. A small section of this railway from Haidarpasha along the coast of the Sea of Marmara to Ismid, which had been built by a British company, was bought by the Deutsche Bank for six million francs.

The Ottoman government guaranteed the Deutsche Bank an annual income of 15,000 francs per kilometer to cover amortization and interest payments and pledged the income from tithes in the districts through which the railway line was to be built. In return for the concession, Constantinople asked for the acceptance of a loan of 30 million marks. In view of the great interest which the British ambassador had shown in the railway

project during the preliminary discussions and encouraged by several con-
versations with British businessmen, the Deutsche Bank definitely expected
British banks to participate in raising the loan and financing the railway.
But these expectations were disappointed when it came to the nitty-gritty
of financial problems. The London City banks cold-shouldered Siemens;
nor did other German credit institutions offer any of the assistance which
Siemens and Steinthal had hoped for. Salomonsohn and Alfred Lent of the
Disconto-Gesellschaft politely rebuffed their overtures, and Mendelssohn
and Bleichröder also kept aloof. Finally the Deutsche Bank brought a loan
consortium together which included the Berliner Handels-Gesellschaft, the
banking house of Robert Warschauer & Co., the Württembergische Vereinsbank and the Deutsche Vereinsbank of Frankfurt.

To build and operate the railway to Angora, the Deutsche Bank founded
the *Anatolische Eisenbahngesellschaft* in 1889, in which the Württembergische Vereinsbank and the Deutsche Vereinsbank also had a stake. The
execution of the building works were taken on by a building company in
which the Deutsche Bank had a direct involvement. The railway to Angora
was completed in 1893. Siemens had planned to raise the profitability of
the Haidarpasha-Angora railway by connecting it to a railway network in
the European parts of the Ottoman Empire which at that time still included
Albania, Epirus, Thrace and the whole of Macedonia. For this purpose the
Deutsche Bank, together with the Wiener Bankverein, acquired most of the
shares in the *Betriebsgesellschaft für Orientalische Eisenbahnen* comprising
1,260 kilometers in European Turkey from 'Türkenhirsch' in 1890 (see
above p. 45). The value of this railway network had increased greatly with
the completion of the Vienna-Belgrade-Constantinople railway line in 1888.
In 1890 the Deutsche Bank, in co-operation with the Wiener Bankverein
and the Schweizerische Kreditanstalt, promoted the Bank für Orientalische
Eisenbahnen in Zurich as the bank concerned with railways in the Ottoman
Empire.

Whilst building work was still in progress on the Haidarpasha—Angora
railway line, Abdul Hamid let the Deutsche Bank know of his plan to continue this railway beyond Angora to Baghdad. But with the collapse of the
Northern Pacific already looming on the horizon, Siemens was very reserved towards this idea. However, in order to meet the Sultan, the
Deutsche Bank proposed building a railway from Eskişehir — on the
Haidarpasha-Angora railway line — to Konia in the southeast. This railway
was expected to be more profitable since it could be linked up with two
terminal branch-lines leading to the coast. It was also for this reason that the
Banque Impériale Ottomane, which owned one of those branch-lines,
supported the project. In 1893 the *Anatolische Eisenbahngesellschaft*
received the concession for the Eskişehir-Konia line and another one for
a line from Angora to Kaiserije which had not been requested at all, but
which the Government saw as a further stage along the desired link with
Baghdad. At the same time the Ottoman Bank group and Nagelmackers
Fils & Cie. of Liège obtained a concession to extend their line from Izmir-

Alashehir to Afium-Karahissar, which provided a connection with the *Anatolische Eisenbahn*. The Eskişhehir-Konia section was completed in 1896.

Abdul Hamid was not yet satisfied, however. He was still without his strategic line to Baghdad. From 1896 onwards, he pressed even harder that the railway line be extended to Baghdad. When the Deutsche Bank failed to respond, the Sultan threatened to give the concession to a French company. This threat did not impress the Deutsche Bank very much. It had maintained friendly relations with the Ottoman Bank which would have been the only 'French company' available to build the line to Baghdad. When the *Anatolische Eisenbahngesellschaft* was first promoted, the Deutsche Bank had been in competition with the all-powerful Banque Impériale Ottomane and had acted as its counterweight. But their rivalry changed into a community of interest during the building of the Eskişhehir-Konia and Alashehir-Afium-Karahissar lines. At the beginning of 1898, Siemens wrote to the Banque Ottomane that he attached the greatest importance to the continuation of their *entente* and to an *'accord parfait'* between them. However, in 1897 the Sultan obtained support from the new German Ambassador in Constantinople, Baron Marschall von Bieberstein. In the following year, Emperor Wilhelm II, who had fallen for the Baghdad Railway project during his trip to the Orient that year, added his support. Wilhelm II and Marschall believed that the construction of the Baghdad Railway with German money would offer excellent opportunities for German economic and diplomatic activity in the Middle East.

The shrewd Abdul Hamid took advantage of Wilhelm's interest to engineer a *fait accompli*, which made it impossible for the Deutsche Bank to withdraw short of a political scandal. During the German Emperor's visit to Constantinople, the Sultan declared his willingness to grant the concession for the Baghdad Railway to a German company. Wilhelm II accepted the offer with great pleasure, and the Deutsche Bank had no choice but to go along. Had the Bank refused the offer, the Emperor's rash diplomacy would have been discredited; no less disastrously, the Bank's reputation would have suffered. Its refusal could have been interpreted as a sign of weakness, not to mention the damage that would have been done to its relationship with the German government, had it left the Emperor 'in the lurch'. Thus the Deutsche Bank was forced into its most spectacular venture abroad, a commitment which it had not really wanted.

In the same way as the Anatolian Railway, the Baghdad Railway received political backing as a result of a diplomatic understanding, except that this time the partners were France and Russia. The German and French ambassadors in Constantinople arranged a Franco-German entente to deal with Ottoman financial matters. Russia was reassured about the construction of the Baghdad Railway by means of an agreement concluded in the same year. According to this agreement, all railway building in Northern Anatolia and Armenia, i.e. in those parts of the Ottoman Empire which bordered on Russian Transcaucasia, was to be reserved for Russia. Thus, there existed for a short while and in the shape of an agreement on Ottoman finance and railways, a Continental Union between Russia, France and Germany against Britain, which Wilhelm II kept on talking about between 1896 and 1905.

In 1899 the *Anatolische Eisenbahngesellschaft* obtained a provisional concession to extend its Eskişhehir-Konia line to Baghdad. The Deutsche Bank wanted to internationalize the financing of this link by calling upon the participation of British and French banks. This did not please Marschall, the German Ambassador in Constantinople; he was of the opinion that the Baghdad Railway must become a 'German national concern'. Yet it was impossible for the Germans to finance the railway on their own because German capital resources were limited. Nor did Siemens's international plan succeed as envisaged by him. He secured the co-operation of the Banque Ottomane on account of its earlier *entente* with the Deutsche Bank. Austria-Hungary and Italy could also be relied upon for limited participation. On the other hand, the London banks displayed the same reserve which they had shown during the Anatolian railway project 10 years earlier. J.P. Morgan & Co., which had intimated an interest earlier on, also declined.

After a study group had worked out the technical details, determined the exact routing and submitted an estimate of the costs, the *Bagdad-Bahn-Gesellschaft* was established in 1903. The company obtained a firm concession to build and operate the railway. The construction was scheduled to take eight years. The estimated costs were 450 million francs. The Ottoman Empire reserved for itself the first refusal on repurchase, and the *Bagdad-Bahn-Gesellschaft* was not allowed to sell the railway to another company without the Government's consent. The company's joint-stock capital was 15 million francs. The Deutsche Bank took over 40% of the shares, the Banque Imperiale Ottomane 30%, the *Anatolische Eisenbahngesellschaft* 10%, the Wiener Bankverein and the Schweizerische Kreditanstalt 7.5% each and the Banca Commerciale Italiana, together with a number of Italian and Ottoman banks, 5%. Thus 50% of the joint-stock capital was in German hands. Germany's indirect share was even larger since German capital had direct stakes in the Wiener Bankverein and particularly in the Banca Commerciale Italiana. According to the statutes of the *Bagdad-Bahn-Gesellschaft* both the president and one of the two vice-presidents were to be German, the other vice-president being French. The board of directors was to consist of 12 Germans, eight Frenchmen, three Turks, two Austrians and two Swiss. Georg Siemens died in 1901, two years before the *Bagdad-Bahn-Gesellschaft* was constituted. Arthur von Gwinner took over as the board member in the Deutsche Bank responsible for the management of railway questions in the Ottoman Empire.

In the spring of 1903, shortly before the *Bagdad-Bahn-Gesellschaft* was constituted, Gwinner tried once more to obtain British participation in the company. This time it looked as if he might succeed. Sir Ernest Cassel (a private banker whose family came from Cologne and who had acquired the nickname 'Windsor-Cassel' because of his business and personal contacts with the Royal Family) and the London bank of J.S. Morgan & Co. (which had been owned for many years by Junius Spencer Morgan, John Pierpont Morgan's father) both showed an interest. They received encouragement from Prime Minister Balfour and Lansdowne, the Foreign Secretary. The ministers furthermore induced Baring Brothers to join Cassel and Morgan. Yet when the matter became public, it was fiercely criticized in the press and the House of Commons. The Liberals opposed British participation in the enterprise because of their traditional hatred of Turkey. In the Conservative camp, some were of the opinion that this railway could threaten India's security, establishing, as it did, a fast connection by land between Central Europe and India. The Government and the bankers retreated before the storm of protest and dropped the idea of British participation.

From 1903, French co-operation in the building of the Baghdad Railway also met with strong opposition. At the crucial moment, the political understanding which had existed between Germany and France about their collaboration over Turkish financial matters could no longer be maintained. Delcassé, the French Foreign Minister, made it a condition of his consent to the participation of French capital that, through the inclusion of British and Russian firms in the contracts to finance, supply and build the railways, they would be effectively internationalized. His stipulation remained unfulfilled, because the German government refused to oblige and because the British abstained. When Delcassé demanded equal representation in capital shares and on the board between the Deutsche Bank and the Ottoman Bank, the former declined. Ignoring French government's advice, the Banque Impériale Ottomane took over 30% of the Baghdad railway shares. In retaliation, Paris blocked the trading of Baghdad Railway bonds on the French capital market. They wished to prevent the Germans from gaining control of the venture by obtaining the capital for it in France. In December 1906 Pichon, Delcassé's successor, gave a further explanation of his Government's position on the Baghdad Railway to Jean Constans, to the French Ambassador in Constantinople. The latter wanted to take up an accommodating attitude, but was told: 'Our policy aims to internationalize the line and not to provide the Germans with the means to build it.' The Ottoman Bank nevertheless remained involved in the *Bagdad-Bahn-Gesellschaft* and maintained its close collaboration with the Deutsche Bank for many more years. In April 1905, both banks even concluded an agreement in which they assured one another that each would offer the other a 25% participation in every major financial project in the Ottoman Empire.

The Baghdad Railway became significant and genuinely profitable only after it had been extended to the Persian Gulf. But inevitably it now began to penetrate into areas where British interests were affected, and even in Baghdad itself. The passenger- and goods traffic between Baghdad and the Shatt-al-Arab was in the hands of a British river shipping company. The Deutsche Bank, which had always tried to co-operate with the British, was fully prepared to respect British interests. Nevertheless, a long Anglo-German tug-of-war ensued over the terminal point of the railway link to be built by the Germans. The British wanted Baghdad to be the limit of the German concession. The *Bagdad-Bahn-Gesellschaft,* which was controlled by the Deutsche Bank, on the other hand, wanted to build up to a point some 500 kilometers outside Basra in order to be able to cash in on the pilgrim traffic from Persia to Mecca.

Once Britain and Russia had settled their disputes in Asia between 1907 and 1910, the balance of power in the East changed against Germany and the Deutsche Bank. The latter had a foretaste of this when the Banque Impériale Ottomane began to lean towards Britain. Whereas the Deutsche Bank had previously been keen to co-operate with British banks in the East, it was now virtually forced to do so. Thenceforth, Gwinner courted Sir Ernest Cassel, and the oil resources in Mesopotamia presented an opportunity to initiate collaboration. In 1901, whilst holding a provisional concession for the Baghdad Railway, the *Anatolische Eisenbahngesellschaft* had been granted another concession to develop and exploit Mesopotamian oil. In the meantime, the question of the concession had become precarious. From 1903, railway construction in Mesopotamia was in the hands of the *Bagdad-Bahn-Gesellschaft,* and the oil concession had never been transferred to this company. Was the concession granted to the *Anatolische Eisenbahngesellschaft* still valid, even if it no longer had anything to do with the Baghdad Railway? As long as there was no interest in Mesopotamian oil, it was not important to clarify this issue. But after 1910, Britain became interested in the oil reserves at Mosul. Oil consumption had been steadily rising since the beginning of the 20th century. Above all, Britain had come to realize sooner than the other powers that oil was of significance as a fuel for warships. British interest in oil from Mosul and the unclarified legal position of who owned the concession became the subject of negotiations between the Deutsche Bank and Cassel.

As a result of these negotiations, the Turkish Petroleum Company was founded in 1912 with a joint-stock capital of £40,000, 50% of which was acquired by Cassel and the National Bank of Turkey which he had founded, and 25% each by the Deutsche Bank and Royal Dutch Shell. In the spring of 1914, the British government insisted that the Anglo-Persian Oil Company should also have a direct stake in Turkish Petroleum. This was accomplished by the latter doubling its joint-stock capital and the Anglo-Persian company acquiring all the new shares. At the same time, Cassel and the Turkish National Bank of Turkey handed their shares over to the Royal Dutch Shell and the Deutsche Bank so that they would each retain their 25% participation. After preparatory talks between Cassel and Gwinner, this arrangement was laid down in February 1914 in an agreement between the British and German governments, in which the whole complex of Mesopotamia, including the Baghdad Railway, was settled between the two countries.

Following the Anglo-Russian accord, the British government at first contemplated internationalizing the Baghdad Railway. On 21 January 1911, Sir Edward Grey, the British Foreign Secretary, told the Russian Ambassador in London that his Government would like to internationalize the Baghdad Railway, but that this would require an agreement between Britain, Russia, France and Germany. Britain's plan for an agreement between the four powers was thwarted by a unilateral action on the part of the Russians. In 1911 Russia and Germany concluded a treaty in which Germany recognized Russian interests in Northern Persia; in return the Russians agreed to an arrangement favourable to Germany concerning railway construction in the Mesopotamian area. Under the terms of this agreement, the Russians were to build a railway from Teheran to Khāniquin through Turkish territory near the Persian border; the *Bagdad-Bahn-Gesell-schaft*, on the other hand, was to construct a branch-line from there to Baghdad. Had the project been realized, the Germans and the Russians would have secured for themselves a good share in the profits arising from the journey of pilgrims between Persia, Russian Armenia and Mecca.

The Russian-German treaty forced Britain and France to conclude separate agreements with Germany. The Anglo-German agreement on Mesopotamia was prepared for and facilitated by the accord on the Mosul oil question which the Deutsche Bank and Sir Ernest Cassel had concluded. In February 1914, whilst the Turkish Petroleum Company was being reconstructed, the controversy between Germany and Britain over the Baghdad Railway was also settled. A proposal by Cassel was the basis of a compromise between the two sides. According to this proposal, the *Bagdad-Bahn-Gesellschaft* was to build the railway to Basra. British companies alone were to be allowed to build the remaining link to the mouth of Shatt-al-Arab; the Baghdad Railway was not to grant preferential rates to any nation; British investors were to participate in the company's capital; finally, the British shipping monopoly on the Euphrates and Tigris rivers was recognized by the Germans, and the Germans withdrew their plan to build an irrigation scheme in Mesopotamia. At the same time, Germany and France also came to an accord on Turkish financial and railway questions. Under the terms of a Franco-German agreement of February 1914, the Banque Ottomane withdrew from the *Bagdad-Bahn-Gesellschaft;* its place was to be taken by the British; Germany left railway construction in Syria and East Anatolia to the French in collaboration with the Russians; finally, the Germans and the French agreed to collaborate on the consolidation of Ottoman public finances which were once again in disarray after the Balkan Wars. Thus, on the eve of the First World War, the economic and political rivalries between the great powers in the Middle East had been resolved. They had no bearing on the outbreak of war in 1914.

In order to be able to continue financing the Baghdad Railway, the Deutsche Bank sold the *Betriebsgesellschaft für Orientalische Eisenbahnen* in 1913 to an Austro-Hungarian syndicate of banks which operated a railway network of 1,260 kilometers on the Balkan Peninsula. The rail connection between the Bosphorus and the Persian Gulf was completed only after the First World War. But by then it was no longer a concern of the Deutsche Bank. In 1918, the railway on Mesopotamian territory was handed over to the new State of Iraq; the Anatolian railway system became Turkish state property in 1921 under the terms of the Treaty of Angora.

3. Capital Export and Foreign Policy, 1880-1914

The financially powerful and advanced industrial powers of Britain, France and Germany possessed, in their export of capital, an instrument of foreign policy which the financially weak, less industrialized great powers of Russia, Austria-Hungary and Japan did not command. The United States was in a special position, being, on the one hand, heavily indebted to Europe from about 1890 onwards, and exporting capital on a massive scale to the Caribbean and to a lesser extent to the central and southern parts of South America and to China, on the other. To be sure, long before the period of 19th-century industrialization and imperialism, foreign policy had been supported by financial levers. Rome and Athens had been very good at it, and in early modern times England and France strengthened their policy of alliances through systematic financial subsidies, with the French going considerably further than the British in this respect. The British paid subsidies to allied states only in wartime, whilst the French granted several states subsidies in times of war and peace, on condition that they provided auxiliary troops in the event of war or granted French troops free passage through their territory or simply remained neutral. This costly foreign policy had been one of the causes of the desperate state of French public finances in the 18th century.

If compared with the policy of subsidies in earlier centuries, capital export obviously represented a wholly different kind of financial relationship between two countries. The subsidies were payments made by one government to another in return for political and military services that had already been rendered or were expected from the recipient. Such subsidies were not therefore credits on which interest was due and which had to be paid back; and they were given exclusively for political rather than economic reasons. The export of capital, on the other hand, involved business transactions in the private sector of the economy, i.e., investments and long-term credits from commercial banks and other private investors. In these cases, the point of private economic activity was a decisive factor: amortization and the interest-bearing capacity of capital. The governments of capital exporting countries could pursue diplomatic aims so long as these did not collide with the economic objective.

The banks of the major industrial powers have at times also been prepared to undertake such international financial transactions which their governments had encouraged or urged them to engage in. Basic developments in international political relations have been greatly advanced by the international activities of banks. On the other hand, the banks were not always prepared to follow their governments' schemes and wishes. British investors participated in politically motivated foreign investments only when they had been given government guarantees. After a number of setbacks, Foreign Secretary Grey, in a House of Commons speech shortly before the First World War, regretted that the British government was unable to exert an influence on the foreign business of British banks.

Nor were the governments in France and Germany entirely happy with the way in which the policies of the banks were attuned to their foreign policy, even if they had greater opportunities to influence international banking business and were at least able to prevent exports of capital which were politically undesirable. The French Ambassador to Rome, Camille Barrère, reported to Paris on 11 October 1910 that German banks subordinated their business dealings to the national interest. French banks, by contrast, evaded diplomatic influence. The French government viewed the participation of the Banque Ottomane in the *Bagdad-Bahn-Gesellschaft* as negatively as it did the earlier collaboration of the Comptoir National d'Escompte de Paris and the Société Générale with the Disconto-Gesellschaft and the Bleichröder bank in the Rumanian state loan. Of course, it looked different when seen from abroad. As Count von Wedel, the German Ambassador to Vienna, remarked in his report of 8 July 1907 in no other country was capital so devoted to serving national policy as in France. Yet, in comparing the attitude of French and German bankers towards their governments' policies, one could agree with Barrère that the German banks generally displayed greater 'national discipline' than their French counterparts. On the other hand, the combined efforts of French foreign policy and capital export were, in so far as they got off the ground, incomparably more effective than those of Germany. It is that which makes Wedel's judgement plausible.

It was considerably simpler for both the French and German governments to prevent undesirable capital exports than to encourage politically desirable ones. They had sufficient institutional leverage to do this (see above pp. 119ff. and pp. 123ff.), and the French government in particular made extensive use of these opportunities.

Just as governments were seeking to utilize the banks' international business for foreign policy purposes, so the banks in turn wanted their governments' political backing for their foreign transactions. Until the end of the 19th century governments harboured many reservations about this. Bismarck's reply to the Deutsche Bank of the summer of 1888 in connection with the Anatolian railway concession (see above p. 139) is typical not only of the Reich Chancellor's attitude towards these questions, but also characterizes more generally the position of contemporary statesmen towards the problem of protecting foreign trade against risks. The British government was likewise of the opinion that British citizens investing their money abroad did so at their own risk. It is important to emphasize this, since the image of the British government sending a gunboat to the main port of a state which was in arrears with its payments to its British creditors, thus presenting a kind of order to pay, was firmly fixed in the minds of many Germans. This popular idea is mistaken. It cannot even be supported by reference to the British intervention in Egypt in 1882. British troops occupied Egypt after Arabi Pasha's revolt in 1882 not in order to protect the interests of private British creditors (quite apart from the fact that the British Suez Canal shares were in possession of the Government), but to establish military control over the Suez Canal, the shortest sea route to India. Only later, under Grey, was the Foreign Office prepared to offer more help in protecting private British investments abroad. Thus, on 10 July 1914, Grey declared in the House of Commons that his Government was prepared to give 'the utmost support we can' to British capital investment 'in any part of the world', so long as there were no serious political objections. His determination to back private foreign investment was also designed to encourage private investors to make such investments abroad as would be particularly desirable from the viewpoint of British diplomacy.

Political support for private foreign investments was most marked in the United States from the 1890s onwards, in particular from 1897 when President McKinley took office and the imperialist tendencies of the Republicans fully asserted themselves. These tendencies were rooted in economic and social crises which set in when the opening-up and settlement of the continent came to an end. There was also the collapse of railway speculation in 1893 and a change in the flow of immigrants, which was no longer dominated by natives of Western and Central Europe, but by people from Southern and Eastern Europe. At the same time, American business witnessed how the non-European markets and sources of raw material were being carved up among the European great powers and, above all, how European capital began to dominate in South America. The South American capital market was then controlled by nine big banks of which seven were British, one German and one Italian with strong German capital participation. There were, however, strong internal obstacles to attempts to conquer a separate American colonial empire. The United States had emerged from a fight for independence against colonial rule, and the rejection of colonial rule *per se* remained so strong that it was impossible to contemplate the conquest of colonies. These traditions had to be taken into account by the supporters of American imperialism.

America's territorial expansion was therefore restricted to naval bases in Puerto Rico, Hawaii, Guam, the Philippines, one of the Samoan Islands and the Panama Canal Zone. An 'informal empire' was established in the Caribbean, thanks to the joint effort of the Government, banks and big commercial companies. This empire consisted of monopolies and concessions to American companies in return for accepting state loans for the Central American states concerned. Due to the unstable political conditions in Latin America these investments were exposed to greater political risks than investments in European countries or in colonies. This gave the American government cause to send warships and marines to protect American investments and to prop up governments which co-operated with American investors or to push a defaulting debtor state into meeting its commitments. Thus the United States intervened in Nicaragua in 1909 and in Haiti six years later. The expression 'dollar diplomacy' was coined to describe the interplay of capital export and power-political expansion in establishing the 'informal empire'.

In order to reconcile dollar diplomacy with the principles of American foreign policy as laid down in the Monroe Doctrine, President Theodore Roosevelt, in a message to Congress of 6 November 1904, produced an amendment to that Doctrine in which he stated that the United States had the duty to intervene, should an American state commit or permit acts harmful to the rights and interests of American citizens. In 1912, William H. Taft, his successor, provided something like an official definition and interpretation of dollar diplomacy: 'The diplomacy of the present Administration seeks to respond to modern ideas of commercial intercourse. This policy has been characterized as substituting dollars for bullets. It is one that appeals alike to idealistic humanitarian sentiments, to the dictates of sound policy and strategy and to legitimate commercial aims. It is an effort frankly directed to the increase of American trade upon the axiomatic principle that the Government of the United States shall extend all proper support to every legitimate and beneficial American enterprise abroad.'

In 1913, Woodrow Wilson, a Democrat and professed opponent of dollar diplomacy, took office as President, and this seemed to signal the end of dollar diplomacy. In his foreign policy programme, he proclaimed that his diplomacy would no longer be guided by the notion of economic exploitation nor by the selfish interests of a small group of financiers. The Under-Secretary in the State Department, William J. Bryan, informed the banks that they had no legal claim to the U.S. Government protecting their foreign investments. On the other hand, Wilson recognized that the United States could not simply abandon the role they had assumed during the previous 15 years. And just as Taft had gone into Nicaragua in 1909, Wilson intervened militarily in Haiti in 1915, where the domestic situation had run out of control and sizeable American investments were threatened. The connection between capital export and foreign policy in the diplomacy of the dollar was not a unilateral one, however, in which the initiative came exclusively from the banks and companies which invested abroad, with the flag merely following in order to protect them; bankers were often pressed by their government to undertake certain capital investments in some Latin American country because such investments were regarded as a useful device by the United States to gain political control at a later stage.

During the first two-thirds of the 19th century private bankers conducted loan transactions with foreign governments without their own governments interfering or seeking to gain political advantages. From the last quarter of the 19th century, however, the governments of capital exporting countries have tried continuously to turn the export of capital to good use in their pursuit of foreign policy objectives. The impact of international financial relations on diplomacy will now be examined by reference to a number of important events before 1914.

The political effect of the export of capital was first reflected in Russo-German and Franco-Russian relations in 1887, when Bismarck issued the ban on Russian securities (see above p. 123). If Bismarck believed he could put the Russians under pressure by excluding their securities from the German capital market, he was mistaken. His ban on guarantees promoted the very Franco-Russian rapprochement which he had feared and wished to prevent when he concluded the Reinsurance Treaty of 18 June 1887. The French willingly took on the task of supplying Russia with credits. By the end of 1888, French loans to Russia had reached 1.4 milliard francs. By contrast, the Reich's total debt amounted to just 721 million marks by the end of the same year.

Thenceforth the financial relationship between France and Russia grew closer and closer. By the time the Franco-Russian Military Convention was signed on 18 August 1892, Russia had received from France more than six milliard francs in loans. These capital movements did much to smooth the path for the Franco-Russian Alliance, though they obviously did not do so alone. It was hastened by Germany when Leo von Caprivi, Bismarck's successor, refused to renew the Russo-German Reinsurance Treaty. He took this step despite Russian willingness to scrap the Treaty's top secret appendix which, if it had been leaked, would have compromised Germany's relations with Austria-Hungary. Yet the origin of the Franco-Russian Alliance can be traced back to the period before Caprivi's failure to renew the Reinsurance Treaty: it was rooted in Bismarck's decision to exclude Russian securities from the German capital market. And it was certainly not Bleichröder, Bismarck's banker and friend, who counselled this ill-considered and fateful decision. Bleichröder was a 'Russophile' among his colleagues and very much involved with the Tsarist Empire. Not surprisingly, he also worked for the abolition of the ban in later years. It must be concluded, therefore, that Bismarck himself undermined the Reinsurance Treaty. What is more: the ban on guarantees was triggered off by a minor incident, i.e. a decree by the Tsar which excluded foreigners from acquiring and utilizing real estate in the western provincial districts of the Russian Empire and which affected the Germans most.

French loans continued to provide the cement which held the Franco-Russian Alliance together. Several of these loans helped to finance the construction of strategically important railways in the western *guberniyas* of the Russian Empire. The French general staff kept pressing for this, believing it to be of the utmost importance that, in the event of war with Germany, the Russian army should be capable of relieving the French in the West through speedy mobilization and swift attack along Germany's eastern frontier. This was the rationale behind the construction of the railway network in western Russia. It was to make the quick assembly and movement of troops possible. To finance these railways, loans were placed on the Paris capital market in 1898, 1900, 1901 and 1913.

At the same time that France replaced Germany as Russia's foremost creditor, Italy began to move away from France and towards Germany. Following the renewal of the German-Austrian-Italian Triple Alliance in 1887, the French banks sold the Italian government bonds in their possession and bought Russian securities. But German banks came in to fill the gap left by Paris. By 1890, the state of Italian public finances had become so precarious that France was once more approached, again without success. The head of the Paris Rothschild Bank, Baron Alphonse de Rothschild, complying with an agreement he had made with the French Foreign Minister Alexandre Ribot, refused the issue of a new Italian state loan. Thereupon German banks formed the 'Consortium for Italian Business' and took over the loan. It appears that the German government exerted some pressure on a number of banks to join in. This emerges from a remark by Gerson Bleichröder who complained to Herbette, the French Ambassador to Berlin, in November 1890 that he had taken part in the scheme only because the Emperor, through Undersecretary Marschall, had appealed to his patriotism.

From 1892, the Continental powers regrouped to form two blocs: the Triple Alliance and the Franco-Russian military alliance. Britain persisted in her 'splendid isolation'; but, with Russia expanding her influence in the Far East and with war against France threatening over the Sudan, Colonial Secretary Joseph Chamberlain and Balfour, the Chancellor of the Exchequer and future Prime Minister, thought it prudent to look around for an ally. The Reich seemed to be a potential partner. There had been occasional frictions with Germany; but there were no major conflicts of interest of the kind that existed with France and Russia. In the spring of 1898, Chamberlain, with Salisbury's knowledge and cautious approval, began to explore the possibility of an alliance with Germany. The plan came to nought. Salisbury had no confidence in German policy; Wilhelm II, Bülow and Holstein did not trust the British. The only result of the Anglo-German negotiations in the spring and summer of 1898 was a financial and colonial agreement which Balfour and the German Ambassador to London, Count Hatzfeld, signed on 30 August 1898.

This agreement came about because of the chronic financial plight of the Kingdom of Portugal. In 1898 representatives of the Portuguese government were in London to negotiate a loan to be granted by the British government. Desperate to obtain the money, the Portuguese let it be known that they would, if necessary, pledge the income from, and jurisdiction over, their colonies as collateral. The German government, learning about this, intimated to the British government that it had an interest in the fate of the Portuguese colonies. Thus the question of the Portuguese loan and its guarantees came to be connected with the explorations of an Anglo-German alliance. And some progress was made: the two countries agreed that, should Portugal receive a loan from one of the two governments against a pledge of customs duties and other revenues from Angola, Mozambique or Portuguese Timor, the other government would be informed and be given an opportunity to participate in the loan scheme. In a secret supplementary convention, both governments agreed that they would be given control over those areas whose returns had been pledged to them, in the event that Portugal would be unable to meet her financial obligations and thus be forced to surrender her own sovereignty rights in the colonies. Ultimately, these conventions did not help in the Germans' quest for further colonies. The British government informed the Portuguese of the contents of those parts of the Anglo-German agreement which were not secret. By waving this agreement about in Paris, the Portuguese government came to a new arrangement with its creditors in France. A little later, Portugal was able to place a loan on the London capital market without British government participation. Above, all, in 1899 Britain secretly guaranteed Portugal's possessions under the terms of the Treaty of Windsor. The German government had been duped.

Later attempts to create an Anglo-German alliance also ended in failure, and in 1904 Britain came to an agreement with France, her former rival in world politics: Morocco and Egypt were to become French and British spheres of interest respectively. This agreement laid the foundations for the Anglo-French *Entente Cordiale*. In the years preceeding its conclusion, a large volume of French money kept pouring into London. It appears that the diplomatic negotiations between the two governments were boosted by politically inspired financial activities, even if the French government abstained from using the *'arme financière'* at this time. In order to finance the Boer War, Britain had issued three big loans abroad in 1900, 1901 and 1902; but they were placed with American rather than French banks, as British bonds were not traded on the Paris capital market in those years. This did not prevent French money from flowing into Britain after 1900, largely because of the attractively high rates of interest arising from a shortage of capital following the outbreak of the Boer War. Towards the end of 1903, against the background of financial recovery, the Bank of England lowered its discount rate which was followed by a reduction in the bank rate. After this, the flow of French money into London dried up quite suddenly and before the Anglo-French negotiations had been successfully concluded.

However little the influx of French money into Britain between 1900 and 1903 had been motivated by political considerations, France's position as a creditor was massively exploited both as a means of exerting political pressure and as a bait in French diplomacy *vis-à-vis* Russia and Italy between 1904 and 1906, i.e. from the Russo-Japanese War until the end of the First Moroccan Crisis. When in the autumn of 1904 Russia ran into military and financial difficulties during the war against Japan, the Tsarist government tried to obtain a loan on the Paris capital market. Maurice Rouvier, the French Finance Minister, who was himself a banker set several conditions for admitting the loan to the Paris stock exchange, which did not please the Russians. Arguing that the French capital market was already saturated with Russian government bonds, Rouvier stipulated that the loan should not be issued before 1905 and that it was to be offered for international subscription. Furthermore, the Russian government was asked to commit itself to ordering war supplies in France. Russia refused and took up a loan of over 500 million marks at 5.5% on the Berlin capital market. The Berlin

banks accepted the loan at a rate of 90.5% and issued it at a rate of 95%.
Russia was very soon in need of another loan to finance the war. In
March 1905, the Russian government began negotiations with a group of
Paris banks headed by 'Paribas' about a loan of 600 million francs. But
when news of the Russian defeat at Mukden arrived later that month, the
French dropped out. The whole plan now seemed unsound to them. The
Russian government had asked Maurice Bompard, the French Ambassador
to St. Petersburg, to advise his superiors in Paris that this negative attitude
might have unpleasant consequences for France. The significance of this
message emerged in May. As in the previous autumn, Finance Minister
Kokovtsov turned to the Berlin banking community and was offered a big
loan to clear the Russian government debt. However, the Berlin banks were
not in a position to provide the money from their own resources. Consequently they offered the Paris Rothschild Bank and the Crédit Foncier de
France a participation in the loan. Both institutes declined in July 1905.

Russia found herself in a critical situation at this time: the largest part
of her fleet had been destroyed at Tsushima; the Russian army had suffered
serious losses in land warfare against Japan although it had not been decisively defeated; since the end of January 1905, strikes and unrest had
spread across Russia; the deficit in the Russian budget had become enormous;
out of consideration for Britain, France had maintained strict neutrality,
much to the disappointment of her Russian ally; after all, they were under
no obligation *vis-à-vis* Britain in the event of a war involving Japan. Wilhelm
II and Bülow believed — the latter more sceptically — that they should take
advantage of this situation and induce Russia to join a defensive alliance
with Germany in which France was to be included at a later stage. Wilhelm
II's old dream of forming a Continental Union against Britain re-emerged
with this plan. However, as the German banks were in no way able to
satisfy the Russian government's credit requirements without French
participation, the Emperor's attempt first to form a Russo-German alliance
and to offer France no more than the possibility of joining later, did not
stand much chance of success. Wilhelm II and Bülow wanted to achieve
more than was politically feasible and more than Germany had the capacity
to pay in the form of credits. Friedrich von Holstein, the head of the
Political Department at the Foreign Ministry, correctly appreciated this.
On 22 July 1905, two days before the Emperor and the Tsar met on the
Finnish island of Bjoerkoe, he wrote in a note to Bülow: 'Our stipulation
that Russia must first sign up with us before she starts to negotiate with
France about a triangular association is out-of-date for two reasons: The
Rouvier Cabinet, it is true, will not be so totally opposed to Germany's
affiliation as Delcassé would have been. However, Russia is today more
dependent on France in financial matters than she was six months ago;
this means that she would not wish to take such a grave step without
France's prior consent.'

Although Wilhelm II was able to persuade Tsar Nicholas II to sign a
treaty on 25 July 1905 which he had drawn up before the Bjoerkoe meeting,

no Russian or German Minister or Undersecretary of State had been present and those responsible both in Berlin and St. Petersburg disagreed with its text once they saw it. Whereas Reich Chancellor Bülow objected only to a few sentences and insisted on eliminating them before ratification, the Russian Ministers rejected the treaty *in toto*. Even Witte, who generally favoured a rapprochement with Germany, was opposed to ratification. He made it clear to the Tsar that Russia needed France from the financial point of view and that the Berlin capital market was no substitute for the Parisian one. He also aptly remarked that the loan which the Berlin bankers were offering could not be floated without French help. In order to avoid ratifying the Bjoerkoe Treaty without offending the Germans too much, the Russian government decided to propose to the Germans such changes to the text as would render it worthless, whereupon the whole project was quickly buried.

The loan which the Berlin banks had been planning to raise with French help failed because the latter refused to participate. Subsequently negotiations were started to raise an international loan to be issued in France by the 'Paribas', in Britain by the Baring Brothers, in Germany by Mendelssohn & Co. and in the United States by J.P. Morgan & Co. When, owing to continued internal unrest, the price of Russian government securities fell, St. Petersburg broke off negotiations fearing that the rate of issue — and thus the yield of the loan — would be too low. In the meantime, the Russian financial situation deteriorated further. Something had to be done. In January 1906 Kokovtsov approached Rouvier with a plan to place a Russian state loan of over 1.2 milliard francs on the Paris stock exchange. This time the French Prime Minister insisted on two conditions before a loan scheme would be admitted and turned into a success: the first was that Russia would have to make a successful transition to a constitutional monarchy, as promised by the Tsar in his Manifesto of 17/30 October 1905, to help stabilize the country internally; secondly, the Algeciras Conference on the Moroccan problem which had just opened would have to yield a result satisfactory to France. Quotation of a new Russian state loan on the Paris stock exchange would be possible only after these conditions had been met. These were, no doubt, very far-reaching and stiff political demands. Concealed in the formula that the Algeciras Conference must lead to a result satisfactory to France was the idea that Russia support French interests unconditionally, in sharp contrast to the neutral attitude which France had adopted earlier during the Russo-Japanese War. The demand that constitutional reform in Russia must succeed and lead to internal stabilization sprang from France's worries about the political viability of Tsarism and about the safety of her extensive investments in Russia. However understandable the demand may have been, it nevertheless constituted a clear interference in the domestic affairs of Russia. Witte reacted to these tough conditions by obtaining a credit of over 400 million rubles at 5% from the Disconto-Gesellschaft, Mendelssohn, Bleichröder in Berlin.

Rouvier immediately realized that just at the start of the Morocco

Conference, when France needed her ally's political support, Russia had begun to distance herself from Paris and had drawn closer to Germany. In order to prevent a further deterioration of relations, Rouvier hastily mediated a French loan of over 100 million rubles at 5.5%. This still did not cover Russia's deficit, however, and another 600 million rubles had to be found. A loan of 200 million rubles, which was issued in Russia, proved unsuccessful in view of the uncertainty about the future internal development of the Tsarist Empire. In the end, Russia remained dependent on French capital as the Berlin market, though willing, was unable to supply further funds. The problem was that the Russian government needed the loan, and needed it very quickly, because the First Duma was due to assemble in May 1906. Thereafter it would be necessary to obtain its consent for the issue of the loan. In short, pressure of time worsened the Russian government's financial difficulties, and it had no other choice but to take up the loan in France on French terms: 1) the French banks would accept the loan at 83.5%, well below the earlier transfer rate of 90% and above; 2) the loan was to be disposed of to the public at a price of 88%, again well below the customary rate of 95%; 3) no further Russian loan was to be issued in France for two years; 4) the French government was to be informed by Russia of other proposed foreign loans. In order to secure the placing of the loan among the French public, a favourable press was required. To this effect, the Russian government paid 'slush' money to such papers as *Le Petit Journal, Le Petit Parisien, Le Temps* and *L'Auxiliaire* (100,000 francs each, *Le Journal* (80,000 francs), *L'Echo de Paris* (70,000 francs) and *Le Matin* and *L'Eclair* (60,000 francs each). And of course Russia supported France at the Algeciras Conference from which Paris emerged victorious over Germany.

Like Russia, Italy was also prompted to support France over Morocco with the help of a credit which had political strings attached to it. After Italy's attempt to conquer Ethiopia in 1896 had failed, her colonial aspirations shifted to North Africa and aimed at the annexation of Tripolis. As France was herself strongly engaged in that part of the African continent, Italy was compelled to come to an understanding with France. In December 1900, Italy and France agreed that Morocco and Tripolis would be their respective spheres of influence, and in November 1902 both states concluded a secret neutrality treaty. It was the beginning of Italy's gradual alienation from the Triple Alliance. A year later, the Italian government, in an attempt to consolidate the national debt, made a move to convert the 5% loan into a 3.5% annuity. They could hardly expect much help from the German capital market. Prime Minister Giovanni Giolitti and his Finance Minister Luigi Luzzatti therefore applied to the French government for permission to go to the Paris capital market, hinting darkly that should they fail, the present Italian government would be superseded by one headed by Sidney Sonnino, who was reputed to be pro-German. This threat made little impression on the French. They knew very well that their banks had more than once been called upon to assist the German banks with short-term credits. Camille Barrère, the French Ambassador to Rome, turned the tables on the Italian government and demanded in return for financial support *'une marque finale et décisive de confiance en soutenant la France sur le terrain politique'*. After this, negotiations to convert the debt dragged on until 1906. They ended with Italy receiving French financial help in return for a promise to support France at the Algeciras Conference.

The Algeciras Agreement of 7 April 1906 did not settle the Moroccan Question permanently. In 1911, French troops occupied Morocco. Paris established a protectorate, and this led to another crisis between France and Germany. In order to put Germany under pressure, the French banks recalled, on their government's recommendation, all short-term credits from Germany. This resulted in a credit squeeze in the Reich; yet the German money- and capital markets did not collapse, as French short-term credits were replaced by money from American banks. It was the second time that the Americans made their appearance as money-lenders to one of the major industrial and commercial countries. The first occasion was when they helped Britain during the Boer War. The end of the Agadir Crisis did not lead to a resumption of the short-term credit business between German and French banks. The Germans had come to realize in the course of the crisis which had just passed what were the dangers of a strong dependence on French short-term money.

Germany had acquired an influential position in the Ottoman Empire through the construction of the Anatolian Railway and of the Baghdad Railway and by sending military instructors. Their position was put in jeopardy after the Revolution of July 1908. The Young Turks first deposed the Grand Visier and then, in April 1909, Sultan Abdul Hamid, and both had been advocates of a pro-German policy. The new Government tried to re-establish closer relations with Britain. In September 1908, the Turkish Ambassador to London mentioned to Grey that his government was anxious to obtain a British loan of one million Turkish pounds. He requested the British government's help in mediating this loan. Grey first approached the Rothschild Bank in London. But Nathaniel Rothschild refused to accept the Turkish loan. The British public had purchased very few Turkish bonds in recent years and to issue a Turkish loan in London ran the risk of failure. Baring Brothers also thought it impossible to place a Turkish loan on the London capital market and hence refused. Grey was forced to inform the Ambassador that, much to his regret, it was not possible at present to provide help. Mindful of the strong support which French policy in the Middle East was receiving through the Banque Impériale Ottomane and which Germany gained from the Deutsche Bank, Grey now turned to Sir Ernest Cassel. London society still reguarded Cassel a half-foreigner, and he was keen to prove his loyalty to his country. He was therefore much more willing to consider an approach by the British government than the other London bankers. In 1909 and with Grey's backing, Cassel founded the National Bank of Turkey as a bank to deal with Turkey's credit and investment business. The Government demonstrated its interest in the bank by nominating a high civil servant as its president. Yet British investors failed to give support to the National Bank of Turkey, and it was unable to fulfil the expectations of its founders.

After the rebuff in London, the Young Turks made another attempt to obtain a loan in 1908, this time with the help of the Ottoman Bank. In 1910 the Turkish government needed more money; but, after consultation with the French government, the Ottoman Bank laid down very stiff conditions. The French government wanted to use the government of the Ottoman Empire as a lever against the Deutsche Bank to give way to French demands over the *Baghdad-Bahn-Gesselschaft*. Resisting a French *diktat*, the Turks turned to London, where their prospects were better than in 1908, now that the National Bank of Turkey had been established. Sir Ernest Cassel was prepared to mediate a loan for them on favourable conditions. At this point, the French government intervened in London. It informed the British government through its Ambassador, Paul Cambon, that Cassel's behaviour contradicted the spirit of the *'Entente Cordiale'*. At the insistence of the Foreign Office, Cassel dropped his offer to the Turks. Through the good offices of the Deutsche Bank, the Ottoman Empire finally received a loan of over six million Turkish pounds on the German capital market. It served to strengthen German-Turkish relations which had been weakening since the Revolution of 1908.

In much the same way as the French government had accelerated Italy's alienation from the Triple Alliance by attaching political conditions to loans, it also tried to undermine the relationship between Germany and Austria-Hungary. The first opportunity arose in 1909 when the Hungarian government requested a loan. The Hungarians had tried to place a loan of over 500 million francs on the Paris capital market. The French banks were prepared to accept it, and the French government was even keener to admit this loan to the Paris stock exchange. Here was an opportunity to counteract Hungary's financial dependence on German capital. However, the project miscarried when the Russian government protested in Paris and the German government intervened in Vienna and Budapest. Faced with an urgent request by the Reich government, the Berlin banks, though saturated with Hungarian securities, were prepared to issue the Hungarian loan. Another opportunity presented itself to France in 1911, when Austria-Hungary's Foreign Minister, Baron Alois Aehrenthal, explored the possibility of a loan in Paris. This project also miscarried, as Aehrenthal was not prepared to give the political guarantees demanded by the French government. The French hoped the Austro-Hungarian government could be persuaded to give an undertaking not to use the loan for military purposes. But the latter wanted the money precisely for this purpose. There was another factor which contributed to the failure of the Franco-Austrian negotiations: the Russian government objected vehemently because a French loan would strengthen the Dual Monarchy, their main opponent.

Anglo-German relations had deteriorated seriously when Germany intervened in Morocco. There was also the naval rivalry which had grown since 1905 to a point where Britain preferred to come to an understanding with Russia, its main opponent in world politics since 1815. According to a hypothesis which was promoted by both German nationalists and Marxists, the Anglo-German antagonism was a result of their economic competition. This hypothesis is perfectly plausible as long as one knows nothing about Anglo-German economic and commercial relations. If, on the other hand, the statistically measurable traffic of goods between the two countries is considered, the hypothesis loses its persuasiveness. Next to the British Empire, Germany was Britain's main supplier and main customer, and Britain was Germany's main trading partner. There were cartels of German and British enterprises. For these reasons, leading enterprises and entrepreneurs in both countries tried to improve their political relations. In 1906 Adolph Salomonsohn, one of the owners of the Disconto-Gesellschaft, together with representatives of Berlin businessmen, the Saxon textile industry and the firms of Haniel and Bayer (Leverkusen) promoted a campaign for an Anglo-German understanding, which was also supported by a number of academics and artists.

In Britain similar views were represented by the Anglo-German Union Club, whose members included the bankers Schroeder and Beit, the latter being the financiers of Cecil Rhodes. The effect was not impressive. The efforts made by Albert Ballin, the director of HAPAG, and by Sir Ernest Cassel were much more far-reaching. The Hamburg banker Max M. Warburg, who had known Cassel since his apprenticeship in London in 1891, introduced Ballin to 'Windsor-Cassel'. The German shipowner and the London banker acted as intermediaries in the naval talks which the German and British governments had been holding since 1909. On Ballin's and Cassel's initiative the British War Minister Haldane visited Berlin in 1912, in a final attempt to achieve a general Anglo-German understanding. Its failure was due not to economic rivalry, but to the Reich government's firm commitment to naval armaments and also to the two countries' mutual political distrust which became unbridgeable.

In summarizing the relationship between capital export and international relations before 1914, the following picture emerges: the international movements of capital did not contribute to the origins of the First World War. However, in some cases they played a role in the grouping and regrouping of alliances. The banks did not take the initiative in this but, on the contrary, complied with their governments' requests. French capital export was the most effective politically, certainly in Russia and Italy. By contrast, half of Germany's foreign investments went to countries which sided with the Reich's enemies during the First World War. German capital export had obviously been determined more by economic than by world-political calculations. On the whole, however, it should not be overlooked that, where it mattered, the greater political effectiveness of French capital export was not due to the fact that French banks could be deployed more easily for political aims than German ones, but that the French capital market was considerably better supplied with funds than the German one.

In this respect, French foreign policy had an advantage over German diplomacy, and it used this advantage with great skill. It seems that in this ability to influence the power relations of two rival capital exporting countries lies the most important political effect on the export of capital before 1914.

VI Banking Systems in the Major Industrial and Commercial Countries before 1914

1. Britain

The British banking system was — and still is today — remarkable for the clear division of functions between different types of banks: the big deposit banks structured as joint-stock banks, the merchant banks, the overseas- and colonial banks, the post-office savings bank and private savings banks. Issuing- and investment business, excluding foreign government loans, was undertaken by special institutions which did not belong to the banking sector. Thus large areas of business which the major German banks and the French *banque d'affaires* carried out as a matter of course were handled in Britain by firms which were not regarded as banks. A further characteristic feature of the British banking system was its high degree of concentration which existed even before 1914: in 1884, 118 joint-stock banks and 207 private banking firms operated in England and Wales; by 1913, there were only 43 joint-stock banks and about 70 private banking houses. In this connection, another peculiarity must be mentioned. The statistical data on concentration in British banking refer only to England and Wales; Scotland and Ireland, though part of Britain by this time, had a different banking structure and their credit institutions enjoyed special privileges. Finally, the London Bankers' Clearing House is also a special feature of the British banking system.

The Bank of England, with its Banking Department, was the biggest of all deposit banks before the First World War. As a central issuing bank the Bank of England was a public institution and became a state bank in 1946. Special legislation had been required at the time of its foundation. There were also strict regulations relating to the issue of notes which was in the hands of the Issue Department. The Bank's shareholders, however, were exclusively private persons, and so the Banking Department hardly differed at all from those deposit banks which were private joint-stock companies. The Banking Department of the Bank of England maintained a special and continuous relationship with the British government. It kept the state accounts. All income from taxes, customs, stamp duties and the surpluses of the postal and telegraphic services were paid into the Government's account at the Bank of England; the Banking Department also remitted all the Government's outgoings for public expenditure. The Banking Department administered the state debt and placed new state loans for subscription.

The British government did not entrust a bank or banking syndicate with the issue of its loans, but had them issued by the Bank of England. Interested private parties could buy their state securities in Threadneedle

Street, the Bank's head office, or in one of its 11 branches. The Banking Department was the largest deposit bank in terms of its own capital funds. The Bank of England's joint-stock capital and reserves of approximately £18 million were almost as large as the capital and reserves of the then two biggest private joint-stock banks, the London City & Midland Bank and Lloyds Bank, taken together. The Banking Department was not the largest as regards deposits; but it was certainly one of the biggest deposit banks in the country, with all the deposit banks as well as the Government keeping deposits in the Banking Department. These 'bankers balances' were used partly for clearings between the London Clearing Banks. In the main, however, they represented the cash reserves of the deposit banks. Private commercial banks were not obliged by law to keep any reserves in the central issuing bank; nor did the Bank pay interest on deposits. This did not deter the commercial banks from keeping most of their cash reserves with the Bank of England. They did so because the Bank of England was regarded as particularly safe on account of its large capital and the highly favourable balance of its own capital funds against outside resources. Furthermore, it always had the government to fall back upon, if difficult situations arose. 'Safe as the Bank' (of England), as the saying went.

The deposit banks, which functioned as joint-stock companies and whose institutional and organizational development has been described (see above pp. 66ff.), supplied their clients with working capital and bridging loans. They preferred to give overdrafts rather than loans. By granting overdrafts, they in fact advanced money for the export trade. They also guaranteed reliable securities on a short-term basis and discounted bills of exchange. Originally there was a division of labour between the London deposit banks and the Country Banks in serving their respective clientele. The metropolitan institutions did business with the large business firms based in London and with the families of London's high society; the country banks found their customers among the landed aristocracy and in the industrial and commercial companies of large and medium-sized towns. This division became blurred when, at the end of the 19th century, the metropolitan banks began to establish branches in the provinces. It was only a one-way development, however, which worked in favour of the big London banks, as they began to serve the customers who had hitherto been looked after by the country banks. It was in this way that the big London banks began to absorb the provincial banks.

However, the London banks were only able to expand their business throughout England and Wales. They were not allowed to establish branches in Scotland and Ireland and this has remained the pattern to this day. In Scotland and Ireland, joint-stock banks were dominant from the start. The few private banking firms which had been operating there soon folded up, in Scotland by the mid-18th century, in Ireland in the course of the 19th century. Scotland and Ireland had public issuing banks, the Bank of Scotland and the Bank of Ireland, which also operated as commercial banks. The eight Scottish banks and five of the eight Irish banks had also been granted note-issuing privileges, but the note issue of Irish and Scottish banks was restricted following the passage of Peel's Bank Act. They were protected against competition from English banks which were not allowed to establish branches in Scotland and Ireland. By contrast, Scottish banks could establish branches in London, and naturally the London banks were up in arms about this undesirable competition. Yet the Scottish banks remained restricted in the scope of their business; their London branches did not so much get them new customers as establish closer links with the London money market.

British deposit banks have developed a set of banking rules in their business acitivity which have served them in lieu of bank laws. These rules are also observed outside the British Isles and cannot be violated by a banker with impunity. The central point concerns liquidity: the so-called cash ratio — the cover of all liabilities in cash and credit balances at the central issuing bank — was to be at least 10%; and the liquidity ratio — the cover for all liabilities held in cash and note balances in the bank, treasury bills, nostro balances in other banks and first-class trade bills discountable at the issuing bank — was to be at least 30%. These percentages were regarded as 'sacred'. The cash ratio of Barclays Bank, Lloyds Bank, the National Provincial Bank of England, London City & Midland Bank and of the London County & Westminster Bank varied between 13-15% in the twenty years preceding the First World War, and the liquidity ratio more often rose to over 40% than that it would sink below 30%.

The British deposit banks and the major banks hardly made an impact internationally. Their scope of activity was almost exclusively confined to Britain, as they preferred to handle British domestic credit business and internal payment transactions. It was the merchant bankers who took up international banking. They undertook the issue of foreign state loans, engaged in international bill brokerage, and credit-financed the British import trade. In this connection they made particular use of the acceptance credit which they developed into an important instrument for financing international trade. They provided credit to absolutely reliable customers; more precisely, they lent their good name and international reputation rather than providing a direct cash loan by allowing the customer to draw bills on them endorsed with their acceptance. With this acceptance, the importer was able to meet his liability to the foreign supplier. A bill which had been accepted by an internationally respectable English bank, well-provided with capital, was always taken as payment. A promissory note which simply bore the merchant's name and signature would certainly not have met with a similar trust. By sending it with the bank's acceptance, the customer could defer payment himself until the accepted bill matured. If he was unable to pay at this point, the bank would be obliged to honour the presented bill. The bank did not give its acceptance without collateral, however. The customer had to hand over the shipping documents for the goods he had bought on the bank's acceptance guarantee until his debt was cleared, and the bank had the right to dispose of these goods (see above p. 77).

Among the merchant bankers there were an extraordinarily large number of firms which had been founded by immigrants. In no other European country did immigrants play such a big role in banking as in England. And it was precisely the big merchant banks, founded in most cases by immigrants, which turned London into the leading money market of the world in the 19th century. From the period of the Seven Years' War, and particularly during the 19th century, foreign merchants and bankers had been attracted by the British Empire, with its world-wide trade relations, to set up commercial and banking firms in London. Originally the merchant banks were more involved in trading than in banking and many of them were founded by immigrants from Germany. These included the Baring Brothers, the London Rothschild Bank, John Henry Schroder & Co., Wm. Brandts Sons & Co., Kleinwort Sons & Co. and Frühling & Goschen. The founder of this last banking house, Wilhelm Heinrich Goschen, was the son of Georg Joachim Göschen, the founder of the *Göschensche Verlagsbuchhandlung*(Göschen Publishing Company) in Berlin. Sir Ernest Cassel, himself an immigrant from Germany, was also a merchant banker. Carl Joachim Hambro, who had founded the banking house of C.J. Hambro & Son, came from Denmark. The merchant bank of Lazard Brothers & Co. developed from the London branch of the Paris banking house of Lazard Frères & Cie. The merchant bankers engaged in international business with European countries and with the United States, whilst the 72 overseas and colonial banks discussed above (see pp. 116f.) were involved in overseas business.

As to the British savings banks, the main shift to occur was from the private trustee savings banks to the Post Office Savings Bank, founded in 1861. In 1913, deposits in the Post Office Savings Bank amounted to £185 million, almost three times as much as the deposits of all private savings banks taken together. However, these were insignificant sums in comparison to bank deposits. The London City & Midland Bank alone, with £93 million deposits, had half as much as the Post Office Savings Bank's total and hence considerably more than all private savings banks taken together.

Membership of the London Bankers' Clearing House determined whether or not a British bank was among the leading banks in the country. The Clearing House was set up by the larger London banking houses as a counting office to avoid transporting money from bank to bank. After all, there were innumerable remittances between them every day. The Clearing House cleared the movements of money between its members at the close of the day and balanced their accounts every evening, settling their payments in Bank of England notes. Almost all London banks joined the Clearing House. The new joint-stock banks which, as unwelcome competitors, were for a long time debarred from joining, succeeded in gaining admission only in 1854. When they became members, the practice of balancing accounts at the end of every day was changed. Thenceforth this was no longer done with ready cash, but by means of transfers to the Bank of England avoiding the use of cash. For a time after the joint-stock banks had gained membership of the Clearing House, every bank based in London was admitted as long as there were no doubts about its solvency. This changed when the Bank of England became a member in 1864. From then on, the members of the London Bankers' Clearing House, mindful of exclusivity, no longer admitted new members. And so, with the concentration movement getting underway, the number of members dwindled from 125 (Bank of England, 111 joint-stock banks, 13 private bankers) in 1867 to 17 in 1913. Blatant self-interest lay behind this desire for exclusivity; for the greater the number of cashless transfers, the more commission there was to be earned by the clearing banks when they undertook clearing settlements as a service to those banks which did not belong to the Clearing House.

Because the different types of banks specialized in financing different business activities and because of Britain's numerous overseas and colonial banks, her banking system met the needs of her great colonial and commercial empire. On the other hand, it did not recognizably influence or advance her industry which, until 1892, manufactured the largest volume of industrial goods in the world and was still the third biggest industrial power in 1913. Nor did the banking system adjust to rapid industrial development. There was nothing like the universal banks of Central Europe and the United States, or the specialized investment banks of France. Investment remained the domain of special investment trusts which were outside the banking system. Only much later did deposit banks incorporate such companies as subsidiaries. Nor did Britain's credit institutions provide long-term credit to finance investments. Not even the large and truly unique process of concentration within British banking was directly related to the concentration of economic power in industry.

2. France

Before 1914 the French banking system was characterized by the following special features: the central issuing bank, the Banque de France, had the largest gold reserves in the world. The big joint-stock banks had divided their operations, according to the type of business they pursued, into deposit and investment banking. Through the expansion of the big banks, the immediate importance of the private bankers, the *haute banque*, had been greatly reduced, though they still retained great influence in economic life as the principal shareholders in joint-stock banks, railway companies and industrial enterprises. The system of consortia was well-developed; the larger provincial banks had combined to form a syndicate.

With the change from bimetallism to the gold standard, the Banque de France had gradually reduced its originally very large silver reserves — in 1910 the bank still held silver worth about 800 million francs — and accumulated large amounts of gold instead. Its gold reserves rose from 600 million francs in 1881 to about four milliard francs by 1910. Thanks to this large stock of gold in the central issuing bank, French notes had the highest gold cover (65-70%, with the total metallic cover, gold and silver, fluctuating between 75-90%); at the same time France had the largest note circulation of all European states amounting to 5.6 milliard francs. Transactions by cheque and the transfer business were still underdeveloped. The large gold reserve also enabled the Banque de France to assist the Bank of England with gold credits in cases of financial difficulty in Britain, as in 1836-7 or during the Baring crisis of 1890, or in 1906, 1907 and 1909. For the other banks, the Banque de France functioned chiefly as a rediscount institution. It accepted bills for discount, provided they bore three signatures and the customer presenting the bill — usually a bank — had an account with a *'faculté d'escompte'* at the Banque de France. From 1880 onwards it also granted loans on securities. However, it accepted as collateral only French state loans and securities guaranteed by the state as well as bonds of the Crédit Foncier de France and of the *Départements* and cities.

Although the Governor of the Banque de France and his two deputies, the *sous gouverneurs*, were appointed by the President of the Republic on the Cabinet's recommendation, the central issuing bank was not dependent on the State. Its policy was determined by the *conseil général*, where the shareholders wielded the decisive influence; they elected the 15 regents and three censors, who made up this council together with the Governor and the two *sous gouverneurs*. The *conseil général* was elected by the *assemblée générale*. The 200 largest French shareholders in the Banque de France belonged to this Assembly. But each of them had no more than one vote, no matter how many shares they owned. The families of these 200 largest shareholders were the 200 *'grandes familles'* of French society. The Banque de France did not have to win its independence from the Government by a majority vote of the elected members of the *conseil général* over the state-appointed Governor and his two deputies. Instead the governors had developed a tradition of representing the independent expertise of the issuing bank *vis-à-vis* the Government and its political considerations. This tradition survived the nationalization of the Banque de France. Until the end of the 19th century there were three types of joint-stock banks in France, distinguished by their field of business: deposit banks, investment banks and universal banks. Both the Crédit Lyonnais and the Société Générale had gradually wound up their investment business after the bank crisis which had been triggered off by the collapse of the Union Générale in 1882. They became deposit banks, and the French joint-stock banks divided their business functions; they split up into deposit banks for short-term banking transactions and *banques d'affaires* (investment banks) for the promotion of industry and long-term credit.

Three of the deposit banks gained a dominating position as major banks: the Société Générale, the Crédit Lyonnais and the Comptoir National d'Escompte de Paris. Their assets far outstripped those of other joint-stock banks. In 1909, the Société Générale had a joint-stock capital of 400 million francs, almost as much as that of the 17 largest regional and local joint-stock banks taken together (430 million francs). And when the joint-stock capital of the Crédit Lyonnais (in 1909, 250 million francs) and the Comptoir National d'Escompte de Paris (in 1909, 200 million francs) is added, the three major banks' capital was approximately twice that of the next 17 large joint-stock banks taken together. The dominant role of the Big Three was even more evident in their business operations. Each of them had by far more deposits than the 17 largest provincial and local banks. Whilst all of these together had just under 860 million francs at their disposal in 1909, the Crédit Lyonnais had deposits amounting to 1,880 million francs at this time, followed by the Société Générale with 1,380 million francs and the Comptoir National d'Escompte de Paris 1,100 million francs. In terms of short-term loans and overdrafts, the three big institutes each surpassed the regional and local joint-stock banks taken together. In 1909, these had claims totalling 1,160 million francs, whereas the claims of Crédit Lyonnais reached 2,260 million francs, those of the Société Générale 1,490 million francs and the Comptoir National d'Escompte de Paris 1,325 million francs.

The three big deposit banks became this powerful after they extended their branch network throughout the whole of France and penetrated into the domain of regional and local banks. Although their expansion in terms of geography and business activity took place at the expense of the provincial and local banks, there were, unlike in England and Germany, very few mergers with regional and local banks prior to the First World War. As to liquidity regulations, the Société Générale followed the English banking rules very strictly. Its cash ratio generally exceeded 10%, its liquidity ratio never dropped below 40%. The Crédit Lyonnais' cover in cash and notes rarely reached the 'sacred' 10% and came on average to 8.5%. On the other hand, the Crédit Lyonnais always maintained a very high liquidity ratio of generally more than 50%, with the rule requiring at least 30%. The Comptoir National d'Escompte de Paris reached an average cash ratio of 8.1% and a liquidity ratio of 47.5%. The liquidity ratio of major banks was quite stable and showed only insignificant fluctuations.

Two of the provincial and local banks began to grow into supra-regional major banks: the Crédit Industriel et Commercial at Paris and the Crédit du Nord at Lille. The Crédit Industriel et Commercial, unlike the other Paris deposit banks, did not establish branches outside Paris, and as it did not compete against them in the provinces, the provincial banks preferred to collaborate with it. After the First World War this collaboration developed in many cases into capital participation in the Crédit Industriel et Commercial; ultimately a group of 15 banks was formed which comprised institutions at Strasbourg, Lyon, Nancy, Nantes, Rouen, Valenciennes, Lille, Blois, Bordeaux and other places. The Crédit du Nord, which had a large branch network in the north of France, moved beyond its regional boundaries in 1913 when it extended its branch network to the South of France.

The large-scale expansion of the big Paris deposit banks with their branch networks in the provinces moved the provincial banks to form a Syndicat des Banques de Province in 1899. In a sense, this syndicate was to be a permanent consortium of participating provincial banks; it was to provide its members with better information and, above all, enable them to participate more effectively in the issue of securities. Since the syndicate was not recognized by French law, its members founded a joint-stock company, the Société Centrale des Banques de Province, in 1905 to act on behalf of the syndicate. Over 400 regional credit institutions joined the syndicate, among them all the larger regional joint-stock banks, such as the Crédit du Nord, The Société Marseillaise, and the Société Nancéienne. For the small member-banks with limited business and limited capital, the syndicate served only as a source of information; on the other hand, it opened up fresh business opportunities for the larger members. It must remain an open question how far the syndicate provided support for the expansion of its most powerful member, the Crédit du Nord.

After the Société Générale and the Crédit Lyonnais had withdrawn from the promotion and investment business, this became the main field of activity for the big investment banks: the Banque de Paris et de Pays Bas, the Banque de l'Union Parisienne and the 'Rouvier Bank' (Banque Francaise pour le Commerce et l'Industrie). Among their principal shareholders were the firms of the Paris *haute banque*. They were also represented on the supervisory boards of these *banques d'affaires*. It was in this way that the families of the *haute banque* became indirectly engaged in industrial investment. A number of private banking houses were directly involved in this particular line of business. The leading institution among them was de Rothschild Frères, which also came to head various consortia underwriting the issue of industrial shares. The old banking house of Mirabaud & Cie. collaborated closely with Rothschild in this area. Demachy & Seillière, Lazard Frères & Cie. and Louis Dreyfus & Cie. also took part in the promotion business. These three were not banks in the genuine sense, but had originally been wholesalers. Demachy & Seillière had started off as Seillière and had supplied the army during the First Napoleonic Empire. It moved into the credit business after Napoleon's fall. Lazard Frères & Cie. had been in the cotton import and export business; Dreyfus combined a wholesale trade in grain with banking. Of the investment banks, the Banque de Paris et des Pays Bas was the strongest and the most active, though its main interests lay abroad. It was deeply involved in financing the Russian railways and had investments in Russian mines, metallurgical plants, shipyards and banks. In 1905 it founded the *Société Norvégienne de l'Azote et de Forces Hydro-Electriques*, which was soon to conclude an agreement with the *Badische Anilin- und Sodafabrik* and with the AGFA (*Aktiengesellschaft für Anilinfabrikation*) relating to the joint utilization of Norwegian water power. The Banque de l'Union Parisienne also preferred to invest abroad. The 'Rouvier Bank' kept in the wake of the 'Paribas' as a participant in syndicates headed by the latter.

Among the old *haute banque* firms, Hottinguer & Cie., Mallet Frères & Cie., de Neuflize & Cie., Vernes & Cie. and Heine & Cie operated an extensive short-term credit business which consisted primarily of bill brokerage. The Paris *haute banque* was able to maintain its position more successfully than British or German private bankers. It demonstrated economic solidarity and co-operation and, despite religious and party-political differences, remained a rather homogeneous group socially. The Crédit Foncier de France (see above pp. 103ff.) held the monopoly in the field of mortgage credit until 1877. Thenceforth other banks were also allowed to provide mortgages. Nevertheless, the Crédit Foncier retained a monopoly-like position because it was the most popular and widely used public institution in the field of communal credits; its organization not only extended over the whole of France, but also enjoyed several legal privileges. Yet the significance of credit co-operatives and savings banks was slight before the First World War.

Although France's banks were highly developed and well-provided with capital, the two largest sectors of the economy, industry and agriculture, complained of insufficient support by the domestic credit institutions. In view of France's large capital resources, the repeated allegation that her vast capital export was a burden on domestic industry is greatly exaggerated. The complaints by industry referred less to a lack of credit than to the fact that capital exporters did not provide more help in securing orders for French manufacturers. If investment banks had more commitments abroad than in their own country, this was because French industry, which had relatively few large-scale enterprises before the First World War, only made modest use of the richly equipped French capital market. It was a different matter with agriculture. The Crédit Foncier narrow-mindedly preferred to grant mortgages on urban properties, and as the agricultural credit co-operatives were still suffering from teething troubles the credit base for agriculture remained insufficient.

3. Germany

Pre-1914 Germany had developed a very differentiated credit system with a multitude of institutions and many different types of banks. Nevertheless, there was not the same clear-cut division of labour between the individual types as existed in England. In fact, the very strong trend in Germany towards the universal bank caused the demarcations between joint-stock banks, private bankers, credit co-operatives and savings banks to become blurred. This development continued and accelerated throughout the 20th century. Thus the difference between various types of banks was not so much that they were involved in different kinds of banking, but rather that the relative importance of divergent business spheres varied. On the whole, the characteristic features of the German banking system were: a close connection between credit institutions and industry, a marked concentration (in respect of the number and size of its bank mergers Germany was second only to England), a strong development of agricultural credit, large numbers of credit co-operatives and finally, a dense network of savings banks.

The Reichsbank had quickly assumed the role of the central issuing bank. It also became the central rediscount institution, largely thanks to the note-tax privilege which it enjoyed. The law stipulated that the Reichsbank and existing private issuing banks must keep a gold reserve of at least one-third of the total notes in circulation. But the Reich had imposed a 5% note-tax on notes not covered by gold. Only a limited quota was tax-exempt, but in the case of the Reichsbank the contingent (250 million marks) was almost twice as high as that of all the private issuing banks together (135 million marks). The latter therefore kept their issue within the limits set by their gold reserve and their tax-free contingent. When they had to cope with a greater demand on the money market, they dealt with it not by increasing the issue of notes — thereby exceeding their contingent and becoming caught in the tax-net — but by refinancing themselves through discounting parts of their holdings of bills at the Reichsbank. This was cheaper for them than to pay the note-tax. The Reichsbank, as the last rediscounting institution in the line, basically had two options, if it wanted to avoid exceeding its tax-free contingent of notes too often and by too much: it could put up the bank rate, thus increasing the cost of refinancing and depressing demand on the money market; alternatively, it could try to increase its cash reserve by buying up gold. The Reichsbank tended to prefer this second option as a matter of principle and so systematically allowed its gold reserve to grow. In 1913, it held a gold reserve of 1.17 milliard marks against a note circulation of 2.6 milliard marks, providing a gold cover of over 45%. If one compares these figures with those of the Banque de France whose gold reserve was four milliard francs and note circulation was 5.7 milliard francs, it becomes clear why France was able to engage in a much larger capital export, despite the fact that Germany had outstripped her in terms of industrial production and trade as early as 1870.

The Reichsbank kept the bank rate generally low in order to satisfy domestic demand for money. It also endeavoured to develop the giro transfer business; under the provisions of the Banking Act, the growth of giro money required neither an increased gold reserve nor a tax on notes. The cover regulations were merely concerned to guarantee that notes could be converted into gold at any time. What had been overlooked here was that giro money, or bank deposits, could also be transformed into cash at any time and hence represented gold claims. This error in monetary theory had no practical consequences, except that it kept the Reichsbank from pursuing a deflationary monetary policy which in turn would have slowed down economic growth in Germany; it was never that worried about its liquidity.

The major German banks (Deutsche Bank, Disconto-Gesellschaft, Dresdner Bank, Berliner Handels-Gesellschaft, Bank für Handel und Industrie, Nationalbank für Deutschland, Commerz- und Discontobank, and the Schaaffhausenscher Bankverein) had very large capital funds of their own in comparison with British and French banks. In 1913, they owned an equity capital of 1,635 milliard marks; funds borrowed from outside sources totalled 5.15 milliard marks. Thus the ratio between the two factors was 1:3.5 at a time when it was 1:13 for the big British banks. In this connection it must be borne in mind that, as universal banks, the German banks needed a higher share of equity capital. They had to guarantee deposits and to bear the risks of long-term investments. As for the rest, the fact that the major German banks had a capital ratio of 1:3.5 sprang less from a purposeful business policy than from the accident that various sections of the large German middle class decided to deposit their savings in savings banks. In 1913, cash ratios for the big German banks were an average 7.4% and hence considerably lower than the 'sacred' figure of 10% established by the English banks. They offset the lower cash ratio by a substantially higher liquidity ratios which averaged out at 50.7% in 1913. In that year, credit granted by all major banks reached 4.9 milliard marks.

The closeness and durability of the link between the major German banks and industry can also be gauged from the fact that the banks occupied large numbers of seats on the supervisory boards of industrial enterprises and in many cases also supplied the board chairman. The distribution of board seats by individual branches of industry also provides evidence of the ties between the banks and specific industries. The Deutsche Bank had the largest number of representatives on supervisory boards: 78 seats in 73 enterprises, and it supplied the chairman to 15 industrial companies. The Schaaffhausenscher Bankverein had 78 seats, distributed among 60 industrial enterprises, in 16 of which a member of the board of directors of the Schaaffhausenscher Bankverein acted as chairman of the respective supervisory board. The Berliner Handels-Gesellschaft held 74 seats in 56 industrial concerns, providing the chairman in 13 cases. The Disconto-Gesellschaft had over 67 seats on 47 supervisory boards and chaired them in 11 companies. The Dresdner Bank had 49 seats and supplied the chairman in 11 cases. The Darmstädter Bank für Handel und Industrie took up 63 seats on 59 supervisory boards, the chairman being a board member of the Darmstädter in 14 of them. When breaking these figures down according to the branches of industry involved, it becomes apparent that the Schaaffhausenscher Bankverein and the Berliner Handels-Gesellschaft occupied by far the largest number of supervisory board positions in the coal, steel and metal industries; the Deutsche Bank and the Berliner Handels-Gesellschaft were pre-eminent in the electrotechnical industry; the Darmstädter Bank had the closest ties with the chemical industry, taking up more than one-third of the total number of seats held by the big banks; the Schaaffhausenscher Bankverein and the Deutsche Bank were particularly closely linked with the engineering industry; by comparison, supervisory board seats in the textile industry which were occupied by bankers, were distributed fairly evenly amongst the six largest banks.

Alongside the eight major banks there were in 1913 a further 309 provincial banks which were constituted as joint-stock companies. A third of these banks had their own branch networks and half of them had balances of over one million marks. Taken together, these 150 larger provincial banks represented an equity capital of 2.1 milliard marks in 1913. This was 500 million marks more than that of the major banks. However, they were trailing behind by well over 500 million marks as far as deposits were concerned, which amounted to 4.5 milliard marks. In this field they had to face vigorous competition from the branches of the major banks as well as from the savings banks. In the matter of credit provision, the 150 larger provincial banks exceeded the major banks by five milliards; but there were considerable differences in the size of the provincial banks. Some of them approached the dimensions of a big bank in terms of joint-stock capital. Thus the Barmer Bankverein of Barmen in the Rhineland had a joint-stock capital of 100 million marks, followed by the Rheinische Credit-bank at Mannheim (95 million marks), the Allgemeine Deutsche Credit-Anstalt of Leipzig (90 million marks), the Bergisch-Märkische Bank at Elberfeld (80 million marks) and the Bayerische Hypotheken- und Wechselbank of Munich (65 million marks). However the other provincial banks were mostly rather small. Their joint-stock capital often came to no more than one to three million marks. Their number declined following the economic crisis of 1901-2, when bankruptcies in industry lost all banks a lot of money. Ten of them disappeared through mergers with bigger banks in the aftermath of the crisis. Others survived, but found that the major banks and big regional banks had acquired parcels of shares in about 40 of them.

Almost all the regional and local joint-stock banks operated like the major banks, as universal banks. One exception was the Frankfurter Bank. Before the founding of the Reich, it had been the second largest issuing bank after the Preussische Bank (see above p. 13). In 1901, it suspended the issue of notes which, since the establishment of the Reichsbank, had increasingly lost its earlier significance. Moreover, the Frankfurter Bank had become involved in the trusteeship business. This meant that it could only engage in certain short-term credit transactions. In short, it was not a universal but a deposit bank, like the English joint-stock banks.

Almost all the major German private bankers had participated in the founding of joint-stock banks until the early 1870s. For a long time they did not regard joint-stock banks as competitors but virtually as auxiliary institutions which they could use for particularly costly and risky pro-motion and issuing operations. But things did not work out as planned. The big joint-stock banks, whose equity capital and balance-sheet total had increased enormously, drove the private bankers from the dominating position they had held in the credit system since the beginning of the 19th century. The joint-stock banks did not take over the financing of industry as the 'auxiliaries' of the private bankers, but acted entirely at their own discretion; consequently, they also had a greater influence on the industrial economy than the private banking firms who merely played a subordinate role. The declining importance of private bankers may be compared to the diminishing economic influence of the landed gentry relative to that of the wealthy industrial middle class. There is also the fact that the landed gentry formed an important part of the private bankers' clientele, whereas the industrial middle class preferred to collaborate with big joint-stock banks. The Stock Exchange Law of 1896 reinforced this development. It was a belated reaction to the uncontrolled and often fraudulent stock exchange transactions of the *Gründer* years of 1870-73. It contained, among other things, the stipulation that shares of newly-founded companies were not to be admitted to the stock exchange for a full year after their issue. However, since these companies needed the capital that came in from the sale of their shares, they had to arrange for an advance from a bank. The latter kept the shares in its portfolio until their admission to the stock exchange, i.e. for a minimum of 12 months. Only the big joint-stock banks, with their voluminous deposits, were in a position to carry out such transactions which tied up a considerable part of their assets for at least a year in an operation whose success was by no means certain. Thus the Stock Exchange Law in fact ousted, albeit unintentionally, both the private bankers and the small joint-stock banks from the financing of industry when it introduced a provision which was in effect designed to protect the public.

Private bankers were also taken over by the joint-stock banks in considerable numbers. By 1911, the eight major banks had absorbed 51 private bankers. The Darmstädter Bank für Handel und Industrie and the Dresdner Bank were the most active in this merger movement, each absorbing 16 private banking houses. Apart from those directly taken over by big banks, a further 30 private banks were merged with subsidiaries founded by the Disconto-Gesellschaft. The provincial banks also absorbed private bankers' firms. Thus, by 1911, the 41 joint-stock banks belonging to one of the five groups formed by the major banks had taken over 116 private banking houses. Generally speaking, it was the smaller firms which ceased to exist in their own right and, as a rule, continued as branches of the adoptive institutions. Only three of the big private banking firms were absorbed by a major bank: A. & L. Camphausen of Cologne was integrated into the Schaaffhausenscher Bankverein in 1903; Erlanger & Söhne in Frankfurt was incorporated into the Dresdner Bank in 1904, and Warschauer & Co. at Berlin was taken over by the Darmstädter Bank für Handel und Industrie in 1905. Two distinguished Berlin banking houses, Delbrück Leo & Co. and Schickler Brothers, amalgamated in 1910 to form the banking house of Delbrück Schickler & Co. in order to increase survival prospects against competition from the big banks. This merger was initiated by Ludwig Delbrück whose father had been co-founder and first chairman of the supervisory board of the Deutsche Bank.

With many private banking houses disappearing either through liquidation, mergers with joint-stock banks or the extinction of the owner's family — as happened with the Frankfurt house of M.A. Rothschild & Söhne in 1901 — new private bankers started up continuously. By 1913, there were 1,221 private bankers in Germany. Contrary to Adolf Weber's assertion, most of these firms were in fact independent and not subordinate to a major bank by limited partnership ties. Between 1900 and 1914, the number of private banking houses which had such partnership ties actually declined because they were taken over by the major banks. On the other hand, not all of the 1,221 private bankers continued to be active in banking. A number of them, and the precise figures cannot now be fully ascertained, retained the name 'banking house' out of tradition, even though they had decided to confine their business to looking after the assets of a few major customers.

Private bankers had no specific branch of business which was exclusively or predominantly their domain. They worked alongside the joint-stock banks, either in competition or in collaboration. Their business included offering short-term credit through the discounting of bills. However, this was profitable only in the biggest commercial centres, and only occasionally was it pursued by firms in small provincial towns. Some, such as the bankers of Frankfurt, Berlin and Hamburg with their far-reaching business connections, also dealt in securities and money market securities which they purchased as cheaply as possible on the capital market in order to sell them to the highest bidder in a different place. In the field of industrial and commercial finance, private bankers were important credit institutions, particularly for those medium-sized commercial and industrial firms in the provinces which were not yet serviced by the big banks and had no links with savings banks and credit co-operatives. Several of the larger private banking houses, like the big joint-stock banks, also maintained strong ties with commercial and industrial joint-stock ccompanies and strengthened them by investing in these firms. The private bankers who had close links with industry included the banking houses of Delbrück Schickler & Co. and F.W. Krause & Co. in Berlin; in Düsseldorf it was the firms of C.G. Trinkhaus and B. Simon & Co., in Essen, Simon Hirschland, in Cologne the banking houses of Sal. Oppenheim & Cie., J.H. Stein and in Munich Merck Finck & Co. Nevertheless, as far as the size of their business was concerned, their ties and direct investments were on a much more modest scale than those of the major banks.

In one field, however, the big private bankers were virtually on a par with the big banks until 1914. This was the international and national state loan business. The large part which the Mendelssohn, Bleichröder, Warburg, Behrens, Oppenheim banks played in the issue of state loans has already been described (see above pp. 124ff. and 127ff.). Their co-operation in placing German state loans was no less important. Two large and permanent state loan consortia had been formed for this purpose: the Prussian Consortium and the Reich Loan Consortium.

The origin of the Prussian Consortium dated back to the summer of 1859. At that time the Prussian Prince Regent Wilhelm and future Wilhelm I mobilized the whole of the Prussian army after French and Sardinian troops had won a first great victory at Magenta in their war against Austria. Wilhelm and his ministers feared that Napoleon III, following his uncle's footsteps, would first inflict a military defeat on Austria and then attack solitary Prussia. The mobilization of the Prussian army helped to bring about a speedier conclusion to the war and easier peace terms for the

Austrians; but it cost the Prussians 30 million thalers. In order to raise this sum the Prussian State took up a loan of over 30 million thalers. Adolph Hansemann, who owned the Disconto-Gesellschaft together with his father, took the initiative in forming a consortium to guarantee the loan and to sell the bonds to the public. The following banks took part in this consortium which was headed by the Disconto-Gesellschaft: the Berliner Handels-Gesellschaft and the Berlin private banking houses of Bleichröder, Mendelssohn, Magnus, Gebr. Schickler and Warschauer & Co. When Prussia issued further loans to finance her wars of 1864, 1866 and 1870-71, consortia were again formed to raise them; they included the same banks which had been involved in the deal of 1859. The number of members had grown by the addition of the Cologne banking house of Sal. Oppenheim & Cie., the Frankfurt Rothschild Bank, the Berlin banker Plaut and the Preussische Seehandlung; the Seehandlung took over the chairmanship of the consortium from the Disconto-Gesellschaft. Thenceforth, the banking consortium established to raise Prussian state loans was led by the Prussian state bank and became known as the 'Prussian Consortium'.

Following the creation of the North German Confederation, the Hamburg private banking house of L. Behrens & Söhne as well as the Norddeutsche Bank were added. The Deutsche Bank was excluded from the consortium until 1877, thanks primarily to the Disconto-Gesellschaft rather than to the private bankers. The Deutsche Bank was admitted to the Prussian Consortium only after it had agreed to the demand of the Seehandlung that it would accept a Prussian state loan single-handedly and in competition with the Consortium. The Deutsche Bank was never very happy with its role in the syndicate; its quota was a mere 7.5% — the same as the newly-admitted Bank für Handel und Industrie of Darmstadt; the Disconto-Gesellschaft and Bleichröder, by contrast, had a quota of 19.4% and 12.5% respectively. For a modest commission, the Consortium guaranteed the state a certain agreed yield from the issue of loans. The advantage of this arrangement for the Government was that it was not dependent on the successful outcome of the subscription to the issue.

On the other hand, the Prussian government was loath to rely exclusively on the Consortium or to concede to it a monopoly for mediating state loans. This is why it made several attempts to place loans through the Preussische Seehandlung or through outsiders. However, these attempts did not meet with much success; the public was very sceptical about state loans which were not issued by the Prussian Consortium and the Government received less than it would have done had the Consortium been entrusted with the matter. Only once did a loan placed without the Consortium yield a large return. This was in 1899 when the Deutsche Bank — to the great annoyance of the other Consortium members — took over a Prussian loan worth over 75 million marks and successfully sold it to the public. A coup of this kind was possible only once, though. Nor could the Deutsche Bank afford to outdo the Disconto-Gesellschaft, Bleichröder and Mendelssohn more than once. After the turn of the century the Prussian

government therefore placed its loans via the Prussian Consortium.
From the 1880s onwards, the circle of consortium members became
much enlarged. At the Government's insistence other, and above all non-
Prussian banks, participated directly in the Consortium for reasons both of
Reich policy and the need to broaden its financial base. Owing to this expansion, the original Consortium members had to accept an inevitable
reduction in their quotas. They were divided into four categories, each with
a uniform quota according to their presumed capacity to handle loans.
Thereafter the composition of the Prussian Consortium remained unchanged
until the end of the Hohenzollern monarchy in 1918.

The same banks which belonged to the Prussian Consortium also formed
the Reich Loan Consortium, with the same quota allocations and chaired by
the Reichsbank. The Reich Loan Consortium came into being in the 1880s
after Bismarck's attempt to secure a profitable source of income for the
Reich through a Reich tobacco monopoly had miscarried. His failure was
due to the opposition of the Reichstag between 1880-81, tempting the
Government further to resort to a balancing of budget deficits with the help
of loans.

On the eve of the First World War, private bankers were still participating
in the Prussian Consortium and their combined quota was 28%. This was
quite a considerable share; on the other hand, if one remembers that in
1877 they had participated in the Consortium to the tune of 45.4%, it becomes apparent that the joint-stock banks had stolen the march on them.

Two State Banks were also members of both consortia: the Preussische
Seehandlung and the Bayerische Hauptbank (Staatsbank), which had its
head office in Nuremburg at that time. The State Bank of the Duchy of
Brunswick, the Herzogliches Leihhaus (see above p. 28), operated as the third
state bank. The Herzogliches Leihhaus functioned, like a savings bank,
without capital resources of its own and was largely a mortgage institute. In
1899, over 80% of its credits were mortgages. The Bayerische Staatsbank,
like the big regional banks, operated as a universal bank. The Preussische
Seehandlung was both a commercial bank and the bank of the House of
Hohenzollern, covering Prussian state-owned enterprises and negotiating
credits for the Prussian State and for the municipalities of the Kingdom.
It specialized in long-term credits against securities for which it usually
charged lower than normal rates of interest, but made stricter demands
on the solvency of borrowers and the provision of collateral for securities.
Its special position caused the Seehandlung carefully to avoid open
competition with private commercial banks.

4. The United States of America

The passage of the National Banking Act in 1863 established two legal
banking systems in the United States. One system created joint-stock banks
which were subject to the regulations of the National Banking Act; they
obtained their charter from the Government of the Union and were known

as National Banks. The other system comprised all credit institutions which
conformed to the less stringent legal regulations of individual Federal States
and obtained their charter from the Government of their home state. These
included the State Banks (which were commercial banks structured as joint-
stock banks), trust companies and property management companies which,
having expanded into banking, also obtained their charter from a State,
although legal regulations other than those for the State Banks were
applicable to them. Finally the savings banks were also subject to Federal
State legislation. Thus there were three different types of banks in existence
within the American banking system at State level. Beyond the two banking
systems there was in fact a third one, not subject to any special legal
regulations and therefore not in need of a concession or charter. These were
the 'unincorporated banks', the private bankers.

    Before the Federal Reserve System was introduced in 1913-14 and the
12 Federal Reserve Banks started business (see above pp. 15ff.), the United
States had no central issuing bank. The National Banks issued notes under
the supervision of the Comptroller of the Currency who was to make certain that they observed the regulations of the National Banking Act.
Another task which central banks fulfilled elsewhere, i.e. to supply the
banking system with liquid funds could to a limited extent be met by the
Treasury Department by making part of its funds available as deposits to the
National Banks in the Reserve Cities. Between 1900 and 1914 an average of
30-40% of the cash (gold, coins, notes) circulating in the American national
economy was held by the banks and 10% by the Treasury Department.

    During this period there occurred a shift in the balance of different types
of banks in the credit system, both as regards the total number of institutes
and in their capital and deposits. The number of private bankers – some
5,000 in 1900 – declined continuously although the absolute number of
credit institutions of all kinds increased. In 1914 there were more than three
times as many State Banks (14,512) as there had been in 1900 (4,369). By
contrast, the number of National Banks merely doubled during the same
period of time from 3,732 to 7,525. The number of savings banks also
doubled, even if their absolute number of 2,100 remained rather small. In
the case of trust companies, the greatest increase took place between 1900
and 1914 when their numbers grew more than fivefold from 290 to 1,564.
As regards equity capital and deposits, the National Banks ranked first both
in 1900 and in 1914. But the share of the State Banks and, in particular,
the trust companies, was considerably larger on the eve of the First World
War than at the turn of the century. In 1900 the equity capital of all the
National Banks amounted to $622 million and was 75% larger than that
of all the State Banks ($237 million) and trust companies ($127 million)
taken together. In 1914 the equity capital of the National Banks was
only slightly larger at $1.06 milliard than the combined total of State
Banks ($501 million) and trust companies ($464 million). This shift was
even more marked as far as the distribution of deposits is concerned. By
the turn of the century, the National Banks had accumulated deposits of

$2.5 milliard, much larger than both the State Banks ($1.3 milliard) and the trust companies ($1 millard). By 1914, on the other hand, the trust companies (with $3.94 milliard) and the State Banks (with $3.23 milliard) taken together had more deposits than the National Banks (with $6.3 milliard).

Two developments caused this shift by which the State Banks, and especially the trust companies, caught up with the National Banks as regards equity capital and deposits. To begin with, American bankers found much less incentive to acquire the status of a National Bank, as the major European banks had shown them that the privilege to issue notes was not as important for a bank's business as they had assumed during the last third of the 19th century. But as interest in the right to issue notes diminished, so did the willingness to pay the price for this privilege. After all, the liquidity regulations of the National Banking Act were very strict (see above pp. 93f.). The State Banks, on the other hand, were required to maintain considerably lower reserves in relation to their commitments. The regulations affecting this ratio varied from one Federal State to another, but were much more liberal everywhere. Even more generous stipulations applied to trust companies which, at the time of their foundation, had not been banks at all. The virtual absence of legal restrictions was certainly a factor behind the large numerical expansion of banks of this type after 1900.

The second reason why National Banks lost their pre-eminent position after the turn of the century was that, from 1902, the Comptroller of the Currency had so restricted their activity in the issuing and investment business that they no longer played a role in this field. This benefited the trust companies above all. They had much larger capital funds than the State Banks, and through the administration and investment of properties they had access to extensive funds from outside sources. Shortly after the Comptroller of the Currency had driven the National Banks out of the investment and issuing business, two new trust companies were founded in New York: the Bankers Trust Company in 1903 and the Manufacturers Trust Company two years later. These companies immediately became two of the biggest banks in the country in terms of their capital resources. The National Banks themselves adapted to the changed situation by transferring the investment business (in which they were not allowed to engage) to subsidiaries which they founded by obtaining charters from the Federal States.

The biggest of the National Banks were based in New York. The principal shareholders of the National City Bank of New York were the Rockefellers. James Stillman, the Bank's President between 1891 and 1909, was a personal confidant of John D. Rockefeller. From 1907 the private bankers John Pierpont Morgan and Jacob Schiff were also principal shareholders in the National City. From 1863 to 1909 the First National Bank of New York was led by its co-founder, George F. Baker, who put the Bank into close contact with Morgan. John Thompson and his sons, who, having founded the First National together with Baker, withdrew from it in 1877 and founded the third of the three big New York banks. They named it the

Chase National Bank of the City of New York after the initiator of the National Banking Act.

The three biggest trust companies (Guaranty Trust Company of New York, Bankers Trust Company and Manufacturers Trust Company) also had their head office in New York. In Cincinnati, following the merger of a savings bank and a trust company, the Provident Savings Bank and Trust Company emerged in 1902 which, in addition to banking, also rendered services to immigrants, such as procuring ship's tickets and dealing with immigration formalities. In this way it gained customers for its banking business among the immigrants. Eventually it developed into one of the largest American travel agencies which is still being operated as a subsidiary by the bank today. Under the legislation concerning trust companies, Arthur J. Morris founded the Fidelity and Savings Trust Company in Norfolk, Virginia, in 1910. This Bank was to specialize in granting small credits to small and medium-sized tradesmen. It became the model for a new type of industrial bank which advanced small credits and developed during the First World War and immediately afterwards.

By comparison with the National Banks and the trust companies, the majority of the State Banks were rather small joint-stock banks. On average, individual National Banks had three times and individual trust companies nine times as much joint-stock capital as individual State Banks; and, as far as deposits were concerned, the average ratio between trust companies, National Banks and State Banks was something like 11:4:1. Nevertheless a number of State Banks in New York grew into major banks. These included the Chemical Bank which emerged from the New York Manufacturing Company in 1844, and the Corn Exchange Bank which had been founded in 1853 by members of the New York grain exchange for interim financing.

Because of the steadily growing competition from joint-stock banks, more and more private bankers gave up. Only the great private banking houses of J.P. Morgan & Co., Kuhn Loeb & Co., Winslow Lanier & Co., Brown Brothers & Co., all of which had their head offices in New York, were able to stand their ground alongside the major joint-stock banks because of their extensive interests in industry, railways and shipping. Indeed, the dominating figures in the American credit system during the first quarter of the 20th century were two private bankers, John Pierpont Morgan Senior and Junior.

The legal differences between the various types of banks were considerably more marked than the differences in their business activities. All of them accepted deposits and granted short-term commercial credit. The savings deposits in the savings banks were naturally greater than deposits on current accounts; however, since there were fewer savings banks, the other types, if compared with German, British or French joint-stock banks, also had unusually large savings deposits, amounting to between a quarter and a third of all deposits held in State Banks and trust companies. In principle, every type of American bank was a universal bank. This statement must be qualified with reference to National Banks in the period after 1902. It was from this date onwards that they were able to engage in long-term finance only indirectly through subsidiaries which had the status of State Banks. Similarities between different types of banks also existed in another very important respect. They were all, in principle, local banks; they were all equally affected by the ban on the establishment of branches other than in the area where they had their head office (see above p. 93). Of course, they all had an opportunity to circumvent this ban quite legally by founding subsidiaries, or by acquiring a large stake in other banks. And due to the credit balances which they would have with some other bank, there existed very close business connections between all these different types of banks.

In addition to their tight liquidity reserve in the form of cash, the banks and trust companies kept larger liquidity reserves in the form of deposits in the National as well as the State Banks. On 28 April 1909, the State Banks had cash balances totalling $226 million, with deposits in the National Banks amounting to $326 million, and credit balances in other banks of $160 million. On the same day, the trust companies had cash balances totalling $256 million, over and above $397 million kept as deposits in the National Banks and another $185 million in the form of credit balances in other banks. The National Banks did not have their head offices in a Reserve City, and so maintained three-fifths of their legal liquidity reserve in a National Bank in one of the Reserve Cities. And the National Banks in the Reserve Cities in turn kept deposits at National Banks in one of the three Central Reserve Cities as additional liquidity reserves. This re ciprocal network of credit balances enabled individual banks to provide sufficient liquidity support to others; but it could not increase the liquidity of the banking system as a whole.

New York as the largest commercial centre in the United States, was also the country's banking centre. More than one-third of the total of American exports and three-fifths of her imports were transacted in New York, a further reason for American banking to be concentrated there. Of the 22,500 banks presenting annual reports in 1909, 153 were New York credit institutions. These New York banks had at their disposal one-seventh of the entire equity capital of all American banks; they had attracted almost one-quarter of the total deposits; they supplied more than one-fifth of all bank credits; and three-fifths of all bank clearings were cleared in New York. The New York banks had founded a New York Clearing House Association on the model of the London Bankers Clearing House with about 60 members drawn exclusively from the National and State Banks. Trust companies were not admitted to the Clearing House on principle, because the National Banks and State Banks regarded them as unwelcome rivals which were privileged by virtue of their legal status, i.e. the very lax regulations concerning their liquidity reserves. The Clearing House attended to the clearings between its members. Banks not belonging to the Clearing House could participate in the clearings provided their business was attended to by a member bank and for a fee.

After the recession of 1901-2, the United States, like the other industrial countries, experienced a strong economic upturn between 1903 and 1906. This had certain unpleasant side-effects: speculation, reckless business dealings as well as criminal activities. Just as in the German *Gründer* crisis of 1873 reckless and shady business dealings contributed in no small way to the sharp economic downturn of 1907. The first symptoms of a recession were apparent in the winter of 1906-7 when there was a shortage of money and the cost of borrowing went up. A drastic fall in stock exchange prices in March 1907 served as a prelude to a recession, causing several highly quoted securities to slump by almost 30 points within a month. Further slumps in prices took place in the summer and autumn of 1907. The commodity markets began to stagnate following speculative over-production. In October 1907, the banks were given a taste of these economic problems by a short, but sharp, banking crisis.

This crisis was directly caused by the failure of a massive coup in the copper market. A group of speculators had brought eight New York banks under their control to help them finance their copper transactions. The plan misfired, and they made enormous losses. When these became public, customers first started a run on the banks connected with the copper deals. It was then rumoured that one of the biggest trust companies in New York, the Knickerbocker Trust Company, had business connections with the copper speculators, and soon that company was dragged down as well. Within a few days it lost $8 million of its $60 million in deposits. After this, the crisis was aggravated by the notorious rivalry between the trust companies, on the one hand, and the National and State Banks, on the other. On 21 October 1907 the National Bank of Commerce, which had thus far undertaken the clearings for the Knickerbocker Trust Company at the Clearing House, declared it would no longer do so. This announcement started a general run by its own customers, and the company suspended its payments on 22 October 1907. This action by a major bank triggered off a run on all banks. Depositors withdrew their money to hoard it at home. Some 243 banks, including 31 National Banks, had to suspend payments; for weeks and months many other credit institutions accepted only partial cash withdrawals.

Seen with the benefit of hindsight, the run was not really that massive, but it hit the banks at a very unfortunate time and with disastrous repercussions; for it happened during the period when the grain exporters purchased grain from the farmers in the Mid-West. They paid them with the help of credits taken up in New York, and money was therefore tight. Since the grain was exported to Europe, it took until winter for payment to reach New York. The Treasury Department stepped in to help the banking system out of the crisis. Undersecretary Cortelyou had already placed an extra $28 million at the disposal of the New York banks to overcome the seasonal shortage, in addition to the $157 million of public money held by the commercial banks as deposits. Then the panic struck New York. Three days later, on 22 October 1907, he transferred $35 million. This left the Treasury Department with a mere $5 million. However, Cortelyou's rescue action was insufficient. Urged by the New York banking community, old John Pierpont Morgan formed a committee with Stillman and Baker in an attempt to organize a joint self-help operation. These three men, and Morgan in particular, enjoyed such great authority that the banks adopted their proposals which facilitated the mobilization of funds to support those institutes most at risk and prevented further bankruptcies.

The committee's work helped to reassure the public, and in the next two months gold worth over $100 million flowed into America. Some of this represented the returns on the grain exports of the previous autumn; some was attracted by New York's high interest rates. The sensitivity of the American money and credit system had been exposed by this brief, but sharp crisis. The New York market fluctuated violently between utmost strain in the autumn and surplus supply in the spring and summer. It revealed that the New York National Banks were not in a position to provide the banking system of the whole country with the necessary liquidity, and certainly not in critical situations. The fact that the Treasury Department backed the New York Banks by placing almost the whole of their liquid funds at their disposal could not alter this conclusion. The banking crisis of 1907 therefore prompted investigations and proposals which led to the creation of a central banking system, the Federal Reserve System, six years later (see above pp. 18f.).

5. Japan

Japanese banking has been strongly influenced by foreign models. When they drafted their first Banking Act in 1872 and began to establish National Banks, the Japanese were guided by the American National Banking Act and the American National Banks. The Bank of Japan (Nihon Ginko), on the other hand, was founded in 1882 on the model of the West European central issuing banks. The Japanese mortgage banks took the Crédit Foncier de France as their example, and the credit co-operatives imported their ideas from Germany. The Japanese government, however, introduced extensive banking legislation and established big public commercial banks. Consequently it had a much stronger and more direct influence on the development of the country's credit system than its counterparts in Europe and North America. Three laws were passed prior to 1914 which were designed for the commercial banks in general: in 1872 they were invested with the right to issue notes under certain conditions; this right was revoked in 1884, two years after the foundation of the Bank of Japan; in 1890 a new law regulated the admission and control of commercial banks. The organization and activity of mortgage banks was regularized by several laws and revised many times after 1896. The savings bank system obtained its legal basis in 1890. Laws relating to public banks were also ratified. The intensive legislative activity of the State was largely due to the fact that it had initially introduced foreign models. Later it was found that amendments had to be drafted to adjust them to Japanese conditions, once several years of practical experience had been gained. The initiating role which the Government played must be seen as a special feature of the Japanese banking system before 1914. Two further characteristics were the major zaibatsu banks (see above pp. 99ff.) and the specialized banks.

Japan had a silver currency until the Sino-Japanese War of 1894-5. Under the terms of the Peace of Shimonoseki of 1895, China had to commit herself to pay a war indemnity of £37,836, payable in three instalments. This was considerably more than the war had cost the Japanese; but the excessive indemnity was looked upon as compensation for the Liao-tung peninsula which the Japanese had occupied and which they had had to return to China under pressure from Russia, France and Germany. The Japanese government deposited the greatest part of the war indemnity with the Bank of England and used it to buy the warships and arms which had been ordered from Britain. However, Finance Minister Matsukata who was the decisive force behind Japan's central banking institutions between 1880 and 1900 insisted that the Government set aside part of the war indemnity to purchase gold and move to the gold standard. This finally happened in 1897; a gold yen was valued at approximately half a dollar.

From the very beginning the Bank of Japan had kept part of their monetary reserve not in gold, but in foreign exchange which could easily be converted into gold. Thus, strictly speaking, Japan had a gold exchange standard. At the time of the Russo-Japanese War, the proportion of the gold exchange reserve was 80%, whilst by the outbreak of the First World War it was 40%. Monetary reform was accompanied by a new banking policy. Thus far the Bank of Japan had maintained business relations only with the Government and with other banks. This had been very profitable for the commercial banks as they were lending money, which they borrowed from the central issuing bank at low interest, at considerably higher rates. The Bank of Japan was severely criticized for this practice by industrialists and wholesalers, and so, from the summer of 1897, it started to make credits available to firms other than banks. Although this did not happen on a large scale, the mere availability of direct credits from the central issuing bank, and the opportunity for other enterprises to obtain them, were sufficient to lower the interest on commercial bank loans. In this way the original objective had been achieved.

The specialized public banks were another peculiar feature of the Japanese credit system. The oldest of the specialized public banks was the Yokohama Specie Bank. It had been founded in 1880 by a number of businessmen; but the Japanese government had immediately taken over one-third of its joint-stock capital and given its support to the Bank. In 1887, the Yokohama Specie Regulations converted this private commercial bank with state participation into a public bank under government control. The new bank was earmarked for a special task: to bring the country's foreign trade under Japanese control and generally to promote it. This applied in particular to the export trade which, up to this time, was in the hands of foreign banks and merchants.

The Yokohama Specie Bank was supported by the Government and, from 1882 onwards, also by the Bank of Japan which made low-interest loans available. Tea and raw silk were Japan's main exports at this time, and when the goods were shipped the bank advanced the selling price (minus the usual charges) to the exporters. In this way the exporter had the advantage of receiving immediate payment, which the Yokohama Specie Bank made in Japanese notes. The Bank subsequently arranged for one of its agents to collect the debts for the goods at the place of destination. Payment was to be made in the currency of the country of destination or in precious metal (silver and, from 1897 gold). It was with this foreign currency and coinage that the Bank repaid the credit received from the Government and the central issuing bank. The foreign currency and gold and silver reserves not used for this purpose were converted into Japanses notes with which Japanese exporters could in turn be credit-financed. Thus the Yokohama Specie Bank fulfilled two functions: it promoted exports and saw to it that the foreign currency and metal reserves netted from exports were concentrated in the hands of the Government and the central issuing bank. Thanks to an agreement with the Bank of Japan, the Yokohama Specie Bank owned the monopoly on the financing of foreign trade and on all international payment transactions in Japan. It set up branches in London, San Francisco and New York, the monetary markets and commercial centres of prime importance to Japan.

Other specialized public banks were established around the turn of the century. The Nippon Kangyo Ginko, which started business in 1897, collaborated with 46 regional mortgage banks which relied on it as a credit institution for agriculture and the textile industry. The Industrial Bank of Japan (Nippon Kogyo Ginko) was founded in 1900 to provide long-term finance for the iron and steel industry, transport and shipbuilding and electricity generation. It granted credits for up to five years and accepted securities; following a change in its status in 1911, it also gave credits secured by mortgage. Three specialized banks were destined to assist the development of colonial and strategically important areas. The Hokkaido Colonial Bank (Hokkaido Takushoku Ginko), established in 1899, was to help firms participating in the economic development of the northern peninsula of Hokkaido which was of military importance to Japan. It provided long-term credits against the pledge of shares and debentures. When Taiwan became a Japanese colony in 1895, the Japanese government set up the Bank of Taiwan as an issuing bank whose notes remained convertible to silver until 1906, the date up to which Chinese silver coins continued to be in circulation in Taiwan. The Bank of Taiwan was the main financier behind the island's economic development. The third public Japanese issuing bank, the Bank of Chosen, was founded in Korean Seoul in 1909; Korea had become a Japanese protectorate in the wake of the Russo-Japanese War, before it was formally absorbed into the Japanese Empire in 1910.

From the 1890s, Japan rapidly developed into a powerful industrialized country and a major naval power. The key areas of her economic growth were the iron and steel industry and shipbuilding. A process of concentration in banking began which parallelled the rise of heavy industry, with its own large-scale enterprises. In 1901 there were 1,867 commercial banks and 441 savings banks constituted as joint-stock companies. By the end of 1914, there remained only 1,593 of these 2,300 credit institutions — not counting the 2,000 or so credit co-operatives. The concentration process was particularly beneficial for the larger banks. In 1903, 39% of all bank deposits were in the possession of the 25 largest banks at Tokyo and Osaka. By 1914 these banks had 46% of all bank deposits in their hands.

Japan's rapid economic growth in the early 20th century is reflected in the growth in deposits and loans. In the 11 years between 1903 and 1911, the deposits of all commercial banks increased threefold, from 566 million yen (ca. $280 million) to 1.52 milliard yen. Current bank credits grew from 725 million yen to 1,727 million yen in the same period.

VII Financing the First World War and its Consequences

1. The Financing of the War in the Major Participant Countries

General Problems

In the First World War, the economic and technological potential of the highly industrialized countries was for the first time fully and wholly employed in the service of power politics, for the conduct of war. At the beginning of the War, not one of the belligerent countries was in a state of readiness. Nowhere had serious economic preparations been made for this war, such as the stockpiling of raw materials essential to the war effort. Consequently, each side quickly ran into great difficulties. By the winter of 1914-15, the supply of ammunition was threatened, and it was only now that all economic resources were mobilized for the war effort.

Up to the mid-19th century, the main economic problem posed by warfare had been how to finance it. Countries found it much more difficult to raise funds than to produce and supply the materials for war. It was also less expensive to equip an army. Weaponry consisted mainly of small arms as well as knives, sabres and bayonets. As late as 1850, an army corps would be equipped with no more than 20-25% of the guns that troops of the same strength had at their disposal in 1914. In the First World War the mechanized mass armies required almost unlimited supplies. The main problems facing the war economies of Europe concerned the supply of essential raw materials, the mobilization of labour for the armaments industry and the organization of the production and transport of war materials. Germany and her allies were moreover confronted with the problem of food supplies following the imposition of the British naval blockade. This problem became increasingly insurmountable as the war continued.

On the other hand, the circulation of money, the movement of credit and the financing of the huge and continuous rise in state expenditures in the years between 1914 and 1918 could, if nothing else, at least be fairly easily regulated in all the countries concerned. The price for the way the war was financed had to be paid only after 1918, leading to the Great Inflation and harsh currency reforms in 1923-24.

In the history of money and credit the First World War represents the end of the international gold standard and the reversal of previous international capital movements and financial relations. Most belligerent countries rescinded either *de jure* or *de facto* their convertibility requirement and prohibited the export of gold. Within a few days of the outbreak of war, the Reichsbank and the Banque de France were freed from their obligation to convert their notes into gold. The German government immediately tied the abolition of convertibility to a ban on the export of gold. France had access to very large gold reserves in the Banque de France and in private hands and therefore banned exports only in the summer of 1915. In the following year, it was made illigal to invest French capital abroad. In Britain the cover regulation of Peel's Bank Act, which had been suspended many times during economic crises (see above pp. 9f.), was again lifted so that the Bank of England could put more notes into circulation without having to increase its gold reserve. However, it was still required by law to convert its notes into gold, even if this was made rather difficult in practice after the introduction of administrative obstacles. The British government did not ban the export of gold; in fact it had no need to do so. The insurance premiums for gold shipments had risen so sharply because of the war at sea as to make exports totally uneconomic. By 1917, the response to unlimited German submarine warfare endowed the British government with further administrative powers to control unwanted exports: now it also controlled shipping space. When the United States entered the war in 1917, they reduced the gold cover for the Federal Reserve Banks' note circulation along British lines. The export of gold was not formally banned, but government permission had to be obtained.

Japan found herself in a considerably better position than the other belligerent powers. Although Japan had declared war on the Reich in August 1914, her troops were only mobilized and in combat during the battles of Tsing-tao, the German naval base, between 2 September and 7 November 1914. Otherwise, Japan's involvement in the war was limited to the supply of ammunition. The First World War was therefore no burden on Japan; she actually increased her exports and there was a heavy influx of gold. From July 1914 until November 1918 the Bank of Japan's gold reserves increased from 217 million yen (ca. $400 million) to 716 million yen. The number of notes in circulation rose in approximately the same proportion during that time from 450 million to 1,145 million yen. Japan became a creditor to her European allies during the war. The Japanese government placed British, French and Russian short-term loans amounting to 641 million yen (ca. $320 million) on the Japanese money market and bought government bonds of its European allies for some 134 million yen. Moreover, it exchanged 182 million yen worth of gold deposits which it had been keeping abroad for treasury bills from its allies and redeemed Japanese state loans worth almost 300 million yen which had been accepted by English and French banks before the outbreak of the war.

Unlike Japan, Britain, France and Germany found their position as creditors to other countries seriously weakened. They had to sell part of their foreign investments in an effort to offset, if only partially, the large deficit in their war-time balance of trade. France's balance of trade deficit during the war years totalled 62 milliard francs, whilst Britain's amounted to £2.1 milliard. Germany's unfavourable balance of trade of 15.3 milliard marks was a great deal smaller than that of her enemies because the blockade had not only throttled German exports, but also greatly reduced her imports.

The fact that these hitherto major creditor countries sold off their foreign investments to reduce their balance of payments deficit was not the only reason for the decline in the foreign investments. Investment in an enemy country was appropriated and confiscated as enemy property. Germany lost five milliard of her six milliard or so dollars of foreign investments in this way. At the end of the First World War, she also lost the bulk of her capital investments in those countries which were allies of Germany, Austria-Hungary and the Ottoman Empire because the territories where capital had been invested were reconstituted into states which belonged to the Allied camp: Czechoslovakia, Poland, Rumania, and French and British protectorates in the Middle East. Thus, Germany's only surviving foreign assets were basically her investments in Spain, Brasil, Argentina and Chile. France had half of her foreign assets wiped out totalling over $4.0 milliard of some $8.6 milliard. The largest part of these losses consisted of state loans to Russia after the Bolshevik government refused to pay off Tsarist debts. Britain, which had placed 94% of her total foreign investments abroad, got off with losses of $600 million sustained in Russia and the Ottoman Empire.

Before we consider state expenditure during the war years and how individual countries tried to cover it, it is necessary to discuss briefly the data relating to the cost of the war. In calculating their war expenditure, individual countries have applied different criteria by which to differentiate between expenditure for purposes of war and expenditure for civilian purposes. Some countries include the debt service as part of their war costs, others include it as a civilian item; some countries count war-induced burdens (pensions, for example) as war-related, others as civilian expenditure. This is why it is not possible to compare the data provided by individual governments. Nor do annual budgets and accounts permit more than limited comparisons because items of expenditure under various headings cannot be clearly divided into civilian and military uses either.

In view of these methodological difficulties, Horst Mendershausen, in his *The Economics of War* (1941) applied a technique for reaching approximate, yet internationally comparative figures on the cost of the war which appears to be promising. He assumed that the national budgets would have had the same volume of expenditure had there been peace between 1914-18 as in the last year of actual peace. All increases are hence deemed to have been caused by the war. State expenditure in the last year of peace would indicate the 'normal' civilian expenditure during the war years. The total war expenditure then emerges from the difference between actual state expenditure during the war years and the fictitious 'normal' expenditure. Using this method, Mendershausen calculated that Britain, excluding the Empire, had to fork out $43.8 milliard. The United States figures with $36.2 milliard. The figure for the Reich was $47 milliard. The assumption that state expenditures would have remained at the 1913 level in all countries had peace been preserved, is of course rather unrealistic. The error which is inherent in this assumption is not serious, however, as the growth rates in state expenditures before 1914 were relatively small.

To inquire into the overall cost of the war is a prerequisite of determining the share of the actual conduct of war in the enormously increased state expenditures between 1914 and 1918-19. The financial policy of all countries was to provide cover for all public expenditure and not merely for that of the war. An interpretation of the figures on war finance of the four major industrial powers – Britain, France, Germany and America – should therefore be based on the sum total of their respective state expenditures, and not on the amount of their military expenditure, however they may be defined. The financial policies of the belligerent states had to pursue three goals simultaneously: 1) to meet government's enormous financial needs; 2) to keep war-related price increases, if they could not be avoided altogether, within the narrowest possible limits; and 3) to curtail private demand sufficiently in order to facilitate a shift from peacetime to wartime production in industry.

In order to achieve these goals, it was necessary to skim off surplus private purchasing power. This could be done through taxes or loans. Germany and France at first thought they would be able to spare their population increased tax burden. Both countries opted for financing the war with the help of credits which the defeated enemy would have to repay in the form of reparation once victory had been won. This policy had been adopted after the Franco-Prussian War of 1870-71 and the Japanese-Chinese War of 1894-95. It was only in the second half of the First World War that the tax screw was tightened in Germany and France. Britain and the United States, on the other hand, took the other approach and tried, from the very beginning, to cover as large a part of their additional expenditure as possible by increased income tax and by using internal loans only as a source of subsidiary finance. Hence the amount which taxation and other regular public revenues contributed in both Anglo-Saxon countries to the raising of funds for state expenditure between 1914 and 1918 was approximately twice that of the two Continental countries. In the United States, ordinary revenue contributed just over 29% to the budget during the two years America was at war. Britain provided over 28% of her state expenses through taxes and other ordinary revenues in the years 1914-1918. The percentages for France and Germany were 15.4% and 13.7% respectively.

Germany

Total Reich expenditure amounted to 161 milliard marks between 1914 and 1918. This figure does not include the public expenditure of the Federal States. Only 21.8 milliard of these 161 milliard marks were raised in the ordinary way. A third of this sum (7.3 milliard marks) were taxes on war profits which were imposed in 1916, compelling joint-stock companies to pay an excess-profits tax at a rate of between 10% and 50%. The basis of assessment were the average profits made during the last five years of peace. Individual citizens had to pay a capital gains tax covering the years 1913-16. This was levied for the first time in 1916, and later on the rate of income tax was increased to up to 50% above the 1913 base-line.

It was only in 1917 that the tax on war profits yielded high returns. Although this war levy was the most just and impartial tax that could be devised, the Reich government flinched from launching it for so long that it lost milliards of possible revenue. In 1915, Undersecretary in the Reich Treasury Karl Helfferich defended the rejection of heavy taxation on income and wealth in the face of Social Democratic criticism in the Reichstag. The Socialists were demanding the ruthless taxing of war profits. Helfferich argued that such a tax would have a detrimental effect on the economy. This argument was of course fallacious; the war years produced no more than a pseudo-prosperity which led to a shift in the distribution of wealth, but did not result in an increase in national wealth. After all, war production was unproductive in the sense that it destroyed itself.

Next to these extraordinary war taxes, taxes on consumption contributed most to the Reich budget, namely 5.2 milliard marks. Taxes on profits made by the Reichsbank and the Reich's loan banks produced some 4.1 milliard marks, and were hence also of great importance. The British blockade caused German imports to dwindle and revenue from duties with them. In 1913, these duties had yielded just under 680 million marks and 560.8 million marks in 1914; but in 1918, revenue from this source had slumped to 133 million marks. The combined income from duties during these years totalled 1.64 milliard marks. In 1916, a turnover tax was introduced with a tariff of one promille of turnover. In 1918 the base for the turnover tax was increased to five promille; but this did not yield more than 150.5 million marks. Even if it had wanted to, the Reich government was unable to change the rate of direct taxes, because the Constitution had left this source of revenue to the Federal States.

Ultimately the Reich had to borrow about 140 milliard marks. Of course, there was no question of substantial borrowing abroad. The big capital markets of London and Paris belonged to the enemy camp, and the New York capital market was also very close to London and Paris. A loan of 150 million guilders could be placed in the Netherlands which was a very small amount when compared with the Reich's actual credit requirements. Credit therefore had to be mobilized at home. Between September 1914 and September 1918 the Reich issued altogether nine loans which raised a total of 96.9 milliard marks. The 8th War Loan of March 1918 produced both the largest number of subscribers and the highest yield. This was the time when, following Russia's and Rumania's withdrawal from the war, a decisive German offensive on the Western front was expected. The final War Loan of September 1918 yielded more than either the first or the second issues. Yet when it was issued, the High Command had already come to the conclusion that the war was lost. As this was kept secret, the public who subscribed the loan still believed that Germany would win the war.

The successes of the war loans notwithstanding, a considerable part of the Reich's expenditure still had to be raised by way of short-term credits. At the end of the War, the Reich's short-term debt had reached 51.2 milliard marks, representing the total of the non-interest-bearing treasury bonds that the Government had issued and of interest-bearing 90-day treasury bills. Until the autumn of 1916, 80-95% of all treasury bonds and bills were in the Reichsbank's portfolio almost all the time. From the winter of 1916-17, the commercial banks accepted more and more of these certificates, so that by 1917 on average only about one-half of the treasury bonds and bills were in the hands of the Reichsbank. From 1918, this figure declined progressively to less than one-half.

Although the Reichsbank was freed from the obligation to convert marks into gold in August 1914, there was no relaxation of the rules concerning cover which remained unaffected by legislation throughout the War. Accordingly, the Reichsbank had to keep a primary cover in gold of one-third of the total of notes in circulation, with the law permitting the other two-thirds to be held in first-class trade bills. For the duration of the War, treasury bonds and bills were put on a par with trade bills so that the Reichsbank could use them as secondary cover next to gold. By the end of the War, private trade bills had been almost completely replaced by Reich treasury bonds and bills. This was a result of the great increase in money circulation which increasingly caused trade bills to lose their significance as a means of payment.

The growth in the money supply was brought about by the Reichsbank's monetary and credit policy. Between June 1914 and November 1916, note circulation trebled from 2.4 milliard marks to 7.3 milliard marks. At the same time, however, the Reichsbank had also increased its gold reserve from 1.6 milliard marks to 2.5 milliard marks, having succeeded at the beginning of the War in laying its hands on both the majority of the gold coins still in circulation and some of the privately hoarded gold. Thus the legal requirement of a one-third gold cover was officially maintained until the late autumn of 1916. After that, reserves began to fall short of the required minimum. By November 1918, a note circulation of 18.6 milliard marks was backed by a gold reserve of 2.3 milliard marks.

In reality, however, note circulation was much higher and had fallen below the minimum gold cover by December 1915. Side-by-side with its official note issue, the Bank operated an indirect and camouflaged system of note issue which did not appear in the Reichsbank's published accounts; for in August 1914, the Reichsbank had established at all its branch offices a Reich Loan Bank, whose management, though legally autonomous, was linked with the respective branch office through joint directorships. These loan banks were to meet the credit needs of the private sector which was particularly pressing at the beginning of the War; they were to provide short-term credit for up to three months against collateral in goods or securities. Loan banks were allowed to issue substitutes for money up to the total sum of their collateral loans, known as 'loan bank notes', in order to satisfy the increased demand for currency. 'Loan bank notes' were covered by the claims which the Reich Loan Banks had against their debtors. The Reichsbank was permitted to include these 'notes' next to gold as primary cover. Even though they were not legal tender, they were accepted as such by all public banks and came to be used as a means of payment in private business. In fact they became bank notes for all practical purposes. For a year the loan banks' issue of money substitutes remained limited to little more than one milliard marks, half of which came into free circulation, whilst the other half was kept in the Reichsbank's cover reserve. From the winter of 1915-16, there was a large increase in the issue of these 'substitute notes'. By November 1918, loan bank notes totalling 14.1 milliard marks had been issued, 9.7 milliard of which circulated freely, so that at the end of the War total note circulation had reached the actual figure of 28.3 milliard marks.

The use of short-term loans to finance state expenditure and the increase in note circulation triggered the inflation of the country's currency which reached its peak only several years after the War. Until the end of 1918 there was no sign yet of galloping inflation. On several occasions the Reichsbank had sold gold to neutral foreign countries in order to support the mark's rate of exchange. The sale of German capital assets to neutral foreign countries also strengthened the exchange rate. Thus the decline of the mark's exchange rate was kept within reasonable limits between 1914 and November 1918. In June 1914, one dollar cost 4.20 marks; by the end of the War, the dollar was quoted at 7.45 marks.

The mark's domestic purchasing power declined much more drastically than the rate of exchange. The index of wholesale prices which was at 100 in 1913 had risen to 234 in aggregate at the end of the War, with the food index climbing to 238; the index for industrial materials was 227. However, it has to be borne in mind that these figures only register the officially quoted and permitted price-rises for rationed goods. The real loss of purchasing power would only become apparent, were it possible to ascertain the average of black market prices which differed greatly from region to region and of which no official statistical survey was ever made.

The credit institutions experienced a large increase in their deposits. Deposits at major banks rose almost fourfold from the end of 1914 until the end of 1918: from 5.3 milliard marks to 19.7 milliard marks. Total deposits in the provincial banks grew two and a half times, from 4.3 milliard marks to 10.3 milliard marks, during the same period. Deposits at savings banks rose much more slowly and increased by 50% from 20.5 milliard to 31.8 milliard marks from the end of 1914 to the end of 1918. The customers of savings banks were predominantly people on a medium or low income. The nominal growth rate of their income was lower than the rise in the cost of living, and they had hence little scope for building up reserves. On the other hand, industry, as the principal customer of the joint-stock credit banks, achieved a greatly improved liquidity through very high nominal profits and a reduction of their stocks.

As the liquidity position of private companies was so favourable, they made relatively little use of credit on current account. Accordingly the credit granted by the major banks rose from three milliard marks in 1914 to 4.2 milliard marks in 1918. This was very little, considering that the volume of money saw a more than threefold increase during the same period. At the same time, this meant that the granting of credits to private individuals, which had after all constituted two-thirds of the major banks' total business in the last year of peace, had shrunk to less than 30% of their business in 1918. The State became the main borrower from private commercial banks. Over half of the major banks' funds were made available to the Reich. Of debts of approximately 11.5 milliard marks which the Reich had run up with the major banks by the end of the War, only 542 million marks were consolidated debts; almost 11 milliard were short-term. The major banks had thought it of the utmost importance to preserve the greatest possible liquidity, since 55% of their deposits were repayable within seven days. It was for this reason that they had accepted no more than a few of the Reich loans and preferred to acquire treasury bills. Although these bills had to be prolonged all the time and hence represented short-term bills only in a very formal sense, confidence in them was maintained by the Reichsbank's rediscount pledge.

The savings banks, on the other hand, with their different deposit structure, had accepted a considerable number of Reich loans. At the end of the War, the Prussian savings banks held 9% (8.5 milliard marks) of all the loans which the Reich had issued during the War. Even more striking was the decline in the share of credits to private industry given by the Reich loan banks. Until 1916, the private sector (banks, trade and industry, agriculture) called upon 75% of the loan banks' collateral loans. By 1917, the situation had been reversed: some 75% of all loan banks' credits were taken up by public authorities in the Federal States and municipalities. By 1918, this figure had risen to 84.5%. Thus the financing of the War produced a credit system which was primarily geared to providing public credit.

France

France was hardest hit by the ravages caused by the battles of the First World War. For more than four years, her *Départements* in the North-East and North were the main theatres of war. In view of this, the French Finance Minister, as early as December 1914, expressed the opinion that one could not expect a country so seriously damaged by the War to bear even higher tax burdens. It was for this reason that the French government, like its German counterpart, shied away for a long time from introducing new taxes or from increasing existing rates. The introduction of income tax, which had been adopted shortly before the War, was deferred until 1916 because of the War. In the same year, a tax on war profits was finally introduced at a rate of 50% on profits in excess of the average during the last year of peace. Later this rose to 80%. The French government's reluctance weighed all the more heavily on state finances, because the mining and industrial areas around Longwy, Briey, Lille, Roubaix and Valenciennes, with their large tax potential, were in the hands of the Germans for almost the entire duration of the War and hence yielded no revenue. Until the end of the War, income tax, with its low rate of 2%, together with the tax on war-profits raised a mere 1.7 milliard francs. This was not even 7% of the ordinary state revenues of 1914-18. These amounted to 26.2 milliard francs and were largely raised in the traditional way by direct and indirect taxation.

These revenues covered no more than 15% of the 170.6 milliard francs spent by the French state during 1941-18. The trouble was that the debts of the Third Republic were already exceptionally high before the outbreak of the war, totalling some 32 milliard francs. About two-thirds of this sum was *rente perpetuelle*, a special characteristic of the French financial system (see above p. 31). Since the state debt was so high and a further loan had been issued in July 1914, the French government did not consider it advisable to call upon the public to subscribe to a war loan. The first of the four War Loans was issued in November 1915, all of which were sold as *rente perpetuelle*. They yielded a total of 24.1 milliard francs. The Government relied more heavily on the capital markets of foreign countries than on the Parisian one. Because of the strong international creditor position which France occupied in 1914, she obtained financial help not only from her allies, but also from neutral countries. Thus, from 1914 to 1918, the French government received credits from abroad amounting to 32 milliard francs, two-thirds of which came from Britain and the United States. France passed a portion of this money — some 7.7 milliard francs — on to Russia, Belgium, Serbia, Rumania and Italy, her European allies.

The war loans and foreign credits met less than half of the Government's requirements. The gap had to be filled by means of short- and medium-term loans. The Banque de France granted the first of these credits immediately upon the outbreak of war. It did not have to comply with any cover regulations and was, at regular intervals, allocated a certain note quota. This quota was increased several times in the course of the War, and each time the amount of short-term credit which the Banque de France was allowed to provide for the State was revised upwards. At the time of the mobilization, the Bank had made available its first credit, amounting to 2.9 milliard francs, against the deposit of short-term treasury bonds (*bons du trésor*). Until the spring of 1919, short-term credits to the Government rose to about 27 milliard francs. The latter also obtained its funds by issuing *bons de la défense nationale*. These had a duration of between three and 12 months and, in representing a liquid investment, were eagerly accepted by the public. Throughout the war *bons de la défense nationale* and *bons du trésor* were issued, totalling 55 milliard francs. As in Germany, the issue of short-term certificates of this kind was conceived as no more than a stopgap measure. These debts were to be transformed and consolidated into a loan as soon as possible; yet both countries had but little success in attaining this objective.

The high war-time import surplus, the increased note circulation and the huge short-term debt greatly endangered the stability of the exchange rate of the franc. The French government, the Banque de France and the commercial banks counteracted this danger vigorously. For a while the decline of the franc was slowed down. The Banque de France sold gold to foreign countries, and particularly to the United States, France's main war-time supplier. The Bank had the largest gold reserve of all issuing banks, amounting to almost four milliard francs. Once the War had broken out, it received more than 400 million francs in gold from private hoarders. The owners had been asked to show their patriotism and to convert their gold into Banque de France notes. In the first year of War, the Bank was therefore able to sell gold worth more than 500 million francs to other foreign countries. At the same time, the French government endeavoured to support the rate of exchange by using foreign credits not only to balance the budget, but also to obtain foreign currency. Finally French foreign investments worth around 700 million dollars were sold in order to reduce the deficit in the balance of trade and to mitigate its effects on the franc. Consequently, the franc's loss of value remained quite small. In 1913 one dollar was 5.18 francs. In the first months of War, the franc even gained a temporary advantage over the dollar and in December 1914 the exchange rate was 5.16:1. Soon, however, the rate began to shift against the franc. On 31 December 1915, it reached its lowest level during the War: one dollar was 5.86 francs. Subsequently and with the help of foreign currency credits, the Government succeeded in stabilizing the currency at 5.735:1. After the United States had entered the conflict, the rates of exchange between the pound, the franc and the dollar were pegged for the duration of the War. Whilst the French government was successful in keeping the international value of the currency approximately stable, the excessive creation of money and credit led to a tangible loss of internal purchasing power. Next to Italy, France had the highest price increases of all belligerent Great Powers up to the end of the War. In 1918, the wholesale price index, which had been at 100 in 1913, reached 340.

Britain

According to a declaration by David Lloyd George, the Chancellor of the Exchequer, the British Government intended to raise part of the increase in expenditure incurred in the budget by war through higher taxes. In May 1915, Asquith reshuffled his Cabinet and Lloyd George took over the Ministry of Munitions. Reginald McKenna was his successor at the Treasury. He elaborated on the aims of the fiscal programme: it was designed, he said, to cover expenditure for civilian purposes and for the servicing and amortization of the state debt (including war loans) from ordinary revenue. This objective was basically achieved. In the fiscal years 1914-15 to 1918-19, during which state expenditure totalled £9,593 milliard, £2,733 milliard were actually raised through taxes, customs and other ordinary revenue.

Income tax and income tax surcharge rates for very high incomes were doubled as early as November 1914. In the years up to 1918, income tax rates for earnings in the lowest category were increased from 6% to 13.8% and at the top of the scale from 8.1% to 42.6%. In respect of capital gains, the top rate rose from 15.1% to 50.3%. When compared with a French income tax rate of 2%, which was not even raised before 1916, this constituted a heavy burden on private incomes. Since both wages and prices doubled between 1914 and 1918, whilst the ceiling below which earnings remained untaxed was simultaneously lowered, the number of people liable to income tax increased from 1.13 million before the outbreak of war to three million in 1917-18. From July 1915, a tax was imposed on 'controlled firms' in the armaments industry. This tax was introduced more for social reasons than for fiscal ones. On the strength of the Munitions of War Act of July 1915, the Government had secured large powers to influence the labour market and particularly to recruit labour for the armaments industry. At the same time trade unions had to renounce traditional rights, in particular the right to strike for the duration of the War, at least as far as 'controlled firms' were concerned. By way of compromise, all profits of these firms in so far as they exceeded the average of 20% or more of profits in the immediate pre-war years, had these gains taken away from them. In practice, the revenue derived from this Munitions Levy was quite small because the firms concerned were able to manipulate the calculation of their profits. In the very same year, an excess-profits duty was introduced for businesses, though not for individuals. It provided for 50% of the surplus profit, calculated from a base-line of the immediate pre-war years, to be creamed off. In 1917 the rate of this excess-profits tax was increased to 80%. The Munitions Levy whose revenue had been insignificant was integrated into a general excess-profits duty, and it was this tax which yielded no less than 25% of the total war-time tax revenue.

In the last peace-time budget, direct taxes had raised £94 million or 57.5% of total tax revenue. In 1917-18, the income from direct taxation had risen to £508 million which corresponded to 80% of total tax revenue.

The Government treated the increase and extension of indirect taxes much more cautiously than it handled direct taxation. Such caution was motivated by a concern for social justice; indirect taxation burdened the poorer classes most heavily. But there were also economic considerations which called for restraint in matters of indirect taxes. In so far as such taxes do not apply to luxury goods, they tend to raise the prices of consumer goods for the working population. An increase in taxes on consumption was particularly likely to provoke a corresponding increase in wage demands. Wage increases raised the manufacturing costs and would be passed on in higher prices. Since the State was the main customer for most industries during the War, it would, in the last analysis, have had to finance a tax increase on essential consumer goods by having to pay higher prices for the goods it needed. Hence, in the field of indirect taxes, only the duty on sugar and tobacco was heavily increased. Beyond this, two new duties were introduced: an amusement tax and 33% purchase tax on cars, bicyles, watches and musical instruments. Imports of such goods, and demand for cargo space for them, was to be discouraged by this tax. In order to finance the War and to control foreign trade, Britain gave up her free trade policy and imposed tariffs.

Under Britain's war-time fiscal policy, war costs in the narrower sense, as well as credit for her allies, were to be raised through loans. This meant that payment was to be postponed until after the War. The war-time budgets approved by Parliament granted the armed forces unlimited expenditure. Because of the credit-financing of the War, the internal British state debt grew from £650 million at the outbreak of war to £6.1 milliard by the beginning of 1919. Some £1.4 milliard, almost one quarter of those £6.1 milliard, were short-term, unconsolidated debts. The first war loan was issued in November 1914; two more followed in June 1915 and January 1917. With every loan the debts became more expensive for the State. The last loan was issued at an interest rate of 5.3%; in peace-time, the interest on British loans had been 3.25%

In the major coalition wars of the 18th and 19th centuries, Britain had contributed to the joint conduct of warfare in three ways: through her fleet she had gained control of the seas in order to keep sea routes clear for her allies and to close them to enemy shipping; she took part in battles on land with relatively small contingents of her own; and she invariably granted her allies financial help in the form of subsidies. The subsidies were not repayable credits, but grants. At first, Britain played her traditional role in the First World War: the sea routes were blocked to the German enemy; a small expeditionary force of high combat effectiveness was sent to the French theatre of war; and financial aid was granted to the Allies, this time in the form of credit. However, from the winter of 1914-15, Britain also had to participate massively with her own expeditionary army in land operations. The six infantry divisions which Britain sent to France in 1914 had grown to 70 by the last year of war. Because of her own huge military effort, Britain was no longer able to supply her Allies with funds from her own resources as in previous wars. Thus to some extent her role was changed from that of a creditor to that of a mediator of credits; in order to provide some seven milliard dollars' worth of credits which she had granted her Allies by the end of the War, Britain herself had to take up credit in the United States amounting to $3.7 milliard (see below, pp. 202ff.).

During the War, the Bank of England and the Scottish and Irish issuing banks increased their note circulation of £200 million in June 1914 to £383 million in July 1918. At the same time the Bank of England increased its gold reserve from £40 million to £107 million. This considerable growth in the gold reserve to more than double its size was due to two factors. Firstly, the Bank of England was able to attract, like the central issuing banks in Germany and France, some of the gold coins in circulation in 1914 as well as part of private gold hoardings. Secondly, it obtained the privilege to purchase gold from Australia and South Africa for the duration of war.

Like Germany, Britain put quasi-bank notes into circulation alongside the established notes. At the beginning of the War, the Exchequer gave the banks currency notes as an additional means of paying depositors during the expected run. The currency notes represented a loan from the Exchequer to the commercial banks at the Bank of England's bank rate. When the expected run failed to materialize, the commercial banks returned the currency notes to the Exchequer. Why should they pay interest on a loan they no longer needed? From then on, the Exchequer sold the currency notes to the public through the Bank of England which was obliged to open a redemption account for them. Since the treasuries of public authorities accepted them as a means of payment they were also generally accepted. The public used them in lieu of gold coins which were being hoarded either privately or in the Bank of England. Once again it provided proof of the old rule that bad money drives good money out — as long as there is only one place which is forced to accept the bad money. In 1914, another £34 million worth of currency notes were issued. By the end of the War, £299 million of these notes were in circulation. Whereas the amount of ready money (notes, currency notes and coins) rose by less than £500 million, deposits in commercial banks and savings banks increased by about £1.5 milliard up to the summer of 1919.

The State's high short-term indebtedness, the deficit in the balance of trade, the increase in the money supply, together with a simultaneous shortage of goods and labour, and finally the price rise in freight insurance as a result of the submarine warfare, all undermined the purchasing power of the pound. However, its international value could be stabilized at quite a high level. In the summer of 1914, the rate of exchange actually rose slightly. The pound was the most sought-after currency on the European foreign exchange markets during the July crisis of 1914 and at the beginning of the War, as it was believed to have the greatest stability. From the autumn of 1914, the pound began to fall slightly against the dollar. At the end of 1915 it was still quoted at $4.74, as compared to $4.866 on 31st December 1913. From 1916 until 1918 it was stabilized at 1:$4.7645. As soon as the rate of the pound had begun to fall in the autumn of 1914, the British government intervened in the foreign exchange markets in order to support the currency. In the course of 1915, gold worth 328 million dollars, mostly from Canada, was transferred to the United States for this purpose. From the end of 1915 the British government acquired dollar assets in British private hands to use them as payment for American supplies of war materials. Since private individuals did not sell their bonds in sufficient quantities, the Government obtained authorization in January 1917 to sequestrate the foreign securities owned by British citizens, should this be necessary. Thus, around $3.5 milliard of British assets, half of which were held in the USA, were sold to reduce the deficit in the balance of trade. The United States began to change from being a debtor to a creditor country.

The pound's internal purchasing power developed less favourably than the rate of exchange. The wholesale price index, which was at 100 in 1913, had risen to 227 by the end of the War. This was a little less than the decline in the mark's purchasing power, and overall it was the mildest inflation of all those countries which participated in the War from the start. Only Canada, Japan and the United States had lower inflation rates.

Contrary to the Government's and banks' expectation, there was no run on the banks once war had broken out. Nor was there one in Germany and France. The public reacted to the outbreak of war with a tremendous nationalist enthusiasm and confidence, and these moods did not create a climate of panic-like withdrawals or hoarding purchases. The banks were as apprehensive and worried about the declaration of war as Britons were enthusiastic and confident. The joint-stock banks recalled their credits to institutions specializing in international bill brokerage and to acceptance houses. At the same time, they increased their assets with the Bank of England, expecting that only part of the foreign bills would be honoured and that acceptance houses would then need sizeable refinancing credits. The Bank of England reacted to the increase in deposits from the commercial banks by increasing the bank rate to an alarming 10%. Worried by the behaviour of the banks, the Government proclaimed five bank holidays from 2-6 August 1914. It was this very mood of alarm which prompted the Treasury to provide the commercial banks with the currency notes on loan. Currency notes and postal orders were temporarily declared legal tender. At the same time a moratorium was announced for the discharging of bills and, at the Government's instigation, the Bank of England signalled its willingness to rediscount all bills issued before the date of the moratorium. The Government undertook a guarantee of £500 million for these bills. Except for a small proportion, all the guaranteed bills were actually redeemed so that the guarantee was not too costly. The banking public remained calm even after the bank holidays, and the Government's massive protection of the banks proved unnecessary; the City which exerted a strong influence on the Liberal Party in power had over-reacted.

In the last two years of the War, the concentration movement in English banking reached its peak and a first conclusion (see above pp. 71f.), when it became clearer that the role of the United States would change from a debtor country to Europe's creditor. At the beginning of the War, there were still 38 independent joint-stock banks in England and Wales, with a total of 5,900 branches. The big banks, the 'Big Five' by this time, had become so pre-eminent that they disposed of 83% of all bank deposits in England and Wales.

The United States

In the relatively short period of her involvement in the War, the United States had made a major military effort. In 1914, she had the third largest fleet in the world after Britain and Germany. When America entered the War, her land forces (territorial forces included) numbered no more than 300,000, with no heavy artillery. By the autumn of 1918, the army was reinforced by over three million men equipped with modern heavy arms, two million of whom were sent to the European theatre of war. In spite of her own large military presence, the Americans raised more money to finance her allies in the First World War than for her own conduct of the war. As a result she developed, within a few years, from a debtor to the main creditor country in the world. In 1914 the Europeans, by acquiring assets in America, had altogether around seven milliard dollars' worth of claims against the United States; in 1919 the Europeans were indebted to the Americans to the tune of $12 milliard.

After war had broken out in Europe, America endeavoured to maintain strict neutrality. It was for this reason that, until the spring of 1915, American banks did not receive government consent to provide credit for the Entente Powers to finance their armaments contracts with American firms. The Americans had traditionally had great sympathy for France; the Anglo-Saxon element in the United States felt most akin to the British. On the other side stood the Americans of German descent and the strong contingent of Irish immigrants whose sympathies were with the Central Powers. Several prominent American bankers, such as Otto Kahn, Jacob Schiff, Paul and Felix Warburg, James Speyer and Charles Hallgarten, came from Jewish families with branches still domiciled in Germany. Thus they had family, friendly and also business ties with Central Europe.

In the meantime neutrality became increasingly problematical for the United States. Even before the War, their economic relations with the Entente Powers were incomparably closer than those with the Central Powers. In 1913, 77% of America's exports went to the countries and colonies of Britain, France and Russia. Britain's naval blockage caused American exports to Central Europe to shrink from $169 million in 1914 to precisely one million dollars in 1916. This represented the value of the goods which actually arrived in Germany and Austria-Hungary through the trade channels of neutral states in Northern and Western Europe. American exports to the Entente countries, on the other hand, rose from $825 million to $3.2 milliard during the same period. Thus the economic community of interests between the United States and the Entente Powers was becoming steadily closer. The boom which the American economy experienced during the First World War was almost solely due to her exports or war materials, foodstuffs and raw materials essential to the war effort in Britain, France and Russia.

As a result of these economic interests, the United States drew closer to the Entente from 1915. When the Entente Powers' foreign currency and gold reserves dwindled and it was feared that their arms orders might have to be reduced, Washington abandoned its negative attitude towards its own banks. In May 1915, credits were made available to the governments of the Western Powers and Russia. And yet it was not merely economic interests which induced the United States to enter the war against Germany on the side of the Western European powers in April 1917. As late as November 1916, the Board of Governors had warned the American banks against accepting too many loans from the belligerent countries since their servicing might become uncertain. At the same time, Democratic Party managers organised Woodrow Wilson's presidential election campaign under the slogan 'He kept us out of the War'. Although by the end of 1916 Wilson was convinced that it was scarcely possible to prevent the United States from becoming involved in the conflict, the general mood was still against it. Nevertheless, that the United States finally entered the War and that the Americans greeted this step enthusiastically, was largely due to the impact of German submarine warfare and Germany's scant regard for the United States.

On 1 February 1917 the Reich recommended unrestricted submarine warfare. Three days later, President Wilson broke off diplomatic relations. In the second half of February, a German submarine sank the British luxury-liner *Laconia* in a torpedo attack off the Irish coast; there was no prior warning. This time there were American citizens on board, and they lost their lives. Three days later, the 'Zimmermann Telegram' became public. Arthur Zimmermann, the Secretary of State at the Reich Foreign Ministry, had informed the German Ambassador in Mexico, in a coded telegramme, of the resumption of unrestricted submarine warfare. He added that Berlin counted on the continuing neutrality of the United States. However, should the Americans refuse to remain neutral, it would be necessary for Germany to enter into an alliance with Mexico against the United States. The Mexicans were to be guaranteed the return of the American Federal States of Texas, New Mexico and Arizona, which had once belonged to Mexico. The British, who had cracked the German Foreign Ministry's code, had intercepted and deciphered the telegram, and informed the Americans about it. These two events, the sinking of the *Laconia* and the publication of the 'Zimmermann Telegram', brought about a change of mood in the United States. When four more American merchant ships fell prey to German submarine warfare during March 1917, America was prepared to enter the War.

In the two years that America was at war in 1917 and 1918 her state expenditure reached a total of 15.9 milliard dollars. Some $5.3 milliard, about one-third, were raised through ordinary revenue. By September 1916 direct taxation had been increased: income tax remained the main source of revenue, yielding 50% of the ordinary budget in the two years of war. In 1914 income tax from individuals amounted to $41 million; the figure for 1918 was $1.13 milliard. The yield from corporation tax rose from $39 million in 1914 to 653 million in 1918. With America's entry into the War, the Treasury Department issued short-term bonds to prefinance the war expenditure, known as 'Treasury Certificates of Indebtedness'. Some $22 milliard in these bonds were produced and placed mostly with banks. But short-term debts could be substituted almost completely by long-term state loans. From May 1917 until July 1918 four 'Liberty loans' were issued on the basis of four Liberty Bond Acts. They yielded $17 milliard. In April 1919 a further war loan, the 'Victory loan', was issued which raised another $4.5 milliard. Over half the returns from these war loans were passed on to the Allies (see below pp. 204f.). As a result of financing her own war and even more so that of her Allies, the American state debt rose from $1.2 milliard in 1916 to $25.5 milliard in June 1919. However, only $175 million of these were floating debts. Because the proportion of short-term debts in the state debt was so small, the balance of trade so favourable and, finally, the decline in the exchange rates of other currencies so much sharper, America had the smallest increase in prices of all belligerents. The wholesale price index rose from 100 in 1913 to 194 in 1918.

The outbreak of the war in the summer of 1914 triggered off a brief economic crisis which forced the Americans to take energetic counter-measures. Cotton plantations had a record crop that year; but it could not now be sold to the usual principal customer countries that were at war. In order to support the cotton producers, bank syndicates placed interim credits and depreciation credits at their disposal. Since many European holders of American securities tried to mobilize their American bonds in order to obtain liquid assets, the New York Stock Exchange was swamped with selling orders from Europe in the last two days in July. To forestall a fall in prices of American securities, the Stock Exchange was closed on 31 July 1914. Stock Exchange business started again on a limited scale by the end of November 1914. A committee decided in every single case which bonds were to be admitted for trading. It was only from 1 April 1915 that the Stock Exchange operated without restrictions again.

The initial crisis did not last for long. Soon the United States stepped up their deliveries of war materials to Britain, France and Russia and this led to an economic boom. In order to be able to pay for these deliveries the governments of the Entente Powers had to rely on credits from the American banks. The majority of the big banking firms was prepared to give this financial support well before the Federal government in Washington ruled that credits granted to belligerents did not constitute a violation of neutrality. However, there was strong opposition in the American public and press to this policy. The pacifists argued that the war would be pro-longed by these credits. But there was also a very sober economic calcu-lation against financing the Entente Powers. Many questioned whether they would be able to repay their debts later. This question was very pertinent as, indeed, only part of the debt was repaid after the War. As late as October 1915, the economist Edward S. Meade, writing in the *Magazine of Wall Street*, warned against the purchase of foreign securities. He believed that it would be better to invest this money in the building of canals, railways, streets, factories and housing in the United States. As he put it: 'The nation should keep its money at home.' Other political economists objected to such arguments by referring to the example of England and Germany in the pre-war period. They pointed out that Britain and Germany had been able to promote their foreign trade with the help of credits to foreign countries.

The critics did not deter American bankers from lending to belligerents. Most of them felt that Germany alone was no longer credit-worthy because her foreign trade had almost collapsed under the impact of the British blockade. J.P. Morgan & Co. was most prominently involved in loan transactions for Britian and France. In the first three years of war, Morgan transacted all British and French loans in the United States, or at least headed the consortium concerned with these transactions. The assets of the two Morgan banks in New York and Philadelphia rose from $228 million to $481 million between 31 December 1914 and 31 December 1917. Morgan's largest deal involved the placing of a Franco-British loan worth over $500 million in October 1915. This was not an easy operation because the German and Irish elements in the United States offered fierce opposition. Further difficulties arose when Kuhn Loeb & Co. pulled out. Jacob Schiff, the bank's head, had originally agreed to participate. He then learned that Russia would benefit indirectly and refused to provide aid to a country where anti-Jewish pogroms were taking place. And as it was generally known that Britain and France passed some American money on to Tsarist Russia, Kuhn Loeb & Co. did not issue any British and French state loans until after the fall of the Tsarist regime. Following Schiff's retreat, Morgan formed a consortium of 61 New York banks and trust companies, which was joined by 1,570 firms throughout the country. In Chicago, pro-German feeling was still so strong in the autumn of 1915 that only one bank was prepared to join the consortium. In the end, most of the money for this $500 million loan was raised by the consortium banks themselves, as the public still considered such a big loan to be incompatible with American neutrality.

Morgan mediated four further loans for Britain in 1916-17, totalling over $950 million. He was also deeply involved in the issue of French loans. In August 1914, the French government had entrusted the Morgan Bank to look after their financial interests in the United States. In the following year, France obtained a $100 million loan, mediated by Morgan. To facilitate this, he formed a trust company, the American Foreign Securities Company, registered in the State of New York, which included, *inter alia*, the First National Bank of New York, the Mellon National Bank, the Guaranty Trust Company, the Chase National Bank, the Hanover Bank of New York, the Farmers' Loan & Trust Company, and the banks of the Brown Brothers, Dillon Read & Co., and Lee Higginson & Co. The French government deposited as collateral government bonds in neutral countries, together with shares in the Suez Canal Company and shares of American companies.

Whereas the American capital market was open to the Entente Powers, the governments of the Central Powers found but very limited credit facilities across the Atlantic during the period of American neutrality. In March 1915, Chandler & Co. of New York placed German Treasury bills for $ 10 million with banks and trust companies in New York and with private individuals in cities with a strong German immigrant element, such as Cincinnati and Philadelphia. But support dwindled quickly when, in the autumn of 1915, Zimmermann & Forshay offered denominations of the third German War Loan at the low rate of 84%. In the end, it became a loss-making venture for the Bank, and Kuhn Loeb & Co. did not issue any German war loans despite friendly and familial ties with Germany. In 1916, Jacob Schiff was quite prepared to participate in a loan for a number of major German cities such as Berlin, Hamburg and Frankfurt. He had to drop the plan when President Wilson and the Federal Reserve Board voiced their disapproval. Kuhn Loeb & Co. floated a loan for French cities instead. Although the credit America gave to Germany before she entered the War remained insignificant, it was still possible, with the assistance of American banks, to mobilize at least part of Germany's capital investments in America. American shares worth around $ 300 million were sold off by German investors up to the end of 1915.

American banks mediated loans amounting to $2.16 milliard to the belligerent countries from the summer of 1914 until the United States entered the War in April 1917. Some 2.124 milliard of these dollars went to the Entente Powers; the Central Powers received no more than $35 million . The British government was the main recipient of American credits and received more than half, i.e. $1.25 milliard. The French Government got just under one-third ($640 million). Russia was able to place loans worth $107 million in America, followed by Japan with $102 million; Italy, whose need of financial aid was chiefly met by Britain, received a mere $25 million from American banks. The banks also arranged the repurchase of more than $3 milliard of American securities from the belligerent states. When compared with their extensive foreign business, the placing of internal American loans was of less significance for the big banking firms. Nevertheless, the proportion of short and medium-term bank credits in internal American banking business increased sharply. And companies which wanted to take up consolidated loans had to pay considerably higher interest rates than before the War because demand by foreign governments was pushing rates up.

The situation changed with the American entry into the War. Now the Federal government became the largest borrower, and credit to the govern-ments of the Allies was no longer granted directly by the banks but by Washington. In the last analysis, however, American banks remained the creditors in this procedure; the funds which the Government advanced to its Allies originated from the credits which the banks had made available to Washington. The Allies took up about $12 milliard in loans in America until the end of the War. Some $2.1 milliard of this were debts which the Allied governments owed the American banks, and almost $10 milliard were debts to the American government.

2. The Inter-Allied Debts

The international creditor-debtor relations which existed before the First World War were of a commercial nature, regardless of any political conditions and regardless of whatever consequences they may have had.

This is also true of the international debts of governments. When a government appeared on the international money markets, this was done indirectly through commercial channels and agreements with foreign banks. During the 19th century, there were a few cases of 'political' debts. This happened when creditor-debtor relations were formed temporarily between two governments in the wake of political events and agreements, such as the payment of a war indemnity by the defeated party. It was described in a neutral fashion as a 'war indemnity' or just *'paiement'*; the pejorative term 'reparations' only came into use as a result of the passions and sufferings of the First World War. All war indemnities imposed in the course of the 19th century were assessed in such a way that they could be paid within a short period of time. As a consequence there were no long-term creditor-debtor relations of a political kind before 1914. The political debts created by the First World War, on the other hand, were so enormous that, according to contemporary calculations, it would take decades for their repayment to be completed. Even before the United States entered the War, political debts between the Allied governments began to pile up in connection with the credits which Britain and, to a lesser extent, France granted to Russia, Italy, Belgium, Serbia and Rumania. From April 1917 the American government became the main creditor of these inter-Allied debts. Finally, under the terms of the Versailles Peace Treaty, France, Britain, Italy, Belgium, Rumania, Greece, Yugoslavia, Japan and Portugal all became the creditors of Germany's reparation debts.

The size of the inter-Allied debts owed to the United States grew by another $800 million after the War. This was because the Americans supplied both Allied and friendly countries with some of the military equipment which was used in the European theatre of war. Until 1920, the American government moreover sent cereals and food on credit to the destitute peoples of the Baltic States, Russia, Poland, Armenia and the successor-states of the Austro-Hungarian Monarchy. In compiling their inter-Allied claims, the United States arrived at the sum of $10.34 milliard, of which $9.598 milliard were cash advances to the Allies during the War and to Czechoslovakia. The total value of the military equipment was estimated at $599 million. Some $407 million worth remained in France. The rest was supplied to Belgium ($30 million), Poland ($83.7 million), Yugoslavia ($25 million), Rumania ($12.9 million), the three Baltic states ($18.8 million) and Czechoslovakia ($20.6 million). The postwar cereal and food supplies were worth $141 million.

Britain had received about 45% of the total cash advances made by the American government: $4.277 milliard. France was given $2.997 milliard, and Italy was the third largest debtor with $1.648 milliard. Belgium collected a further $349 million in addition to military equipment. During the Kerenski period, Russia received $187,729 million. The young Czechoslovak Republic, whose Provisional Government was formed in Paris on 14 October 1918 and recognized by the United States five days later, was given a further $61.97 million in cash advances by the American government.

British credit to her Allies was not much less than the sums forked out by the Americans. It reached a final total of $8.3 milliard, i.e. almost twice the sum that Britain had herself received from the United States. Russia was given the largest amounts ($2.47 milliard); $1.855 milliard were advanced to Italy, followed by France with $1.683 milliard. The remainder was distributed among the Dominions, Serbia, Rumania and Portugal. The French government granted her allies credits to the tune of $2.238 milliard. However, these claims were balanced by French debts to the United States and Britain which had risen to over $5 milliard.

The European countries regarded the inter-Allied debts as part of their joint war effort which were to be made good by German reparations. The United States, on the other hand, viewed these debts as commercial commitments between countries which had to be honoured. America found herself in a special position within the system of inter-Allied debts. Not only was she the main creditor in this complex web of creditor-debtor relations, but also the only country which was exclusively a creditor.

Britain's attitude towards the problem of inter-Allied debts differed substantially from that of the United States. Britain, to be sure, was more creditor than debtor. But leading British politicians of the early post-war years, Lloyd George, Churchill, Balfour and Baldwin among them, became convinced by John M. Keynes's argument that the best way to settle war debts was to annul them. Lloyd George, the British Prime Minister, had tried unsuccessfully to convert President Wilson to this view during the Paris Peace Conference in 1919. A year later, Foreign Secretary Balfour argued in a memorandum to the American government that all inter-Allied debts be cancelled for the sake of 'the future prosperity of the world'. He was not merely speaking on behalf of the debtors, but also as a representative of a creditor nation and announced that Britain would certainly not claim more from her debtors than she herself would have to repay her creditors, above all to the United States, with insignificant amounts owed to Canada and Japan. The American response was again negative. Thenceforth Britain tried to settle her debts with the United States on a treaty basis. In 1923, the American Treasury Secretary Andrew Mellon and Stanley Baldwin, the new British Prime Minister, negotiated the Mellon-Baldwin Agreement which specified that British debts were to be repaid within 62 years. The amount of the debt was fixed at $4.3 milliard plus $300 million of accrued interest, the 5% interest agreed upon at the time of the borrowing having been reduced to 3.3%. Interest inceased the total payment of the debt from $4.6 milliard to $11.1 milliard.

The other debtor countries who arranged the contractual settlement of their debt repayment at a later date, got off considerably more lightly than Britain. In 1926, Finance Minister Bérenger succeeded in reducing France's rate of interest to 1.8% under the terms of the Mellon-Bérenger Agreement. In this instance the French debt, which was likewise to be repaid within 62 years, was fixed at four milliard dollars, including the accrued interest. As a result of the reduced interest rate, France's total payment rose to

$6.8 milliard. By comparison, Britain had to pay rather dearly for her efforts to achieve a speedy settlement of her debts in accordance with international law. In the end, Britain was the only country to pay back more to the United States than she herself received from her Allied debtors and from German reparations.

The British view that it would be best to cancel inter-Allied debts completely and to use German reparations for reconstruction was not rejected out of hand only by America's leading bankers and by the Federal Reserve Board. When Balfour's memorandum of July 1920 was published, Paul M. Warburg, John Pierpont Morgan Jr. and Clarence Dillon all spoke up for a cancellation of inter-Allied debts. Benjamin Strong, the Governor of the Federal Reserve Bank of New York, did not favour annulment, but advised that repayment be deferred. American bankers recognized that the European allies would not be able to repay their debts unless they stepped up their exports to the United States; but such competition was precisely not in the interest of the American economy.

Against the views expressed by the leading bankers and the Federal Reserve Board, the American government remained stubborn on the issue of inter-Allied debts. Washington argued that the United States had taken up fresh credit to the tune of over $24 milliard in order to finance the inter-Allied debts as well as her own war effort; should the inter-Allied debts not be repaid, they would be charged to American taxpayers. This was also the argument put forward in the American press, and, of course, it went down well with the public. The Americans were disappointed with the attitude of their war-time European allies and so, turning away from a hopelessly divided Europe, isolationism dominated both public opinion and official policy. This isolationism did not create a congenial atmosphere for co-operation with the Europeans.

On the other hand, the American government's unbending insistence on the repayment of inter-Allied debts resulted in the Europeans being no less inflexible over German reparations. Although the Americans did not admit in the first post-war years that there was a link between German and inter-Allied reparations, this connection in fact reinforced their own attitude towards their Allied debtors. Of course, in the end they had no choice but to recognize it when they were forced to participate in the settlement of German reparations. As the United States insisted that inter-Allied debts be repaid, they had to help the Germans pay reparations to the Europeans so that these countries would in turn be able to make payments to America.

3. The German Reparations Issue up to the Young Plan

Both sides had geared the financing of the war to the expectation that the costs of the conflict could be imposed on the defeated enemy at a later date. On the German side, Undersecretary of State Karl Helfferich expounded this idea in the Reichstag in the summer of 1915: 'The instigators of this War deserve to carry the mill-stones of these milliards (of marks), and it is they who should be weighted down by them for decades, not us.' Historical experience has shown that the defeated side has always to take upon itself responsibility for a war and hence also the bulk of the costs, and in 1918 it was the Germans who were to bear the weight of these milliards. Having approved Helfferich's words in 1915, the Germans had no moral grounds to condemn the large claims made against them by the victorious Entente Powers. All one might criticize is the inadequate economic expertise which for a long time characterized the formulation of reparations policy.

Germany's liability was based on Article 231 of the Versailles Treaty. In this Article, it was declared that Germany and her allies 'were, as instigators, responsible for all losses and damages' suffered by the Allies and their citizens during the War. Subsequent clauses described Germany's reparations obligations in greater detail. These were: to hand over all merchant ships of over 1,600 tons, constituting 90% of the German merchant fleet (the second largest in the world in 1914), and to deliver machines, factory equipment, building materials, breeding cattle and 40 million tons of coal per annum for 10 years. The amount of reparations payable in cash was to be fixed later.

In a subsequent series of conferences, at first of the Allies themselves and from 1921 with German participation, negotiators sought to agree on a global sum and on the methods of payment and its distribution between the recipient countries. In June 1920, French Premier Millerand, Prime Minister Lloyd George, Lord Curzon, the British Foreign Secretary, the two Chiefs of Staff, Marshal Foch and Field-Marshal Wilson had a meeting at Boulogne with the Foreign Ministers of Italy, Belgium, Greece and Japan. A plan was accepted, which remained provisional for the moment and under which Germany was to pay a total of 269 milliard gold marks in 42 annual instalments. At a subsequent conference in Spa in July 1920, the creditor states reached an agreement on the distribution of German payments: France was to receive 52.5%, Britain 22%, Italy 10%, Belgium 8%, Yugoslavia 5%, Rumania 1.1%, Japan and Portugal 0.75% each and Greece 0.4%. However, in the winter of 1920-21 the currencies of most European states deteriorated. In terms of its 1914 value, the exchange rate of the pound had declined by 27.5% against the dollar; the franc saw a 17% drop against the dollar.

In view of this, another conference was convened at Paris in January 1921. It modified the reparations plan which had been unofficially accepted in Boulogne. Germany was now to pay a fixed sum of 226 milliard gold marks in 42 annual instalments; there was a further sum of 43 milliard gold marks which could be revised. Finally, the Reich was to cede 12% of its earnings from exports for the next 42 years. This plan served as a blueprint for the London Conference of February-March 1921, to which Germany had also been invited. The German government presented the Allies with a counter-proposal: they estimated that 269 milliard gold marks over 42 years had a current value of 50 milliard gold marks. By handling over her merchant fleet, railway stock and other equipment in the areas occupied by the Allies and taking into account the deliveries already effected, Germany was said to have paid reparations amounting to 20 milliard gold marks in assets; this supposedly left the country with debts of 30 milliard at current value. The Allies were not convinced by this calculation. Germany refused to accept the plans drawn up at the Paris Conference and sanctions were imposed: in March 1921, Allied troops occupied Düsseldorf, Duisburg and Ruhrort.

In April 1921, the Reparation Commission, at Britain's insistence, reduced the total sum to 132 milliard gold marks. The German government under Reich Chancellor Fehrenbach maintained its negative attitude. The Allies now issued an ultimatum, and on 5 May 1921 the German government was ordered by Britain, France, Japan, Belgium and Italy to declare within six days that Germany was prepared to meet the conditions set down by the Reparation Commission unconditionally, to comply with the disarmament measures stipulated by the Peace Treaty and to try her war criminals. The Fehrenbach government resigned on 4 May 1921 in anticipation of the ultimatum. On 10 May, Joseph Wirth formed a new cabinet, which was joined by Walther Rathenau as Foreign Minister. This government also considered it impossible to meet Allied reparations demands; but did not want to assert this merely in public declamations. By endeavouring to comply with Allied conditions, it wanted to demonstrate Germany's good will, but also the impossibility of fulfilling the demands. This was the purpose of the 'policy of fulfilment' which Wirth and Rathenau conceived and which was immediately decried and disparaged by intransigent German nationalists. Wirth's government accepted the London Ultimatum with the intention of proving that the reparations programme was unrealistic in practice. Germany paid an initial one milliard gold marks, which was followed later by a further remittance of 700 million gold marks. However, the rapid depreciation of the country's currency meant that by 1921-22 reparations were chiefly paid in kind. By the end of 1922, Germany was once more in arrears with her deliveries. At this point Paris lost patience and, after giving formal notice, French and Belgian troops occupied the Ruhr on 13 January 1923 to collect the payments in kind by themselves.

Galloping inflation (see below pp. 218ff.) and economic chaos in the summer and autumn of 1923 jeopardized Germany's ability to make any reparation payments at all and indeed during 1923 hardly any payments occurred. At this point, the creditors appealed to the United States, arguing that they were unable to repay their inter-Allied debts. In this way the United States were drawn into the German reparations question. If they wanted to recover their inter-Allied credits, Germany had to be helped to make her reparations payments again. However, the Americans also realized that Germany's inability to pay had in part been caused by French political pressure. Under the slogan: 'Business, not politics!', they therefore demanded that political considerations should be excluded from the reparations question and that the problem must be put on a commercially viable footing. At Washington's insistence, a commission of experts was convened in January 1924 under the chairmanship of the American financial expert

Charles G. Dawes to examine how to restore Germany's ability to pay and which payments Germany would be capable of making at all.

Germany had, up to this point, raised cash reparations worth 1.7 milliard gold marks. All other reparations payments prior to 1924 were made in kind. Estimates of their money value varied greatly between the German government and the Reparation Commission. The greatest difference of opinion arose over the estimated value of the merchant ships and confiscated German private property in the creditor countries. According to Germany's calculations, the merchant ships represented a value of 4.48 milliard gold marks; the Commission was of the opinion that this was the original value of the ships, but taking into account depreciation, a total value of only 712 million gold marks was assumed to be left. German private property confiscated in former enemy countries was estimated by the Germans at 10 milliard gold marks. The Commission, on the other hand, rated it at only 13 million gold marks. This estimate was certainly much too low. If one does *not* include those German foreign investments which had been confiscated during the War, the value of the German navy, of the Reich- and state property in the lost territories and of the labour of German prisoners of war, the Reich paid, according to credible German calculations, 20.7 milliard gold marks in reparations from the end of the War until 31 August 1924, of which 1.7 milliard gold marks were cash payments and 19 milliard gold marks were in assets.

In April 1924 the Commission of Experts presented its report, the so-called Dawes Plan. A week later, the German government had agreed to the plan. The Dawes Plan was signed in London on 16 August 1924. It was an agreement between the United States, the reparations creditors and Germany and had the force of an international treaty. The Plan came into operation on 1 September 1924; at the same time Germany introduced a new currency (see below pp. 221 ff.), and the occupation forces evacuated the Ruhr.

The Dawes Plan did not provide for a comprehensive settlement of German reparations and did not fix a new overall sum, but left this latter question open. In this sense it was no more than a temporary settlement. Although the stipulation that Germany must pay a total of 132 milliard gold marks was not lifted, it was overtaken by a provision in the Dawes Plan which removed payments in kind. This meant that the sum total to be determined at a future date had to be higher than 132 milliard marks, if it was to remain in line with the 1921 figure. The Dawes Plan laid down how much Germany would have to pay in the following years in annuities, how these annuities were to be raised within Germany and how the money was to be transferred to the creditor countries. Up to 1927-28, the annuities were to rise from an initial one milliard Reichsmark (RM) to 1.74 milliard RM. From 1928-29 onwards, regular annuities of 2.5 milliard RM were to be paid. In order to make certain that these sums were available, a mortgage was put on all German industrial enterprises amounting to five milliard RM. Furthermore the *Reichsbahn* (Reich Railways), which was transformed into a joint-stock company for this purpose, had a mortgage of 11 milliard RM imposed on it. Industry and the *Reichsbahn* were to pay 5% interest on these mortgages; amortization was fixed at 1%. These payments were to yield 960 million RM annually. Finally revenues from certain customs duties and indirect taxes were pledged as collateral, and the Reich government was allowed to use the revenue from these sources before the reparations annuity had been paid for the current year. An international Reparations Agent, the American banking expert Parker Gilbert, was appointed to supervise and regulate Germany's reparations payments. The Reich government paid the annuities in German currency to him, and he kept an account at the Reichsbank for this purpose. Gilbert was entrusted with the distribution of the annuities among the creditor countries according to the scheme which had been agreed in 1920. He also dealt with the transfer of the sums in foreign currency to their central banks. He was required both to control and to protect the reparations debtor. It was he who had to examine whether Germany's balance of payments would be threatened by the transfer of funds to the creditor countries. Indeed reparations could be transferred only when Germany's balance of payments was favourable. In case of an unfavourable balance, he was empowered to leave the annuities in his account at the Reichsbank.

From 1924 until 1929 Germany paid out eight milliard RM in reparations. This amount was in fact transferred, as the country's balance of payments was healthy from 1924 to the onset of the Great Slump; this was because foreign credit flowed into Central Europe on a large scale, once the Dawes Plan had come into force and the German currency reform had been enacted (see below p. 230).

Within two years of the ratification of the Dawes Plan, efforts and preparations were made to replace it with a final settlement of the reparations question. Four contradictory positions emerged during these preparations. The French were the first to try to replace the Dawes Plan. From July 1926 the new French Premier Poincaré worked together with Emile Moreau, the Governor of the Banque de France, to re-stabilize the franc (see below (pp. 223ff.). In order to achieve this objective, he considered it desirable to obtain France's reparations from Germany more quickly. One solution seemed to be to increase the mortgage on the *Reichsbahn*. With her 52.5% share in reparations, France was a creditor of the *Reichsbahn* to the tune of over 5.5 milliard RM. However, under the stipulations of the Dawes Plan, France could not turn these claims into liquid funds, just as mortgage certificates cannot normally be sold; she was merely entitled to annual interest and amortization payments. Poincaré and Moreau now had the idea to quote the French share of the *Reichsbahn* mortgage on the stock exchange. They expected to sell approximately four milliard RM of *Reichsbahn* mortgage bonds on the American capital market. At least this is what they had been promised by the New York bank of Dillon Read & Co., which hoped to enter into business relations with the French government in this way. The sale of French reparation claims to private persons and commercial banks could, of course, only succeed, if intending buyers were able to sell the bonds at any time. In short, Poincaré and Moreau wanted to remove the transfer protection provided by the Dawes Plan, and for this they needed German approval. The French believed they would be able to obtain this approval, if they hinted at the possibility of a political favour in return, such as an early evacuation of the occupied areas in the Rhineland and the Palatinate.

These were the financial and monetary aspects which formed the historical background to the Franco-German rapprochement of the summer of 1926 and which reached its sensational climax in the talks between Briand and Stresemann at Thoiry in September 1926. The meeting had no tangible results, partly because Briand, on the French side, promised more in return for a 'commercialization' of the German reparation debt than Poincaré was prepared to concede; but above all, because the project had meanwhile been deprived of its economic basis; the American government and the Federal Reserve Board refused to place *Reichsbahn* bonds on the American capital market so long as the repayment of French debts to the United States had not been settled. It was only in 1929 that the Mellon-Bérenger Agreement was ratified by the French Chamber. Fortunately, France's financial position improved in the winter of 1926-27, and the franc could be stabilized. Consequently, French interest in an early revision of the reparations settlement diminished. Nevertheless, in principle the French government continued to pursue the 'commercialization' of the German debt in exchange for concessions relating to the evacuation of the Rhineland.

Meanwhile Parker Gilbert worked very hard for a revision of the Dawes Plan and a final settlement of the overall reparations figure. He urged the Germans and the French to come to a quick agreement, using opposite arguments to convince the two sides. He made it clear to the French that it was imperative for them to fix the final figure without delay because an economic crisis was expected in Germany. If it were fixed in an economic crisis, France would be the worse off, whereas she stood to receive more, if the figure was agreed at a time when Germany's economy was booming. And booming it was in the summer of 1927. Gilbert took a different line in his negotiations with Stresemann, the German Foreign Minister, and Julius Curtius, the Reich Minister of Economics. He put it to both of them that a speedy settlement of the final reparations figure was in Germany's best interest; for, from 1928-29, regular annuities of 2.5 milliard RM would be due as laid down by the Dawes Plan. Should Germany be able to raise the full amount of the first annuity, her creditors would continue to insist on this amount in future. Germany would hence be better off, if a final settlement with lower annuities could be agreed before she undermined her claim that she was unable to pay by actually raising those 2.5 milliard RM.

It is not clear what Parker Gilbert intended to achieve with his double-game. Some of his statements suggest that he genuinely expected an economic crisis in Germany and that he did not wish to get embroiled in a conflict between the claims of the reparations creditors, on the one hand,

and his duty to protect Germany's currency, on the other. At the same time, he was not prepared to grant transfer protection in case there was a deficit in the German balance of payments or to defer the remittance of reparations. The German government learned this much when it decoded Gilbert's telegrammes to the American government. This enabled them to follow the confidential exchange of telegrammes between the Reparations Agent and Washington.

After fruitless preparatory talks with the French government in the summer of 1926 and its negotiations with Parker Gilbert, the Reich government came to see the benefits of revising the Dawes Plan. It could expect some relief on the political and financial front by agreeing to waive the clause on transfer protection. The Germans also knew only too well that transfer protection would not in practice be upheld in an emergency, and hence felt free to use it as a political bargaining counter in the negotiations. The financial price at which transfer protection could be sold was a reduction of the 'regular annuities' under the Dawes Plan. Gilbert suggested this possibility. The political price for waiving the transfer protection was the elimination of a number of restrictions on German sovereignty. As the French and Gilbert had hinted, an early evacuation of the Rhineland, the removal of the institution of the Reparations Agent and a lifting of international controls on the Reichsbank seemed to be within reach.

The British government and the presidents of Britain's and Germany's issuing banks, Montagu Norman and Hjalmar Schacht, on the other hand, thought little of a speedy final settlement of reparations. London and the two presidents of the issuing banks all expected an early economic crisis. They anticipated that a lower final figure and lower annuities would then become inevitable. And the British government also hoped that an annulment or reduction of the inter-Allied debts might be obtained at the same time. Schacht, who had not been told of Gilbert's decoded telegrams and who therefore still regarded the transfer protection as valuable, did not wish to waive the protective clause in the face of the expected economic crisis.

In the autumn of 1928 the German government reached agreement with France, Britain, Italy, Japan and Belgium that negotiations to revise the Dawes Plan were to be opened and that they were to include an early evacuation of the Rhineland. After preliminary negotiations, it was decided the criterion for the settlement of annual reparations payments should be Germany's ability to pay. This meant that a committee of financial experts had to determine first of all the country's economic capacity before the governments could begin to negotiate a revised reparations agreement. Because German reparations and inter-Allied debts were interconnected, the United States had to come in as well. However, in the autumn of 1928 the campaign for the American presidential elections was in full swing. The new President would not be sworn in before January 1929 and major political decisions could not be expected in Washington during that period.

The Conference of Experts therefore did not start in Paris until

9 February 1929. The chair was taken by Owen D. Young, the President of the Board of Directors of the American General Electric Company. The second American delegate was John Pierpont Morgan, Jr. The head of the French delegation was the Governor of the Banque de France, Emile Moreau. The first Belgian delegate was Emile Franqui, who had moved from the Board of Directors of the Société Générale de Belgique to the office of Vice-Governor of the Banque Nationale de Belgique in 1923. The British experts were Sir Josuah Stamp who sat on the Board of the Bank of England and Lord Revelstoke of Baring Brothers. On the German side, Schacht, the President of the Reichsbank, Ludwig Kastl, member of the executive committee of the *Reichsverband der deutschen Industrie* and Carl Melchior of the Hamburg banking house of M.M. Warburg & Co. were appointed. The appointment of Schacht as head of the German delegation was certainly justified on account of his expert knowledge; but it was nevertheless not a happy choice. There had been so many misunderstandings and so much mutual distrust between Schacht and the Reich government of Reich Chancellor Hermann Müller that not only did they fail to co-operate, but they even disavowed each other on more than one occasion. This led to a crisis which almost brought the conference to the brink of collapse. If Germany nevertheless realized some of her objectives, she owed it not to her own diplomacy, but to the Americans and the British, who worked hard for a practicable and generally acceptable solution.

The experts adopted the Young Plan of 7 June 1929. With a few minor modifications, agreed at two further conferences, it became an international treaty and was signed at The Hague on 20 January 1930. Germany's remaining reparations debt was fixed at a current value of 34.5 milliard RM. It was to be paid in 59 annual instalments until 1988. In the first 37 years, the annuities were to rise gradually from 1.6 to 2.2 milliard RM, after which they would again diminish. Because the debt repayments were distributed over a period of 59 years and included accumulated interest, the total sum came to 110.7 milliard RM. Some 660 million RM of each instalment were to be transferred as a matter of course. In an economic emergency, the Reich government could apply for a transfer deferment of up to two years for that part of the annuity which exceeded those 660 million RM. Thus, the total sum of the payments still to be made had at last been fixed. The annuities for the years until 1940 were to be 500 million RM less than the regular annuities under the Dawes Plan. The abolition of the transfer protection implied a weakening of Germany's legal position; in practice it carried little weight, since, in Gilbert's view, it could not be invoked, anyway. But the Young Plan gave Germany various political gains: the immediate evacuation of the Rhineland by the occupation forces five years ahead of schedule, the abolition of the Reparations Agent's office and of international control over the Reichsbank. As soon as the Dawes Plan had been accepted, Germany was granted an international loan of 800 million gold marks; she received another international loan nominally valued at $351 million and with an effective yield of $300 million.

Several obvious advantages notwithstanding, the ratification of the Young Plan by Germany was accompanied by furious protests from the German Nationalists, the National Socialists and the *Stahlhelm* veterans' association. They demanded that criminal proceedings be initiated against those Reich ministers and representatives who had signed the final treaty document. Schacht, who had initialled the Young Plan, also joined the ranks of chauvinist critics and ostentatiously resigned as President of the Reichsbank. He justified his U-turn with spurious arguments to the effect that the Young Plan had been altered to Germany's disadvantage in the final version at The Hague, a statement which was quite simply false. The actual reason for his disassociation was that during the domestic German disputes about the Young Plan he recognized the strength of the nationalist opposition. It was on this opposition movement that he now staked his political future in the expectation that it would eventually gain power.

The Young Plan also influenced the history of banking in the 20th century. It initiated the foundation of the first international public bank, the Bank for International Settlements (BIS) at Basle. As the office of the Reparations Agent had been closed and the transfer of reparations had been 'commercialized', it seemed necessary to establish an official, though politically independent, bank to carry out the large-scale international business arising from the transfers and the international loan transactions connected with it. Implementing a proposal by Schacht, the Young Plan established an international bank. It was set up by the states participating in the reparations agreement with its registered office in a neutral country. Consequently, the central issuing banks of Germany, Belgium, France, Britain, Italy and Japan founded the Bank for International Settlements as a joint subsidiary. Its head office was in Basle. It was constituted as a joint-stock company in accordance with Swiss law. The board of directors was made up of the presidents of each of the promoting banks and a second representative. A group of commercial banks in the United States acquired a parcel of shares of the BIS. In 1931, the central issuing banks of Switzerland, the Netherlands and Sweden also participated. The Bank was equipped with a large joint-stock capital of 500 million Swiss francs. Its tasks consisted of carrying out, on a trusteeship basis, the international operations assigned to it by the central issuing banks. It thus handled the reparations transfers and was involved in the international loan- and gold business.

4. The Course of the German Inflation

The main reason why a scheme for reparation payments came into being only in 1924 was the confused state of Germany's currency. This confusion lasted for several years after 1918. Germany's inflation after the First World War is a model case of hyperinflation. It has therefore posed a challenge not only to economic historians, but also to economists and monetary theoreticians who have investigated and analysed it. The latter have basically employed three theories to explain the causes and economic relationships behind Germany's inflation: the balance of payments theory, the inflation theory and the purchasing-power parity theory. The advocates of the balance of payments theory, such as Karl Helfferich and Moritz Julius Bonn, saw the main cause of inflation in the fact that Germany's balance of payments had been consistently unfavourable after 1914. It was this that caused the exchange rate to fall; import prices rose and domestic price levels were forced up. They attributed the unfavourable balance of payments to the reparations payments, the flight of capital and impeded German exports, and to the loss of income from Germany's merchant fleet which had been surrendered to the Allies in 1919. The soundest argument in favour of this theory was that until August 1923, the mark's exchange rate declined on the whole more rapidly and more steeply than prices rose on the German domestic market.

The supporters of the balance of payments theory, most of whom were German, were criticized for attempting to use their theory for political purposes to prove that the burden of reparations was intolerably high; it was not based on sufficient scientific evidence. The inflation theory — of which Gustav Cassel, Ludwig Albert Hahn and Alfred Lansburgh were prominent advocates — argued that the causal link worked in the opposite direction from that which the balance of payments theorists assumed. The inflation theorists regarded the enormous public indebtedness and the increases in the money supply as the cause of inflation. These two factors in turn led to the rapid deterioration of the rate of exchange. In its early and rather schematic formulation — later and more differentiated versions of the inflation theory cannot and need not be considered here — this theory was a continuation and extension of David Ricardo's currency theory (see above p. 8). The strongest argument supporting the inflation theory was that the excessive increases in both the public debt and the money supply had set in during the War and hence several years before Germany made her first reparations payments.

Finally, in making a comparative analysis between Germany's hyper-inflation and cases of very much lesser inflation in the victorious nations, Gustav Cassel developed his purchasing-power parity theory. This theory held that, when considering the inflation of two currencies, the 'normal' rate of exchange between them equals the old rate of exchange multiplied by the quotient of the rate of price increases in the two countries. Cassel's theory won wide recognition in the 1920s, above all through the writings of Keynes, Hahn and Lansburgh. However, it only fits the very improbable case that there are no restrictions on international trade and that there are no significant capital movements which might also influence the exchange rate. Neither of these conditions were fulfilled between 1918 and 1924.

Whilst these three theories certainly further our understanding of individual problems of the Great Inflation, they explain neither the inflation itself, its causes and its dimensions, nor the fissures and leaps in its development. On closer inspection all these theories examine isolated factors and so become monocausal explanatory models, which are of little value in dealing with such a complex phenomenon. Above all, a purely economic explanation of economic developments which were so closely intertwined with political factors as the collapse of the German monetary system after 1918 must inevitably miss the mark. If economic historians for a long time rightly criticized political historians for neglecting economic history in their interpretations of history, economic historians must take care not to fall into the other trap of neglecting politics in their analysis of economic events.

Germany's inflation began in 1914 and was related to the way in which the War was being financed. We have seen that higher direct taxes were imposed very late and that the Reich resorted primarily to borrowing. By the end of the War, the exchange rate and the mark's internal purchasing power had fallen to 50% of the corresponding pre-war figures. The value of money continued to fall after the end of the War. The exchange rate of the mark against the dollar had slumped to an eleventh of the pre-war ratio by the end of 1919. In December 1919 one dollar was on average 46.80 marks. After the Treaty of Versailles had come into force in January 1920, the rate of exchange deteriorated in the following weeks to approximately 99 marks for one dollar. This sudden change in the rate of exchange was apparently related to the flight of capital from Germany. We can only assume this today; it is difficult enough to ascertain the flight of capital quantitatively in the balance of payments statistics, but it is even more difficult for the historian to demonstrate in retrospect that a flight of capital had in fact occurred.

From the spring of 1920 until June 1921, there was a period of relative stability when on average 64 marks equalled one dollar. At the end of May 1921, when the first instalment of reparations amounting to one milliard gold marks had been paid following the London Ultimatum, the decline in the mark's rate of exchange began once more. The pace of the deterioration was now considerably faster than it had been in 1919. In June 1922 the dollar was quoted at 317.50 marks. After the assassination of Foreign Minister Walther Rathenau on 24 June 1922, the rate of exchange slumped to 493.20 marks for one dollar in July 1922. Thenceforth galloping inflation set in when the Reichsbank introduced its inflationary credit policy to which we shall return in a moment. By December 1922, the dollar was quoted at an average of 7,592 marks. Once French and Belgian troops had occupied the Ruhr district and the Germans had begun their passive resistance to which the French responded with their own counter-measures, the fall into the abyss could not be stopped. In January 1923, the dollar was on average 17,972 marks and in July 1923 between 300,000 and 400,000 marks. From August 1923, the collapse was so enormous that the mark lost its *raison d'être* as a currency, and the German economy found itself in a state of disintegration. On 15 November 1923, 4,200 milliard marks were paid for one dollar. This is the last available quotation before the totally devalued paper-mark was replaced by an interim currency: the rentenmark.

If one looks for the causes of hyperinflation, the Reich's long-standing and large budget deficits must come first in the chronological order. This applies not only to the beginning of the inflation during the First World War, but also to its post-war development when the Reich budgets remained in deficit. In the first years of peace, ordinary revenue could not even cover half of the Reich's expenditure. In the financial year 1920-21, 34% of Reich expenditure were covered in this way; the figure for the financial year 1921-22 was 44% and 38% for 1922-23. In the immediate postwar years, budgets were burdened with the costs of demobilization, the deployment of troops to cope with local and regional revolts and the maintenance of Allied occupation forces in the Rhineland and the Palatinate. All these items made the return to a balanced budget even more difficult. The Reich also suffered a great loss of income through inflation itself; a period of up to 18 months would elapse between the assessment and collection of taxes such as income tax and corporation tax had been completed. The devaluation of money which took place in the meantime was to the detriment of the Reich and the *Länder.*

From time to time the Reich government came under fire from abroad. It was reproached for deliberately failing to balance its budget in order to take advantage of inflation and to flout the payment of reparations. This charge may not be quite fair. The Reich government seriously attempted to open up larger and more abundant sources of revenue when introducing the Erzberger financial reform of 1919-20. At the same time it tried to distribute tax burdens more justly by taking considerably more from the rich than from the lower income groups. The latter policy was wrecked by hyperinflation. Only those who had large incomes and great wealth profited from the inflationary devaluation of the tax debt and only if taxes were collected after assessment. The Reich government was unsuccessful in eliminating this damaging fiscal effect of inflation. But worst of all was that, because ordinary revenue covered only a small fraction of expenditure, over half of the Reich budget had to be financed by means of short-term treasury bills. As no-one in his right mind would have subscribed to a long-term loan at this time, Germany's short-term debt mounted further. The overall debt rose from 50 milliard marks at the end of the War to around 800 milliard marks in July 1922.

What role did reparations play in the Reich's budget deficit? At 1.7 milliard gold marks, the share of cash reparations was quite small. But reparations in kind, amounting to 19 milliard marks, which were delivered until 1924, burdened the budget. These goods had to be bought and paid for by the Reich government on the home market; they were withdrawn from the national economy to be dispatched as reparations in kind. By 1924, however, the bulk of these losses had been replaced. Dismantled machinery had made room for new machinery. The German merchant fleet, which had shrunk from 5.13 million BRT in mid-1914 to 0.4 million BRT in the summer of 1919, regained much of its former size and was at 2.9 million BRT by the beginning of 1924. By this time the *Reichsbahn* had

made good the losses of locomotives and rolling stock which had occurred
through wartime wear and tear and reparations deliveries. Indeed it
possessed more rolling stock than the various railway companies of the
German Empire had had before 1914, and they had operated a larger network. The devaluation of money made it easier to renew these goods in kind
on credit. In 1921 and 1922, reparations had used up almost all of the
Reich's ordinary revenues. The remaining items in the budget, which
included the replacement of *Reichsbahn* reparations, were almost exclusively
financed by further borrowing. In short, there is a very tangible connection
between reparations, and particularly reparations in kind, on the one hand,
and Germany's budget deficits, public indebtedness and continuing
inflation, on the other.

However, this causal link does not explain the enormous extent of
inflation from the summer 1922. At this stage it is necessary to examine the
actions and responsibilities of the Reichsbank itself. From the summer of
1922, the Reichsbank provided private enterprise with inflationary credits
at rates of interest so far below the actual level of devaluation that, by their
maturity date, they represented but a tiny fraction of their original value. In
the summer of 1922, when the currency had dropped to 1% of its 1914
value, the Reichsbank charged a 25% rate of interest; the rate was 85% in
the summer of 1923, when the value of the mark had fallen to one
millionth of its value of the summer of 1914. This credit policy can be
traced in the Reichsbank's balance sheet by looking at the steep rise in the
bills of exchange portfolio which began from the moment it provided its
first inflationary credits. From 30 June to 30 September 1922, the Bank's
holdings of bills rose from 4.8 to 50.2 milliard marks, a ten-fold increase,
whereas the price index rose no more than four- to five-fold. These
inflationary credits not only made it easy to pay for the replacement of
reparations in kind, but they also favoured investment and hence triggered
off a big wave of investments. In this sense it may be said that inflation
helped the German national economy to renew its industrial machinery and
infrastructure.

However, it would be wrong to conclude from this that the Reichsbank
and the Reich government deliberately pursued an inflationary policy, or at
least allowed inflation to take its course without adopting any counter-
measures. The Reichsbank and the Government tried to stabilize the
currency until the winter of 1922-23. The Bank endeavoured to obtain a
stabilization loan from American, Dutch and Swiss banks against the pledge
of the Reichsbank's gold. Yet such a loan would have been given only if
Germany's reparations payments had been suspended for several years; this
proved impossible to obtain. These attempts at stabilization could, of
course, not be reconciled with the inflationary credits which the Reichsbank
continued to supply. But the management of the Reichsbank under its
President Rudolf von Havenstein was apparently not aware of this incon-
gruity. The Bank pursued an inflationary policy not from malice, but
from ignorance of monetary theory. Until the autumn 1922, the board of

directors not only failed to realize that a catastrophe was threatening, but was also in no way pessimistic about the prospect of breaking out of the fatal inflationary spiral. This is revealed by the arguments which Havenstein and his Deputy, Otto von Glasenapp, presented to the Government. In view of the political and social conditions of the immediate postwar years, the Reichsbank and the Government considered it impossible to introduce tough credit restrictions, as Schacht, Havenstein's successor, succeeded in imposing after the currency reform of 1924. It would have brought the danger of massive unemployment, and this would in turn have sharply increased the political instability of the Weimar Republic.

By pointing to the threat of mass unemployment and its political consequences, the representative of the interests of industry had little difficulty in ensuring that fiscal and credit policies were handled in such a way as to facilitate the financing of large investments. In fact, until 1924 unemployment in defeated Germany was infinitely less than in the Netherlands, Sweden, Belgium or Britain. In October 1922, 1.4% of German workers organized in trade unions were unemployed, in contrast to 14.1% in Britain, 9.6% in Holland, 15.5% in Sweden and 3.9% in Belgium. Even bearing in mind that these figures must be used with caution because of the differing levels of trade union organization in the above-mentioned countries, the German unemployment rate remains exceptionally low. In view of this, trade union opposition to the financial policies of the time was not very strong. The practices which favoured the entrepreneurs spelled full employment for the workers, and this at a time of heavy unemployment in other countries.

Events began to turn only when the Ruhr was occupied in January 1923. The Reich government had been threatened with this action long before it actually occurred. Germany was in arrears with a relatively small quantity of reparation goods, and the Government could almost certainly have delivered them by the appointed date to prevent the occupation of the country's industrial heartland. Nevertheless, Reich Chancellor Wilhelm Cuno risked the invasion of the Ruhr by French and Belgian troops. It has been suspected that the Government pursued a deliberate policy of total bankruptcy and collapse in order to rid itself of reparations. But apparently this was not what it was aiming at. Rather it wanted to put France and Belgium in the wrong in full view of the rest of the world. If the penalty for an insignificant delay in the delivery of Germany's reparations was so severe, then — so the leaders in Berlin reasoned — her moral position would be strengthened in future reparation negotiations. Berlin had not reckoned with the collapse of the German monetary and financial systems. But it did expect supply difficulties (coal shortages) as well as mass unemployment and, in its wake, political unrest which might 'escalate into a dissolution of the Reich', as the Undersecretary in the Reich Chancellery put it in a memorandum. These calculations and fears were well founded. Germany achieved comparatively better reparations terms under the Dawes Plan, once the occupation of the Ruhr ended. But it was paid for with the complete

collapse of her financial and monetary system. Furthermore, the threat that
the Reich might break up into several states loomed large in the autumn of
1923 when there were uprisings in Bavaria and separatist activities in the
Rhineland and the Palatinate.

The immediate consequence of the Ruhr occupation was to accelerate
the deterioration of German currency. The Reich's government called upon
the population to counter the occupation with passive resistance, which
took the form of a general strike. France reacted to this by blocking the
transfer of taxes from the whole of the occupied area to the unoccupied
territory of the Reich. The loss of tax revenue from the largest and richest
industrial area was temporarily made up by short-term loans and ultimately
by the increased issue of bank notes. It was now only a question of time
before Germany's economy and finances would collapse. From the summer
of 1923 onwards, serious plans to overcome inflation were being worked
out. Hyperinflation was by now so catastrophic that nobody profited from
it any more. Unemployment also rose sharply. In many sectors of the
economy, payment with worthless money was replaced by barter. The
dangers which it had been feared in 1922 would result from an anti-
inflationary financial and credit policy — i.e. mass unemployment and
political unrest — were now brought about by hyperinflation. From the
summer of 1923, inaction in the face of galloping inflation had become
totally indefensible.

The end of passive resistance in the Ruhr was a *sine-qua-non* of a return
to a stable currency. The Reich's expenditure could only be reduced once
the struggle in the Ruhr had ended. This would also facilitate the
resumption of tax collection from the Ruhr district. Only thereafter would
there be a hope of balancing the budget again, and no policy of stabilization
could be carried out without a balanced budget. At the end of September
1923, passive resistance in the Ruhr was called off.

The first plan for a currency reform was presented in August 1923 by
Helfferich who, as Undersecretary in the Treasury, had been in charge of
public finances between 1915 and 1917 and who had in fact set off the
inflationary spiral during the War. Since the Reichsbank's holdings of gold
and foreign currency were insufficient to keep a stable one-third cover and
to issue the required amount of legal tender, Helfferich proposed to issue
a new currency, the 'rye mark', which was based on a cover in kind: the
yields of the rye harvest. The 'rye mark' could not become a stable currency
as the price of rye was exposed to strong fluctuations, depending on the
results of the harvest. A month later, the Social Democratic financial
expert Rudolf Hilferding, who was Reich Finance Minister in 1923 in
the Grand Coalition government of Gustav Stresemann, submitted a new
currency plan. He proposed to establish a Central Bank (whose note issue
would be exclusively based on gold) by providing it with a capital of 180
million gold marks. This Bank would then issue double the amount of its
capital in notes. However, it is clear that 360 million marks would have
been too little. In the end, the Hilferding Plan, like Helfferich's before it,

was rejected by the Cabinet. Hilferding resigned in October 1923; the former Reich Minister of Food, Hans Luther, succeeded him.

Luther combined Helfferich's and Hilferding's plans by preparing a 'currency in kind' as a transitional currency; later there was to be a return to the gold standard. Luther took industrial real estate as cover for the temporary currency. These assets represented a quite stable value which he mortgaged to the total value of 3.2 milliard gold marks. The mortgage was distributed between the individual companies affected in accordance with the valuations which had been made in 1913-14, following the introduction of a national 'defence contribution'. The mortgages bore an interest rate of 6%, and a public bank which was independent of the State, named Deutsche Rentenbank, became the creditor of this mortgage debt. On 15 November 1923, the bank note printing press was stopped, and the Deutsche Rentenbank began to issue the new money, the rentenmark. At first 2.4 milliard in rentenmarks were issued. Cover for the new notes was provided by land annuity securities, which were issued as mortgage bonds on industrial real estate. The Reich received 1.2 milliard of this total as non-interest-bearing credit, with the remaining 1.2 milliard rentenmarks being given to the Reichsbank to be passed on to the commercial banks. The rentenmark circulation was later increased to 3.2 milliard, the full amount of the mortgage on the industrial real estate. The devalued paper-mark was traded in at a ratio of one billion marks to one rentenmark.

The new currency could be kept stable because its circulation was limited to 3.2 milliard marks and could not be increased. It was also a purely domestic currency and was not related to any international rate of exchange; but it had a reliable cover. It could be converted into land annuity securities of 500 rentenmarks each, and these represented a secure capital investment, a claim on the industrial real estate. The Government and the Reichsbank, with Schacht as its President from December 1923, adjusted their strategy to the new monetary situation by pursuing a deflationary financial and credit policy. Numerous and severe cuts were made in the budget which resulted in a surplus of income over expenditure. Imports were curbed by temporary exchange controls in order to eliminate the deficit in the balance of trade. As was to be expected, this was unsuccessful; a certain volume of imports was indispensable for restocking. The Reichsbank reduced its credit to commercial banks and industry, and for a time it even blocked credit altogether.

The rentenmark was only a transitional currency, as Germany was obliged to return to the gold standard. This was one of the conditions of the Dawes Plan; but it was also desired by both the Reich government and the Reichsbank. The London Agreement of 1924, which ratified the Dawes Plan, contained in addition to the numerous clauses on reparations precise regulations relating to Germany's future currency and the status of the Reichsbank. This meant that the monetary structure was subject to international control and could not be changed unilaterally by German legislation.

In accordance with the stipulations of the London Agreement the

German monetary system was revamped on the basis of four currency laws
ratified on 30 August 1924. The Reich was put back on the gold standard
with the Reichsmark (RM) as the new monetary unit. The Reichsbank was
obliged to maintain a reserve at least 40% of which was in gold or in foreign
currency. Not less than three-quarters of this latter cover had to be in gold.
For the rest, a cover of first-class short-term trade bills was accepted as
sufficient. The Reichsbank was obliged to convert its notes, but it had a
choice. It could offer either gold coins, ingots or foreign bank notes,
calculated on the basis of the market value in gold of the currency
concerned. No gold coins were brought back into circulation so that the
restored gold currency was not a gold circulation currency but in fact a
gold exchange standard. Mindful that the dependence of the Reichsbank
on the Government, particularly in the question of the Reich debt, had
played a fateful role during the inflation, the amount of credit the central
issuing bank could grant to the Reich was now limited to 100 million RM
for a maximum of three months. The Reichsbank was allowed to buy Reich
treasury bills up to 400 million RM, but was not permitted to use them as
part of its cover. The Reichsbank was also permitted to provide the two big
Reich-owned companies, the *Reichsbahn* and the *Reichspost*, with working
capital to a total of 200 million RM.

On paper, the Reichsbank's independence of the Reich government had
been established as early as 1922, but as the Bank continued to be managed
by Havenstein, the ageing President of the Reichsbank who had been
appointed for life, its policy remained unaffected by this clause. Indeed,
galloping inflation set in only after the Reichsbank had become independent
and was to some extent a result of the Bank's disastrous credit policy. The
new Bank Law strengthened the independence of the central issuing bank at
the insistence of Germany's reparations creditors. It stipulated that the
Reichsbank's General Council alone could elect the President of the Reichsbank. The Reich President was to confirm the appointment. Of the 14
members of the General Council, seven were to be foreigners, with one
representative each to be nominated by Britain, America, France, Italy,
Belgium, the Netherlands and Switzerland. One of these foreign representatives was to control the bank's note issue as Note Commissioner. By
inserting this international control mechanism, Germany's creditors wanted
to prevent another inflation and remove the threat it posed to reparations
payments. But international control also affected Germany in a positive
way. By reducing the risk of inflation, the new law bolstered the credit-
worthiness of a country which had experienced hyperinflation only a year
earlier.

Inflation and the stabilization of the currency had a number of
consequences for the development of the Weimar Republic. The reform
enabled the Reich and the *Länder* to rid themselves of their debts very
cheaply. German industry had rescued its assets through the inflation. In
some areas at least, it had even been able to renew stocks and machinery
with the help of rapidly depreciating, and hence very cheap, credits.

Agriculture had likewise shed most of its debts. Of the 16 milliard marks in mortgage debts on real estate which had been pressing agriculture very hard in 1913, only four milliard RM were still outstanding in 1924. Agricultural debts would have been completely eliminated had the conversion ratio of 1:1 billion been applied to it in the same way as it was employed elsewhere in the economy. However, a ruling by the Reich Court in the autumn of 1923 enforced the revaluation of mortgages at 25%. Social considerations similarly led to the revaluation of savings deposits on savings books at 25%. Of course, in most cases there were hardly any savings balances left to be revalued.

Those who lost out badly in the inflation and currency reform were the banks and all those who had invested their wealth on fixed terms. By 1924 less than two milliard RM were left of the banks' total capital funds (excluding private bankers). In 1913, these funds had amounted to at least 7.1 milliard marks. Total deposits in German banks (excluding private bankers) had dwindled from 33.6 milliard marks in 1913 to 9.8 milliard RM in 1924. The extent to which the inflation had ruined the middle classes becomes even more apparent when a comparison is made between deposits in savings banks in 1913 and 1924. In the last year before the War, 19.7 milliard marks were kept in German savings banks; by 1924 slightly less than 600 million RM remained. The destruction of their wealth contributed to the loss of confidence of the middle classes in the young Weimar Republic and made them receptive to political radicalism. Indeed, the expropriation of the middle classes was the real social revolution which took place in Germany after the end of the First World War.

5. Inflation and the Re-Stabilization of the Franc

France's financial and monetary position was not much better at the end of the First World War than that of the Reich; her methods of financing the War had been very similar to Germany's. At the time of the armistice, the French Republic had an internal debt of 130 milliard francs in addition to foreign debts of about five milliard francs. Approximately half of the internal state debt was short-term. The French budget also remained in deficit after the end of the War. Her national budget was heavily over-burdened with the costs of demobilization, and, until September 1919, the support of troops which intervened in the Russian civil war. Some 700,000 men were kept under arms after demobilization in addition to the colonial contingents. Yet the anticipated German reparations payments fell far short of France's expectations. In 1920, her deficit of 38 milliard francs was nominally as high as it had been in 1917, a war year. The French managed to reduce the annual deficit by 1924, and they also succeeded in reducing the advances the Banque de France made to the Treasury from 27 milliard to 22 milliard francs. But at this point, the French budget was burdened with further extraordinary expenditure: in April 1925, the Rif-Berbers revolted in Morocco under Abd el Krim, and in July of the same year, the

Druzes in Lebanon rebelled as well. Strong troop reinforcements had to be deployed against the rebels in the Protectorate of Morocco and the Mandate of Lebanon. During these colonial wars, the Banque de France had to increase its advances from 22.35 milliard to 38.35 milliard francs within 15 months.

The substantial increase in short-term state debts during the War also affected note circulation. Since 1870 the note circulation of the Banque de France had not been subject to any cover regulations, though notes could be issued only up to a certain maximum amount determined by law. In 1911, the issue of notes was limited to a maximum of 6.8 milliard francs. Up to 1919, the maximum amount of notes in circulation was increased to 40 milliard francs. In the following year the issue was restricted to a maximum of 41 milliard francs. This remained the limit until April 1925. From March 1924 the issuing bank, with the Government's knowledge and approval, repeatedly exceeded this maximum. These breaches were concealed from the public and the Chamber of Deputies by a manipulation of the balance sheets. In April 1925, the Cabinet of Edouard Herriot requested an increase in advances from the central issuing bank to the State from 22 to 26 milliard francs. The ceiling for notes in circulation was correspondingly raised by four milliard francs to 45 milliard francs. It was only at this point that it was disclosed to the public that the limit had been exceeded. Later that year, the maximum amount of notes in circulation had to be increased twice so that it finally amounted to 58.5 milliard francs.

During the War the franc could be maintained at a level only 5% below its 1913 rate of exchange — thanks to sales of gold, to foreign credits and to agreements with the British and American governments. When Britain and the United States suspended their financial aid to France in March and July 1919, the exchange rate of the franc *vis-à-vis* the dollar fell to less than half of its 1913 level and continued to slide downwards until the end of 1919. By December 1919, one dollar was 10.99 francs. The rate of exchange stabilized somewhat in the following two years and fluctuated between 12.30 and 13.70 francs to the dollar. After France's intervention in the Ruhr, the franc's rate of exchange began to slip once more. At the end of 1923, one dollar cost 19.61 francs in Paris; in March 1924 the dollar was quoted at 27.20 francs. When Poincaré became Prime Minister at the end of July 1926 and also took charge of the Finance Ministry in order to stabilize finances and currency of the Third Republic, the international value of the franc had fallen to just a little more than 10% of its pre-war level. On 20 July 1926 the dollar was quoted at 49.22 francs. By this time the wholesale price index, which had been at 100 in 1914, had reached 854. Thus the loss in internal purchasing power corresponded approximately to the losses in the franc's international value.

Changes took place with Poincaré's new government. To begin with, Poincaré eliminated the budget deficit and thus re-established public confidence. Within the next two years he also succeeded in stabilizing the currency. In 1926 he managed to balance the budget after the Chamber had granted him the full powers. He increased taxes on consumption, put up the price for tobacco to be charged by the tobacco monopoly and raised postal, telegramme and telephone charges. The developments in Lebanon and Morocco strengthened his policy of fiscal stabilization. After the collapse of the Druze revolt and the capitulation of Abd el Krim, the troops had achieved their mission and the military budget could be reduced.

In order to gain public confidence, Poincaré, following the advice of a committee of experts, founded the Caisse Autonome d'Amortissement in August 1926. This Bank was to help repay the existing state debts. For this purpose it was provided with administrative autonomy and equipped with a secure source of income. By virtue of its autonomous status it was independent of government directives. In order to be able to fulfil its task, the Bank was granted revenue from several sources which had so far been under the authority of the Treasury: the net profits of the state-owned tobacco monopoly, the yields from death duties and the newly created change-of-ownership tax. It was also to receive any surplus which might arise at the end of the fiscal year. All this was laid down by law, so that these sources of income could not easily be withdrawn should the majority change in the Chamber of Deputies. Finally, the Caisse Autonome d'Amortissement was allowed to issue consolidation loans totalling 48 milliard francs. This amount was determined by the current total circulation of *bons de la défense nationale* and *bons du trésor* which was 49.5 milliard francs.

Since redemption of the debt was now safeguarded institutionally, public confidence was restored fairly quickly. In anticipation of a stabilization and revaluation of the franc, medium- and long-term state bonds were being purchased again. Consequently the Caisse Autonome d'Amortissement was able to convert the *bons de la défense nationale* into medium-term securities with a duration of two years (hitherto three to twelve months). Up to 1929, the circulation of *bons* was reduced by 20 milliard francs. The Government simultaneously strove to reduce the amount of its short-term debts at the Banque de France. Between July 1926 and the spring of 1928, the '*Avances directes à l'Etat*' were cut back from 38.35 milliard francs to about 20 milliard francs.

The stabilization and gradual strengthening of the franc went hand-in-hand with a policy of stabilizing public finances. There were two opposing trends. On the one hand, Poincaré wanted to return to the pre-war parity of the franc, because of the country's moral obligation as debtor towards the large number of owners of state bonds. Considerations of political prestige contributed to these aspirations. After all, in 1924 defeated Germany had re-established the gold parity of 1914; Britain had done the same in 1925. Clearly it was a matter of national honour that the franc, which had been a strong and highly valued currency from 1803 until 1914, should be returned to its pre-war parity. Poincaré was opposed by Emile Moreau, the Governor of the Banque de France, and *sous gouverneurs* Charles Rist and Leclerc. They believed that, in view of the deflationary effects which the return to pre-war parity had had in Germany and Britain, only the franc's rate of exchange should be stabilized. From the end of December, the Bank accordingly used its powers to purchase gold, silver and foreign currency against francs to acquire sterling and dollar reserves. This was to prevent an unwelcome sharp and rapid rise in the franc's exchange rate as a consequence of a rising confidence in the franc and of the speculation which could be expected in anticipation of a revaluation. Indeed, by the end of December 1926, the value of the franc on the foreign exchanges had already risen sharply. On 20 July 1926, one dollar was 49.22 francs and one pound sterling was 240.25 francs. Five months later, on 22 December, the ratios were 1:25.16 francs and 1:122.25 francs respectively. The foreign currency purchases were itemized as *comptes divers* in the Banque de France's balance sheet, and these *comptes* increased from 4.8 milliard francs to 31.3 milliard francs in the 18 months period from the end of December 1926 to 21 June 1928.

In 1927 the Banque de France repaid a British foreign currency credit which had been granted in 1916 against the pledge of gold worth 600 million francs and moved the equivalent of 462 million francs of this gold back to Paris. A year later, in May 1928, the influx of foreign currency into the Banque de France was so large that it bought gold worth 168 million dollars in New York because it was unable to neutralize its foreign holdings.

In April 1928, Poincaré's government gained a large majority in the elections to the French Chamber. The outcome of the elections increased the pressure on the Prime Minister to re-establish the franc or at least to introduce a parity as close to the pre-war level as possible. Moreau also appreciated that the fixed long-term investments of the French bourgeoisie must not be allowed to be destroyed by inflation, as had happened in Germany. He was encouraged in his efforts by the French entrepreneurs who were worried about the deflationary effect of revaluation. To maintain jobs in the export industries, Léon Jouhaux, the chairman of the socialist French Trade Union movement, Confédération Générale de Travail (C.G.T.), also turned against over-valuing the franc. He was motivated by a concern to preserve jobs in the export industries. It was at this point that Poincaré gave in.

On 25 June 1928 the gold standard was re-established by law, but with a gold parity of only one-fifth of the pre-1914 franc. The 'Poincaré franc', as the new currency was called in common parlance, was a gold exchange standard; for, although the Banque de France had to convert its notes, it was to do so only when a minimum of 215,000 francs was presented. In comparison with the old Banque de France constitution, the Law of 25 June 1928 brought one important change: the size of note circulation was no longer determined by the cover regulation; instead the Bank had to keep a gold reserve of 35% to cover its note circulation. With the gold parity of the franc fixed in this way, the Bank had a gold reserve of 28.9 milliard francs on 25 June 1928.

The Banque de France now began to exchange its large holdings of foreign currency into gold. Until May 1929 the Bank bought up gold worth 7.7 milliard francs, five milliard of which was acquired in New York. In the following theee years, until the spring of 1932, the Banque de France increased its gold reserve to 75 milliard francs. These heavy withdrawals of gold affected the big international commercial centres of New York and London and had a deflationary effect there, accelerating and sharpening the Great Slump which began in the autumn of 1929. It has often been argued and assumed that it was not only the desire to maintain as high a gold reserve as possible, but also political motives which provided, from time to time at least, the incentive to convert foreign currency into gold. So far such statements have been based on mere speculation and on the fact that certain of France's political actions coincided with significant movements of gold to France. Convincing direct evidence seems to be lacking; but the whole question will concern us again when we come to discussing the banking and monetary crises of 1931 (see below pp. 258f., 263, 280).

6. International Financial Relations from the End of the First World War until the World Economic Crisis

By comparison with pre-war times, international financial relations were conducted under greatly changed conditions after 1918. Next to the international creditor-debtor nexus, the political transfers of money which arose from inter-Allied debts and German reparations were important new factors. Since we have already dealt with the problem of political debts and the way they can be traced back to the way the War was financed, we can restrict ourselves to international capital and money transfers here. In this connection it should be borne in mind that the inter-Allied debts and German reparations arose not only as a new form of international financial relations, but also influenced existing patterns. The Dawes Loan of 1924 and the Young Loan of 1930 to the German government were traditional international loan transactions; but they emerged in the context of political debts. A veritable merry-go-round of commercial and political debts was started. By granting commercial loans, the Reich was put in a position to pay its political debts, i.e. the reparation annuities. The recipients of the reparations used the monies to honour their own commitments, the inter-Allied debts, to the United States. In the United States, where the money and capital market was very liquid, investment opportunities could only be found for a fraction of the repayments from Europe. Thus the funds flowing into America were re-invested abroad, with Germany, where interest rates were high, being one of the beneficiaries. Parts of the reparation annuities returned to Germany in the form of American credit. The great merry-go-round had transformed the Reich's political debts into the commercial debts owed by German cities, banks and businesses.

The monetary aspects of international financial relations also saw major changes when compared with the period before 1914. The direction and extent of this shift were influenced by inflation and strong fluctuations in exchange rates until the second half of the 1920s. The inflation in Germany and in France described in the previous chapters are the most significant and momentous of these monetary developments. Like Germany, Britain also re-established the pre-war gold parity of her currency. This was done by the Conservative government under the Prime Minister James Baldwin in the spring of 1925. When the exchange rate of sterling against the dollar had reached roughly its pre-war level in April 1925, Winston Churchill, the Chancellor of the Exchequer, decided to re-establish gold currency at pre-war parity. He induced his ministerial colleagues to take the appropriate decision. Churchill was later repeatedly reproached for over-valuing the pound when Britain returned to the gold standard. But with the exception of Keynes, who was regarded as rather eccentric at that time and Reginald McKenna, the former Chancellor of the Exchequer, the other financial and monetary authorities whom Churchill consulted — Montagu Norman, the Governor of the Bank of England, Lord Bradbury, Otto Niemeyer, Ralph Hawtrey, J.P. Grigg — recommended the return to the old gold parity. Although they saw that the British price levels in the spring of 1925 were 10% above America's, they expected prices abroad to rise, whilst believing they would be able to keep Britain's price levels stable. Japan was the last country to return to the gold standard in 1930.

International financial relations after 1918 differed from those before the War in yet another respect. This was the extraordinary volume of international short-term credits. Measured against the money capital that was actually available and the demand for long-term credits, the international capital market had insufficient funds after the First World War, whereas the international money market was oversupplied. It is no longer possible to make a statistical survey of the total international short-term capital movements in the 1920s. Nevertheless, the relative weight of short-term capital movements can be established. In 1931, the volume and number of short-term credits frozen during the banking crisis became known, to which must be added the sums of foreign money recalled from Germany between 1930 and July 1931. As it turned out, 57.8% of Germany's foreign debts were short-term, to be repaid within three months, unless, of course, they were prolonged.

The international movement of capital restarted from 1920, and when the world economic crisis began, long-term foreign investments had reached about $55 to 60 milliard. In the field of purely commercial financial relations, Britain was still the largest capital exporter and creditor in the world at the beginning of the world economic crisis. Until 1931 the British were able to reverse the decline in their foreign investments almost completely. These had dropped from $19 milliard in 1914 to $14.4 milliard in 1919. In 1931, British foreign investments once again totalled $18.75 milliard. Some 41% of the new foreign investments went to India, Australia and New Zealand, 8% to Canada, 13% to the British dominated parts of Africa, 16% to Latin America and just under 22% to various European countries. Thus British foreign investments shifted more markedly to

Commonwealth areas; in fact more than 50% of the total foreign investments were placed in the Commonwealth.

The long-term foreign investments of the United States were not much smaller than Britain's. From 1919 to 1930 American capital investments abroad increased by $10 milliard to reach $17.2 milliard. About 33% of these funds were invested in Latin America and 25% in Canada. Just under 30% went to Europe. Canada and Latin America had become areas for American capital investment before 1914. By contrast, the sizeable export of capital from America to Europe represented a reversal of the capital movements of the pre-war period.

There are only rough estimates of French foreign investments after 1918 which cannot be regarded as reliable. All they do is to illustrate their range in an appproximate fashion. After the deduction of wartime liquidations and losses, France's foreign wealth amounted to 18.5 milliard francs at pre-war parity in 1919. New long-term foreign investments were only possible in the French colonial empire until 1926, as the ban on capital export issued during the War remained valid until that time. Thus for seven years after the end of the War, French banks and other capital owners were directed by law to make only short-term investments abroad. It seems that before Poincaré brought the situation under control, there had been a flight of capital into foreign shares; but this suspicion cannot be verified by the available statistics. Until 1931 France's long-term foreign assets had grown again to about 20 milliard francs (old parity). As compared to the pre-war period, the colonial empire now played a greater role as an area for investment; in the 1930s France placed about 30% of her total long-term foreign investments in her own colonial empire. Her long-term investments in Europe were approximately of the same size and about another 30% were divided between North America, Latin America and Asia in equal portions. Though smaller overall than before 1914, short-term investments in New York and London and to a lesser extent in Germany and Austria were also of considerable importance after 1918. This becomes apparent when one looks at France's withdrawals of money from New York and London in the years after 1931.

Thus of all the large capital exporting countries of the pre-1914 period, Britain, which had suffered the least losses in foreign investment during the War, had maintained its leading position as a commercial creditor. As before, France remained a major creditor country, though less so in respect of long-term foreign investments. The United States had become a large exporter of capital. If the inter-Allied debts are added, she had in fact grown into the largest creditor nation in the world. However, the United States continued to be a large debtor country. About $1.7 milliard of foreign capital investments in America survived from the pre-war period. In the 1920s American securities were once again popular with European investors. Until 1930 overseas buyers acquired about $1.5 milliard in new American securities. Foreigners also invested about $500 million directly. The short-term assets of foreign banks — probably most of them French and British —

which were placed with American institutions, rose in the second half of the
1920s to an estimated $2.5-2.7 milliard.

Germany, which had been the third largest creditor country in the world
before 1914, became the largest debtor country in the world both in terms
of political and commercial debts. Germany lost her creditor position
through the expropriation of five milliard of her six milliard dollars of
capital investments in Allied countries and in areas ceded to countries in
the Allied camp in 1919. By 1924 she had taken her place among the
leading debtor countries. She was a country with high interest rates due to
the demand for capital after the currency reform. There were also the
regulations of the Dawes Plan, which imposed a bank rate of at least 5% on
the Reichsbank. Between 1925 and 1930 interest rates on the capital and
monetary market in Germany were on average twice as high as the corresponding foreign rates. In addition, investments in the Reich were regarded
as particularly safe once international control of the Reichsbank had been
established in 1924. Foreign credit now flowed into Germany on a large scale.

In 1930, Germany had foreign debts to the tune of 32 milliard RM.
Some 6.8 milliard of these were foreign capital investments in shares, other
direct business investments and property. About 25.6 milliard RM were in
foreign debts, with 14.8 milliard of these being short-term. Almost 40% of
Germany's foreign credits (5.6 milliard long-term and 4.4 milliard RM
short-term credits) came from the United States. The Netherlands were
Germany's second largest creditor with 1.9 milliard RM in long-term and
2.7 milliard RM in short-term credits. Britain supplied 1.1 milliard RM in
long-term and 2.6 milliard RM in short-term credits. The Reich owed
Switzerland some 1.1 milliard in long-term and 2.3 milliard RM in short-
term credits. France played a subordinate role with 500 million RM in long-
term and 800 million RM in short-term credits. Of course, Germany's claims
in foreign countries and long-term capital investments abroad, which
totalled 9.7 milliard RM, must be set against these debts. Canada had debts
of 7.6 milliard dollars, which was not much less than Germany's commitments. But her debts abroad represented long-term capital investments
which accelerated the pace of her industrialization. Germany, by contrast,
had abnormally high short-term commitments to foreign countries. Worse,
almost 75% of the foreign currency coming into the country in the form of
credit between 1924 and 1930, was used to balance Germany's trade deficit
and to enable her to pay reparations. She incurred commercial debts in
order to pay off her political debts.

VIII Structural Changes in the Banking System after the First World War

1. General Developments

From the closing years of the 19th century, concentration was the dominant structural feature in the development of national banking systems, and it continued after 1918. It was most pronounced in Britain, Germany, Japan and the United States. The concentration movement which first took place in Britain in 1917-18 with the merger of a number of major banks (see above pp. 71f.), did not occur in Germany until the inter-war period. On the other hand, a similarly high degree of concentration did not spread to other countries — France, the United States and Netherlands — until after 1945.

Like the concentration process, increasing governmental influence on the credit system likewise affected the structures of banking after 1918. One reflection of this influence was that legislation in most countries became both more extensive and differentiated. The credit system experienced two waves of legislation: the first was at the end of the First World War during the transition from a wartime to a peacetime economy once the financial requirements of reconstruction had become clearer; the second wave came during the world economic crisis and was triggered by banking crises and by the job creation schemes of the early 1930s. Banking legislation apart, the supervision of banks became an instrument of governmental influence on the credit system. It was first introduced in the United States well before the beginning of the 20th century. Those incorporated banks which, as 'State Banks', received their charter from a Federal State, were supervised by authorities of that State. National Banks founded after the ratification of the National Banking Act of 1863 were supervised by the office of the Comptroller of the Currency established in the Treasury Department in the same year. When the Federal Reserve System was created in 1913, similar supervision rights over its member banks were introduced. In practice, it restricted itself to controlling the State Banks which had volunteered to become members of the Federal Reserve System, leaving the supervision of the National Banks which were obliged to belong to the Federal Reserve System, to the Comptroller of the Currency. The supervision system of Japanese banks was modelled on the American example. Under the Bank Regulations of 1890, the Finance Ministry exercised control over Japanese banks. In 1928 the supervisory powers of the Minister of Finance were decisively enlarged; he was now empowered to see the books and intervene in the business- and personnel-policy of the banks.

The other nations introduced controls of banking only during the Great

Slump: in 1931 they were promulgated in Germany, in 1934-35 in Belgium and in 1935 in Switzerland. France delayed the decision until 1941. Unlike the other countries, Britain does not have any legal or formal control of her banks to this day. Instead there is personal contact between high government officials and Bank of England board members. There are also 'recommendations' which the Government and the Bank of England make to the banks.

Increasing governmental influence on the banking system finally took the form of an expansion of the public sector within the credit system through the foundation of state-owned or public credit institutions. In most cases these were specialized banks. For instance Federal Land Banks were founded as state-owned agricultural credit institutions in the United States in 1916. In 1923, there emerged the Federal Intermediate Credit Banks. In Germany, the Reichs-Kredit-Gesellschaft was established as a new state bank to act as the 'house bank' for the Reich's nationalized industries. The financial problems which arose from combatting the crisis of the 1930s impelled many countries to found other state-owned or public banks, such as the Reconstruction Finance Corporation in America, the Caisse Nationale des marchés de l'Etat in France or the Société Nationale de la Petite Propriété Terrienne in Belgium.

During the last years before the Second World War, new types of banks were established in Germany and the United States in the form of employees' banks, trade union banks and civil servants banks. In terms of their objectives, they are best compared to rural and trade credit co-operatives, as they were supposed to meet the credit requirements of a particular social group in a similar way. The employees' and trade union banks adopted either the co-operative or the joint-stock company principle.

In both Britain and America, Building Societies were well established before the 20th century. After the First World War, they experienced a big boom in the United States. At the same time they also proliferated in Germany.

Investment trusts and investment companies remained primarily Anglo-Saxon institutions until the Second World War. These are unit trust companies which invest money deposited with them in securities on the joint account of their depositors. The idea is to spread the risk. In other words, these companies make profitable investments for their members, but do not administer their property; for, to do the latter they would have to provide additional services and, in particular, to take over the management of their clients' real estate. Investment companies are institutions whose main interest is in long-term finance. In this respect their activities overlap with those of regular banks. Investing and managing a person's assets has been the domain of the private bankers and of the trust companies in America. The long-term financing of businesses and of public corporations through the acquisition of securities (shares, bonds, state and communal loans) was, and is, the main business of all investment banks, which is why the Société Générale de Belgique and the Crédit Mobilier may be regarded as forerunners of the investment companies. At the same time, investment banks are credit institutions. They do not have profit-sharing schemes for their depositors, but guarantee them fixed rates of interest. From the start, insurance companies were also involved in long-term financing. They invested their income from premiums in securities, but did so on their own account with the aim of augmenting funds for their services to the insured parties and for improving their own profitability.

The specialized investment company originated in Britain where no investment banks existed. The fundamental idea was to mobilize the funds of the small investors who, unlike their wealthier counterparts, did not have the expertise and skill to put together a mixed portfolio of securities. The Scottish-American Investment Company was founded as the first investment company in 1860. By 1890, over 50 investment companies had been established, the majority of these during the boom period of 1860-75. The Baring crisis and the stock-exchange crisis of 1890 brought this development to a halt, and it was not until the economic upswing of 1922-29 that investment companies were once again founded in large numbers. They experienced their most rapid expansion in the United States in this period, very few companies having been founded up to then. But the mighty boom of the 1920s pushed the price of securities up and thus kindled speculation in securities. The steadily increasing demand for securities also stimulated the establishment of investment companies. More than 700 of them were founded between 1924 and 1929.

Whereas periods of peak prosperity (1860-75, 1922-29) led to the foundation of a particularly large number of investment companies in the Anglo-Saxon countries, such companies were established in France, Switzerland and Japan only after 1930 and only in small numbers. Most of them were built up during the Depression and were intended to stimulate business in securities when it was very slack. But the real development of investment companies in these countries, as well as in Germany and Belgium, stimulated by the American example, took place only from the end of the 1950s. It is problematical to include investment companies with banks. Certainly in Anglo-Saxon countries they do not belong to the banking sector. For this reason they are not subject to banking controls, but are supervised by the Stock Exchange, particularly in the United States, where their control through the Securities and Exchange Commission was introduced in 1934. They also occupy a special place in France and are subject to the control of the Stock Exchange Committee. On the other hand, they have been classed as bank-like institutions in Switzerland since 1967 and explicitly as credit institutions in the Federal Republic of Germany since 1957. Irrespective of whether the law links investment companies to banks or to the stock exchange, they are in close contact with the commercial banks in all countries and the latter invest in them.

2. National Developments

Britain

In Britain the 'Big Five' which emerged from the concentration movement of 1917-18 — Barclays Bank, Midland Bank, Westminster Bank, Lloyds Bank and the National Provincial Bank — continued their merger policies in the immediate post-war years. This time, three Scottish joint-stock banks came under their control. In 1919, Barclays Bank took over virtually the total joint-stock capital of the British Linen Bank in Edinburgh. In 1920, the Midland Bank acquired the joint-stock capital of the Clydesdale Bank in Glasgow and that of the North of Scotland Bank in Aberdeen four years later. The National Provincial Bank took over the joint-stock capital of Coutts & Co. in 1920. Although these banks lost their independence when their capital was acquired, they carried on under their old name. The concentration process in British banking was in effect an expansion of the Big Five, which either completely absorbed small and medium-sized banks or incorporated them through the acquisition of their joint-stock capital.

Nevertheless, there were several small and medium-sized banks which similarly grew as a result of mergers. In 1927-28, Martins Bank in Liverpool and in 1935 the District Bank in Manchester both expanded through mergers to regional banks of national importance in the wake of mergers. One of the various mergers for which Martins Bank was responsible was with the old London goldsmith bank of Duncombe & Kent, which was a founder member of the London bankers' Clearing House. It was thanks to this take-over that Martins also gained membership in the Clearing House. The District Bank became the newest member of the Clearing House following its merger with the County Bank in 1935. In order to challenge the Big Five, a Scottish issuing bank, the Royal Bank of Scotland, in conjunction with the two London Banks of Glyn Mills & Co. and Williams Deacons Bank, formed 'The Three Banks Group' which it took under its control. The Williams Deacons Bank had been a subsidiary of the Royal Bank of Scotland since 1930. The two London banks brought the group its membership of the Clearing House. The Williams Deacons Bank also had a special link with the Bank of England, and this tradition was continued by the Three Banks Group once the reorganisation had taken place.

The number of independent banks in Britain had shrunk greatly as a result of the concentration process. By the time of the Second World War, only the Big Five, Martins Bank, the District Bank, as well as three Scottish and three Northern Irish banks were actually still independent. These latter institutions were: the Bank of Scotland, the Royal Bank of Scotland, the National Bank of Scotland, the National Bank (which was based in London, though it operated mainly in Northern Ireland and the Irish Republic), the Northern Bank and the Provincial Bank of Ireland. The other credit institutions, even if nominally still independent, were attached to, or at least under the influence of, one of the above banks.

The distribution of deposits at the end of 1938 reveals the extent to which the Big Five had achieved supremacy in the concentration process. The Big Five had attracted about £2.3 milliard in deposits. The other banks in England and Wales, by contrast, held a mere £248 million and those of Northern Ireland £151 million.

After 1918, British banks continued to pursue their traditional business policy. As before, they preferred to give short-term commercial credits, to discount bills, and to deal in gilt-edged securities. They avoided direct investments in industry or long-term industrial loans. However, after 1918 British industry was no longer in a position to self-finance its investments or to rely on local resources in the same way as in the 19th century. The rate of saving had declined sharply after the War. Net investments, which had amounted to 17% of the national income in 1911, had slumped to just 6-7% by 1938.

With industry no longer able to rely primarily on self-financing and on investment by a few wealthy people, new sources of finance were required. In July 1931, the MacMillan Committee came to the conclusion that Britain should emulate Germany where the banks invested in competing industrial enterprises. This, it was argued, would lead to a rationalization and strengthening of industry because ruinous competition would be eliminated and cartels formed. Sporadic collaboration between industry and banks was deemed insufficient. What was needed was an 'intimate co-operation over years'.

In individual cases this was already happening. In the immediate post-war years several banks had been compelled to change frozen assets into industrial investment. The Bank of England had also come into the possession of industrial securities after participating in a number of rescue actions. In order to administer these securities, the Bank of England founded a holding company in 1930. This was the Bankers Industrial Development Company, a quarter of whose joint-stock capital of £6 million was issued by the bank itself. The other shares were acquired by the major banks. This company supported the *Lancashire Cotton Corporation*, the *National Shipbuilders Security Ltd.* and the steel industry during the economic crisis.

In order to give aid to smaller firms in the form of long-term credits, the Credit for Industry Ltd. was founded in 1934 with the participation of the Bank of England; the firm was an investment trust. The steep rise in the number and size of investment trusts in the 1920s was closely connected with the growth in earnings of the lower middle class and the working class. Disposable incomes were higher after the First World War than before 1914. Between 1901 and 1913, small savings deposited in insurance companies and in building and consumer co-operatives amounted to about 13% of the total net capital formation. Between 1924 and 1935, they amounted to more than half. Small savings were tapped through insurance companies and the building co-operatives for the long-term financing of industry. Next to the banks, these institutions were purchasers of shares and bonds with which the investment trusts procured long-term capital.

Merchant bankers and discount houses experienced a contraction after 1918. Above all, the discount houses specializing in the discounting of bills experienced a decline, once private bills were replaced by credit on current account. In the 1920s, trade bills totalling between £400 million and £650 million were discounted annually; in the 1930s the average was £300 million. This decline was not simply the result of the Depression. Indeed, economic recovery had set in around 1932. The contraction in the trade bills business was in part made up by dealings in treasury bills in which the discount houses continued to be involved.

France

As in Britain, the concentration process in the credit system also continued in France after 1918. Local banks were particularly affected. Of the 3,000 local banks in existence at the end of the 19th century, only 75 remained in 1937. The main beneficiaries of this development were the big regional institutes rather than the major banks. The major deposit banks in Paris declined in significance after 1918, whereas the regional banks made relative gains. In 1913 the four big Paris deposit banks held over 75.9% of all bank deposits; by 1924, their share had been reduced to 52.7%, and in 1929 it was at 53.1%. By contrast, the regional banks' share of total deposits increased from 13.7% in 1913 to 24% in 1924. Five years later, their share amounted to 23.7%.

In 1914 three of the four big Paris deposit banks possessed a large branch network. After the First World War, they continued to expand this network. Thus, the Crédit Lyonnais had 415 branches, the Société Générale 668 and the Comptoir National d'Escompte de Paris 285 in 1913. By 1932, the number of the Crédit Lyonnais branches had grown to 1,469, that of the Société Générale to 1,511 and of the Comptoir National to 496. On the other hand, the Crédit Industriel et Commercial operated without a branch network of its own even after 1918, but concentrated on fostering its close links with the provincial banks (see above p. 166) and on building up a banking group. In 1932 ten regional banks belonged to the group — including the Banque Scalbert in Lille, the Société Normande de Banque et de Dépôts in Rouen and the Crédit Industriel d'Alsace et de Lorraine in Strasbourg — apart from four local banks and three overseas banks, among which the Banque Transatlantique was the largest.

Because of the growing economic instability, the big deposit banks attached more importance to high liquidity than they had done before 1914. At the end of 1926, shortly after the re-stabilization of the franc had been initiated the big deposit banks kept their cash liquidity at an average of 17.9%. Once the re-stabilization policy had been brought to a successful conclusion, they permitted themselves a somewhat smaller cash liquidity of 17.2% at the end of 1929. When, at the end of 1931, the world economic crisis reached its climax, the major French banks maintained an average cash liquidity of 31%. They were much better prepared for the huge run on the banks than were the big German banks (see below p. 270). Short-term commercial credit and the underwriting of treasury bills remained the main type of credit business of the major deposit banks and amounted to about two-thirds of the total credits granted. Overdrafts were the second most important. But the volume of overdrafts was not half as large as the volume of acceptance credits. Their holdings of securities and shares were quite insignificant, amounting to less than 1% of the balance-sheet total throughout the inter-war years. Since the major deposit banks, constantly preoccupied with their liquidity as they were, practically never granted any medium-term or long-term industrial credits, no matter how strong the demand for them, the big and regional deposit banks founded several special institutions for this purpose. In 1919 the Crédit Lyonnais, together with the Comptoir National d'Escompte de Paris, established the Union pour le Crédit à l'Industrie Nationale as a bank for medium-term credit and the Omnium Financier pour l'Industrie Nationale for long-term credit. The C.A.L.I.F. (Société Anonyme de Crédit à l'Industrie Française), an institutuion for medium- and long-term credits whose volume of acceptance credits was roughly equal to that of its direct investments, was founded as a subsidiary by the Société Générale in 1928. The Crédit Industriel et Commercial and Crédit du Nord group trusts also established subsidiaries for the provision of long-term credits to industry, the former founding the Union des Banques Régionales pour le Crédit Industriel in 1929, the latter the Union Bancaire du Nord a year earlier.

Two of the big regional banks to benefit from the concentration movement developed into major deposit banks after 1918: the Crédit Commercial de France and the Banque Nationale de Crédit. Originally neither of them was French. The Crédit Commercial de France had been founded in 1894 as the Banque Suisse et Française with Swiss capital at Paris. Swiss capital still has a large share in the Bank to this day. During the First World War the firm changed its name to Crédit Commercial de France. Its name notwithstanding, the Crédit Commercial de France was never a deposit bank for commercial credit alone, but a *banque mixte*, a universal bank. The Swiss banks which founded it used the Central European universal banks as their model. It therefore maintained longer-term credit ties with industry, in particular with the chemical concern of *Etablissements Kuhlmann* and with the *Compagnie Générale d'Electricité*. The Banque Nationale de Crédit was of German origin. It emerged from the Mülhauser Diskontokontor/Comptoir d'Escompte de Mulhouse which had been established in 1901 in the then German Alsace-Lorraine. Since entrepreneurs residing in Alsace maintained close business ties with Eastern France, the Diskontokontor set up branches in France as well. These French branches of the Diskontokontor joined the Banque de Province syndicate. Franco-German relations deteriorated so seriously during the Second Moroccan Crisis of 1911 that the hitherto close international collaboration of German and French banks came to an end; the French branches of the Diskontokontor had to sever their links with the central office and were almalgamated into a French regional bank, the Banque Nationale de Crédit in 1913. When Alsace became French in 1918, the Diskontokontor became affiliated with its former branches and merged with the Banque Nationale de Crédit. Its German origin had a lasting effect on the bank's operations; like the Crédit Mobilier, it operated as a universal bank. Thus France had three different types of major bank after 1918: four major deposit banks, two new universal banks and two big investment banks (*banques d'affaires*): the Banque de Paris et des Pays Bas and the Banque de l'Union Parisienne.

In order to gain direct access to the capital market, several branches of industry and industrial groups founded their own banks. In 1920, *Schneider-Creusot*, with the support of the Banque de l'Union Parisienne, established the Union Européenne Industrielle et Financière as a holding and financing company for its industrial interests in Central and South-East Europe. The French coal and steel industry, which was headed by de Wendel and the Pont-à-Mousson group, founded the Union des Mines in 1923. Several of the banks' branches, including the Banque Cotonnière and the Union Financière Française et Coloniale, were set up with strong participation of the Banque de Paris et des Pays Bas. These banks were universal banks. They granted acceptance credits, overdrafts, managed share issues and acquired shares in enterprises. By 1929, the volume of securities and participations held by the Union des Mines equalled the amount of its joint-stock capital (270 million francs), whilst its commercial credit totalled 590 million francs and its overdrafts 184 million francs.

The companies of the *haute banque* continued to work with insurance companies and big industrial joint-stock companies whose financial transactions they managed. The most important of their other operations were the discounting of bills and reimbursement credit. Lazard Frères were primarily involved in reimbursement credit. During the Popular Front government of Léon Blum, the families of the *haute banque* lost their hitherto large influence in the Banque de France. The Bank's statutes were changed by a law of 24 July 1936 which Vincent Auriol, the Finance Minister and future President of the Fourth Republic, had introduced. The rationale behind this law was that, by reinforcing the Government's influence, the issuing bank would be more sensitive to general social and economic considerations. As the French Socialists argued, the Bank had until now promoted the interests of its 200 largest shareholders, the '*200 grandes familles*', to gain control of, and even at times to establish a virtual counter-government *vis-à-vis*, the representative institutions of the Republic. Its critics exaggerated the frequent controversies between the central issuing bank and the Government; they interpreted them as evidence of the *haute banque* exerting too much influence on the policy of the Banque de France. Yet these controversies did not stop after the influence of the *haute banque* was eliminated in 1936. Left-wing criticism was justified, however, as far as the General Council was concerned which was seen as an oligarchy of financiers who were only interested in perpetuating their position. Among the 15 Regents who, together with three Censors, the Governor and two Deputy Governers, made up the General Council as a

board, the Mallet, Hottinguer and Rothschild families were invariably represented. A seat on the General Council of the Banque de France was virtually
hereditary for these families, like a seat in the House of Lords was for the
families of the British aristocracy. Membership in the general meeting of the
200 largest shareholders was, of course, inherited with a parcel of shares.

Under the terms of the Statutes of 1936, the number of Regents on the
General Council was increased from 15 to 20, only two of whom were
elected by the general meeting which to date had elected all of them. Nine
Regents were state officials and included the Governor of the Crédit Foncier
de France, the Director of the state-owned Administration of Debts and the
Director General of the Caisse des Dépots et Consignations. One Regent was
elected by the staff of the Banque de France. The Finance Minister selected
the remaining eight from lists of candidates submitted by agricultural, industrial and trades associations. In this way the representatives of the *haute
banque* were replaced on the General Council by government representatives
and trustees. The dominance of the '200 *grandes familles*' in the general
meeting was also broken; from 1936 onwards, all shareholders formed the
Banque de France's general meeting, each of whom had a vote, no matter
how many shares he owned.

Next to the central issuing bank, the Credit Foncier de France was the
most important public bank. The granting of communal loans gained increasing importance after 1918. Before the First World War, they had
amounted to approximately half of the total of long-term loans; in the
1920s and 1930s, its share rose to an average of two-thirds. Prior to 1914,
French governments had, without success, tried to change savings banks into
savings institutions for members of the lower classes by restricting the upper
limit of savings accounts to 1,500 francs. Post-war inflation of the franc,
however, forced the ceiling upwards, and the original social intention was
completely undermined. In 1931 the upper limit for savings deposits was
finally raised to 20,000 francs. Since savings deposits earned higher rates
of interest than bank deposits and appeared to be more secure, people with
larger sums of money to invest apparently placed some of it in savings
banks; between 1927 and 1937, savings banks' deposits rose from 21.2
milliard francs to 61.4 milliard francs.

A special law of 1919 set up the Crédit National pour Faciliter la
Réparation des Dommages Causés par la Guerre to finance the reconstruction of war-damaged areas and to disburse compensation for war damages.
Constructed as a public joint-stock bank, the largest proportion of the joint-
stock capital was subscribed by the major banks and big industrial concerns. Members of the management were appointed by the President of the
Republic and the Finance Minister; members of the board of directors were
elected by the shareholders. The main function of the Credit National was
firstly to distribute compensation payments. The Bank procured the money
for such payments by issuing debentures for which the State undertook to
pay interest and amortization. After the Dawes Plan came into force in
1924, it was no longer necessary to issue debentures of this sort; by this

time some of the incoming German reparations were being transferred to the Crédit National for the purpose of compensating people whose claims had been recognized. The payment had essentially been made by the time the Second World War broke out. In 1937, the Crédit National paid out a mere 61 million francs in indemnities; prior to this a total of 63.8 milliard francs of indemnity money had been distributed. From the very beginning the Crédit National also acted as a credit institution granting low-interest credits for reconstruction work; it was also engaged in providing medium- and long-term industrial credit of between three and ten years. To finance these credits it was allowed to issue debentures on its own account. In 1926 the Crédit National's long-term loans totalled almost half a milliard francs; in 1932, 1.1 milliard francs, and almost 1.2 milliard francs in 1937. In short, the amount of loans exceeded indemnity payments many times over. The Crédit National had become a public *banque d'affaires*.

In order to stimulate French foreign trade following the end of the War, the Government promoted the establishment of a foreign trade bank, the Banque Nationale Française du Commerce Extérieur. The State did not participate in its formal foundation; nor did it impose restrictions on its operations or try to exercise control over it. It did, however, support the creation of the Bank by providing advances. It was a number of the big banks in Paris which helped to found it. The Bank aimed to encourage French exports by providing reimbursement credits, foreign exchange futures, and by undertaking the collection of bills for its customers abroad. Considering that other banks were already handling such business, the new institute was to undertake those transactions which other banks considered too risky or those requiring special expertise and information. There was concern that it might pose a threat to the other firms involved in export credit, and this is why it was not allowed to set up branches in France.

Apart from establishing specialized public banks, French banking laws were designed to improve the supply of credit on a co-operative basis for the middle classes in the cities and the countryside after the First World War. Up to 1914, the French agricultural credit co-operatives had had little influence, and the foundation of industrial credit co-operatives had been a complete failure. From 1911, plans were made to reform the credit supply for the middle class. These resulted in a law relating to *banques populaires* in 1917. There were only three of the old *banques populaires* in existence at that time. The new law allowed merchants, craftsmen, tradesmen and commercial companies to set up *banques populaires*. The members were to contribute to the basic capital, and a *banque populaire* was permitted to grant short-term credits to its members only. In 1921 the Caisse Centrale des Banques Populaires was founded as a centre for payment transactions. Until the mid-1920s, about 100 *banques populaires* were established, though many of them had to go into liquidation within a few years, not least because their management was often incompetent. The Chambre Syndicale des Banques Populaires de France was established in 1929 to tackle these problems and to provide the State with a mechanism to control the *banques populaires* and supply them with back-up credit. In 1936, 76 *banques populaires* were still active. They proved less effective, as they lacked the co-operative element of a liability company and merely granted credit against tangible securities. But many of those, for whose credit requirements the *banques populaires* had in fact been intended, were unable to obtain credit. The situation improved only after 1945, when guarantee communities (sociétés de caution mutuelle) were established. They were liable for their members, should they take up credits with a *banque populaire* or some other bank.

Unlike the *banques populaires*, the rural credit co-operatives were based on the principle of joint liability. The State had subsidized rural co-operative banks even before 1914, and the system was further extended after 1918. According to the Law of 1920, the *caisses de crédit agricole mutuel* were subsidized and controlled by the State. The Caisse Nationale de Crédit Agricole was founded as a central counting house. By 1930, two-thirds of a total of approximately 10,000 agricultural credit co-operatives belonged to this group of *caisses agricoles*. The remaining third consisted of *caisses libres*. It included the agricultural credit co-operatives of Alsace-Lorraine and the *caisses Durand*, which were based chiefly in Brittany and adhered to the organizational principles of Durand, one of the founders of the French co-operative movement in the Alsace-Lorraine. After 1920, the *caisses libres* operated without state subsidies.

Germany

After the First World War the major German banks continued their expansionist drive. Whilst the Disconto-Gesellschaft and the Berliner Handels-Gesellschaft were still without branches after 1918, the other big banks expanded their networks which, until 1914, had been quite modest in scope if compared with Britain and France. In 1913 the total number of branches operated by the major banks was 153; in 1929 there were 698.

The expansion was achieved not only through the extension of branch networks but also through takeovers. The first big post-war merger took place in 1920 between the Commerz- und Disconto-Bank and the Mitteldeutsche Privat-Bank. Up to this point Hamburg, with its shipping and overseas trade, had been the Commerz-Bank's main area of business; it was also represented in Berlin. But shipping and overseas trade was in the doldrums in the immediate post-war years, and the Commerz-Bank therefore sought to expand its business with industry. This was the purpose behind its merger with the Mitteldeutsche Privat-Bank of Magdeburg. The latter had a branch network stretching from Dresden and Torgau to the Harz Mountains, and it maintained close links with the Saxon textile industry as well as Central Germany's potash, lignite and electrical engineering industries. Both banks had collaborated before. The Mitteldeutsche Privat-Bank had reached the limits of its capacity, whereas the Commerz- und Disconto-Bank was looking for fresh opportunities for expansion. By taking over the Magdeburg firm, the Commerz-Bank increased its joint-stock capital by 60 million marks so that the shares of the Mitteldeutsche Privat-Bank could be converted at par. After the merger it adopted the name of the Commerz- und Privat-Bank.

In the same year the Nationalbank für Deutschland at Berlin absorbed the Deutsche Nationalbank of Bremen. Although it was the smaller of the two, it was the Deutsche Nationalbank which formally made the takeover bid. This procedure was adopted because it enabled the new firm to become a partnership limited by shares as the Deutsche Nationalbank had been. The partnership limited by shares had various advantages over the joint-stock company and this is why it was frequently the preferred form in Germany during this period. Thus the partners who were fully liable had, as directors, a stronger position *vis-à-vis* the supervisory board because they could not be dismissed. And, because of their personal liability, they tended to inspire more confidence in their shareholders than did the appointed, non-liable directors of a joint-stock company. It was also thought that a partnership limited by shares was in a better position to avoid domination by major shareholders. Hence, once the merger had been completed, the former directors of the Nationalbank für Deutschland, among them Hjalmar Schacht, the future President of the Reichsbank, and Jakob Goldschmidt, became its proprietors.

In terms of its business volume in general and its security and investment transactions in particular, the Nationalbank für Deutschland had very little equity capital even after its fusion with the Deutsche Nationalbank. It was therefore looking for a bank which was amply provided with capital. The Bank für Handel und Industrie (Darmstädter Bank) was such an institute. To beat the accelerating pace of inflation this bank was in search of greater investment opportunities. When galloping inflation set in from 1922, the Nationalbank, with its sizeable assets, appeared to be an interesting potential partner, and the first merger of two major German banks was affected in the course of that year. The smaller of the two, the National-bank für Deutschland formally initiated the takeover bid, so that the new institution could retain the legal structure of a partnership limited by shares. The new firm was given the name of Darmstädter und Nationalbank (Danat-Bank). It also inherited the Nationalbank's expansionist, and often speculative, business practices, as was to become apparent in 1931 and with disastrous consequences. In 1929, on the eve of the world economic crisis, two further mergers of big banks occurred. In February of that year, the Commerz- und Privat-Bank took over the Mitteldeutsche Creditbank of Frankfurt and Berlin. The latter's business had been stagnating since the Great Inflation. In 1924 and 1929 two major shareholders decided to sell, and after the second parcel became available the Commerz-und Privat-Bank made a successful takeover bid.

On 27 September 1929, shortly before the crash on the New York Stock Exchange, the banking world in Germany was taken by surprise when the Deutsche Bank and the Disconto-Gesellschaft announced their agreement to merge. Such a merger far surpassed that of the Danat-Bank in order of magnitude. But its size and scope was no less surprising than the names of the partners to the merger. Both banks were known to be old rivals. Their competition on the domestic market had been so intense prior to 1914 that it had led to personal animosities between the leading figures of the two institutions: Georg Siemens and Adolph von Hansemann disliked each other, and so did Arthur von Gwinner and Arthur Salomonsohn, as well as Emil Georg Stauss and Georg Solmssen. In terms of their organizational structures and business styles, the 'Deutsche' and the 'Disconto' had developed in very different directions. The former was a major bank with many branches, the latter had never built up a branch network; the 'Deutsche' was keenly profit-oriented, but after 1923 this policy was bound to undermine its liquidity position; the 'Disconto', on the other hand, maintained a high liquidity in line with an old rule of banking, but did so to the detriment of its profitability.

The Deutsche Bank initiated the merger, having been on the look-out for a big partner since 1926, the year when several large concerns were established in heavy industry, above all the *Vereinigte Stahlwerke*, the *Mitteldeutsche Stahlwerke*, and the *Vereinigte Oberschlesische Hüttenwerke*. The chemical trust of *I.G. Farben* was formed in December 1925. In the face of this newly-created industrial power, the leadership of the Deutsche Bank thought it necessary to create larger banks to maintain their weight in the economy. The case for bigger banks to provide finance for large industrial trusts had first been made by the British 'Big Five' in 1918, to justify their mergers against criticism in Parliament and the press (see above p.   ). The existence of industrial giants undoubtedly encouraged the major banks to increase their equity capital through mergers. On the other hand, it must not be overlooked that the big banks had actively participated in establishing these large industrial concerns in the first place. In other words, they had themselves created the 'compulsion for concentration'.

At first, the Deutsche Bank had considered a merger with the Danat-Bank. In the summer of 1926 negotiations took place between Jakob Goldschmidt of the Danat-Bank and Oscar Schlitter of the Deutsche Bank. Louis Hagen, a private banker from Cologne and a partner in Sal. Oppenheim Jr. & Cie., acted as an intermediary. These negotiations came to nought when the Deutsche Bank's board refused to accept Goldschmidt's conditions. The directors also had personal reservations about him. Later that year, the Deutsche Bank sought contact with the Disconto-Gesellschaft. Schlitter turned to Robert Pferdmenges, a Cologne banker, whom he knew well from earlier times and who was also a board member of the Schaaff-hausenscher Bankverein. The latter had been a 100% subsidiary of the Disconto-Gesellschaft since 1914, and one of the 'Disconto's' proprietors, Georg Solmssen, was also a member of the board of directors of the Schaaff-hausenscher Bankverein. Pointing to the need for additional capital to face a highly concentrated industry and to the desirability of reducing costs, Schlitter made a merger proposal to the Disconto-Gesellschaft which was still a partnership limited by shares. For several years, the Deutsche Bank's courtship met with a sceptical response. The differences concerning the way in which the two conducted their business appeared unbridgeable to them. In the end it was rising costs and declining profits which brought the two banks together in the autumn of 1929. Three years had elapsed between the first preliminary talks and the final agreement. Yet the bankers succeeded in maintaining complete silence about their plans until the merger was signed and sealed. Diplomats of the old school could hardly have been more discreet.

The new bank called itself the Deutsche Bank und Disconto-Gesellschaft, shortened in 1937 to the Deutsche Bank. The subsidiaries of the Disconto-Gesellschaft lost their independent legal status in the merger process and were completely incorporated. The Schaaffhausenscher Bankverein, the Norddeutsche Bank, the Rheinische Creditbank and the Süddeutsche Disconto-Gesellschaft all disappeared and only five major banks remained among the commercial banks. The Deutsche Bank's pre-merger joint-stock capital in the post-1924 period was 150 million RM; that of the Disconto-Gesellschaft 135 million RM. The merger ratio was fixed at 1:1 so that the new joint-stock capital was 285 million RM. The Disconto-Gesellschaft also owned all the joint-stock capital of the four subsidiary banks, and it was hence unnecessary for shareholders to exchange their shares. After the merger the Deutsche Bank und Disconto-Gesellschaft had joint-stock capital which exceeded the total joint-stock capital of all the other major banks. The Dresdner Bank had a joint-stock capital of 100 million RM at that time; the Commerz- und Privat-Bank reached 75 million RM, after absorbing the Mitteldeutsche Creditbank; the Danat-Bank was backed by 60 million RM; and the Berliner Handels-Gesellschaft had the smallest joint-stock capital of all the big banks: 28 million RM. The Deutsche Bank und Disconto-Gesellschaft also far outstripped the other major banks with its 1929 balance-sheet total of 5.53 milliard RM. Although the Danat-Bank was only the fourth biggest commercial bank in terms of its equity capital, it had the second largest balance-sheet total (2.6 milliard RM) thanks to its expansionist business policy. The balance-sheet of the Dresdner Bank came to 2.5 milliard RM, followed by the Commerz- und Privat-Bank's 1.9 milliard RM. The very cautious Berliner Handels-Gesellschaft contented itself with a balance-sheet total of 500 million RM. In this respect, the Deutsche Bank und Disconto-Gesellschaft came closer to the big British and American credit institutions. The Midland Bank had a balance-sheet total which was equivalent to 8.5 milliard RM; the National Provincial Bank, the smallest of the 'Big Five', showed the equivalent of 6.3 milliard RM.

Although the mergers strengthened the position of the major banks within the credit system, they did not thereby gain the same supremacy over all other banks as the 'Big Five' had achieved in Britain. With the big mergers completed and including the Reich-owned Reichs-Kredit-Gesellschaft (see below p. 246), but excluding the private bankers, they had around 20% of the equity capital of all banks in 1929. About 30% of all bank deposits were held by the major banks at this time, and 36% of the total of short-term credit was provided by them. Since all the major banks had transferred their head offices to Berlin, they were known in the inter-war years as the 'Berlin major banks', even though the registered office of the Dresdner Bank remained in Dresden and that of the Commerz- und Privat-Bank in Hamburg.

In comparison with the pre-1914 period, the economic situation of the major banks was much worse in the inter-war years. They had suffered big losses through the confiscation of foreign investments during the First World War, through the devaluation of money during the Great Inflation and the subsequent currency reform. In 1913, the major banks had equity capital totalling 1,635 million marks at their disposal; in 1929, they operated with a total of 917 million RM. On the other hand, the amount of deposits and other funds from outside sources had risen rapidly with the end of inflation and at 12 milliard RM in 1929 was more than twice the 1913 figure of 5.1 milliard marks. In this way the ratio between assets and funds from outside sources changed from 1:3.5 to 1:13. Thus, given their volume of business, the major banks operated from a much weaker position than before 1914. The mergers did not improve this situation. The deterioration in the ratio between internal assets and funds from outside sources apart, the source and payment terms of external funds had also changed to the banks' disadvantage, if compared with the pre-war period. In 1913 all German banks had an approximate total of 600 million marks in deposits and credit from foreign countries. By 1929, foreign money amounted to 8.9 milliard RM. Some 42.5% of the banks' funds from outside sources consisted of foreign deposits and credit. This figure represented the banks' share of Germany's foreign debts which had risen since monetary reform and the Dawes Plan.

The banks' foreign commitments consisted of debts, to be repaid in foreign currency or gold; they were thus particularly crucial from the viewpoint of the national economy. The terms for external sources also developed to Germany's disadvantage. The share of long-term funds diminished, whilst short-term funds increased. In 1913, 13.7% of all outside sources which the major banks had taken in were repayable on terms of more than three months. By 1929, the figure was a mere 2.9%. Of the remaining 97% of short-term external loans (which had to be repaid either immediately or within a maximum of three months), 40% came from overseas. As long as Germany was politically and economically stable, it could be expected that foreign creditors would leave their money in Germany and in German banks. But the danger of massive withdrawals of foreign money loomed large during any economic or political crisis; and this is what was to happen during the German banking crisis of 1931.

One consequence of these realities ought to have been for the major banks to maintain a strong liquidity position. Their liquidity should have been higher than prior to 1914. However, the reverse was true. Their cash ratio was a mere 3.5% as compared to an average of 7.4% in 1913, and the

liquidity ratio had dropped from a 50.7% average in 1913 to 42.4% in 1929.
The deterioration in their capital structure and the high proportion of short-
term money from outside sources meant that the number of long-term loans
and investment had to be cut back in comparison with the pre-war period.
Total long-term investments made by the German joint-stock banks in 1929
were less than half the figure for 1913. In the last year before the First
World War, they amounted to 4.4 milliard marks; in 1929 to no more than
two milliard RM. The situation was even more precarious, if one considers
that many of the nominally short-term loans had been lent out on a long-
term basis. Before the Great Slump people could merely speculate about the
dangers of such unsound financial methods. It was only in 1930-31 that
they became glaringly obvious and quantifiable. These investments became a
nightmare for the banks when, during the Depression, they found them tied
up in bankrupt enterprises.

The liquidity position of the provincial banks developed not unlike that
of the major banks. The cash ratio averaged 3.3% in 1929, and the liquidity
ratio was 42.4%. Nevertheless, they had a sounder capital structure. The
ratio of internal to external funds was 1:6 in 1929; just 24% of all funds
from outside sources were due after three months. More alarming was the
decline of their business. Whilst the number of provincial banks decreased
from 309 in 1913 to 211 in 1929, their balance-sheet total shrank by more
than half.

One of the results of the War and of hyperinflation on the German
banking system was the expansion of public banks. Large numbers of these
had existed before 1914 in the form of state-owned banks, the Prussian
Landschaften, the national and municipal banks and the savings banks. The
War threw up a new major bank, the Reichs-Kredit-Gesellschaft – which
was Reich-owned. Throughout the War the Reich had been founding enterprises, known as 'War Companies', to produce goods and materials essential
to the war effort. A Statistical Office for War Companies was set up at the
Treasury in 1917 as a clearing house for these companies. At the end of the
War, this Office was transformed into the Reichs-Kredit- und Kontrollstelle GmbH, a limited company. This company was to look after the
liquidation of the War Companies and to end the Reich's participation in
them. By 1923 the state-owned companies and the Reich's direct investments had been consolidated in a holding company known as VIAG
(*Vereinigte Industrieunternehmungen AG*/United Industrial Enterprises
Joint-Stock Company); in the following year, the Reichs-Kredit- und
Kontrollstelle changed its name to Reichs-Kredit-Gesellschaft AG. It now
became the state bank of the VIAG; the Reich was the sole owner of its
joint-stock capital of 30 million RM. For statistical purposes, the Reichs-
Kredit-Gesellschaft was included in the group of major Berlin banks.
Because it was a joint-stock company, it also became a member of the
Centralverband des Deutschen Bank und Bankiersgewerbes, where member-
ship was normally reserved for private commercial banks. *De jure*, however,
the Reichs-Kredit-Gesellschaft was a state bank owned by the Reich.

The Bank became a correspondent of many provincial banks and conducted their business for them in Berlin. The provincial banks preferred the Reichs-Kredit-Gesellschaft to look after their affairs, because, unlike the big commercial banks with their branch networks, it did not compete against them. Next to the Reichs-Kredit-Gesellschaft, another big public bank was founded in 1924: the Deutsche Golddiskontbank. It was a 100% subsidiary of the Reichsbank and dealt with business in which the Reichsbank had been involved until 1923. However, under the Dawes Plan the latter was prevented from engaging in credit transactions in support of German foreign trade; nor was it allowed to control the administration of public money, or to operate in the money markets. As the Golddiskontbank was created before the reichsmark had been introduced, its foundation capital was in sterling (£10 million), £1.25 million of which were paid. Its joint-stock capital was converted into 200 million RM in 1931, just prior to the devaluation of the pound. The Deutsche Golddiskontbank was to play an important role in the reconstruction of the big banks after the banking crisis of 1931 (see below p. 267).

The public sector of the credit system was also extended through the further expansion of savings banks and central giro institutions. Unlike their foreign counterparts, most German savings banks were communal credit institutions. Until 1931 they had no legal status but were institutions dependent on local government in urban and rural areas. When, in 1908, they were given the right to negotiate cheques, they established their own giro network for cashless payment transactions. In every Prussian province and Federal State (or *Land* after 1919) of the German Reich the municipal authorities of the savings banks formed a giro association, and these associations founded central giro institutions as clearing centres for their affiliated banks; they also administered the liquidity reserves of individual banks. The first central giro institution came into being in Saxony in 1909 on the initiative of Johann Christian Eberle, the burgomaster of Nossen near Meissen. All Prussian provinces and all *Länder* retained their central giro institutions until 1920. In those areas where public national banks existed as central banks for municipal banks, such as in Westphalia and the Rhein Province, the national banks took on the tasks of a central giro institution in addition to their regular business. In 1918 the *Deutsche Girozentrale* was founded as the centre-point for all central giro institutions. Thenceforth, the savings banks were united through a large giro network covering the entire Reich. And via the *Deutsche Girozentrale* they had also gained access to the money and capital markets.

The expansion of savings banks and central giro institutions did not come to an end once their organizational structure had been finalized. They ventured into spheres of business which had hitherto been the domain of private banks. Until 1914, the savings banks merely kept savings deposits and granted mortgage credits and municipal loans. But from 1908 it became possible for them to handle deposits in giro accounts and transactions on current accounts. This business remained insignificant until the First World

War. In 1913, 99.7% of all savings banks' deposits were in savings. After the end of the War, however, inflation forced the savings banks to expand their short-term credit and deposit business. Following the currency reform, when savings deposits, mortgages and mortgage bonds were revalued at 25%, savings and credit against securities became the savings banks' main business again. In 1930, the German savings banks had a total of 10.67 milliard RM in savings deposits and 1.5 milliard RM in giro deposits; this was slightly more than half of what they held before the outbreak of the First World War. About 70% of their assets were long-term loans and securities (mortgages, loans granted to local authorities, the Reich, the *Länder* and the boroughs). In 1930, in addition to the 8.5 milliard RM in securities and long-term loans and 1.4 milliard RM in liquid assets held in the central giro institutions, the savings banks had further assets of 2.5 milliard RM in short-term claims. The central giro institutions had also granted about two milliard RM in short-term credits so that the group of savings banks and central giro institutions was involved in short-term credit operations totalling about 4.5 milliard RM at the end of 1930. This was almost half the short-term credit which the major banks had granted. In other words, they had now become universal banks in the full sense of the term. Private commercial banks viewed them as troublesome rivals, particularly because, as public institutions, the savings banks did not have to pay national taxes. The private credit banks countered this penetration into their business sphere by moving into savings, on which they paid the same rate of interest as the savings banks.

In short, a process which had set in before 1914, continued to accelerate in the inter-war years. Legal and organizational differences between the divergent types of banks continued to exist, but they increasingly resembled each other in terms of the business they undertook. In Britain, the development took the opposite course: the legal and organizational differences between the various types of banks levelled out; the division in their business activities was maintained.

Measured against economic opportunities, the German banking system of 1929 was too large comprising, as it did, about 1,400 private credit banks (including approximately 1,100 private bankers) 39 mortgage banks, 21,499 credit co-operatives, nine state banks, eight Prussian *Landschaften*, 31 central giro institutions and national banks, 43 municipal banks and 3,100 savings banks.

United States of America

In the United States there were various legal obstacles to bank concentration or, to be more precise, to certain forms of concentration. Only the credit institutions in the State of California were, from 1909 onwards, allowed to establish branches outside the area of their head office. In the other Federal States this remained illegal until 1927. Thenceforth branch offices could be established, but only within the same Federal State. This stipulation made it impossible for big banks to build up a network of branches across the whole country. And yet America experienced a powerful concentration movement within its credit system. From the end of the First World War until the world economic crisis, 7,789 banks lost their independence in the course of some 4,177 mergers. A further 5,000 banks disappeared between 1919 and 1929 through bankruptcy or liquidation, generally small or tiny institutions, mostly in rural areas. At the same time, however, many new banks were established so that the total number decreased by a mere 4,000 from 29,123 in 1919 to 25,330 in 1929.

Since the summer of 1929, the economic situation had been deteriorating — several months before disaster struck the New York Stock Exchange on 24-25 October 1929. It was in this situation that the American credit system saw a renewed merger movement. Large-scale mergers got underway. In 1929, the Guaranty Trust Company of New York, in which Morgan was the major shareholder, took over the National Bank of Commerce. In the following year, Giannini in California consolidated his group which was controlled by the Bank of Italy into a major bank, the Bank of America. It was the fourth largest bank in the United States after the National City Bank of New York, the Chase National Bank and the Bankers Trust Company of New York. The Bank achieved its prominence thanks to its successful business activity and not least its purposeful merger policies. Approximately 500 million of the 1.16 milliard dollars equity capital and external loans which it was able to rely on in 1930 had been produced by mergers.

Since the creation of branch networks had been banned before 1927 and remained confined to certain small areas thereafter, American banks practised two other forms of concentration: chain banking and group banking. Chain banking means that one or several persons control several banks. This form of concentration was most common in the rural areas of the Northwest and developed in the last decades of the 19th century, although its dimensions cannot easily be quantified. Group banking involves establishing a bank holding company which has a stake of at least 25% in the subsidiaries in which it seeks to control. The first major holding company was the Bank of Italy Corporation, founded by Giannini in 1919, which operated under the name of the Transamerica Corporation after 1928. When the Giannini banks merged to form the Bank of America in 1930, the Transamerica Corporation became the Bank of America's major shareholder. In the course of the next few years, the holding company sold Bank of America shares to the public. Between 1925 and 1930, a further 20 or so of these bank holding companies emerged. By the end of 1929, some 2,103 American banks belonged to a group controlled by a bank holding company.

In the course of this concentration process the big banks, or rather the biggest major banks, increased their relative share in the American banking system. In 1914, the biggest banks of New York (Chase National Bank, National City Bank of New York, Guaranty Trust Company of New York, Bankers Trust Company, First National Bank of New York) held over 4% of all funds in the American banking system. In 1930 the five biggest New York banks, which now included the Irving Trust Company instead of the First National, managed 11.4% of all American bank capital. If the Bank of America is included in the figure for 1930, 13.1% of the total equity capital and external funds were in the hands of the six largest credit institutions. The largest American banks — the Chase National Bank and the National City Bank of New York — were by then the largest banks in the world, surpassing the British 'Big Five' in equity capital and balance-sheet totals.

Like their Central European counterparts, those of America were universal banks, at least until the world economic crisis. Most of them accepted giro deposits and savings deposits and hence had quite a favourable capital structure. The national banks' ratio between internal capital and external funds, which had not been affected by inflation in the United States, was still at 1:5.6 in 1929. The distribution of the funds from outside sources in relation to their payment terms changed during the boom years after 1922 in favour of long-term deposits. In 1929 somewhat more than 37% of funds from outside sources were long-term. In the wake of the investment boom of the 1920s, the issue of shares and debentures also saw a steep rise, and the demand for securities turned into feverish speculation. This, in turn, pushed share prices up and stimulated banking business. The banks enlarged their own portfolios although the share of securities as a percentage of total assets rose only slightly from 29.9% in 1919 to 30.7% by the end of 1928. On the other hand, loans on securities and mortgage credits made up an extraordinarily high proportion of the credit business, to the detriment of commercial credit. The proportion of mortgages calculated in terms of total credits rose from 6.3% in 1919 to between 13.7 and 14.7% in 1925-28. Loans which were granted to stockbrokers and other customers for the purchase of securities had for some time been playing a major role in the American credit system. In 1919, 23.8% were loans on securities; by 1929, their proportion had risen to over 35%. These credits were to become part of the enormous losses suffered by American banks during the Great Slump when the collapse of share prices deprived the loans on securities of their cover.

Long-term agricultural credit did not develop much in the United States until the First World War. Before 1914, two study groups had been sent to those countries in Europe which had considerable experience in this field. Germany had the most extensive agricultural credit system. But two different types of agricultural credit institutions were in existence there: the public institutions of the Prussian *Landschaften* and the innumerable agricultural credit co-operative societies. Which type was preferable, considering that the United States knew neither public nor co-operative banks at that time? The first public banks were set up in 1914 when the 12 Federal Reserve Banks were established. American credit banks were opposed to public agricultural credit institutions, but were reproached by the farmers for failing to supply agriculture with long-term credit. Agriculture therefore preferred public banks. Since both the farmers and the bankers had powerful lobbies, there was no way of settling the controversy until a compromise solution was reached in 1916. The Land Banks Act introduced two types of rural mortgage banks — public and private. A Land Bank Commissioner was installed as the authority to supervise the two types of banks. The Act of 1916 established 12 public Federal Land Banks whose districts corresponded to those of the 12 Federal Reserve Banks. Their joint-stock capital was to be raised by private subscribers. Because of opposition from the private banks, private subscription was so small that the Federal government had to provide each of the 12 Federal Land Banks with a foundation capital of $750,000. The farmers had to join National Farm Loan Associations, which were expected to furnish the Federal Land Bank concerned with a guarantee of half of every single loan granted to their members. By the beginning of the 1930s, the loan balance of the 12 institutions had reached $1.1 milliard.

Apart from these public agricultural credit banks, the Act also legalised private agricultural credit institutions in the form of joint-stock companies. These Joint-Stock Land Banks began to build up their mortgage business during the boom years after 1922. When agricultural prices collapsed during the world economic crisis and farmers ran into financial difficulties, the Joint-Stock Land Banks refused to grant them further credit and ruthlessly insisted on their claims. They even made a profit when they repurchased their mortgage bonds whose rates had fallen sharply. These business practices created so much ill-feeling against the Joint-Stock Land Banks that, when the New Deal began, the banks were ordered into liquidation by law, a process which lasted until 1950.

Setting up the organizational framework for long-term credit did little to solve the problems of agriculture. In 1921 farming was hit by a short, but deep crisis, when the harvest could not be fully sold. This led to strong pressure on agricultural prices. Certan measures, which were later implemented to meet the farmers' demand for 'fair prices', had already been put on the agenda, following a Congressional investigation into the predicament of agriculture. These measures involved a restriction of the arable area and state subsidies. But the Republican Administration of that time would have nothing to do with this form of state control; the Republicans firmly adhered to the idea of economic liberalism. The only tangible result of the discussions on the situation of the farmers between 1921 and 1924 was the establishment, in 1923, of 12 public Federal Intermediate Credit Banks designed to provide agriculture with interim loans to tide it over the critical phase between harvests and the receipt of payment for its crops. These credits were covered by the collateral of agricultural claims on commerce and on the food industry.

Japan

The structural development of Japanese banks between the end of the First World War and the world economic crisis was very turbulent and profoundly affected by disasters, bank panics and legislation. The War put a stop to the pre-1914 boom when Japan became more of a supplier of war materials than a belligerent nation. The boom was followed by a depression. Recovery from this depression had barely begun when, on 1 September 1923, the country was shattered by a major earthquake which devastated Tokyo and the large seaport of Yokohama. This catastrophe left 105,000 dead or missing; material damage was estimated at 5.5 milliard yen. The Government imposed a 30-day moratorium on all financial commitments dating from before 1 September 1923. Reconstruction of public buildings and of transport and supply facilities was financed by the issue of special treasury bills, known as 'earthquake bills', totalling 2.5 milliard yen. These bills were purchased by the Nihon Ginko (Bank of Japan) and by the 96 biggest banks in the country.

The number of credit institutions had been on the increase until the period immediately after the end of the War. In 1920 the banking system was hit by a liquidity crisis which followed the postwar depression. Bank deposits dwindled during the depression, and the small banks in particular sought to secure new deposits by offering higher rates of interest than those fixed in an agreement which the banks concluded in December 1918. The banks were forced into risky credit and loan transactions in order to be in a position to pay these high interest rates. The Nihon Ginko helped over 50 banks with bridging loans totalling 255 million yen.

In 1927 there was another disaster which was triggered off by the collapse of the Suzuki concern. The company was a product of the wartime boom which had brought high profits to the sugar merchant Suzuki of Kobe. He used the profits as well as large bank credits, primarily from the Bank of Taiwan, to purchase shares in various industries during 1917-18. Ultimately, he directly or indirectly controlled some 65 firms. However, his conglomerate of companies stood on shaky foundations. Many of his firms were unsound, others were badly managed. After 1923, the more solid companies suffered from the consequences of the earthquake. From 1926, the concern's financial difficulties escalated. Credits totalling 68 million yen from the Bank of Taiwan were locked up in these enterprises. As Suzuki's difficulties became more widely known, the Bank of Taiwan became the subject of rumours about its involvement with the former. In March 1927, the run on the Bank of Taiwan began; within two weeks it had lost one-third of its deposits and creditors. The Bank immediately suspended further credits to Suzuki, and on 5 April 1927 the latter had to cancel its own new credits. Three days later, the 65th Bank of Kobe, in which Suzuki was the major shareholder, had to close down. After this, the run on other banks could no longer be stopped. Most of them were faced with massive withdrawals of deposits. On 21 April, the 15th Bank of Tokyo had to close its doors. Its insolvency created a particularly big stir, for it was well known that the Bank had acted as a trustee in transactions for the Imperial State Ministry. The following two days (22 and 23 April 1927) were declared bank holidays by the banks in Tokyo and Osaka, the two main financial centres. The Government imposed a three-weeks' moratorium and restricted withdrawals to 500 yen per day and per account during this period.

Some 37 banks were unable to make even these limited payments during this period. They included such big institutions as the Bank of Taiwan and the 15th Bank. Thanks to the Government's speedy intervention and the preparedness of the Nihon Ginko to help banks which were in difficulties, public anxieties began to subside. The Bank of Taiwan was refloated with credits from the Nihon Ginko. Several medium-sized Tokyo banks merged and carried on their business under the name of the Showa Bank. The 15th Bank had to reduce its joint-stock capital to one-fifth before it was able to resume business. The big zaibatsu banks, on the other hand, weathered the crisis without losses and also without difficulties. The savings banks and Post-Office savings banks were also barely affected by the panic. These groups of banks were thus the 'winners' of the bank panic. Within a year of the crisis, the five big banks (Mitsui, Mitsubishi, Sumitomo, Yasuda, Dai-Ichi) had increased their deposits by approximately 30% from 2.2 milliard yen to 3.2 milliard yen. At the same time savings banks deposits increased by about 28% from 1.1 milliard yen to 1.4 milliard yen. The Post-Office Savings Bank finally almost doubled its deposits from 1.2 milliard yen to 2.11 milliard yen. Meanwhile deposits in the other commercial banks dwindled by almost one milliard yen from 6.95 milliard to 6.1 milliard. That the five big banks weathered the crisis without damage, was because their customers showed great faith in them and did not panic and because their long-term loans hardly suffered. They had granted credits to first-class and sound enterprises only. The Savings Bank Act of 1922 had put the savings banks under strict governmental control; they were merely allowed to acquire state and municipal bonds, and such further securities as had been cleared by the Finance Ministry. They were also permitted to grant mortgage credits, although they were forbidden to provide large credits. This strict control and limitation of risks protected the savings banks from a run during the crisis of 1927.

The crisis induced the Japanese government to introduce new regulations for private commercial banks. They were designed to prevent a repetition of the crisis that they had just experienced. Under the terms of the 1927 Bank Act, only those companies which accepted deposits, granted short or long-term credits and discounted bills were regarded as banks. Bill traders and bill brokers were no longer considered part of the banking sector. Every private commercial bank had to include the designation 'Ginko' (bank) in its company name. No other enterprises were allowed to use this term. All banks had to accept a joint-stock company structure. Those banks with a head office or a branch in one of the two main banking centres of Tokyo or Osaka had to have a joint-stock capital of at least two million yen; banks in other cities had to have a joint-stock capital of at least one million yen. It was only in small towns of less than 10,000 inhabitants that a minimum capital of 500,000 yen was sufficient. These regulations did much to encourage bank concentration. Only 418 of the

1,420 private commercial banks in existence before the banking crisis, remained by 1936. The proportion the five big banks possessed of the deposits of all private commercial banks rose from 24% to 30%, and their participation in the transaction of securities went up from 26% to 41%. State supervision of banks which had existed since 1890 was endowed with almost perfect powers of control. Members of the banks' boards of directors had to obtain the Finance Ministry's permission before they could accept top managerial positions in another company. Branches could be only established with the Finance Ministry's approval, a regulation which was designed to prevent unwelcome competition. Finally mergers also required permission from the Finance Minister. A twice-yearly report had to be submitted to the Finance Ministry, and the Minister was able to call for the dismissal of board members and, should he consider it in the customers' interest, to close a bank down in order to save the deposits.

The five big banks emerged from the turbulent decade following the end of the First World War with their position reinforced. In 1919 the Mitsui Ginko increased its capital from 20 million yen to 100 million yen. It was the first occasion that shares were bought not just by the Mitsui zaibatsu, but were also offered to the public. Mitsui differed from the other zaibatsu banks in that it conducted its business outside the zaibatsu to which it belonged. In 1924 a mere 7.2% of the bank's total deposits came from Mitsui companies. Seven years later, it was 15.9%. Credit transactions in support of the Mitsui companies were even smaller. At the end of 1928, 97 firms with a total capital of 1.6 milliard yen were members of the Mitsui zaibatsu. The policy of the Mitsubishi Ginko was the exact opposite. Until 1919, the Bank was a department of the Mitsubishi Goshi. In August 1919, the bank was restructured and turned into a separate firm within the larger concern. It engaged primarily in credit transactions with companies of the Mitsubishi zaibatsu. During the 1927 banking crisis, many customers of other commercial banks transferred their funds to the Mitsubishi Bank, whose deposits rose from 329 million yen to 471 million yen within a short period. Two years later, the Bank's joint-stock capital was increased to 100 million yen. By the end of 1928, some 65 firms with a total capital of 713 million yen, belonged to the Mitsubishi zaibatsu.

The Sumitomo Bank built up its foreign business after the War and established branches in the United States, Britain, India and China. It was second only to the Yokohama Specie Bank. At the end of 1928, the Sumimoto zaibatsu comprised 30 firms with a capital of 244 million yen. The fourth largest of the zaibatsu banks was the Yasuda Bank. In October 1923 it merged with 11 other banks, several of which had already absorbed smaller banks. The Yasuda Bank acquired the largest deposit account of all Japanese banks through this merger. It also ran the most extensive network of some 210 branches, whereas the other big banks had no more than a few (Mitsui 20, Mitsubishi 15) at that time. After the merger the resources of the Yasuda Bank amounted to 93 million yen joint-stock capital and 46 million yen reserves. Until the end of the 1920s, the Yasuda Bank continued to adhere to the business practices of its founder, Zenjiro Yasuda, who had engaged in credit and investment deals only with well-known enterprises and individuals. He had always refused to grant small credits on a massive scale. After 1929, the Yasuda Bank's position deteriorated under a less purposeful management.

The effect of the Bank Act in furthering the concentration movement was actually reinforced by the world economic crisis. The biggest merger in those years was that between three big banks in Osaka (34th Bank, Yamaguchi Bank and Konoike Bank), which combined in order to rationalize their operations and reduce costs. The result was the emergence of the sixth big bank, the Sanwa Ginko of Osaka, in 1933.

IX Money and Credit during the Great Slump

The world economic crisis of 1929-30 had deep-rooted and complex causes. The most important of these were: 1) the erroneous belief that the backlog of demand at the end of the War reflected post-war society's normal requirements; 2) the overoptimistic estimates of the market's capacity to absorb new industrial products (such as cars, photographic and film technology and synthetic materials); 3) the creation of overcapacities as a consequence of these two misjudgments; 4) excessive speculation in securities; 5) the long-term investment of funds borrowed on a short-term basis; 6) the international transfer of money which was unrelated to commodity production or service industries; 7) the disruption of international trade relations as a result of protectionist measures taken by individual countries, and in particular by the United States. The Great Slump which followed was an international catastrophe; and just as the causes of the crisis were international, so its resolution ought to have been an international problem. Yet the fight against the Depression was conducted by individual countries on the basis of national economic policies without international collaboration; indeed, it turned into a policy of all-round protectionism and even militant discrimination. In the 1930s the traditional division of labour on the world market turned into a struggle for economic and social survival under the motto of *'sauve qui peut'*! Worse: the world economic crisis exacerbated international political tensions. This was particularly true of the Far East and the Pacific, where Japan's 'export offensive' was accompanied by military aggression. Monetary policy was deliberately used for the first time in the 1930s as a means of national economic policy and as a commercial weapon. Country after country abolished the convertibility requirement of its issuing banks. Germany introduced exchange controls. Of the countries whose monetary and banking history is under discussion here, Britain, Japan, the United States, and France all devalued their currencies. The international gold standard, which had been painfully re-established after the First World War and the subsequent Great Inflation, fell victim to this monetary policy.

The threat of illiquidity loomed large over the banks as the Depression deepened with no end to it in sight. Notices of withdrawal were given on deposits; assets became eroded or worthless, as a growing number of debtors went to the wall. The banking systems in Germany, the United States and Belgium were hit by violent crises which ushered in far-reaching structural changes. The problems were less serious in Britain and France; the Japanese banking system had experienced a major crisis in 1927. In other words, it was the countries with universal banks which found that their credit institutions were affected by such great difficulties as to require direct state aid. Many people now came to regard the universal type of bank as one of the sensitive points in the credit system and a focus for reform. This view gained general acceptance in the United States, Belgium and Italy and determined the shape of the new laws which the crisis produced. Between 1933 and 1936, universal banks were banned in these countries. In Germany, too, men such as Hans Luther, the President of the Reichsbank, and Bernhard Dernburg, the former banker and Reich Finance Minister, proposed that universal banks be abolished. Germany's bankers, however, succeeded in persuading the Government to retain this type of bank; and as the Reich had abandoned normal parliamentary legislative procedures in March 1930, the Reichstag never had an opportunity of discussing the problems which had arisen within the banking system.

Yet it was not only divergent economic pressures and structural factors that shaped the development of banks in different countries during the Depression. Rather more decisive was the question of whether the banks had pursued sound or hazardous business practices. What the banking crises clearly revealed was the value of traditional banking rules and the consequences of observing or ignoring them.

1. The German Banking Crisis of 1931
and the End of Reparations

German banks were first affected by the world economic crisis in two areas. To begin with, a number of their major industrial customers ran into difficulties; the banks granted many of them further credits in order to keep them afloat. This was obviously very risky; for in so doing they became even more dependent on their major debtors. Certainly this policy violated the ancient banker's rule that you do not prop up a shaky client with good money. The second neuralgic point at which the Depression affected the banks concerned their holdings of securities. They owned a large volume of shares, parts of which had been acquired when they took a hand in the creation of trusts during the 1920s. As long as industrial share prices were high, they represented a considerable asset, and the dividends helped the banks to establish hidden reserves. But once the crisis had begun, this source of income was lost. The price of shares fell below their nominal value, and the balance-sheet position deteriorated correspondingly.

These first warning signals did not unduly alarm the banks, particularly as their foreign creditors were not yet knocking on their doors. All this changed abruptly with the Reichstag elections of 14 September 1930. Reich Chancellor Brüning had dissolved Parliament because it had called for the withdrawal of a presidential emergency decree which approved cover for the Reich budget. Brüning hoped that fresh elections would provide his minority cabinet with a broader parliamentary base. But the Reichstag election ended in disaster for the coalition parties. Their share of votes dropped from 36.8% to 31.7%. The National Socialists were the main victors and increased their share from 2.6% to 18.3%.

The electoral success of an intransigent and revolutionary nationalism shook the confidence of Germany's foreign creditors in the political stability and credit-worthiness of the Weimar Republic. In the first six weeks after the election, over 700 million RM in foreign credits and deposits in the major German banks were recalled. When it became apparent that the Brüning government had not been completely paralyzed by the outcome of the September elections the pace of foreign withdrawals slowed down, but there was no influx of new money to balance the withdrawals. In the first four months of 1931, a further 400 million RM were recalled. Germany's four main creditors, the United States, Britain, the Netherlands and Switzerland each withdrew funds in roughly equal shares.

Following the electoral success of the Nazis, bank shares also began to slip. Until late in the summer of 1930, bank shares had remained steady at a considerably higher level than industrial shares. But after the Reichstag elections they, too, went into a nose-dive and finally dropped below par. Share prices do not, however, present a reliable yardstick for measuring the actual strength of a particular company, since the formation of stock prices is influenced by many and often volatile factors. On the other hand, they are measures of the standing and confidence which a firm enjoys. It is of course most awkward for a financial institution which depends heavily on the confidence of its depositors, if the price of its shares falls sharply or even drops below the nominal value. In this situation all the major banks, except for the Berliner Handels-Gesellschaft, took supportive action to eliminate the fluctuations in stock prices and began to buy up their own shares. The flexible regulations of German company law did not prevent them from adopting this policy; it was nonetheless a dubious practice. After all, by acquiring its own shares, a joint-stock company's net assets — as well as its liable capital — are being reduced by a corresponding amount.

Events in Austria were the final straw which precipitated an acute banking crisis in Germany. On 11 May 1931, the Österreichische Creditanstalt, the biggest commercial bank of the country, published its annual balance-sheet for 1930. It showed that the Bank had suffered enormous losses which almost exhausted its total internal capital. Much of the credit which the Creditanstalt had given to Austrian industry had been frozen, and their large holdings of industrial shares had been devalued by the fall in share prices. The publication of the accounts prompted a run on the Creditanstalt. By July 1931, the Bank had been put back on its feet with the aid of an international credit mediated by the Bank of England. However, concurrently with the crisis of the Creditanstalt and other Austrian banks there began a run of foreign creditors on the major German banks.

Most observers and authors maintained at the time, and have continued to argue until very recently, that it was the French banks which triggered off the run on the Austrian and German banks when they withdrew their short-term credits. According to this analysis, France took this action in order to put pressure on Germany and Austria to abandon the project of a German-Austrian customs union, to which the French government was strongly opposed. This hypothesis may sound convincing and logical, but it does not tally with the actual course of events; for the French did not recall any credits at this time. This emerges from a country-by-country break-down of foreign credits held by Germany during those critical weeks and months. It is also important to remember that France's short-term credits to German banks were not so large that a recall would have put them into difficulties. It was only late in the crisis that Paris tried to combine financial policy with diplomatic objectives.

It is not surprising that the predicament of the Österreichische Credit-anstalt quickly affected the German banking system. There was a close parallel between the former and the major German banks in that they all had an unfavourable ratio between internal capital and external resources; they were badly hit when industrial bankruptcies immobilized their credits and the value of their shares collapsed. What had happened to a reputable and major bank like the Österreichische Creditanstalt, which included the Viennese Rothschild bank amongst its major shareholders, could also happen in Germany at any time. Consequently the foreign creditors of Berlin's big banks became alarmed, and recalled a total of 288 million RM in short-term credits in the second half of May 1931. In the following weeks, foreign anxieties continued to be aroused by further chilling economic or political news, and there was no respite for Germany's banking system.

At the end of May two major firms — *Karstadt*, the department-store chain, and *Nordstern*, the insurance company — ran into difficulties. These developments accelerated the pace at which foreign credit was withdrawn. At the beginning of June, nervousness abroad increased when the Reich government issued a statement which, though prompted by domestic con-siderations, made a disastrous impression abroad. Worse, it was backed up by an emergency decree which demanded new sacrifices from the German population. It promulgated salary cuts, reductions in unemployment benefit and the introduction of a new tax. In order to make these measures more palatable, Brüning thought it necessary to publish, along with ⋅the emergency decree, a statement announcing that steps would be taken to ease Germany's reparations burdens. This announcement, he hoped, would reduce the pressure exerted on him by the National Socialists and German Nationalists. The Reichsbank President strongly advised him not to issue such a declaration because it would cause alarm abroad and lead to massive withdrawals of foreign credit. But Brüning considered the expected effect at home to be more important than the possible harmful repercussions abroad, and the statement was put out. Luther's worries were only too well-founded. Within four days of the declaration, the Reichsbank had to supply 400 million RM in foreign currency to the commercial banks to enable them to repay foreign credits which had been recalled. A few days later, the Brüning government was temporarily threatened by paralysis when it faced a common front in the Reichstag of the parliamentary groups of the Nazis, the German Nationals, the German People's Party, the Social Democratic Party and the Communists. It was no doubt a unique and extraordinary show of unity. Within a day of this move, a further 220 million RM of foreign credits were recalled.

After this, the Reichsbank adopted a tighter monetary policy and increased the minimum lending rate from 5% to 7%. The aim was to make it too costly for commercial banks and their customers to buy foreign exchange at the central bank by discounting trade bills. They were to be encouraged to use their own foreign exchange reserves instead. Until mid-June 1931, the Reichsbank had to surrender more than half of its foreign currency holding, and in the first half of June 1931 the gold and foreign currency cover fell from 59.9% to 48%.

No sooner had the German economy weathered this crisis than it was shaken by the collapse of *Nordwolle*. This textile company had suffered a loss of 200 million RM in speculative transactions. With an internal capital of 97 million RM and assets worth 140 million RM the firms had debts totalling 170 million RM. It was known that two major banks, the Danat-Bank and the Dresdner Bank, had granted large credits to *Nordwolle*. After *Karstadt* and *Nordstern*, the *Nordwolle* concern was the third large company to run into difficulties within three weeks. As contemporary English and Swiss press comments show, this contributed to a disastrous loss of confidence abroad in the viability of German industry. On the day following the publication of the *Nordwolle* crisis, the Reichsbank had to make 70 million RM of foreign currency available for the repayment of foreign credits which had been recalled.

The Bank now found itself in a precarious situation. On 19 June 1931, its gold and foreign currency cover was a mere 100 million RM over the legally and internationally prescribed minimum. Within a few days, the Bank would either be unable to sell any more foreign currency to the commercial banks so that they could honour their foreign obligations (in which case Germany's credit-worthiness abroad would have been in ruins), or it would have to lower its cover limit below that stipulated by the Young Plan (in which case the Government would have found itself in the embarrassing situation of having to violate an agreement which had been in force for barely 15 months).

At this point Herbert Hoover, the U.S. President, came to Germany's rescue. He had been informed of her financial situation by Frederick M. Sackett, the American Ambassador to Berlin. On the night of 20 June, Hoover proposed a one-year moratorium on all international political debts, reparations as well as inter-Allied debts. This seemed to be the salvation. Should the moratorium come about, the Reich stood to save 1.6 milliard RM out of its total budget of 10 milliard RM. This would relieve the pressure on the German money markets and represented a saving of

1.6 milliard RM in foreign currency for the next 12 months. It was hoped that once a moratorium had been announced, foreign creditors would view Germany's situation more favourably and suspend, or at least restrict, their credit withdrawals.

In fact the withdrawals of capital from Germany almost came to a halt, but only for a few days. On 27 June 1931, they were resumed on a large scale. How did this come about? The problem was that Hoover's proposal had met with resistance in France. It was understandable that France felt no particular enthusiasm for a moratorium. After all, the moratorium was to apply to political debts only. This meant that Germany was to be freed from paying her political debts for one year in order to be able to pay her commercial debts. Her commercial and private creditors were hence given priority over her political creditors. However, unlike the United States and Britain, France had but a few commercial credit claims against Germany; on the other hand, she was Germany's main reparations creditor. The French government agreed to the Hoover Moratorium only after further negotiations which dragged on for two weeks.

French resistance to the Hoover Moratorium revived the anxieties of foreign creditors. The Reichbank's weekly returns, published on 23 June 1931, revealed that the country's note cover had fallen to 40.3%. The Reichsbank sought to obtain a foreign rediscount credit in order to replenish its foreign currency holdings. It received a joint credit from the Bank of England, the Banque de France, the Bank for International Settlements and the Federal Reserve Bank of New York, but this amounted to a mere 100 million dollars. In order to cover up the small size of this credit, the Bank's board of directors decided to announce no more than that a 'rediscount opportunity of sufficient size' had been received. However, a New York newspaper leaked the actual amount of the credit. The source of this leak has remained unknown, but the cat was out of the bag. The Reichsbank was now compelled to disclose the amount in a communiqué published on the evening of 25 June. In the eyes of foreign creditors, the situation once more looked far from rosy. Hoover's proposal for a moratorium, the Reichsbank's balance-sheet and its effort to obtain international rediscount credit clearly revealed that Germany had reached the limit of her capacity to pay. The amount of the international credit was so low that it would only marginally improve Germany's capacity to pay in foreign currency. Thus, if foreign creditors wanted to retrieve their capital from Germany before the Reichsbank blocked the sale of foreign exchange which had reached its lower cover limit, they had to take immediate action and withdraw their credits before it was too late. Within 36 hours of the disclosure of the amount of the above-mentioned rediscount credit, massive withdrawals of capital from Germany set in. By that time, it no longer made any difference that the Hoover Moratorium came into force on 7 July.

The renewed run by foreign creditors not only caused the Reichsbank's foreign exchange reserves to dwindle, but also endangered the liquid assets of commercial banks. Germany was hence threatened not only with having to default on her debts abroad, but also with being unable to maintain the country's money economy at home. This danger intensified when, in the first days of July, German investors and savers themselves became nervous and started to recall their deposits in banks and savings banks on a large scale. The Darmstädter Bank und Nationalbank was most at risk, followed by the Dresdner Bank. The Berliner Handels-Gesellschaft, on the other hand, remained totally unaffected. Its directors, Carl Fürstenberg and Otto Jeidels, had on principle not taken up any foreign credit of less than six months. They had also been very cautious in their lending policy. This caution meant that the Berliner Handels-Gesellschaft was the only major private bank to emerge from the crisis without capital reconstruction and Reich aid. This clearly shows that entrepreneurial skill continued to be a tangible factor in economic development in the face of anonymous structural forces and trade cycles.

By July 1931, the savings banks and central giro institutions also found themselves in great difficulties. The main cause of this was not the high level of short-term foreign debts; they had but few. Rather the savings banks and central giro institutions fell victim to the massive borrowing of the local authorities. These local authorities and municipalities were their principal debtors. But as many communities had to suspend their payments, a large part of municipal credits became frozen. What is more, many savings banks did not keep a liquidity reserve, stipulated by standard statutes, of at least 10% of their deposits in the appropriate central giro institution, and even the reserves that were kept could not be turned into liquid assets; they were tied up in short-term municipal loans.

The Government and the Reichsbank had been in constant touch with each other since 1 July 1931. Brüning and Luther at first hoped to avoid government intervention and to allow the forces of the market to deal with the crisis. They proposed that the big banks should form an association of guarantors to assume liability for the commitments of those banks which were faced with collapse, starting with the Danat-Bank. It is impossible to say, even with hindsight, whether such self-help would have been sufficient at that time. And in any event, it did not materialize because the Deutsche Bank refused to participate. The banks did not want to take an incalculable risk. Bankers and economists reproached the Reichsbank President — and almost all of them have continued to hold this view to this day — for deserting the banks by pursuing a policy of tight money during the most serious phase of the crisis. This criticism would have been justified, if the run had involved the domestic market alone. But the run by domestic customers did not begin until the final stages of the banking crisis. It was not responsible for the predicament of the banks nor for the decisions of the Reichsbank. The crucial factor was the size of the short-term foreign exchange debts to other countries. At the beginning of July 1931, the big banks alone still owed foreign banks 5.5 milliard RM in short-term foreign currency. At this time the Reichsbank had a gold and foreign exchange reserve of 1.7 milliard RM. Even if the Bank had reduced this currency reserve to nil, it would have done no more than delay the big banks' inability to pay the foreign countries by two weeks at most; certainly it would not have been able to prevent it.

The Reichsbank had made a rescue attempt which failed. On Luther's initiative a so-called 'Guarantee Syndicate' of all major German companies was formed by an emergency decree which the Reich President signed on 8 July. This syndicate was to give a guarantee of up to 500 million RM for the credit transactions of the Golddiskontbank, a subsidiary of the Reichsbank. Luther travelled to London, Paris and Basle to explain the purpose of the syndicate and to obtain new credit from the issuing banks of Britain and France, and from the Bank for International Settlements. The Bank of England was prepared to provide credit on condition that the Banque de France participated. Thus the decision about international credit was in the hands of Paris. Luther negotiated with Clément Moret, Emile Moreau's successor at the Banque de France; he also saw Pierre-Etienne Flandin, the French Finance Minister. The French were prepared to grant Germany a credit of 1.5 milliard dollars, but with certain political strings attached: Germany was to abandon her proposed customs union with Austria. It would not have been difficult to comply with this demand. The project had already been written off in Berlin in the face of strong international opposition to it.

However, the other political conditions were such that no German government would have been able to accept them. The French insisted that for the duration of the loan Germany must abandon, once and for all, its attempts to revise the reparations settlement. The implication was that Germany was to receive one milliard dollars in order to pay, without further procrastination, reparations of 4.8 milliard dollars during the ten-year duration of the loan. Politics apart, this would have been bad business from Germany's point of view. Finally, the Reich was to abandon, for the next 10 years, the construction of further 10,000-ton battle cruisers beyond the one already completed, although she was permitted six under the terms of the Versailles Treaty. This French demand was tantamount to a revision of the disarmament clauses of the Treaty to Germany's disadvantage. Flandin's offer and the political conditions related to it were repeated ten days later when Prime Minister Pierre Laval had a meeting with Brüning. The latter rejected the offer just as Luther had done before him. By combining offers of credit with specific political demands, France put her capital export, or rather her export capacity, into the service of her foreign policy.

After Luther's attempt to obtain international credit had foundered in the face of French demands, the collapse of the Darmstädter und National-bank could no longer be averted. It had lost 50 million RM during the *Nordwolle* affair. Some 35 million RM of the Bank's joint-stock capital of 60 million were in its own shares. Thus its liable capital came to a mere 25 million RM. For the last eight weeks, the Bank had had to repay 650 million RM, and it continued to have short-term commitments of 1.5 milliard RM, 460 million RM of which represented foreign claims. By early July, the Bank's liquid funds were exhausted, and Jakob Goldschmidt, one of the proprietors, informed the Reich government that his bank would keep its doors closed on the following Monday, 13 July 1931. At the same time the Reich government heard that the Landesbank der Rheinprovinz which functioned as a central giro institution for the Rhine Province had run into liquidity problems. On receiving this crisis news, feverish discussions and negotiations took place in the Reich Chancellery during the weekend of 11/12 July. The leading men from the big banks were called in; their participation was of little use. They did not fully inform the Government of the seriousness of their own situation. Thus the representative of the Dresdner Bank declared their firm to be fully solvent; yet 36 hours later, it was forced to announce the exact opposite. There was also no consensus among the leading bankers as to what measures should be taken to overcome the crisis. Some of them pleaded for bank holidays; others opposed this solution. The one thing that was certain was that the Danat-Bank would not open its doors on 13 July. Consequently the Government at first confined itself to guaranteeing the liabilities of the Danat-Bank and to laying the management of the Bank into the hands of a trustee.

On July 13 1931, the doors of the Danat-Bank remained closed whereupon the big run on all banks and savings banks set in. Within a few hours, most financial institutions decided to pay out only 20% of the sums their customers wished to withdraw, which was tantamount to a suspension of payments. The Reich government now proclaimed two bank holidays which enabled the banks to avoid an open and complete suspension of payments. Payments were not made again until three weeks later, on 5 August 1931.

The bank holidays were no more than a brief respite. Drastic measures had to be taken during this interval or the crisis would have continued until the total collapse of the German financial and credit system. Two goals had to be achieved: firstly, the banks had to regain their liquidity in order to be able to conduct normal business; secondly, the massive withdrawals of foreign credit had to be curbed. Both goals had to be achieved as quickly as possible. Furthermore, it was necessary to undertake capital reconstructions in the case of those banks which had been most seriously affected.

When the banks reopened, they had to brace themselves for further withdrawals at high levels; their customers had not been able to obtain money for three weeks; nor had the bank holidays allayed public disquiet and distrust. The banks could expect to calm the situation and return to normalcy only if they resumed payments in full. However, the liquid resources available were still far from sufficient to meet the first wave of withdrawals. In order to obtain cash, the banks theoretically had two possibilities. They could recall their own claims; but this was not practicable as a large part of these claims were either frozen or their repayment would have led to the collapse of the company concerned. The second alternative was to rediscount bills with the Reichsbank which they had themselves accepted. Yet the Reichsbank only accepted first-class trade bills with a maximum term of three months, and the banks had very few such bills left after the big run.

Dernburg, a former Reich Finance Minister and Secretary of State for the Colonies under William II, found a way out of this difficulty which was as brilliant as it was simple. He proposed the establishment of a new financial institution, well funded with capital and authorized to discount bills. This Akzept- und Garantiebank, as it came to be known, was equipped with a joint-stock capital of 200 million RM, 25% of which was paid up. By the end of 1931, the Akzept- und Garantiebank had mediated credits of close to 1.75 milliard RM to commercial and savings banks.

This institution did no more than help to keep domestic payments going and to support domestic credit. Yet the greatest source of danger remained the high level of short-term foreign debts. The Reichsbank's gold and foreign exchange reserves were not sufficient to meet all short-term foreign commitments. At first an attempt was made to increase Germany's foreign exchange reserve by acquiring private holdings of foreign currency and transferring these funds to the Reichsbank. Hence the introduction of foreign exchange controls. In fact, Germany was the first country during the world economic crisis to resort to such means: from 1 August 1931, all foreign exchange in private hands had to be sold to the Reichsbank, and private dealings in foreign exchange were forbidden. But this was insufficient to repay short-term foreign currency debts. The Reich also tried to obtain a moratorium on foreign commercial debts similar to the one on reparations. Help came once more from President Hoover. He was anxious to overcome the German banking crisis for fear that it might spread to American banks. Many of these were creditors of the German banks and Hoover proposed negotiations aiming at a moratorium on German commercial debts.

With Hoover's proposal on the table, ministers, diplomats and bankers from the creditor countries met with the Reich Chancellor and the Reichsbank President in London on 21-23 July to negotiate an agreement. The London Conference formed the Wiggin Committee, composed of banking experts from the most important creditor countries and from Germany, to determine, as a first step, the size of the foreign debt and to investigate the use to which foreign capital was being put. This Committee submitted its findings in a report which was edited by Lord Layton, a British banking expert. On the basis of this Layton Report, a moratorium was agreed in August 1931 between representatives of the creditor banks and the German debtor banks. The Germans were granted six months in which to repay their short-term debts. But the story did not end there. The moratorium was extended several times and each time the size of the debt to which the moratorium applied was reduced by a small amount. The final instalments of the short-term credits which had been taken up in the 1920s were not repaid until after the London Debt Agreement of 1953.

The Layton Report also pointed to the crucial role of reparations in causing Germany's high levels of foreign indebtedness. It showed that of the 25.6 milliard RM in foreign currency which Germany had received in foreign credit between 1924 and 1930, 10.3 milliard RM had been spent on reparations and 7.8 milliard on balancing her foreign trade deficit. Layton now pointed the way for a revised reparations settlement, and the British government seized the initiative. After preliminaries which dragged on for some time, the Lausanne Conference assembled on 16 June 1932. All the reparations creditor countries as well as the Reich were represented. Ramsey MacDonald, the British Prime Minister, proposed that reparations be cancelled altogether. He realized that Germany's large commercial debts and catastrophic economic situation would not permit her to pay her reparations within the foreseeable future. He also believed that, if reparations could be waived, he would be able to exert moral pressure on the United States and induce Washington to relent on the repayment of inter-Allied debts. Ever since the immediate post-war years the British government had been aiming to have all political debts cancelled (see above pp. 205f.).

Edouard Herriot, the French Prime Minister, on the other hand, insisted, not least out of consideration for French public opinion, that Germany should, if nothing else, make a final payment once her economy had recovered. Franz von Papen, Brüning's successor, offered Herriot a payment of two milliard RM. But he demanded at the same time that Article 231 of the Versailles Treaty which declared Germany guilty of unleashing the First World War be annulled. Herriot declined such a bargain. British mediation also paved the way for the Lausanne Agreement which was finally reached on 9 July 1932. Under the terms of this Agreement, Germany's reparations debt was assumed to have been discharged after a final payment of three milliard RM. The sum was not immediately due, but payment was to restart after three years and in such a way that the German government would issue three milliard RM worth of debt certificates (bearing 5% interest) to the Bank for International Settlements. For all practical purposes this was the end of the German reparations saga; the settlement sum was due in 1935, but the Nazis never paid this.

If the British had hoped that, by abandoning reparations, they would also achieve the cancellation of the inter-Allied debts, they were to be disappointed. Another American presidential election campaign was underway at the time, and, assessing his chances of re-election, Hoover was loath to explain to his fellow-countrymen that America's claims against Europe had been scrapped. After the Hoover Moratorium had expired in December 1932 and a further instalment was due, only Britain, Italy and Finland paid anything. The other debtors, including France, defaulted. Meanwhile Hoover had been defeated by Franklin D. Roosevelt; but whereas the new President was not prepared to cancel inter-Allied debts, he accepted the fact that the money would not be forthcoming. Consequently, Britain and Italy made a small 'symbolic' payment in the summer of 1933 before they, too, suspended the servicing of their debts in the following year. Only Finland repaid her inter-Allied debts in full.

The immediate danger facing the German banking system was averted by the Moratorium of August 1931. Other measures adopted by the Reich government were aimed at a reorganization of the system itself. Berlin had been prevented from intervening in good time because it had been given false information about the situation by the country's credit institutions. Now, in September 1931, a supervisory authority was imposed on them. The illiquidity of the savings banks and central giro institutions was largely the result of the illiquidity of local authorities; moreover, the savings banks were not independently incorporated institutions, but part of the local administrative structure. In order to extricate the savings banks from too close an involvement with local finance and local politics, they were transformed into institutions in public law by an emergency decree which the Reich President signed on 6 October 1931. The local authorities remained liable for the commitments of the savings banks. However, the central giro institutions and savings banks were barred from providing credit to municipalities and other local authorities. This ban was not relaxed until 1939.

The Reich government made a total of about 1.25 milliard RM available to cover the losses and to change the capital structure of the country's credit institutions. Of these, some 223.5 million RM were contributions *à fonds perdu*; some 845 million RM were in advances, and 187 million RM were in bank shares which the Reich acquired. The reorganization of the banking system had been achieved by the spring of 1932. The Danat-Bank and the Dresdner Bank were merged following the combination of their capital stocks earlier that year. The Reich owned some 66% and the Golddiskontbank 25% of the new Dresdner Bank's joint-stock capital which initially amounted to 220 million RM and was reduced to 150 million RM at the end of 1932. The Commerz- und Privatbank was merged with the Barmer Bankverein, one of the major provincial banks, on the basis of a 10:3 capital ratio. The joint-stock capital of the new firm was fixed at 80 million RM. The Reichsbank, through the Golddiskontbank, had a direct stake of over 50% in the new Commerz- und Privatbank. The Reich held some 14% of the shares. The Deutsche Bank und Disconto-Gesellschaft had to reduce its joint-stock capital from 285 million RM to 72 million RM. Subsequently, 72 million RM were issued in new shares of which the Golddiskontbank acquired 50 million RM. This meant that the latter had a direct participating investment of close to 35% in the Deutsche Bank's total joint-stock capital of 144 million RM. In 1933, the Deutsche Bank had to reduce its capital to 130 million RM for the second time; this meant that, throughout the 1930s, the Dresdner Bank was the most powerful German commercial bank. Of the big private banks, the Berliner Handels-Gesellschaft alone weathered the crisis without government aid and without reducing its capital. It absorbed the losses inflicted by the crisis by using part of its reserves. Its proprietors, Carl and Hans Fürstenberg, Otto Jeidels, Siegfried Bieber and Gustav Sintenis, had observed the rules more conscientiously than most.

The interventions of the Reich government and the Reichsbank resulted in the quasi-nationalization of Germany's three biggest commercial banks. The Reich and its Bank had a 91% stake in the Dresdner Bank, with 70% in the Commerz- und Privatbank and nearly 35% in the Deutsche Bank. Many authors, Gustav Stolper and Rolf Lüke among them, are of the opinion that the nationalization of the big banks helped Hitler to consolidate his power more rapidly in 1933, because he was able to take over an integrated banking system and thus achieve immediate control over the economy via the big nationalized banks. This may sound plausible, but it is hardly tenable. In fact, the nationalization of the banks was rescinded after 1933. Up to 1936, the shares of the big banks which the Reich and the Golddiskontbank held were quietly repurchased by a consortium of private bankers. In order to gain control of the economy, the Nazis employed methods other than those of a state socialism. They used the Enabling Act of March 1933 and the replacement of Luther by Hjalmar Schacht, one of Hitler's supporters, to achieve their aims.

The nationalization of big banks was no more than an ephemeral result of the banking crisis which had no far-reaching consequences. However, the banking crisis contributed in a most important way to the deepening of Germany's economic depression. Before the crisis, the big Berlin banks had pumped some 9.8 milliard RM into Germany's economy; by 1932, these credits to industry dwindled to 4.5 milliard RM. In other words, the bank crash accelerated the decline in manufacturing output and the rise in unemployment. In 1931, manufactured goods still represented 80% of Germany's total output for 1929; a year later, output was down to 58% of the 1929 figure. In the summer of 1931, 4.4 million people were unemployed in Germany; by the summer of 1932, the total was 5.1 million.

The banking crisis revealed a large number of flaws in the structure of the German banking system. For the future it seemed vital to ensure that the traditional rules of banking would be observed and that bank deposits be safeguarded by law. In preparing this legislation, a comprehensive statistical history of banking since the Great Inflation was initiated in 1932, though it was carried out only after the National Socialists had seized power. This study instituted the keeping of bank statistics in Germany and provided the raw material for the Banking Act of 1934. The Act itself, whose basic stipulations apply to this day, was the first attempt to draw up comprehensive regulations relating to this branch of the economy. It stipulated that every bank required a licence from a supervisory board *(Bankenaufsicht)* to which it had to report every month. Banks were obliged to spread risks; they also had to notify the *Bankenaufsicht* of large credits exceeding one million RM. Finally, the new supervisory body could force banks to keep a certain minimum of liquid reserves.

Whereas the Banking Act of 1934 remained unaffected by the ideology of National Socialism, the private Jewish banking houses fell victim to anti-Semitic persecution. Jews, however sound their business, were forced either to liquidate their firms and to move their business to other banks — as happened in the cases of S. Bleichröder, Mendelssohn & Co., Lazard Speyer-Ellissen and others in 1938 — or they had to accept 'Aryanization', i.e. the Jewish owners and partners had to withdraw. The names of such firms had to be changed. For example, the banking house of M.M. Warburg & Co. became Brinckmann Wirtz & Co. in 1938, to be renamed Brinckmann Wirtz Warburg & Co. in 1970; Sal. Oppenheim Jr. & Cie changed its name to Pferdmenges & Co., to become Sal. Oppenheim Jr. & Co. again in 1946. Nazi anti-Semitism also forced the departure of Otto Jeidels and Hans Fürstenberg from the Berliner Handels-Gesellschaft in 1936.

2. British and French Banks

Britain was also badly affected by Germany's banking crisis. How far the development of the pound was influenced by it during the summer and autumn of 1931 will be discussed in another connection (see below pp. 279f.). The London money market was given a taste of the German crisis in mid-July 1931. At that time, British banks were hit by Germany's exchange controls, while short-term foreign funds had begun to be withdrawn from Britain. Finding it impossible to obtain money from Germany, American, Swiss and Dutch banks recalled their short-term credits from Britain in order to strengthen their own liquidity position. From mid-July until 20 September 1931, £200 million of short-term foreign credits were withdrawn from British debtors. On 23 July, the Bank of England increased the discount rate from 2.5% to 3.5%. A week later, it was raised to 4.5% and finally, on 20 September, to 6% in order to check this flight.

The merchant banks were most seriously affected by these developments in the money market. Their specialty was the international acceptance credit. This gave them large supplies of short-term foreign funds which they, in turn, extended as short-term foreign credits. Statistical data are available for only ten merchant banks, since not all of them published their balance-sheets. But the figures from these ten firms may be regarded as representative of all merchant banks. They show that their deposits shrank by 38% between May 1931 and May 1932. In absolute terms, the ten merchant banks lost deposits amounting to £23.7 million. In order to be able to repay these funds, the banks had to sell off easily realizable assets and, since they found this difficult, they also had to sell securities; this they could do only at a considerable loss. All in all, the securities held by the ten merchant banks decreased by 39.4% between May 1931 and May 1932. Their nominal value was £4.6 million. Discount houses, on the other hand, were hardly affected by the international movements of money; their foreign deposits were very small and they had granted foreign countries only insignificant amounts of credit. Their customers were primarily British industry and the Commonwealth trade.

The five big banks and the other members of the London Bankers' Clearing House weathered the critical stage between the summer of 1931 and May 1932 without running into difficulties. Their deposits were always covered by more than 10% in cash and they never granted credit above a maximum of six months. Consequently, only small amounts were withdrawn from the London clearing banks even at the height of the crisis.

In July 1931, the ten members of the Clearing House had a total of £1,788 million in deposits; by May 1932, these had fallen to £1,699 million; by September 1932, their deposits had increased again to £1,865 million and this trend continued during the following months. The Clearing House banks had also gradually, but steadily been reducing their debt accounts since the April of 1931. Here the decline was from £940 million in April 1931 to £750 million in September 1933, and this despite the fact that at that time deposits in hand were some £222 million higher at £1,958 million than they had been in April 1931. The decline in debit accounts was matched by a corresponding increase in security holdings. Between April 1931 and September 1933, the Clearing Banks' security holdings rose from £309 million to £563 million. Frozen credit had evidently been converted into direct investments.

From the spring of 1932, the volume of money was shielded against the oscillations resulting from incoming or outgoing short-term foreign capital. The management of this policy was the responsibility of the Exchange Equalization Account which had been set up in April 1932. It was provided with £175 million in Treasury bills and administered Britain's gold and foreign exchange reserves which were used to iron out the fluctuations in the rate of exchange on foreign exchange markets. British importers were able to buy foreign currency at the Exchange Equalization Account.

The bank rate had risen to 6% in the summer of 1931, but was gradually reduced from February 1932 until it was down to as little as 2% on 30 April 1932. By cutting the bank rate so drastically the Bank of England had several objectives in mind: a low bank rate would result in low interest rates and keep out 'hot' (short-term) foreign money; the money market would be stabilized and the cost of credit to the British economy would be correspondingly reduced. All in all, the British banking system survived the world economic crisis without suffering heavy damage; in particular there were no dramatic collapses or insolvencies, since the British banks had a sound capital structure and had observed the traditional liquidity rules.

France found herself in the grip of the world economic crisis only towards the end of 1931. It was at this point that, owing to the devaluation of the pound, the franc lost the edge which its undervaluation had given it. Although, generally speaking, the French economy continued to be strong throughout 1930, French local and regional banks began to run into trouble in the autumn of that year. The crisis was triggered off not by the Great Slump, but was an after-effect of the French inflation and involved the Oustric Trust. This company was a product of the inflation, just as the Stinnes Group had been of Germany's in 1923; and, again like Stinnes, it soon ran into difficulties due to overexpansion on the basis of insufficient equity capital. The firm was shunned by the big banks as a maverick enterprise; but it succeeded in establishing close business ties with the old provincial Banque Adam at Boulogne-sur-Mer, which had once taken the initiative in the creation of the Syndicate of French Provincial Banks. Oustric first became insolvent in 1929. At this point the Banque de France came to its rescue. By 1930, it was again in difficulties. Oustric's attempts to sell part of his empire failed. The big banks to which he turned refused to help him. On 3 November 1930, Oustric's own bank, the Banque Oustric, had to suspend its payments. The losses suffered by people holding Oustric shares and debentures in the wake of the concern's collapse amounted to about one milliard francs. It was a scandal which brought down the Tardieu Cabinet in December 1930. The Banque Adam, closely connected with Oustric as it was, also had to suspend its payments. The bank had large liabilities in relation to its small equity capital, and many of its assets were claims against the Oustric trust which had now become worthless.

After the Banque Oustric and Banque Adam had suspended their payments, the run on those local and regional banks known to have heavy commitments in industry set in. Their customers transferred their money to the big deposit banks. This caused a considerable number of small provincial banks to collapse; but it strengthened the big banks. Total deposits of the eight largest regional banks decreased from 8.7 milliard francs to 5.8 milliard francs between the beginning of 1930 and the end of 1931, whilst those with the big deposit banks rose from 33 milliard to 37 milliard francs. The traditional Banque Adam was revived with the help of 13 big commercial banks and the Banque de France, and it was able to reopen its doors on 14 November 1930. It merged with the Banque Nationale pour le Commerce et l'Industrie in 1936.

The German banking crisis and the sterling crisis of the summer of 1931 did nothing to calm the French public. Many deposits were withdrawn as people switched to gold. France was, and still is, the classic country of private gold hoarding. This time, the renewed run also affected two big banks: the Banque Nationale de Crédit and the Banque de l'Union Parisienne. Both experienced liquidity problems because their assets were tied up in industry. Whereas the Banque de l'Union Parisienne, the main financier of the *Schneider-Creusot* group, was immediately given support by the Government and the Banque de France, the Banque Nationale de Crédit was forced into liquidation. In the following year, the financially sound parts of its business were reorganized and reopened as Banque Nationale pour le Commerce et l'Industrie. The crisis did not touch the big deposit banks, however, as they had maintained a reasonable level of liquidity. The shock of the crisis in fact persuaded them to raise their cash ratio at the end of 1931 to a very high 26% average. A year later, their cash ratios averaged about 21.8%, falling to about 16.7% by the end of 1933. Their excessive caution had entirely unwelcome repercussions upon the economy. It resulted in a credit squeeze and hampered France's battle against the Depression. Only after 1936 was it possible to counteract the exaggerated caution of the banks and only in those branches of industry with orders from the State or other public institutions. On the initiative of several commercial banks, a law was passed setting up the Caisse Nationale des Marchés de l'Etat. This public institution guaranteed short-term and medium-term credit up to a maximum of 12 months to cover such credit as was needed for the interim financing of state orders. The Bank itself did not provide credit, but mobilized it through its guarantee. The actual money came from the commercial banks.

3. The American Banking Crisis of 1932-33 and the American Banking System

On 'Black Thursday', 24 October 1929 (due to the time difference the course of events on the New York Stock Exchange became known in Europe only on 'Black Friday', 25 October 1929), after panic selling of shares and the collapse of share prices had occurred, a number of bankers met at the invitation of Thomas W. Lamont to discuss the situation. These bankers represented America's most powerful credit institutions: Lamont was a partner in J.P. Morgan & Co.; Charles E. Mitchell was Chairman of the Supervisory Board of the National City Bank of New York; Albert E. Wiggin was Chairman of the Supervisory Board of the Chase National Bank of the City of New York; Seward Prosser was a leading member of the Bankers Trust Company; William C. Potter was one of the top men in the Guaranty Trust Company of New York, and George Baker Jr., one of the directors of the First National Bank of New York.

When the New York Stock Exchange learned about this meeting, the panic began to subside, and when a representative of the Morgan Bank offered to buy shares in *United States Steel* above the last quotation, the rapid slide in stock prices was halted. There was a general expectation that the bankers whom Lamont had called together would save the situation in the same way as old John Pierpont Morgan, in collaboration with James Stillman and George Baker Sen., had stopped the run on the New York banks and saved several of them in 1907. The *Wall Street Journal* actually announced victory on 25 October by informing the public that the bankers had stopped the slump in prices and had established a relief fund of one milliard dollars. The first part of the announcement was premature and the second was wrong. Far from having raised one milliard dollars, the bankers did not even have 50 million. Nevertheless, the confidence that had been created lasted for several days and the price of some shares, for which the banking group had made support purchases, rallied somewhat. When, on 28 October 1929, shares were once more offered for sale at a considerable loss, Lamont told a renewed gathering of the group that they did not have, and never had, the intention of maintaining stock exchange prices as such. On the contrary, they merely wanted to preserve a free and open capital market by buying up no more than a few 'pivotal stocks'. Lamont's statement of 28 October 1929 contradicted the most recent press reports and predictions of the group's intentions which had never been denied, corrected or confirmed until the afternoon of the 28th.

After this announcement, the mood changed abruptly. A fresh panic broke out which caused prices to tumble. Worse was to come, as disillusionment changed into distrust of, and bitterness towards, the bankers. Their

high reputation was badly shaken. It was therefore not surprising that those
who imposed controls, regulations and restrictions on the banks during the
New Deal were generally popular. The big banks were castigated not only
for having given the stock exchange public vague information during the
critical days at the end of October 1929 and for 'leaving it in the lurch'
afterwards, but also for their failure to maintain the public's confidence in
their business methods. After this, Democratic and Republican Senators
demanded an investigation of the New York capital market. On 25 April
1932, after several discussions on this problem, the Banking and Currency
Committee of Senate appointed a special subcommittee to examine the
New York Stock Exchange and the security transactions of the New York
banks.

In January 1933, the subcommittee called on the advice of Ferdinand
Pecora, a lawyer of Italian extraction. Pecora had considerable experience,
having examined and exposed shady stock exchange dealings in the 1920s
in collaboration with the District Attorney's office. He became the driving
force in the subcommittee and interrogated all those leading New York
bankers who had played a role in security transactions. Both the big private
banks of J.P. Morgan & Co. and Kuhn Loeb & Co. emerged well from the
investigations into their banking activities. They had not engaged in
speculative dealings and had sold their customers nothing but first-class
bonds. Only a tiny proportion of the securities which these two banks had
issued involved enterprises which had become insolvent during the Great
Slump. On the other hand, the loss accounts which Morgan had drawn up
for 1931 and 1932 and on the basis of which he and his partners did not
pay a single cent in income-tax during those years, inspired both the
members of the subcommittee and the public with rather less confidence.
Criticism was levelled in particular against the Morgan Bank for keeping a
list with the names of prominent personalities — including those of former
President Coolidge, General Pershing, the Commander-in-Chief of the
American forces in the First World War, and a number of influential
Senators — who were privately offered bonds on favourable terms. In
countering this criticism, Morgan maintained that, as a matter of principle,
he always dealt with people he knew well. Nevertheless, the impression
remained that political and economic interest groups had organized a great
give-and-take among themselves without the public being able to do anything to control them.

The investigation revealed what can only be called abuses committed by
the National City Bank of New York and the Chase National Bank of the
City of New York. The National City had sold its customers foreign
securities which the bank itself considered unsound. On one occasion, it
had placed with the public a loan for the Brazilian Federal State of Minas
Gerais, half of which was used by the Brazilians to repay a short-term credit
of four million dollars which the National City itself had given and which
the Government of Minas Gerais would have been unable to repay without
this loan. Albert H. Wiggin of the Chase National, who had been Chairman

of the Wiggin Committee (see above p. 265), was found to have engaged in profitable dealings on his own account, but using his bank's credit facilities. Wiggin's Chase National was among those banks called in by Morgan and Lamont during their effort to stabilize some 'pivotal securities'. It appears that Wiggin took advantage of this and secretly sold his own Chase National shares just when their price had risen. In the end, he and Charles Mitchell of the National City were so compromised that they resigned from their positions even before Pecora had completed his investigations.

Whilst the collapse of the market in October 1929 resulted in a major and lasting blow to the prestige of the major banks, it inflicted financial losses on the banks in general and later led to massive withdrawals of deposits. The main setbacks occurred in long-term investment and credit; but, as the Depression continued, mortgages were also hit. With the collapse of shares and other securities, the value of the banks' own holdings also fell sharply. Many credits which they had extended to customers who wanted to acquire securities depreciated because the devalued securities which served as collateral could not be mobilized for the moment. Two-thirds of their assets (see above p. 250) were affected by this loss in value. Withdrawals of deposits remained limited until the summer of 1931. Between October 1929 and July 1931 deposits in all banks declined by a mere $2 milliard, from 53.9 milliard to 51.8 milliard. Only the outbreak of the banking crisis in Germany led to large withdrawals and the private hoarding of gold in the United States. In the second half of 1931 alone, a further $5 milliard were withdrawn. In the course of the following year another $5 milliard were recalled, so that by the end of 1932 the total deposit balance of all banks had fallen to $41.6 milliard. The big banks suffered withdrawals of particularly large sums: Morgan's deposit balance fell from $504 million in mid-1931 to $319.4 million in the summer of 1932. Kuhn Loeb & Co. recorded a decline in deposits from $88.5 million to $15.2 million between 1929 and 1932.

Thanks to their high equity capital and their carefully selected and therefore more crisis-proof assets, Morgan and Kuhn Loeb & Co. survived the heavy decline in their funds. On the other hand, the depreciation of assets and customers' withdrawals proved fatal to many a small bank. In 1930, 1,350 banks had to close down, with a loss of $237 million in deposits. In view of the large number of small and financially weak credit institutions, bankruptcies were nothing unusual in the United States. Year after year, hundreds of banks became insolvent. But 1,350 bank insolvencies in one year was extraordinarily high even under American conditions. By the end of that year, two medium-sized banks also went under. The Bank of the United States with deposits of $200 million had to close in December 1930. This Bank had emerged from the Second Bank of the United States (see above p. 16) and had carried on its investment business in New York. Its note issue, on the other hand, had been temporarily continued by the United States Bank of Pennsylvania, but without much success. The old Boston banking house of Kidder Peabody & Co. fared somewhat better than

the Bank of the United States. When its difficulties became public, the
Morgan Bank, together with the Chase National Bank, three New York and
four Boston banks, raised a supporting credit of $10 million; Morgan
subscribed $2.5 million of this. In view of his manifold personal and
business ties with Kidder Peabody & Co., Morgan was keenly interested in
preventing the collapse of the Boston firm; as the public knew of these ties,
a collapse of Kidder Peabody & Co. could easily have triggered off a run on
J.P. Morgan & Co. It was years before the Boston banking house, under new
management, regained its profitability.

In 1931, a total of 2,293 American banks collapsed. Their customers lost
almost one-quarter of their deposits, $390 million out of $1,690 million to
be precise. In order to help teetering banks and to pacify the banking public
the banking community, on Hoover's insistence, formed a self-help organization in 1931: the National Credit Corporation. The banks were expected
to deposit a total of $500 million with this Corporation to be used in
support of shaky credit institutions. In the event, only $135 million were
actually brought together of which a mere $15 million were offered as
supporting credit. Since the self-help organization had been so ineffective,
a governmental body, the Reconstruction Finance Corporation, was
founded in January 1932. It was provided with a capital of $500 million,
raised entirely by the Federal Government. In the following years, its capital
was increased several times. Its first President was Charles G. Dawes under
whose chairmanship the Dawes Plan had been worked out in 1924. In order
to finance its credit operations, the Reconstruction Finance Corporation
was allowed to issue debt certificates up to three times its capital. During
its first year of activity, until March 1933, the Corporation granted credits
amounting to $1.24 milliard to banks which had run into difficulties.

The Reconstruction Finance Corporation was established a few weeks
before the Kreuger trust collapsed, followed by Ivar Kreuger's suicide on
12 March 1932. By then, the new organization, backed as it was by the
Government, had gained enough public confidence so that there was no
panic when Kreuger's vast match-manufacturing empire with its international financial connections disintegrated. Only the Boston bank of Lee
Higginson & Co. which had close ties with Kreuger was hit hard by the
collapse of its largest business partner. The losses it suffered through
Kreuger were so enormous and the subsequent withdrawals of deposits so
serious that it was   forced into liquidation in June 1932. Its security
business was carried on by a newly founded joint-stock company, the Lee
Higginson Corporation, in which the proprietors of the old firm became the
directors. The heavy losses which Lee Higginson & Co. suffered in
connection with the Kreuger scandal were found to have been caused by
almost criminal negligence. The Bank had issued Kreuger shares and bonds
totalling $250 million without ever examining the financial position of the
Kreuger concern.

If the number of bank insolvencies decreased in 1932 to 1,453, with
depositors' losses amounting to $168 million, the Reconstruction Finance

Corporation and its success in reviving the confidence of customers must be given the credit for this. These beneficial effects did not last for long, however. The Corporation preferred to give credit to the larger banks. At the end of June 1932, it granted the Central Republic Bank & Trust Company of Illinois in Chicago credit of $90 million. As this decision came only a few days after Dawes had moved from the Reconstruction Finance Corporation to the Central Republic, he created an unfortunate impression and provided the Democrats with fresh ammunition for their presidential election campaign; for Dawes was a prominent Republican who had been Vice-President of the United States from 1925 to 1929 under President Coolidge before becoming American Ambassador to London.

As the Reconstruction Finance Corporation had insufficient means to support the entire American banking system during the crisis, the number of bank failures mounted again from October 1932, causing renewed public anxiety and inducing the recall of deposits on a large scale. These withdrawals, in turn, dramatically worsened the situation of many small and medium banks. And so the pressure continued. As early as October 1932, Nevada had been forced to close the credit institutions in this State for 12 days. In February 1933, developments in Michigan unleashed a general panic throughout the United States. In Michigan a fierce struggle had started between two Detroit banking groups. One of them was supported by Senator James Couzens, the other by Henry Ford. There was a danger that Ford might withdraw large sums from the banks of the rival group, and, on 14 February 1933, the Governor of Michigan ordered all banks in the State to close for eight days. Some 550 banks with deposits totalling $1.5 milliard were affected by this decision. The bank holidays in Michigan were the signal for a run on credit institutions all over the United States. The banks' liquidity reserves disappeared in no time. On 21 February 1933, the banks of New Jersey had to be closed, and on 3 March, a day before the inauguration of President Franklin D. Roosevelt, the Governor of the State of New York imposed a holiday for all banks in his State. As a result, the largest credit institutions in the United States, which were indispensable for both credit and payment transactions throughout the country, remained closed. Subsequently withdrawals of deposits assumed such proportions that most credit institutions were expected to become insolvent shortly. On 5 March, other Federal States therefore declared bank holidays, and on 6 March 1933, two days after assuming office, Roosevelt closed all banks in the United States, invoking the powers of the Enemy Trading Act of the First World War.

Three days later, the American Congress passed an Emergency Act, authorizing the President to decide upon closure, restructuring and re-opening of banks and to confiscate gold coins, ingots and gold certificates in private possession. That Congress was prepared to endow the President with powers of intervention which broke with the country's tradition, cannot be understood simply in terms of a reaction to the critical situation of America's credit system. What contributed to the willingness of Congress

to act swiftly was the negative image which many Congressmen and Senators
had gained of the banks and the big banks in particular. On the basis of the
Emergency Act, the liquidity position of all banks was investigated during the
following days and weeks. The decision on whether and when the banks were
allowed to reopen their doors depended on the results of this investigation.
Some 17,300 banks were examined and just under 12,000 of them were
given permission to resume business from 13 March 1933. This figure
included 4,510 national banks; on the other hand, 1,407 national banks
remained closed for the time being. Of the more than 5,400 institutions to
remain closed in March, 3,298 were able to resume business later on, whereas
2,132 were forced to go into liquidation. The bank panic of the winter of
1932-33 led to the disappearance of some 4,000 American credit institutions.

The Subcommittee of the Banking and Currency Committee of Senate
concluded its investigation into investment banking in June 1934. In the
summer of 1934 Congress passed a reform of the American banking system.
The bill incorporated the experiences of the crisis and the early results of
the Senate inquiries. It was named the Glass-Steagall Banking Act, after
Carter Glass and Henry Steagall, the chairmen of the appropriate
committees of Senate and the House of Representatives. Its adoption was
no less significant for the American banking system than the National
Banking Act of 1863.

The Glass-Steagall Banking Act strengthened the powers of the Federal
Reserve System. To begin with, the reserve banks were allowed to include
in their legal note cover Federal Government bonds which they had
acquired on the open market. Also, in order to prevent insolvencies like
those of the previous years, the Federal Reserve System was authorized to
adjust the level of liquid reserves deposited with it by the National Banks
to changing economic conditions. Hitherto, the reserves held by the Federal
Reserve Bank of a particular area on behalf of the National Banks and State
Banks affiliated to the Federal Reserve System had been prescribed by the
Federal Reserve Act and could only be changed by legislation. The first
findings of the Pecora Inquiry were reflected in new regulations which
stipulated that employees — directors included — of banks affiliated to the
Federal Reserve System could not receive credit from their banks and that
the Board of Governors could dismiss directors of affiliated banks who had
been found guilty of irregularities. Mitchell and Wiggin would have been
candidates for dismissal under these new regulations. The stipulations of the
Glass-Steagall Banking Act regarding the Federal Reserve System were
complemented in 1935 by a bill which Marriner Eccles, the President of
the Board of Governors, had initiated. This bill changed·the federal
structure of America's central banking system in favour of greater centralization. Thenceforth, the seven members of the Board of Governors were to
be appointed by the President. The Board's position *vis-à-vis* the presidents
of the twelve Federal Reserve Banks were also strengthened. Thus it was
given the final authority within the System to intervene in the economy and
to secure fair and open competition.

Mindful that bank customers had lost over $1.25 milliard in deposits between 1930 and 1933, the Glass-Steagall Banking Act introduced a deposit insurance scheme which was strongly resented by the banks. It provided for the establishment of a public deposit insurance company, the Federal Deposit Insurance Corporation. All National Banks and State Banks affiliated to the Federal Reserve System were obliged to join it. The other banks could take out an insurance with the Corporation on a voluntary basis. The size of the insurance contributions was determined by the volume of deposits. The deposit insurance offered 100% cover for accounts up to a certain amount -- at first $2,500, today $15,000. For sums exceeding this ceiling a partial cover was introduced. The bankers objected to the scheme on the grounds that it supported weak banks to the detriment of the national economy and that it might lead others to abandon due caution. Actual developments disproved these counter-arguments. The insurance granted small bank customers security, and as these had been the customers most prone to panic withdrawals, it also gave the banks a substantial guarantee against a recurrence of the events of the previous years.

The Glass-Steagall Banking Act also changed the structure of the American banking system and ultimately eliminated the universal bank. It banned deposit banks from the securities markets after 1935. Thenceforth commercial banking had to be institutionally separate from investment banking. Two-thirds of the private firms which had thus far both accepted deposits and dealt in securities decided to become investment banks. However, both J.P. Morgan & Co. and Brown Brothers Harriman & Co. opted to become deposit banks, handing their securities business over to new firms with whom they maintained close ties. In 1934, three of Morgan's partners and two partners from the parent company of Morgan, Drexel & Co. in Philadelphia founded the Morgan Stanley & Co. investment bank, a joint-stock company. They acquired the majority of shares in the new bank and hence also secured for themselves a decisive influence in Morgan Stanley & Co. In 1940, J.P. Morgan & Co. was converted into a joint-stock company; at this point Morgan Stanley & Co. acquired a parcel of J.P. Morgan shares and so, although the deposit and investment banks were *de jure* separate entities within the Morgan empire, their business ties remained so close that managerial decision-making was co-ordinated through joint directives. Brown Brothers Harriman & Co. likewise detached their investment business. It was taken over by the new investment bank of Brown Harriman & Co., a joint-stock company founded in 1934, whose joint-stock capital was subscribed by the partners of Brown Brothers Harriman & Co. and the investment trust National City Co. Its management was appointed by Brown Brothers Harriman & Co.

In order to improve the capital structure of American banks, the Reconstruction Finance Corporation was invested with greater powers. Hitherto it had not been able to give anything more than supporting and bridging credits to facilitate liquidations; but now the Emergency Act of 9 March 1933 authorized it to acquire shares in commercial banks. Such participations were designed to help banks with their capital reconstruction. It was a solution similar to that adopted in Germany by the Golddiskontbank and the Reich government in the previous year. Because the Reconstruction Finance Corporation was a governmental body, American banks first had the greatest misgivings about handing over shares to it; they were fearful of increased state intervention. However, the business climate forced them to allow the Reconstruction Finance Corporation to buy up their shares, and by May 1934 the Corporation had acquired 31% of the joint-stock capital of the 100 largest banks. As soon as the situation improved, the banks saw to it that, like in Germany, their shares returned into private ownership. State participation in the big banks was thus no less a temporary phenomenon in the United States than it was in Germany. However, the banking crisis and subsequent amendments to the law brought about a much more fundamental change in the structure of the American system than was true of Germany.

4. The Devaluation of the Major Currencies

The Great Depression inevitably also had a profound impact on the world's currencies. When creditors withdrew a large part of their capital from the international markets to prevent losses and to strengthen their own liquidity position, the currency reserves (gold and foreign exchange) of the debtor countries began to disappear, as was clearly demonstrated by the case of the German Reichsbank (see above pp. 260ff.). This meant that central issuing banks in countries experiencing large withdrawals of capital were faced with having to renege on their promise to convert their currencies into gold. Moreover, the struggle to maintain the largest possible share in a rapidly contracting international market sooner or later led most countries to consider whether their own currency was overvalued in comparison to others. A good way of improving one's own foreign trade position was, of course, to devalue one's currency.

The Reichsbank was the first central issuing bank to run into difficulties in the summer of 1931, following a heavy outflow of gold and foreign currency to creditor countries. In July 1931 its note cover fell below the legal minimum. However, in 1924 the reichsmark had been deliberately overvalued, not least in the interest of the country's reparations creditors; on purely economic grounds, it would obviously have been advisable to devalue it in the early 1930s. International agreements made this difficult. The gold parity of the reichsmark had only just been fixed under the terms of the Young Plan of 1930. Nor were there more than a few individuals — such as Wilhelm Lautenbach, the Ministerial Councillor in the Reich Ministry of Economics, and Ernst Wagemann, the President of the Reich Statistical Office — who thought of devaluation as a financial instrument to be used as part of a policy of job creation. Yet both Brüning and Reichsbank President Luther rejected the idea of devaluation knowing that it would have been tantamount to a breach of the Young Plan and that it would have rendered Germany's position more difficult in future negotiations on the reparations question. Germany adopted foreign exchange controls instead of devaluing its currency.

When it became clear in mid-July 1931 that the Reich would default, Dutch, Swiss and Swedish commercial banks, whose credits were tied up in Germany, began to sell their holdings in sterling in order to reinforce their gold reserves. It appears that the French government was also selling sterling at this time. At least there is a striking correlation, discovered by Günter Schmölders in his *Frankreichs Aufstieg zur Weltkapitalmacht*, between the sterling assets held by the French Treasury and the Caisse Autonome in the Banque de France, on the one hand, and the Bank of England's gold reserves during the summer of 1931, on the other. By launching an offensive against the pound, the French government hoped to force London, which had adopted a very different position on the question of Germany's political and commercial foreign debts, to accept the French view. Finally there was the indecisive attitude of the ruling Labour Party. Since mid-July, a strong group within the Party, centered around Ernest Bevin, had been calling for devaluation. This undermined the confidence of foreign holders of sterling in the stability of the pound, and they continued to convert it into gold. The Bank of England twice put up its very low discount rate of 2.5%, but did not dare exceed 4.5% as the deflationary effect of a rise in the cost of credit would have increased the already high rate of unemployment. In order to be able to continue its support of the pound, the Bank, on 24 and 26 July 1931, took a short-term credit of £50 million from the Federal Reserve System and the Banque de France.

However, the news that the Bank of England had been given these credits was not sufficient to allay the fears of foreign holders of sterling. At the beginning of August, Prime Minister Ramsay MacDonald and Philip Snowden, the Chancellor of the Exchequer, realized that Britain would not be able to maintain the gold standard without further foreign loans. Yet she would have been unable to obtain such credit unless Government and Parliament made a determined effort to offset the anticipated budgetary deficit of £120 million. Since the spring of 1931, a committee under the chairmanship of Sir George May had been working on proposals to achieve a balanced budget. The May Report which emerged from this Committee proposed that the deficit be offset by cuts in unemployment benefits; the Bank of England and City banks, after making inquiries in New York and Paris, had insisted that only a reduction in unemployment benefit would be regarded abroad as a serious attempt to balance the budget. Whilst MacDonald was prepared to accept these proposals, Arthur Henderson, a prominent Labour politician and Foreign Secretary, stood up against them and supported the idea of a 10% import tax. The trade unions, on the other hand, led by Ernest Bevin, demanded devaluation. While these disputes were going on, the Bank of England's gold reserve declined by almost 14% during August 1931.

The argument over the May Report split the Labour government which had been in office since 1929. One half of the ministers went along with MacDonald in wishing to cut unemployment benefits; the other half emphatically rejected it and denounced the bankers' demand as an ultimatum. Formally, the bankers had merely expressed an opinion on the situation, but in essence their opinion amounted to nothing less than an ultimatum. The Parliamentary Labour Party and the Cabinet which was only a minority government were at loggerheads. With the consent of the Party's Executive Committee, MacDonald tendered the government's resignation on 24 August 1931. The Labour leadership hoped that, once in opposition, it would be able to settle the internal dispute between its right wing and the Trade Union supporters and re-establish party unity. Against all expectations, the King did not call upon Baldwin, leader of the Conservative Opposition, to form a new government. Instead he asked MacDonald, as Chairman of the strongest party, to form an all-party government to overcome the acute financial crisis. The 'National Government' which was led by MacDonald had the support of both Conservatives and Liberals, but only a small section of the Parliamentary Labour Party. Nevertheless, it had a secure majority in the House of Commons.

Within a few days of the formation of the 'National Government', on 28 August, the Bank of England obtained a further loan from the United States and France totalling £80 million. In September the new Cabinet presented the expected cost-cutting budget. This budget increased income-tax rates and reduced Civil Service salaries as well as social welfare for women and children. Unemployment benefit was also cut by 10%. In spite of these measures the exchange rate of the pound and the gold standard could no longer be safeguarded. Foreign funds continued to be withdrawn from London, partly because the creditors wanted to strengthen their own liquidity position and partly because of fears of a devaluation of the pound. The already tense atmosphere was heightened by reports of a mutiny in the British Fleet. On 16 September 1931, naval units at the small naval base of Invergordon in Northern Scotland, which consisted predominantly of volunteers, refused to carry out orders in protest against the cuts in pay which had been announced. Although order was restored within a few days, exaggerated reports in the press gave the impression that the reliability of the British Fleet, the power-political arm of the Empire, had been seriously undermined. What was to become of Britain? Had not the German Revolution of 1918 also begun with a naval mutiny thirteen years ago? Foreign withdrawals of credit and the exchange of pound notes into gold continued during these critical days.

Having paid out £200 million in gold and foreign currency since mid-July to support the international value of the pound, the Bank of England was freed from its obligation to uphold the gold standard on 20 September 1931. The pound's exchange rate was now left to its own devices, and it dropped by about 30% until mid-December 1931. The greater part of the British Empire and the Commonwealth immediately followed the mother country's example. But Canada and the Union of South Africa adopted a different policy. Whereas Canada devalued her dollar by about half as much as the pound, the Union of South Africa clung to the gold standard until 1936 and joined the British monetary bloc only thereafter. Countries under British influence, such as Egypt, the Sudan and Trans-Jordan as well as the countries whose currencies were aligned with the pound, such as Iceland and Ireland, immediately followed the British lead. Thus the sterling area (or sterling bloc) came into being. This community took on a firmer shape during the Second World War after Britain had introduced foreign exchange controls in 1940. The free movement of capital continued among the members of the sterling area. The bloc members also harmonized their trade policies with Britain's and kept the bulk of their currency reserves in the Bank of England. The joint devaluation and formation of the sterling bloc reinforced the Westminster Statute of 11 December 1931 and the resolutions of the Ottawa Conference in August 1932 at which the members of the Commonwealth and the Empire agreed on a system of preferential tariffs. For those countries which did not devalue at the same time, Britain's 30% devaluation was tantamount to a revaluation of their own currencies by about 40%. This represented a considerable deterioration of the competitive position in the international markets in relation to the sterling countries. Although Britain continued to pursue deflationary economic and financial policies, she did not exploit her advantage by raising sterling bloc prices. On the contrary, the margin between sterling prices and gold currency prices resulting from devaluation was offset by the continued decline of the latter.

Outside the sterling bloc, the Scandinavian countries, Argentina, Portugal and Japan soon followed Britain's lead. In Germany export opportunities were being severely hit by the devaluation of sterling. Various people raised their voice again to advocate a devaluation of the reichsmark. They included Ludwig Albert Hahn, Wilhelm Grotkopp, Wladimir Woytinski, but they remained in a minority. The Brüning government did not want to impair Germany's chances of negotiating a lightening or even elimination of reparations burdens. Devaluation would have breached an international agreement. As Gustav Stolper aptly stated in his *Deutsche Wirtschaft seit 1870*, the Germans were also traumatized by their recent experience of hyperinflation. The spectre of another inflation — even if it was quite unreal — was more terrifying than the harsh realities of long-term mass unemployment. In view of this, neither the Reich government nor the Reichsbank board of directors seriously contemplated devaluation. The only advantage the Germans gained from their policy of inaction was a reduction of their foreign commercial debts in the countries which had devalued. Britain's devaluation and America's devaluation of the dollar in 1933 lightened Germany's foreign currency debts by 1.5 milliard RM.

Like Britain, Japan also suffered heavy financial losses in 1930-31, although the reasons for the withdrawal of foreign credits and the conversion of yen holdings into dollars or gold were more political than economic. Japanese national pride had been wounded by two events. In

July 1929 the American Congress had laid down new immigration quotas for the United States which excluded Asians. And in the spring of 1930, at the London Naval Conference, Japan failed in her attempt to shift in her favour the ratios for battle-fleets which had been fixed by the Washington Naval Agreement of 1921. These two events gave a strong impetus to a militant nationalism in Japan which was furthered by the armed forces. A wave of nationalist agitation swept the country and gave rise to fears for the future. In November 1930 Prime Minister Hamaguchi was gunned down by a young chauvinist and died from his severe injuries 10 months later. In September 1931 the Japanese Kwantung army, which was based in Manchuria, provoked an incident on the Chinese border and, quite arbitrarily and against the wishes of the Tokyo government, launched an offensive which aimed at the complete conquest of this Chinese province. China responded to Japanese aggression with a highly effective boycott of Japanese goods. The withdrawal of gold from Japan accelerated rapidly. Between mid-October and mid December 1931, the gold reserve of Nihon Ginko declined from 700 million to 474 million yen. By December 1931, the country's gold reserves were less than half of what they had been at the beginning of 1930. On 13 December 1931, the Government imposed a ban on gold exports, and four days later Nihon Ginko was freed from its obligation to convert yen into gold. Japan had also abandoned the gold standard.

No new rate of exchange for the yen was fixed. Flexible, but manipulable rates came into operation. Japan now experienced what came to be called 'planned and controlled inflation'. Finance Minister Korekiyo Takahashi initiated and spearheaded this policy. Pursuing a strategy of 'deficit spending' à la Keynes, he increased State expenditure and the central issuing bank's uncovered note issue from 120 million to one milliard yen. He also introduced foreign exchange controls. Takahashi's fiscal and monetary policy was designed to support Japan's export offensive. Through 'planned inflation', Japanese exports were so cheap in comparison with those of their competitors that she was able to increase her share of world exports from 2.9% to 5.4%.

Owing to Britain's devaluation, a number of foreign central issuing banks with large sterling holdings suffered heavy losses. The Banque de France, unlike the French Treasury and the Caisse Autonome, had not reduced its sterling holdings out of a sense of solidarity with the Bank of England. On 20 September 1931 it still held £65 million. The Banque Nationale de Belgique had £12.6 million and the Nederlandsche Bank £11 million at this date. The Schweizerische Nationalbank, on the other hand, had reduced its sterling holdings to £300,000 in good time. The central issuing banks most directly affected by Britain's action were grimly determined never to suffer losses in this way again. After their experiences with the 'Old Lady of Threadneedle Street' they thought little of the much-vaunted solidarity of the central banks. They felt deceived since the Bank of England, to the bitter end, had led them to believe that the pound would not be devalued.

The American Federal Reserve System also felt the tremors of these events. Within two days of Britain's devaluation, the Banque de France converted $50 million into gold and the Banque Nationale de Belgique $106 million. In the first two weeks of October, the Banque de France converted a further $70 million into gold. Clément Moret, the Governor of the Banque de France, informed George Harrison, the President of the Federal Reserve Bank of New York, on 7 October that, following the heavy losses which the Banque de France had sustained in London, it had now come to view its relationship with other issuing banks in a different light. Between 22 September 1931 and 17 December 1931, the Federal Reserve System had to surrender gold worth $755 million. Of this, the Banque Nationale de Belgique took 131 million dollar's worth, the Nederlandsche Bank $77 million and the Schweizerische Nationalbank $188 million. The bulk of what remained went to France.

After their disappointment with Britain's currency policy, a number of European central issuing banks watched the economic and monetary development in the United States closely and warily. The situation in America gave some grounds for these apprehensions; for in no other country was the recession biting so deep. By 1931, the Federal budget showed a deficit of $1 milliard as a result of a dramatic decline in tax revenue. The budgets of the Federal states also ran large deficits. In a report for the *Agence Economique* in Paris, Parker Willis, an economics professor at Columbia University, described these deficits as constituting a source of inflation. The dollar was, next to the pound, the most important international commercial currency and most central banks held fairly large amounts of dollars; a devaluation would have inflicted considerable losses upon them.

In the course of the winter 1931-32, the Federal Reserve Banks began to have problems with their cover limits. Although they were fully able to comply with the 35% note cover in gold as stipulated by law, the economic depression caused difficulties on another front: they no longer had enough first-class trade bills to cover the remaining 65% of notes in circulation, as required by the regulations of the Federal Reserve Act. Of course, the trade bills could have been replaced by gold, had gold reserves in excess of the 35% gold cover been available. However, these reserves had declined substantially after the events of the previous months, and by February 1932 no more than $350 million in gold were available in the Federal Reserve System. In order to help the central banking system out of this dilemma, a law was passed on 17 February 1932 permitting the use of both state certificates of indebtedness and first-class trade bills as cover reserve. Like the Banking Act of 1933 this piece of legislation was named after its protagonists in Congress, Glass and Steagall. More importantly, it was interpreted as evidence that the United States was no longer prepared to defend the gold standard and was paving the way for abandoning it altogether. This caused the Banque de France to convert most of its dollar holdings into gold. By June 1932, the Bank held a mere $10 million. The Nederlandsche Bank likewise reduced its dollar holdings to a minimum.

However, as long as Hoover was President, the United States continued to adhere to the gold standard. Once the French, Dutch, Belgians and Swiss had reduced their dollar assets, the immediate external threat to the Federal Reserve System had been removed. Britain still held considerable amounts of dollars. She was untroubled by the possibility that America might devalue the dollar and so retained her holdings. Hoover's successor did not, at first, contemplate devaluation. Roosevelt's extensive aid and work-creation programmes unavoidably added to the existing deficit and had an inflationary effect. On the other hand, in the spring of 1933 these programmes had barely come off the drawing-board. The pressure to devalue the dollar in effect arose from another quarter. During the Congressional debates on the agriculture bill, the farming lobby which aimed to increase agricultural exports through devaluation combined with the protagonists for a return to bimetalism. Roosevelt announced that he would veto an amendment to the agriculture bill proposed by Senator Sheeler which would have obliged the Treasury Department to provide silver as well as gold cover at a ratio of 16:1. At this point, Senator Thomas introduced another amendment. He moved to give the President full powers to issue up to $3 milliard in bank notes which were not covered in gold to purchase gold and silver and to reduce the gold and silver content of the dollar by up to 50%. Roosevelt went along with this 'Thomas Amendment' on 18 April. On the following day, he ruled that the special permission, which had been hitherto required for the export of gold ever since the bank holidays, be withdrawn. Simultaneously, the Treasury Department began to purchase gold in order to push up the price of gold.

In approving the Thomas Amendment, the United States had effectively abandoned the gold standard. Through its gold purchases, Washington had increased the price of gold and devalued the dollar by a corresponding percentage. In the end a rough figure was put on the devaluation which had been taking place between April 1933 and January 1934, the date when the Gold Reserve Act was ratified. It was 40%. This meant that no new gold parity was agreed, but that the gold price which had by then established itself was now taken as the legally-fixed norm. The Gold Reserve Act also laid down that all gold bars and gold coins in private banks had to be sold to the Treasury Department. Private persons were allowed to keep gold jewellery, but had to surrender ingots and coins. Banks and other firms could purchase gold from the Treasury Department only in order to honour international commitments. The Federal Reserve Banks had to deposit a gold reserve for 25% of their note circulation with the Treasury Department which kept this gold at Fort Knox.

After Britain and the sterling bloc, Japan and the United States had devalued their currencies, the deflationary pressure increased on the economies of the countries in the 'gold bloc', i.e. those still adhering to the gold standard. Whereas economic recovery had begun in Britain and the United States and unemployment was declining, the economies of the gold bloc countries continued to stagnate. Italy, for reasons of prestige, was reluctant to devalue the lira and decided to follow the German example by introducing foreign exchange controls. Belgium devalued the belga by 28% in April 1935.

Thanks to her high gold reserve in the Banque de France and her balance of payments surplus, France had the most stable currency until 1934. But she was unable to offset the advantage gained on the world market by the countries which had devalued with a superior technology or greater industrial productivity. Indeed the French depression was at its worst when other countries were beginning to make a recovery. By 1935, foreign capital was being withdrawn which only a few years earlier had been transferred to an economically stable France. Now the French public began to purchase and hoard gold. The policies of the Popular Front Government of Léon Blum and the wave of strikes that hit the country in 1936 caused a mass exodus of money from the franc area in anticipation of various 'socialist experiments'. By the end of September 1936, the Banque de France's gold reserve which had totalled 82 milliard francs at the end of 1934 had dropped to 50 milliard francs. It was at this point that the Bank suspended the sale of gold and hence also stopped converting its bank notes into gold. The franc was devalued by 25%. After this, Switzerland also felt compelled to abandon the gold standard and to devalue the Swiss franc by 30% in order to correct the distortions in her foreign trade which had become intolerable. The Netherlands devalued the guilder by 25%.

X Financing the Second World War

1. The 'Covert' Financing of Rearmament and of the War and Temporarily Suppressed Inflation in Germany

Having paid for the First World War with run-away open inflation of her currency, Germany's need to finance the incomparably greater expenditure of the Second World War led to a policy of deliberately delayed inflation. Since 1936, if not before, the Third Reich had been living under a virtual war economy, and in order to pay for the enormous costs, first of armaments and later of war, the National Socialist regime took recourse to a method which has been aptly described as 'covert war financing'. During the First World War, loans had been an important source alongside the issue of treasury bills; the National Socialists, on the other hand, covered the deficits in the Reich budget almost exclusively by issuing short-term bonds: treasury bills, 'Mefo' bills and others. These bonds were unquestioningly accepted by the commercial banks because they could be rediscounted at the Reichsbank at any time. In this way, the volume of money was enormously enlarged. Between 1936 and 1945, the circulation of bank notes alone rose from 4.5 milliard RM to 56.4 milliard RM. And yet there was no decline in the exchange rate of the reichsmark nor a rise in domestic price levels. Since the banking crisis of 1931, the exchange rate had been artificially maintained by the imposition of foreign exchange controls so that the exchange rate was prevented from finding its level freely.

After 1934 the system of controls was perfected and tightened up. Thenceforth foreign trade was regulated through bilateral clearing agreements. About 80% of Germany's foreign trade consisted of straight-forward barter. Domestic prices, which would normally have soared owing to the big increase in the money supply and the simultaneous steep decline in the provision of consumer goods, were artificially pegged at their 1936 level by means of a price freeze proclaimed on 10 October 1936. This policy was supplemented by a wage freeze on 25 June 1938. On the other hand, as private incomes were never absorbed by war loans and taxes, the purchasing power of incomes and savings was preserved on paper; but there were no goods on which they could be spent. However, should government controls over the economy ever be abandoned, this purchasing power which had been artificially held back for so many years was bound to trigger off an explosion of prices. It was in this sense that the inflation was delayed during the Second World War.

Soon after his seizure of power, Hitler created the instruments to put Germany's money and capital markets wholly at the service of rearmament.

On 16 March 1933, Reichsbank President Luther who was trying to uphold the Bank's independence, resigned under pressure. He was succeeded by Hjalmar Schacht who was at this point still in basic agreement with the aims of the National Socialists. In July 1933, the Reich Minister of Economics was given full powers to impose bans on investments. Thenceforth, private industry was forced to resort primarily to self-financing. The capital market was reserved for Reich needs. The Reich did, however, subsidize investments which were considered vital for the rearmament programme. In the December of 1934, a law on the distribution of profits in joint-stock companies limited the payment of dividends to a maximum of 6%, and 8% in exceptional cases. Dividends in excess of this were to be remitted to the Golddiskontbank and served as a loan reserve for the Reich.

From March 1935 so-called *Mefo* bills were used as a means of financing armaments production over and above the funding of rearmament through the Reich budget by ordinary, though secret means. *Mefo* bills were accommodation bills in the guise of trade bills. In order to put this novel method of financing state expenditure into practice, the Reich government instigated the establishment of a joint-stock company, known as the *Metallurgische Forschungsanstalt GmbH* or *Mefo*. Four big companies *(Siemens, Gutehoffnungshütte, Krupp* and *Rheinstahl)* subscribed its small joint-stock capital of one million RM. The Reich assumed direct and full liability for all the company's debts and also appointed its management. The *Mefo* was a bogus company; its sole purpose was to pretend that it was trading in commodities for which the use of trade bills was ostensibly necessary. *Mefo* bills were used in the following way: a Wehrmacht supplier would draw a bill on the *Mefo* Company to the amount of his claim against the Reich. The *Mefo* endorsed this bill and so made it acceptable at the Reichsbank. The Reichsbank in turn was empowered to discount a *Mefo* bill after 90 days, and because the Reichsbank accepted these bills, other credit institutions discounted them too. In this way, the Wehrmacht supplier would obtain cash for his bills very quickly and well before the expiry of the 90-day term. Up to the spring of 1938, a total of 12 milliard RM were issued in *Mefo* bills. Then Schacht stopped the issue and made preparations for a repayment of these huge debts — without much success. At the end of the Second World War eight milliard RM of these bills were still in the possession of the Reichsbank and commercial banks. From April 1938, 'delivery treasury bonds' replaced *Mefo* bills to pay for armaments contracts. These reached four milliard RM by the beginning of September 1939.

On 7 January 1939, the Reichsbank's board of directors drew up a memorandum to protest against Hitler's unscrupulous financial policies. The document proposed that public expenditure should in future be financed, without interference in the capital market, by means of long-term loans or higher taxes; if the Government had to go to the capital market, the Reichsbank was to have the exclusive right of decision. All the board members signed what was clearly a courageous statement. Hitler's response was to dismiss both Reichsbank President Schacht and the entire board on

20 January 1939. Walther Funk, the Reich Minister of Economics, was appointed as Schacht's successor and a few of the board members were reinstated. After this purge, a new law was promulgated on 15 June 1939 which stripped the Reichsbank of its policy-making powers. The cover regulations and the restriction on the depositing of treasury bills were removed, and the Bank was directed to provide the Reich with credit 'on the instructions of the Führer and Reich Chancellor'.

In accordance with the 'New Financial Scheme' of Under Secretary of State Fritz Reinhardt, tax vouchers totalling 4.8 milliard RM were issued from March 1939 to pay for supplies to the Reich. Suppliers were given two kinds of tax vouchers in partial payment of their claims. Type A could be offered to pay taxes owed the Reich seven months after its issue; Type B could be used to pay tax 37 months from its date of issue. The first type was non-interest-bearing, the second bore 4% interest per annum. However, Type A vouchers brought tax relief, provided they were held without interruption by the company concerned for a certain minimum period. The Reichsbank neither discounted nor pledged securities on tax vouchers of the first type, although the vouchers of the second type were accepted as collateral. Firms supplying the Reich had to accept 40% of their claims in tax vouchers, half of which were paid out in Type A, the other half in Type B certificates. The capital market was almost completely blocked to private industry not involved in war production. Consequently large amounts of money accumulated in the savings banks and insurance institutions which would normally have been used for short-term or long-term loans to private persons or enterprises.

From 1935, the Reich siphoned these funds off by selling so-called liquidity loans ('Li-Anleihen') to savings banks and insurance companies. These loans were not negotiable on the open market, but 50% of the legally prescribed liquidity reserve could be kept in Li-Anleihen and hence be deposited with the central giro institutions where they bore interest. Immediately after the outbreak of war, income tax was increased by 50%. From 1941, the Reich mobilized the savings which had accumulated because there were no consumer goods to spend them on for long-term loans, thus avoiding, formally at least, the issue of a Reich loan. A decree of 30 October 1941 which aimed at restricting and controlling purchasing power, set up the so-called 'iron savings accounts'. These accounts made it possible for savers to deposit their money tax-free. They could be recalled at 12 months' notice, but only after the war had ended. German-occupied Europe was also forced to contribute to the financing of Germany's war effort. Contributions totalling 85 milliard RM (12% of the Reich's total wartime expenditure) were extorted from these countries during the War.

In his Reichstag speech at the outbreak of war on 1 September 1939, Hitler stated that Germany's expenditure on the Wehrmacht since 1933 amounted to 90 milliard RM. This was an exaggeration, made for propaganda purposes. The actual cost of German armaments in the period between 1933 and 1939 amounted to about 61 milliard RM. During the war, the German Reich spent a total of 657.38 milliard RM, 445 milliard of which were allocated to the Wehrmacht and included allowances for soldiers' families. 184.8 milliard RM were raised through taxation and tax vouchers, 85 milliard RM through the plunder of occupied territories. The rest was in loans. The Reich debt rose from 12.9 milliard RM in 1933 to 31.5 milliard RM in 1938 and 389.9 milliard RM at the end of the war; 251.1 milliard RM were short-term debts. The Reichsbank's note circulation rose from 3.5 milliard RM in March 1933 to an average of 8.3 milliard RM in 1939 and to 56.4 milliard RM in February 1945. The Reichsbank's gold and foreign exchange reserve slumped from 592.7 million RM in 1933 to 77 million RM in 1941-45.

Japan forced the territories occupied by her in the Second World War to contribute to her war costs to an even greater extent than National Socialist Germany. Approximately 80% of the roughly 300 milliard yen which the Government spent between 1942 and 1945 was for the armed forces and armaments. A mere 11% was raised through taxes; some 25% were contributed by banks in the occupied territories in the form of compulsory loans; 64% was raised at home through the 'paper-money credits' of Nihon Ginko. All this caused Japan's public debt to raise from 13.4 milliard yen in 1937 to over 200 milliard yen at the end of the war.

2. The Allies and their Methods of Financing the War

France was under direct German occupation or indirect control for four of the close to six years of the War in Europe and was forced to put her economy into the service of the Reich. Given her early defeat, the resources France mobilized to finance the war effort in 1939-40 were therefore of greater benefit to her enemy than to herself. In 1941, France had to allocate 50.9% of her budget to pay for the costs of the occupation, and she was also forced to credit-finance supplies to the German Wehrmacht. In 1942 the Germans received 51.3% and in 1943 66.3% of France's total budget. Some 48% of government expenditure went into the German war chest as late as 1944, although almost the whole of France had been liberated by mid-August.

Britain once more tried to raise the largest part of her war expenditure through higher taxation, and this time she was more successful than she had been between 1914 and 1918. At least 45% of Britain's entire state expenditure during the Second World War (£28.1 milliard) was recouped through taxes. This was a tremendous achievement. Consequently, Britain's state debt saw a comparatively moderate rise between 1939 and 1945: from £7.2 milliard to £21.5 milliard. High tax revenue was obtained by increasing the rate of income-tax and by taxing away all profits exceeding the average of the immediate pre-war years, initially at 60% and later at 100%. Revenues subsequently rose from £980 million in 1939 to £3,262 milliard in 1944.

The difference between revenue from taxes and government spending was bridged by means of loans. Domestic borrowing totalled £14.8 milliard and reached its peak at £2,972 milliard in 1943. The increased rate of taxation meant that, from 1943 onwards, revenue from taxes exceeded that from credit. Apart from short-term bonds and treasury bills, six months' medium-term bonds were issued, known as treasury deposit receipts. Long-term loans were issued in very small denominations in order to mobilize small savings in the Post Office Savings Bank and trustee savings banks.

The British government's aim was to limit the wartime rise in the cost of living to between 28% and 30%. With this in mind, it subsidized the most important foodstuffs and gave about £1 milliard in food subsidies throughout the War. It more or less achieved its goal of restricting the rise in the cost of living to 30%: in 1939 the cost-of-living index was at 100; by 1945 it had risen to 132.

Britain had not only to finance her own wartime needs, but also assisted her allies with credits, investments and the credit-financing of supplies. Some $171 million of British money were invested in 61 armament factories in the United States. Britain supplied the Soviet Union with ammunition, rubber, fighter planes, boots etc. on credit worth £270 million. British aid to the other allies totalled £126 million.

One of Britain's problems was to pay for her vital imports, as earnings from exports had dropped to a trickle. From 1940, sterling countries which continued to send their goods to Britain had their invoices credited to them in blocked accounts at the Bank of England. Britain's total debt to these countries finally reached £2.7 milliard. India was Britain's main creditor, with over £1 milliard in blocked accounts, largely because of her contribution to the war against Japan. A solution to the balance of payments problem created by the large supplies which Britain received from the United States was postponed in so far as most of these supplies arrived after March 1941 and fell under the Lend-Lease Programme. Whereas postwar Germany had to solve the problem of a delayed inflation, Britain was faced with very high foreign debts after the War.

Like Britain, the United States also recouped a substantial part of its wartime expenditure through higher taxes. Tax revenue covered 40% of government spending in the period 1941-45, leaving 60% to be raised through loans. In numerical terms, government spending in this period totalled $320 milliard, about 80% of which were spent on the war effort and on aid to the Allies. The internal state debt rose from $43 milliard to almost $260 milliard. After her experiences during the First World War, the United States did not, on this occasion, provide the Allies with financial assistance, but supplied them with goods to be returned or replaced after the War. This was the principle of Lend-Lease for which Congress had granted Roosevelt full powers in March 1941. Roosevelt expounded the programme's fundamental idea at a press conference on 17 December 1940. If a neighbour's house is on fire, he argued, there is no time for lengthy discussions with him about the cost of the garden hose which he needs to fight the fire. It should simply be lent to him, to be returned or replaced later.

America was still neutral at the time of this statement, and the Neutrality Act permitted the supply of war materials to belligerents, provided they paid in cash and transported them in their own ships. However, it banned the granting of loans to belligerent countries. By the winter of 1940-41, Britain had exhausted her foreign currency reserves and would not have been able to pay for American supplies. In bypassing the regulations of the Neutrality Act, the Lend-Lease system was primarily intended as a temporary help to Britain. Later on, it proved to be a much more suitable form of aid to all Allies than credits had been during the First World War. Originally Lend-Lease restricted supplies to a maximum of $ 7 milliard. In the end, supplies reached a total of $ 43.6 milliard. Britain and the members of the Commonwealth received $ 30.1 milliard of this total, the Soviet Union $ 10.7 milliard, and the remaining Allies $ 2.8 milliard.

XI Currencies and Banks, after the Second World War

1. Currency Problems

While the Second World War was still raging, Britain and the United States started deliberations on post-war economic reconstruction and the future of international economic relations. Their first aim was to avoid a repetition of those developments which had proved so fatal in the inter-war period and had destroyed the international economy. John Maynard Keynes was the first prominent expert to concern himself with monetary problems. The principal flaw of the international monetary system of the inter-war period, he believed, had been its rigid linkage to gold and the very unbalanced distribution of gold reserves. This had compelled those countries with large balance of payments deficits to conserve their small gold reserves either by adopting a deflationary policy — which resulted in declining wages and increased unemployment — or by introducing foreign exchange controls and develuation which, in turn, inflicted serious damage on international trade and the economies of other countries.

In order to break this vicious circle, Keynes, in a memorandum published by the British Treasury in June 1942 under the title 'Proposals for a Clearing Union', propounded the idea that a Clearing Union be founded which would act as an international accounting house between individual countries. The Clearing Union would use a foreign currency — called 'bank gold' by Keynes — both as an international clearing unit and as a unit of currency. This international currency was to have a specific gold parity and member countries of the Clearing Union were to declare themselves willing to accept 'bank gold' instead of gold or dollars in settlement of their mutual debts. As these international payments were to be settled between individual acccounts at the Clearing Union, a country's credit or debit position would be easily ascertainable. Above all, a creditor country's surplus in gold, foreign exchange or 'bank gold' at the Clearing Union could be made available to provide bridging loans or long-term loans to a country in deficit. Consequently, weaker countries lacking foreign exchange would not be forced into adopting a policy of deflation or devaluation; the Clearing Union would be able to distribute its accumulated reserves of gold and foreign exchange more rationally and efficiently. In order to prevent countries from running up unmanageably large debts, interest would be charged once a certain level had been reached and additional collateral would be required.

Keynes had conceived his plan from the point of view of a country, like Britain, which was bound to have great problems with its balance of payments after the War. The plan did not, however, generate much enthusiasm in the United States. A counter-proposal was submitted on their behalf by Harry Dexter White, a colleague of Treasury Secretary Henry Morgenthau and principal author of the Morgenthau Plan. The Americans wanted to attain the same goal as Keynes and the British, i.e. to stabilize exchange rates as far as was possible so that countries did not have to impose restrictions on foreign trade in order to maintain their exchange rate. White hoped to achieve this objective in a different way, though. He proposed an international exchange equalization fund of $5 milliard in gold or in national currency to which the individual member states were to contribute in line with their share in international trade. The fund was to grant short-term credit to all countries which had difficulties with their balance of payments. Whereas Keynes with his Clearing Union project wanted to abandon the rigid link with gold and replace it with an international clearing system based on the accounts of an 'international central bank', White clung to the gold standard and, through his proposed fund, merely wished to ease the availability of credits to individual members. His proposal was conceived from the point of view of a major creditor and export country with ample gold reserves. But his proposal was much less attractive to the British and most of the other countries. White wanted to apportion control of the fund's financial resources according to the size of each member country's contribution, and this would have given the United States an overwhelming voice in the management of the fund.

In the course of the Anglo-American talks on these questions, which took place during 1943, Britain was forced to drop the Keynes Plan; the White Plan became the basis of subsequent discussions. After 1944, when other countries were consulted on currency matters, the British succeeded in negotiating tangible modifications to the American plan. Finally, in July 1944, delegates from 44 countries – including the Soviet Union– met at Bretton Woods in New Hampshire to discuss the future of the international monetary system.

After three weeks of negotiations, the conference agreed to set up an International Monetary Fund (IMF) and the International Bank for Reconstruction and Development (World Bank) and initialled an agreement on the statutes for these two institutions. Because of differences of opinion among the victorious powers, the Soviet Union did not ratify the agreement; nor did she ever become a member of the IMF and World Bank. By the end of 1945, other countries had ratified the agreement, and the International Monetary Fund and the World Bank were able to start operations in December 1945.

The International Monetary Fund was to further the development of international trade and economic co-operation by stabilizing the rate of exchange between the individual currencies, thus facilitating orderly and unimpeded transactions between the member countries. In order to be able to fulfil its tasks, it was provided with a fund of $10 milliard which was raised by contributions from the members. Every member was assigned a certain quota, and the size of the quota determined the contribution and voting share of each participant. In 1944 quotas of individual member countries were determined on the basis of certain key data on the performance of a national economy. Political considerations also played a part. From an economic point of view, the 11.63% allocated to Britain was too high; but Britain was a political heavy-weight. Members had to pay up their quota contribution in gold and in their own national currency: either 25% of the quota contribution or at least 10% of their own net currency reserves had to be paid in gold or American dollars. As the White Plan had intended, the IMF assumed the role of granting those member states which struggled with major balance-of-payments difficulties short-term credit in the requisite currency. The Fund was allowed to enlarge its capacity to provide such help by selling gold and by going to the capital markets itself. The IMF's own resources were constantly topped up in line with the growing number of members and with international economic growth. At the end of 1967, holdings totalled about $21 milliard. Member states undertook not to discriminate against another member state's currency and to maintain the stability of their own. Variations in the exchange rate were permitted within narrow bands only. Revaluation and devaluation were permissible only if there existed a 'fundamental disequilibrium' and after prior consultation with the IMF. The Fund succeeded in maintaining a system of stable exchange rates only at the price of considerable friction. There developed considerable imbalances between various countries. Moreover, the purchasing power of individual currencies experienced marked fluctuations, depending on the monetary and budgetary discipline of a particular member government. Sheltered by the Fund's protective umbrella, some countries embarked upon careless monetary and fiscal policies. Following the American dollar crisis of 1971, the system of fixed rates of exchange ceased to function. But the Fund has prevented monetary disasters and conflicts of the kind which took place in the 1930s, and it guarantees to this day the regular, institutionalized collaboration of the monetary authorities of the member states.

The International Bank for Reconstruction and Development (World Bank) was founded at the same time as the International Monetary Fund. Like the Fund, it has its head office in Washington. It was equipped with capital of $10 milliard which was paid up by member states in line with their IMF quotas. Every member of the Fund had to become a member and shareholder of the World Bank. Originally, the main task of the World Bank was to provide financial aid for the reconstruction of areas damaged by the War. It later became a major agency of international finance for large-scale development projects and the most important source of development aid.

Whereas the White Plan had reserved a dominant position in the International Monetary Fund for the United States, a compromise was reached at Bretton Woods between countries with high contribution quotas which claimed for themselves a correspondingly high level of influence, and the expectations of the poorer countries which asked for equal rights in the management of funds. Both the IMF and the World Bank were run by a board to which each member delegated a governor and a vice-governor. A board of twenty directors was charged with the management of the respective institutes. The countries with the highest contribution quotas gained a greater influence in so far as the top five were able to appoint a director to both the Fund and the World Bank, whereas the remaining 15 directors for both are elected by the other member states.

By 1945, Germany's currency had been wrecked more totally than any other national currency. Once Nazism was destroyed, the Allies maintained the freeze on prices and wages imposed during the Hitler period in Germany. This plugged a major source of inflation which existed as a result of 'covert' war financing. But other problems arose once the War was over: the Allied programme of dismantling industry widened the gap between surplus purchasing power and the availability of goods; there was also the money in the hands of members of the occupation forces. Thus the artificially retarded inflation continued and crippled the entire economy. Side-by-side with the devalued reichsmark which enabled people to buy no more than the meagre provisions of rationed foodstuffs there existed a second currency, the 'cigarette currency' of the Black Market. It had a vastly greater purchasing power, but was difficult to obtain. In 1948 the three Western Occupation Zones succeeded in introducing a Currency Reform with far-reaching consequences. Although the East-West antagonism between Russia and the Western Allies escalated from 1946, monetary experts of all the four Occupying Powers continued to hold discussions on a joint monetary reform to cover all four Zones until the autumn of 1946. They had, in principle, also come to an agreement that the reichsmark should be replaced by a new currency unit. The Soviet representatives also accepted the Colm-Dodge-Goldsmith Report which the Americans submitted in the spring of 1946 and which proposed a combination of monetary reform and equalization of burdens as a basis for further negotiations. There was no disagreement between East and West until the question arose in the autumn of 1946 as to where the new money was to be printed. The Soviets wanted to print the new German notes in their Zone at Leipzig. The Americans, on the other hand, insisted that they should be produced in Berlin and under the supervision of the Allied Control Council.

Tensions between the Soviet Union and the Western powers intensified in the winter of 1946-47. These developments prompted President Henry Truman, on 12 March 1947, to promise American aid to the free nations of Europe. The 'Truman Doctrine' had been proclaimed. It was to help them 'maintain their free institutions and their national integrity, in the face of aggressive movements which aim to impose totalitarian regimes upon them'. The implication of this was that a joint occupation of Germany was no longer a realistic prospect. The division of Germany had begun. Accordingly, West and East also solved their currency problems separately. In line with American plans, a group of German experts in the three Western Occupation Zones prepared the technicalities of monetary reform between April and

June 1948. On 20 June 1948, the reichsmark was replaced by a new currency: the deutschmark (DM). The exchange ratio between the DM and the old reichsmark was fixed at 1:10. The supply of new money to local authorities, businesses and private persons was at first so limited that there would be no excess of demand in relation to the supply of goods. On the day of the Currency Reform, a per capita amount of 40 DM was issued to every person in exchange for 40 RM. Deutschmark credit accounts were set up for public treasuries and all employers. In the first week following the monetary reform, a total of 4-5 milliard DM was put into circulation.

The new German currency rapidly won the public's confidence, and within a few days of the reform the transition to a market economy was proclaimed on the initiative of Ludwig Erhard, the head of the West German economic administration; finally on 24 June 1948, the 'Law on Guiding Principles for Economic Planning and Price Policy after the Monetary Reform' came into effect. These measures prompted manufacturers and traders to offer goods which they had been hoarding hitherto. The meagre initial supply of new money to private households forced people to economize, and inflationary pressures were drastically reduced. Once the Currency Reform and the return to a market economy had been accomplished, the foundations for West Germany's economic recovery and political stabilization had been laid.

Copying the American example, the three Western Zones (and later the German Federal Republic) were at first given a central banking system. In the winter of 1946-47, regional central banks were established as independent issuing banks in the Federal States (*Länder*). During the preparations for Currency Reform, these Banks founded a joint subsidiary, the Bank deutscher Länder. Its task was to coordinate the activities of individual *Land* central banks and to look after their interests within the deutschmark currency area. It was only in 1957 that this central banking system was replaced by a central issuing bank modelled on the Federal Reserve System and that the Bank deutscher Länder became the Deutsche Bundesbank. The *Land* central banks lost their independence under the law, but remained as branches of the Bundesbank. At the same time, the latter retained a federal element in so far as the *Länder* governments had the right to nominate the president of the central bank in their respective State, and these presidents were *ex officio* members of the Central Bank Council.

Most countries lacked large currency reserves, and particularly gold, after the Second World War. In these circumstances the dollar became a substitute for gold, the more so since the Federal Reserve System was prepared, following the establishment of the International Monetary Fund, to convert American bank notes into gold, if requested by foreign issuing banks. American dollars flowed abroad, above all to Europe and Japan in the form of Marshall Plan aid, payments for the stationing of U.S. troops or as private American investment. The economic recovery of Western Europe and Japan in the 1950s was greatly accelerated by this influx of dollars from America.

However, Western Europe's economic recovery was also furthered by closer political and economic co-operation among the European states. Those European countries participating in the European Recovery Program (ERP), as the Marshall Plan was known, created an organizational structure for their co-operation in which all the European countries outside the Soviet sphere, with the exception of Spain, decided to participate. In April 1948, they founded the OEEC (Organization for European Economic Co-operation) which the Federal Republic of Germany joined in October 1949. The tasks falling to this organization consisted of the co-ordination of recovery programmes and preparations for the free movement of trade and finance. Although all European countries continued to maintain their wartime foreign exchange controls, the European Payments Union (EPU) was founded in September 1950 to facilitate transactions between OEEC members. It functioned as a clearing house for its members, giving monthly accounts of each member's bilateral surplus and deficit. The remaining net surplus or net deficit was balanced out among the EPU members. A country having a balance of payments deficit with other EPU members had to offset 40% of the deficit by paying the Union in gold or dollars; the remaining 60% was advanced as credit. If a country was unable to pay in gold, it had to take credit from the United States or apply for a deferment of payment. The technical banking operations assigned to the EPU were carried out by the Bank for International Settlements.

The European Payments Union was conceived from the outset as an interim solution until the convertibility of currencies had been restored. With this in mind, the Union twice changed its arrangements for balancing net surpluses and net deficits to pave the way for the eventual balancing in gold or dollars. In 1954, the proportion of the net deficit which was immediately due in gold or dollars was increased from 40% to 50%. From 1955, this percentage was raised to 75% and credit advances were available on no more than 25% of the net deficits. In order to calculate and balance surpluses and deficits, fixed parities were introduced for the currencies of EPU members to facilitate the keeping of accurate accounts.

The movement towards the abolition of foreign exchange controls was accelerated in March 1957 when the six member states of the European Coal and Steel Community (Belgium, Federal Republic of Germany, France, Luxembourg, Italy and the Netherlands) founded the European Economic Community (EEC) in Rome. They agreed to secure the free movement of money and capital within four years. Even before this time-limit had expired in December 1958, the EEC countries and eight members of the European Payments Union introduced the free convertibility of their currencies. This step finally eliminated the monetary restrictions which the Great Slump and the Second World War had brought about. After this, the EPU, having accomplished its mission, was wound up.

France had to reconstitute her monetary system before the convertibility of West European currencies could be restored. Since the Second World War, the stability of the franc had been precarious. There were chronic budgetary deficits, recurring balance of payments deficits and, above all, the effect of the wage-price spiral on her economy. In December 1945, the exchange rate was fixed at 119.10 francs to one dollar, and France was admitted to the International Monetary Fund at this rate. By January 1946, inflationary developments in France had forced the rate up to 215:1. However, not even a devaluation of this magnitude was really adequate; it was held at this level for the purpose of clearing the franc with the International Monetary Fund and foreign central banks. As far as commodities were concerned, France soon had to accept a considerably more unfavourable rate of exchange of 350:1. Later, when the devaluation of the pound in September 1948 (see below p. 301) unleashed a wave of devaluations in other countries, the official exchange rate of the franc was brought into line with the 'commercial rate of exchange' of 350:1. It took considerable efforts to maintain this exchange rate until the summer of 1958, when another devaluation became unavoidable and the exchange rate deteriorated to 420:1. France was compelled to announce this devaluation in the autumn of 1958, when the members of the EEC and eight other European countries were preparing the return to free convertibility. The final rate was 493,706 francs to the dollar because adherence to the old rate would have resulted in balance of payments difficulties. At the same time, a new currency unit, the *nouveau franc*, was introduced which corresponded to 100 old francs. In the meantime the Fifth Republic had been established whose constitution had come into force in October 1958. The introduction of the new franc was designed to insure that stability, which France had been lacking under the Fourth Republic, would be achieved both in domestic politics and in financial affairs. The new franc was renamed 'franc' in January 1960 when there was no longer any danger of confusion. During de Gaulle's presidency the franc was once more stable, and the Banque de France increased its gold reserves by converting its dollar holdings into gold at the U.S. Treasury Department. After the events of May 1968, there was a massive flight into other currencies, as France appeared to be less stable than had been assumed. The French government countered this by reimposing foreign exchange controls; the regulations were relaxed in the autumn of 1968, and more money began to leave the country; but de Gaulle rejected devaluation for political reasons; thus the monetary consequences of the Crisis of May 1968 were not drawn until the autumn of 1969, when President Georges Pompidou devalued the franc by 12.5%.

Soon after her Currency Reform of 1948, West Germany managed to have surpluses in her balance of trade and her balance of payments. The deutschmark became a stable, 'hard' currency. This was made possible through a combination of foreign financial aid, a fiscal policy favouring investment, moderate wage demands on the part of the trade unions, a neo-liberal economic policy and the purposeful reconstruction and modernization of the production apparatus. France, as we have seen, also achieved monetary stability between 1959 and 1968. Britain, on the other hand, had to struggle with chronic and at times catastrophic balance of payments and

currency problems after the Second World War. She emerged from the War
with foreign debts of £3.4 milliard — excluding the American Lend-Lease
aid. Some £2.7 milliard of this were for war supplies from countries and
colonies in the sterling area, and these claims had been credited to suppliers
of goods and materials in blocked accounts. It was quite unthinkable for
Britain to pay off her large foreign debts with her own exports so soon after
the end of the War. To begin with, British industry had been geared to the
production of war materials and had to be reconverted to a peacetime
economy. Until British industry was again in a position to satisfy domestic
demand, the United Kingdom depended on imports to supply her population with consumer goods, and increasingly so. There was also, and
irrespective of the effects of the War, a very high demand for imports of
food and raw materials. The main suppliers were the United States and
Canada, and Britain needed dollars in order to pay for these imports. The
British government therefore tried to obtain a large, long-term loan from the
American and Canadian governments, and Keynes was sent across the
Atlantic as chief negotiator.

The loan was granted in December 1945. The United States made a
$3.75 milliard credit available; a further $650 million were provided
to pay off Lend-Lease debts. Canada gave a credit of $1.25 milliard. The
conditions of the loan were quite favourable in a narrow sense: interest
payments and repayment were not to begin until five years from the
receipt of the credit in the summer of 1946, i.e. from the summer
of 1951; the rate of interest was low at 2%, and repayment was over
50 years. It was the 'additional conditions' which were to prove burden-
some and ultimately fatal for the stability of the pound. Britain had
to commit herself to pay her contribution to the International Monetary
Fund not within five years, as required under the terms of the
Bretton Woods Agreement, but by July 1947. By that time she was also
expected to establish the convertibility of sterling against the dollar for
foreign owners of sterling balances; yet these people required large amounts
of dollars in order to buy urgently needed goods in the dollar bloc
countries. Thus Britain had to part with her dollars and gold not only to
cover her own imports but also to convert her sterling assets. The loan
which was originally supposed to tide her over until the repayment date in
1951, was almost completely used up by the summer of 1947. Within five
weeks of re-establishing the partial convertibility of sterling, Britain had to
return to foreign exchange controls. Simultaneously, she imposed a
curb on imports, particularly from dollar countries. These measures
were of little avail. The balance of payments remained unfavourable in 1948
and 1949 although the size of the deficit was considerably reduced. But the
dollar gap remained. Britain's exports were also hampered by the recession
of 1948 and 1949. On 18 September 1949, the Government decided to
devalue the pound by about 30%. Whereas the old exchange rate, fixed at
the beginning of the Second World War, had been 4.03 dollars to the pound,
the new rate was 2.80:1.

The devaluation of the pound unleashed a wave of devaluations in other countries in the autumn of 1949. Most European nations followed suit. They, too, were affected by a recession, and their trade position would have deteriorated further had they not followed the British lead. The Federal Republic of Germany was among these countries. Bonn had a large foreign exchange deficit at this time and held very little gold. The Government therefore thought it vital to increase exports as rapidly as possible. However, the deutschmark was devalued by a mere 20.6%, and the exchange rate against the dollar, which had been fixed at DM 3.33 in 1948, deteriorated to DM 4.20: 1.

Britain profited from her devaluation for no more than one year. Until the early 1960s, her balance of payments vacillated, depending on the world economic situation, between small surpluses and more or less large deficits. Britain's economic policy wavered accordingly between measures designed either to slow down or to revive the economy. It was the period of stop-go. When the Labour Party regained power in 1964, there was another sterling crisis. The Wilson government countered it by imposing an additional import duty of 15% and by obtaining a credit from the International Monetary Fund. For the first time the 'General Arrangements to Borrow' were applied which had been agreed between the so-called 'Group of Ten' (U.S.A., Britain, Japan, Canada, Sweden, Federal Republic of Germany, France, Italy, Belgium and the Netherlands) and the International Monetary Fund in 1962. Meanwhile it had become clear that because of the high membership quotas allocated to the United States and Britain, the Fund had plenty of dollars and sterling, but insufficient amounts of other strong and stable currencies, such as deutschmarks, Belgian francs, Canadian dollars, French francs, Dutch guilders, Swedish crowns or Japanese yen. Precisely these currencies were needed, however, when the United States or Britain required assistance. Consequently, the 'Group of Ten' came to an agreement with the International Monetary Fund that they would, if necessary, provide the IMF with credit in their own currencies up to a maximum of six milliard dollars, with terms of up to five years, in order to meet requests for credit. In this way the British IMF credit was refinanced by the other nine members of the 'Group of Ten' in 1964.

As a result of Britain's poor economic performance, the next sterling crisis occurred in 1966-67. This time, devaluation was inevitable. In November 1967, the exchange rate of sterling was reduced by 14.3% from 2.80 to 2.40 dollars. The devaluation did not prove very effective. Britain's balance of payments for 1967 showed a deficit of £540 million, and so in 1968 her partners in the 'Group of Ten' had to step in again to support the sterling assets of countries in the sterling area. From 1970, and especially after the removal of exchange controls, the pound continued to be one of the most unstable currencies in the industrial world. The main reason for this lay in the fact that Britain had failed to adjust to the change in her economic situation after the loss of her vast colonial empire. With the colonies, she had also lost the sources of cheap raw materials so vital to her former wealth. Nor did the economic, social and political instability generated by the 'stop-go' policies of the postwar period permit her to offset these losses with a programme of far-reaching modernization and rationalization of her industry. Mention must finally be made of another important cause of Britain's weak currency: the heavy military burdens the country had to bear as a major power. The maintenance and protection of bases in Asia (until the military presence 'east of Suez' was abandoned after 1965) and in the Mediterranean, as well as the upkeep of the Rhine Army did nothing to relieve her balance of payments position.

Since 1949, no other industrial country has shown such consistently large deficits in its balance of payments as the United States. However, what caused this large deficit to recur year after year was not the unfavourable balance of trade and services. The trade balance was quite regularly in surplus and fluctuated between $4 milliard and $8.2 milliard between 1949 and 1961. Only in 1959 did this surplus shrink to $200 million. In fact America's deficit was not the result of economic weakness but, on the contrary, of her enormous economic, technical and military strength. Whether they liked it or not, their strength put the Americans in a position where they found themselves providing economic aid against poverty, often accompanied by military aid and protection against an external threat, in various parts of the world. The American government paid out a total of $58.5 milliard in grants or long-term loans to foreign nations. Half of this was earmarked for economic purposes; the other half was in military aid. It was these large sums that were responsible for her balance of payments deficit which, during those years, varied between $700 million (1957) and $5 milliard (1959).

Initially milliards of dollars flowed to overseas countries as part of the Marshall Plan, the stationing of troops and other economic and military assistance. For a long time, these funds were gladly accepted and employed to strengthen currency reserves. After all, since the U.S. Treasury Department had committed itself to converting into gold the dollar notes which foreign issuing banks (though not commercial banks or private persons) would present to it, dollar notes were considered to be virtually the same as gold. Until the end of the 1950s, the foreign owners of dollar notes kept them in safes at the issuing banks, knowing that they could be converted into gold at any time. However, from the end of the 1950s the dollar glut began to arouse suspicions. These feelings were kindled by America's inflation rates which caused the wholesale price of goods to rise by 8% between June 1955 and June 1958. Spread over three years, the rate of inflation was in fact very low in comparison to that of the 1970s; but in the 1950s it was thought to be alarming. Politicians in countries which received large amounts of dollars began to ask themselves whether they were also importing American inflation and whether it would not be more advisable to convert their dollar holdings into gold. Soon the U.S. Treasury Department received requests for conversion on a large scale, and gold reserves declined from $22.8 milliard in 1950 to $17.8 milliard by the end of 1960. In 1960 alone, Washington had to transfer gold worth $1.7 milliard to foreign issuing banks. An attempt was made to persuade foreign issuing banks to retain their dollars and give up their right to exchange them into gold.

For a number of years this policy was generally successful. But by this time private owners had also begun to have doubts about the dollar, and they developed their own methods of parting with them. They used them to buy gold on the London gold market which had been reopened in 1954; or they would use them to buy a comparatively 'harder' currency which was less threatened by inflation. At the end of the 1950s, there were five brokers engaged in the precious metal market in London, the traditional centre of the international gold trade, two of whom, Rothschild & Sons and Samuel Montagu & Co., were also in banking. In 1960 and 1961 private holders of dollars adopted both strategies. They bought up gold in exchange for dollars, whereupon the price of gold soared higher than it had ever been since 1954. In order to counter these price fluctuations, the issuing banks of the United States, Britain, France, the Federal Republic, Italy, Belgium, Netherlands and Switzerland formed a 'gold-pool' following a series of negotiations in 1961 and 1962. They agreed to sell gold jointly on the London gold market, should its price rise sharply as a result of speculative demand; conversely, they would buy gold if its price fell too heavily as a result of oversupply. This was to eliminate the disturbing price fluctuations which, in turn, were having an unsettling effect on both the national and international currency systems. The 'gold-pool' served its purpose for a few years. The hectic 1968 speculation in gold led the pool countries to give up their unsuccessful efforts to stabilize the price of gold.

The switching to 'harder' currencies by private holders of dollars put those currencies under pressure to revalue. The deutschmark and the Dutch guilder were particularly affected, and in 1960-61 the monetary stability of the Federal Republic and Holland was threatened by a heavy influx of foreign currency, consisting not only of dollars, but also of sterling. On 6 March 1961, both countries revalued their currencies by 5%. In 1968, after the events in France, and in 1969 when the pound became very weak, the deutschmark was again under pressure to revalue. But the Grand Coalition government in Bonn was unable to agree on a revaluation. Among the supporters of a revaluation were the Bundesbank board of directors and, from the spring of 1969, Karl Schiller, the Minister of Economics. Franz Joseph Strauss, the Finance Minister, opposed it because he feared that a revaluation would push up the price of German goods on the world market and have a negative effect on exports. The deutschmark was revalued by 9.9% in October 1969, after months of public debate and once the national elections were over and after the Christian Democrats had withdrawn from government responsibility. The new exchange rate was DM 3.66 against the dollar. There were none of the detrimental consequences for German exports which Strauss and others had predicted.

In the meantime, America's balance of payments had deteriorated further. The European allies of the United States had some part in this. The protectionism practised by the European Economic Community had contributed to a reduction of surpluses in America's balance of trade and services. In 1970 her surplus of $2.1 milliard was less than half the 1960 figure of $4.9 milliard. Moreover spending on civilian and military aid had not been reduced. Finally, European protectionism had led many American businesses to surmount the customs barriers of the EEC by founding subsidiaries in Western Europe or by acquiring a stake in indigenous companies. After 1965 and at Washington's request, American industry agreed to a voluntary restriction on capital investment abroad. Banks also cut back on the credit granted to foreign countries. In short, the United States reduced their export of capital. The effect of this was partly offset because American-owned firms did not transfer the returns from their foreign investments back to America, but reinvested them abroad.

The 1960s and 1970s saw no lessening of creeping inflation in the United States. The Board of Governors of the 'Fed' would have been in a position to stop this trend by increasing the reserve quotas, by imposing severe credit restrictions and by raising the bank rate. But the introduction of such measures would have meant a growth in already chronic unemployment. Throughout the 20th century, except for a few years during the First and Second World Wars, the United States has always had fairly high unemployment of 5% on average. In 1970 the rate was 4.9%; but in 1971 and 1972 it began to rise again above the 5% average. The simultaneous combination of inflation and unemployment in the United States — which became known as 'stagflation' — cast doubt upon the argument that, although inflation is unpleasant, it would at least maintain full employment.

In the summer of 1971, Congress began to concern itself with the problems of America's inflation, the balance of payments deficit and the unsatisfactory state of foreign trade. In the first days of August, the relevant Congressional sub-committee submitted a report which asserted that the decline in the balance of trade position and the increase in the balance of payments deficit were caused by an overvaluation of the dollar. The dollar would have to be devalued in order to get the United States out of their difficult predicament. The sub-committee's findings were a signal to foreign holders of dollars. The great *'sauve qui peut'* started, and America's gold reserve tumbled to $10 milliard. In order to prevent further losses of gold, President Nixon suspended the Treasury Department's undertaking towards foreign issuing banks to convert their dollars into gold. He also declared that the dollar was not overvalued and would hence not have to be devalued. In order to achieve a more favourable balance of trade, an import tax of 10% was imposed on the value of all imported goods on 15-16 August 1971.

The rest of the Western world was affected by the dollar crisis in different ways. As early as the spring of 1971, dollars had swamped the money markets of industrial nations. Switzerland and Austria defended themselves against the influx by revaluing their currencies in May. At the same time, the Federal Republic and Holland decided to allow their exchange rates to 'float'. France and Belgium both regarded a split foreign exchange rate as the best line of defence. Consequently the exchange rate was pegged for transfers involving payment for the supply of goods. On the other hand, no guide-lines existed for straight currency operations. Those countries which, like the Federal Republic, resorted to floating early on or, like France and Belgium, split their exchange rates were, on the whole, spared the dollar glut. The industrial countries which floated their currencies only at a later stage were the ones to suffer. Almost all countries have been floating their exchange rates since the dollar's convertibility to gold was abandoned. In view of the fact that, along with gold, the dollar functioned as a currency reserve for many countries, the dollar crisis threw the entire international monetary system into disarray. The postwar order had come to an end. In December 1971, a new exchange rate system was agreed upon after complex negotiations. This time the dollar was devalued by 7.9% against gold; several other currencies were revalued at the same time; they included the deutschmark (revalued by 4.6%) and the yen (revalued by 7.7%). Overall the revaluation of the deutschmark and the yen against the dollar therefore amounted to 13.6% and 16.7% respectively.

2. Banking Systems

International Trends

Two trends which had influenced and changed the structures of the credit systems during the inter-war period continued after 1945. The first was the growing intervention of the state and the rising influence of state-controlled and other public institutions on banking. The second development related to the increase in the number of mergers. As regards the question of public sector growth, it was of no great significance that the joint-stock capital of the issuing banks was nationalized in France in 1945, in Britain in 1946 and in the Federal Republic after the formation of central banks in the *Länder*. The decisive point is not who owns the shares, but how independent the management is from the government. Thus the Banque de France maintained its traditional independence even after nationalization. The same applies to the West German Bundesbank. On the other hand, the nationalization of the biggest deposit banks in France in 1945 and the sharply increased share of business taken by the central giro institutions, national banks and savings banks in West Germany reflected a remarkable structural change which will be discussed in another context (see below pp. 311, 314). Finally, the concentration process in the private sector also continued during the 1950s and 1960s with a series of mergers between big banks.

Since the 1950s new forms of international relations within the credit system came into being with the formation of the Euro-dollar market and of institutionalized co-operation between the big banks of various countries by means of international bank groups. The Euro-dollar market represents an international money market for short-term and medium-term credits outside the United States. Commercial banks, issuing banks and other non-banking institutions inside and outside Europe except for the United States participate in its credit operations. Credit transactions on the Euro-dollar market must involve the participation of at least one European bank. However, the branches of American banks in Europe have the same rights as their European counterparts, as they are subject to the banking regulations of the host countries. The term 'Euro-dollar market' arose because transactions in this credit market are settled in dollars – originally almost exclusively so and still for the most part today. With the dollar losing its position as the leading international currency, there has also been a demand for other currencies on the Euro-dollar market, particularly 'hard' currencies like the deutschmark, Swiss franc and Dutch guilder. In view of these developments the term 'Euro-money market', which has been in use since the beginning of the 1970s, is probably more appropriate.

It is difficult to say when and how the Euro-money market began. We know with some degree of certainty that the credit operations which we call Euro-dollar credits did not begin until 1953. It is also clear that the state banks of the East Bloc countries were initially also involved. These banks preferred to deposit their dollar holdings on a short-term basis in a Western European country, rather than to keep them in American banks. They adopted this policy not because of the Cold War, but because the regulations of the American Federal Reserve Act of 1937 did not allow American banks to accept interest-bearing sight deposits, and, as regards time deposits, the interest rate was determined by the Board of Governors of the Federal Reserve System which before 1970 could not be exceeded. These regulations, which made it unprofitable to keep deposits which could be recalled at short notice in American banks, also persuaded Western European banks to deploy their dollar holdings more profitably in the short-term and medium-term credit business with European and other non-American banks, central issuing banks as well as commerce and industry.

It was in this way that the Euro-dollar market emerged in the course of the 1950s. Its evolution was largely complete when the Western European nations re-established the convertibility of their currencies in December 1958. Regular participants in the Euro-dollar (or Euro-money) market are banks in Belgium, the Federal Republic, France, Britain, Italy, Holland, Sweden, Switzerland and Luxembourg, in addition to the branches of American banks based in those countries. From the legal point of view, all these institutions are subject to the regulations of their own (or, in the case of the latter, their host) country. Whoever wants to lend money, places it, for reasons of profitability, on the Euro-money market where interest rates tend to be higher than in their native country. Those wishing to borrow money, go to the market to strengthen their own liquidity. During the 1960s the volume of the Euro-money market saw a rapid increase. In 1964, the System had funds totalling $9 milliard at its disposal; six years later, the amount was $46 milliard.

In 1964, just under half the funds on the Euro-money market came from Western European countries; by 1970 the proportion had risen to more than 55% ($25.4 milliard). London is the Euro-money market's most important centre. Most European, American and Japanese banks have their branches there and 75-80% of all Euro-money credit transactions take place in London. It has been said from time to time that the Euro-money market might threaten the monetary and credit policies of individual European countries, in the sense that industry might turn to the Euro-market to evade credit restrictions which national governments and central issuing banks may wish to impose to stabilize their economies. It is no doubt difficult to control the Euro-money market because of its transnational character. But governments can use the instruments of monetary policy to counter any unwelcome influx of money from this direction.

From the 1950s, an increasing number of major industrial concerns, in order to gain a firm foothold in foreign markets, began to establish not only branches, but also subsidiaries in other countries which they provided with their own capital. This presented the banks with fresh tasks: as their major customers developed into 'multinationals', they were expected to satisfy the expanded and transnational credit requirements of these large companies. Traditional methods, such as the use of an agency to represent interest abroad or a correspondent to deal with transactions, were no longer sufficient. In order to finance the multinationals, the banks were forced to follow their customers and set up branches or to obtain direct stakes in banks in those countries where the former had their subsidiaries. The multinationalization of the banks followed upon the multinationalization of industry.

Foreign branches, foreign subsidiary banks and direct investments in banks had, of course, been known since the late 19th century, but their number was small until the 1950s. As late as 1966, a mere 66 American banks were represented abroad; they operated a total of 244 branches. By 1971, there were about 30 American banks, with more than 100 branches in Europe alone. There are also, within the EEC, some 13 subsidiaries and 16 European banks in which American banks hold a direct stake. The Deutsche Bank increased the number of its direct investments in foreign banks from seven in 1962 to 33 in 1972.

Long before the First World War, large loan and credit operations had required the co-operation of banks in several countries within the framework of international consortia. But this co-operation never went beyond a specific business transaction and certainly did not create lasting international banking alliances. On the contrary, the banks remained, in principle, open to collaboration with any other foreign bank. The size of the financial operations of the multinationals and the integration of the national economies of Western Europe within the EEC, forced the banks into recognizing the inadequacy of the old *ad-hoc* methods of international co-operation. From 1967, they began to institutionalize their co-operation within the framework of international bank groups and their subsidiaries. This development began in 1967 when the Commerzbank of Düsseldorf, the Westminster Bank, the First National Bank of Chicago, the Irving Trust Company of New York and the Hong Kong and Shanghai Banking Corporation of Hong Kong founded the International Commercial Bank in London as a credit institute for long-term financing. In the same year, the Dresdner Bank, the Bank of America at San Francisco, Barclays Bank, the Banque Nationale de Paris, the Algemeene Bank Nederland of Amsterdam and the Banca Nazionale del Lavoro in Rome founded the Société Financière Européenne, based in Paris and Luxembourg, for industrial finance. In 1968, the Deutsche Bank, the Amsterdam-Rotterdam-Bank, the British Midland Bank, the Société Générale de Banque of Brussels, the Paris Société Générale and the Creditanstalt-Bankverein of Vienna followed suit by founding the European-American Bank & Trust Company and the European-American Banking Corporation in New York. These joint ventures were, in effect, permanent consortia for major credit operations of up to $30-40 million.

In 1970 and 1971 there also emerged four big international bank groups whose members were contractually obliged to engage in close and long-term co-operation. The terms of the agreements included the exchange of information, the mutual servicing of customers, the joint use of foreign branches, the preparation of joint financial operations and the foundation of joint subsidiaries. The first of these international bank groups – the 'Club of Three' – was formed by the West German Commerzbank, the Crédit Lyonnais and the Banco di Roma and came into being in 1970. Within two weeks, the Deutsche Bank, the Amsterdam-Rotterdam-Bank, the Midland Bank and the Société Générale de Banque intensified their previously loose co-operation by founding the European Banks' International Company (EBIC) in Brussels. The Viennese Creditanstalt-Bankverein and the Paris Société Générale came in at a later date. The third international banking group was formed in February 1971, when the Dresdner Bank, the Bayerische Hypotheken- und Wechselbank, the Banque de Bruxelles and the Algemeene Bank Nederland signed an agreement of co-operation. At the same time, the Chase Manhattan Bank of New York, the National Westminster Bank, the Royal Bank of Canada and the Westdeutsche Landesbank Gironzentrale of Düsseldorf and Münster linked up under the name of Orion Group. The members of this Group set up joint subsidiary banks in London, Amsterdam and Hong Kong.

National Trends

Since 1945 the big American banks have been the driving force in the international credit business. The first large-scale mergers took place between them after the Second World War, and they began to lead the field in opening foreign branches and in making direct participating investments. America's commercial banks were already the largest in the world. But after 1945 the Bank of America in San Francisco became the biggest by far. In New York big banks came into being through mergers the size of which definitely surpassed those of their European competitors in terms of capital sums and balance-sheet totals. The American merger movement of the post-war period was launched in 1948 when the Bank of New York took over the Fifth Avenue Bank in New York. In 1954 the Chemical Bank and the Corn Exchange Bank merged to form the Chemical Corn Exchange Bank. This Bank united with the New York Trust Company in 1959 to become the Chemical Bank New York Trust Company (now: Chemical Bank). In 1955 there emerged what are today the second- and third-largest banks in the world as a result of mergers between several New York banks. The combination of the National City Bank of New York with the First National Bank resulted in the First National City Bank, the world's second-largest bank. In the same year, the Chase National Bank of the City of New York and the Bank of the Manhattan Company united to form the Chase Manhattan Bank, which ranks third among the world's commercial banks. The last in this series of big mergers within the American banking system took place in 1959 when J.P. Morgan & Co. fused with the Guaranty Trust Company of New York. These mergers apparently represented the upper limit of concentration which the Government, the Federal Reserve System and Congress were prepared to tolerate. In 1958, the First National City Bank wanted to take over the County Trust Company which would have resulted in an equity capital of $200 million larger than that of the Bank of America; but the merger foundered when the Board of Governors raised objections.

Britain experienced a similar concentration movement ten years later, although her concentration had not come about solely as a result of mergers, but also because of the expansion of group banking since 1950. The American Congress viewed trustification with suspicion; clearly this was more than a mere concentration in banking. These movements quite legally bypassed the ban on universal banks under the terms of the Glass-Steagall Banking Act of 1933. The problem was that the bank holding companies which controlled the banking groups were not counted as banks, even if they owned not only bank shares but also shares in industrial and commercial companies. To meet this challenge, the legal regulations governing group banking were tightened up by the Holding Company Act of 1956 under which the bank holding companies were banned from owning shares other than bank shares. They were obliged to sell their shares in non-banking enterprises which they held in their portfolio; but to protect them from the losses on the stock exchange, they were given an extended period to complete these sales.

Although Britain's banking system had reached a high degree of concentration well before the Second World War, mergers continued or were attempted during the 1960s. In 1968 the smallest two of the Big Five, the

National Provincial Bank and the Westminster Bank merged to form the National Westminster Bank. The new firm became Britain's largest bank and the fifth-largest in the world. At the same time, Martins Bank in Liverpool was looking for a bigger partner. As Martins was the largest deposit bank in the country, the only institutions under serious consideration were the Big Five. Both Barclays Bank and Lloyds Bank, the two largest in this league, were interested in a merger with Martins Bank, and, to everyone's surprise, *both* of them decided to unite with Martins. The implementation of this plan would have created a credit institution with an equity capital as large as that of all the other big banks put together and would have combined 45% of London's Clearing business. This prospect alarmed the Department of Trade, and it referred the case to the Monopolies Commission. The Commission rejected the merger by a small majority of 6:4 votes, and the Government decided to accept this verdict. Although their decision did not constitute a formal ban, the banks chose not to ignore the verdict and abandoned their plan. After Lloyds Bank had withdrawn, Barclays Bank took over Martins Bank, and the British government consented to this more small-scale merger. With London having become the centre of the Euro-money market, merchant banks in the City participated extensively in the Euro-credit business and accepted large foreign deposits. This is also why they are numbered among the 'founders' of the Euro-dollar market.

In the late autumn of 1945, the French Constituent Assembly, dominated as it was by the Communists, Socialists and the left-Catholic *Mouvement républicain populaire*, resolved to nationalize the Banque de France and the *grandes banques*. This affected the four largest deposit banks: the Crédit Lyonnais, Banque Nationale pour le Commerce et l'Industrie, Société Générale and Comptoir National d'Escompte de Paris. The Banque de Paris et de Pay Bas ('Paribas') escaped nationalization out of consideration for its foreign shareholders. It is still not clear why the Crédit Industriel et Commercial was not nationalized. One possible reason is that it did not have a large branch network and that it co-operated with regional and local credit institutions. In essence, the business activity of the big nationalized banks remained unchanged. In this sense it may be said that the French case has demonstrated the pointlessness of nationalizing big banks.

In 1966 there were two further mergers between big banks in France. Firstly, two of the nationalized companies, the Comptoir National d'Escompte de Paris and the Banque Nationale pour le Commerce et l'Industrie amalgamated to form the Banque Nationale de Paris. The Banque de la Compagnie Financière de Suez and the Union des Mines la Hénin followed suit to create the Banque de Suez et de l'Union des Mines. The latter was the bank for French heavy industry; the former acted as the banking house of the Compagnie Financière de Suez, the successor organization of the old Suez Canal Company which had been nationalized by the Egyptian government. The share-holders had been paid a total of £29.15 million in compensation; in 1957, they founded the Compagnie Financière de Suez as a holding company which gradually acquired a direct stake in approximately 130 different companies in a number of countries. In 1958 the Compagnie Financière founded the Banque de la Compagnie Financière de Suez as its own bank, to be responsible for its financial operations and in particular for the raising of capital. The investment business conducted by the Compagnie Financière and its bank was so successful that the shareholders of the old Suez Canal Company were able to recover their losses in full. France's second largest investment bank emerged from the merger of the Suez Bank and the Union de Mines la Hénin. In 1968 it incorporated a deposit bank by acquiring a 34% stake in the capital of Odier Bungener Courvoisier & Cie. in Paris. The creation of the new big *banque d'affaires* prompted the 'Paribas' to conclude co-operation agreements with the Crédit Industriel et Commercial, the Compagnie Bancaire and the Banque Worms and to exchange shares with them.

According to the plans of the Allies, the banking systems of Japan and Germany were to be changed in such a way that they would cease to have a dominating financial influence. Yet the implementation of these plans in Japan and Germany was effective for a few years only. In 1945 the Americans ordered Japan to promulgate an anti-Trust Act. It provided for the dissolution of the zaibatsu. The zaibatsu banks had to sever their links with industry and to adopt a new company name. In 1952 Japan regained her sovereignty after concluding a peace treaty with the United States and the anti-Trust Act was immediately repealed. In the ensuing years, the zaibatsu re-emerged, and the zaibatsu banks re-established their former close links with industry. They also assumed their old company names again. Only the Yasuda Bank retained the company name of Fuji Bank which it had been forced to adopt in 1948. During the 1920s, the Yasuda Bank had been Japan's biggest commercial bank; it regained this position after 1945. The other long-established big banks (Mitsui Bank, Mitsubishi Bank, Sumitomo Bank, Hokkaido Takushoko Bank, Nippon Kangyo Bank, Sanwa Bank, and the Dai-Ichi-Bank) were joined by others after the War, some of which were newly founded or had only recently become big banks. New foundations were the Bank of Tokyo and the Kyowa Bank.

The Bank of Tokyo was established in 1946 as a specialized bank to finance foreign trade. It was designed to fill the gap left by the closure of the Yokohama Specie Bank in 1945. The domestic assets of the Yokohama Specie Bank were transferred to the new foreign trade bank. The Kyowa Bank was established in 1945, representing a merger of nine big savings banks in Tokyo, Osaka and Nagoya. It was Japan's biggest savings bank, but in 1948 it was transformed into a commercial bank. The Daiwa Bank, the Bank of Kobe and the Tokai Bank became major banks after 1945. Since Japan's central mortgage bank, the Nippon Kangyo Bank, operated as a commercial bank after 1950, a new mortgage bank was founded in 1957: the Hypothec Bank of Japan. The capital derived from the liquidation funds of the former Colonial bank for Korea, the Bank of Chosen. The big Japanese banks continued to operate as universal banks after 1945. What helped them to retain this status was that they had a high proportion of longer-term deposits, as Japanese customers preferred to maintain such deposits for their higher returns. Meanwhile the reconstruction and rapid expansion of industry got underway. Capital resources were very small, and the banks were faced with large borrowing requirements and demands for long-term credit in particular. One alarming consequence was, and still is, that the total lending of Japanese banks exceeds their total deposits, and more than once they have had to go to the central issuing bank for refinancing. To date, the Japanese banks have not seen any great danger in this, although it could quickly engulf them in a liquidity crisis should there ever be a major depression.

Japan's trusts were dissolved in 1945, but the banks linked to them remained in existence. In Germany, on the other hand, the big banks were closed in 1945 and 1946 on the order of the Allies. The Soviet Union intervened most effectively in the banking system of her Zone by dissolving all private commercial banks. In accordance with the system of centralized economic planning which replaced the private economy in the Soviet Zone and later in the German Democratic Republic, state-owned, nationally-owned and co-operative financial institutions were set up. There was no competition between them as they had separate fields of activity assigned to them.

In the Western Zones, public institutions (savings banks, central giro institutions and *Land* central banks), credit co-operatives, the private bankers and regional joint-stock banks were allowed to resume their operations in the summer of 1945. The head offices of the big banks, on the other hand, remained closed, and only their branches were permitted to continue; inevitably they lacked the back-up which central offices can provide. In 1947 and 1948, the military governments of the three Western Zones agreed on a joint policy concerning the former big banks. They were to be carved up into separate institutions. In all, 10 new firms were formed out of the Deutsche Bank; the Dresdner Bank was divided up into 11 banks, and the Commerzbank was split into nine institutions. Once the Federal Republic of Germany had been founded, these decisions were cemented by the 'Law on Big Banks' of 1952, except that the total number of separate institutions was reduced. For each of the former three big banks a successor company was established, one of which was to serve the northern *Länder* (Schleswig-Holstein, Lower Saxony, Hamburg, Bremen); the second covered North-Rhine-Westphalia and the third looked after the southern *Länder* of the Federal Republic. Holders of reichsmark shares in the Deutsche Bank and the Dresdner Bank received new deutschmark shares in these successor banks at 10:6.2; the ratio for the successors of the Commerzbank was 10:5. Yet the deconcentration of the big banks did not last for long. Soon after the Federal Republic had regained full sovereignty on 5 May 1955, the supervisory boards of the successor banks agreed to balance profits and losses between their respective companies. This was a first step towards the re-establishment of the former big banks. On 24 December 1956, the 1952 Act was replaced by the 'Law to Terminate the Restriction of the Regional

Scope of Credit Institutions' which cleared the path towards reunification. In the course of 1957, the Deutsche Bank and the Dresdner Bank were re-established, with their new head offices at Frankfurt; the Commerzbank was reunited in 1958, with its main office at Düsseldorf.

However, the re-emergence of the old big banks did not mean that they had gained a dominating position within the German credit system comparable to that of the 'Big Five' in Britain (at present: the 'Big Four'). Nevertheless, they succeeded in increasing the volume of their business enormously. In 1950 business of the successor banks totalled DM 7.9 milliard; that of the three big banks amounted to DM 125.9 million in 1957. They also continued to control the big financial operations. On the other hand, their relative share in the volume of business and in the loans provided by the German system as a whole declined steadily. In 1950 the then successor institutions managed 19.4% of the volume of business and lending of all German banks. In 1960 this share (in terms of volume) was 11.4%; but the lending share was down to 9.9%. Up to 1974, there was a further drop in these percentages to 9.7% and 8.9% respectively.

The main cause for this development lay in the expansion of cashless payments which opened up a large market for the savings banks, co-operatives and local banks. As late as the beginning of the 1950s, most employees had their salaries and wages paid in cash by their employers' pay office. In the mid-1950s, public authorities and public corporations and all big and medium-sized companies began to call upon their officials, employees and workers to open giro accounts at a credit institution so that their earnings could be remitted directly. As the big banks had never been very interested, at least not until recently, in the small customer, the savings banks, co-operatives and local banks took on the cashless remittance of wages and salaries and the maintenance of giro accounts which this required. They succeeded in winning over, as customers, social groups which had hitherto not kept an account and which now also began to use other services offered by these banks.

This enabled several credit institutions to grow into big banks. One of these new big banks is the Bank für Gemeinwirtschaft in Frankfurt. It continued a venture started by the employees' banks in the 1920s (see above p. 232), but operates on a much larger scale and with infinitely greater success. The Bank für Gemeinwirtschaft came into being in 1958 after the merger of six communal banks. It is a joint-stock company with an extensive branch network. The *Deutsche Gewerkschaftsbund* (German Federation of Trade Unions) owns 95% of its joint-stock capital; the *Grosseinkaufsgesellschaft deutscher Konsumgenossenschaften* (Wholesale Buying Association of German Consumer Co-operatives) holds the remaining 5%. The borrowers of the Bank für Gemeinwirtschaft are primarily industrial and commercial enterprises, particularly medium-sized businesses. Like the old big banks, the Bank für Gemeinwirtschaft is a universal bank.

Conclusion

Banks drew their customers from a small stratum of wealthy landowners, manufacturers, merchants and rentiers well into the second half of the 19th century. Up to this period, private bankers also played a dominant role in the business. Their number and even more so their economic importance, on the other hand, experienced a decline since the end of that century. Thenceforth banking was almost exclusively in the hands of those new types of banks which had grown up in the course of industrialization. Today the enormous credit needs of large-scale industry and of modern states with their extended public service networks are being satisfied primarily by the big joint-stock banks. The growth of savings banks and, in Central and Western Europe, of co-operative banks was similarly due to the emergence of industrial society.

There are three trends in the history of banking in this century: 1) the expansion of the big banks as a result of mergers and the formation of trusts and banking groups accelerated the process of concentration and centralization in banking; 2) In most countries the influence of the State in the field of banking has been extended by virtue of increased supervisory powers and of legislation. Regimentation and controls of this kind apart, there are further pressures arising from the establishment and expansion of banks which are state-owned or constitute institutions under public law. France nationalized its four largest banks in 1945, and in 1981 the victories of the socialists in the presidential and the parliamentary elections have resulted in the nationalization of all large and medium-sized banks; 3) The transnationality of banking and other international credit activities, which had been evident for long in the emergence of consortia, foreign branch networks and subsidiaries overseas, was reinforced from the 1960s onwards by the massive expansion of the Euro-dollar market, the proliferation of foreign branches and, above all, by the institutionalization of co-operation among international banking groups. This intensified and institutionalized co-operation on a global scale probably represents the most significant change in recent decades which in the long run is also likely to have the most far-reaching consequences.

Sources and Literature

1. Comments on the Source Situation
and on the Historiography of Banking

For obvious reasons, banks have to take greater care with the preservation of their records than industrial and commercial enterprises. However, this does not mean that the historian has large numbers of bank archives at his disposal for his research. First of all, the use of bank archives is restricted by the secrecy which banks are obliged to uphold even when their business contact with a client has long since lapsed. Therefore archival sources about individual credit operations are not, as a rule, accessible. The use of bank archives is also complicated by the fact that there are only a few which are sufficiently well-ordered and inventoried that an outsider can find his way around them. In many cases, old bank records have simply been destroyed because there was no space. Big banks, generally, maintain their own archives. The same is true of important and traditional private bankers' firms, such as Rothschild or Oppenheim. Occasionally private bankers give their old archival records to a public archive; for example, the older parts of the archive of the Bethmann Brothers banking house have been in the municipal archives of Frankfurt since 1965. The same applies to the older remnants of the archival material belonging to the banking houses of de Neuflize Schlumberger & Cie and Mallet Frères & Cie, which are being kept in the *Archives Nationales* at Paris. Occasionally, public archives obtain archival documents from liquidated banks. In so far as bank archives are accessible to research, they offer source material on the foundation of banks, their legal organization, their basic decisions (expansion, or change of site or kind of business activity) and, naturally, their business reports and balance sheets.

Archives of Foreign Ministries and of Ministries of Economics and Finance also contain sources on the history of banking. Big international financial projects, such as the construction of the Baghdad Railway, or the French loans granted to Russia before 1914, bank disasters like the German crisis in 1931 or bank laws, have been preserved in the records of state authorities. As far as published sources are concerned, there are the monetary and banking laws, business accounts and interim and annual balance sheets, the publication of which was obligatory for joint stock banks since the end of the 19th century. In many countries inquiries were set up after bank crises: in the United States in 1912 and 1913 and in 1933 and 1934 and in Germany in 1933. The results have been published and contain a great deal of information for the economic historian. Bank statistics have been published in Britain regularly since the end of the 19th century, although most countries started to publish special bank statistics only in the course of the 20th century. These statistics raise the same problems as all other statistics: the data on which they are based tends to be flawed. Furthermore, the criteria defining the different types of banks have changed over the course of time. For example, the 1976 *Festschrift* of the Bundesbank includes a volume of statistics which quotes entirely different figures for individual types of banks during the 1920s than does the *Banken-Enquête* volume of 1933. In short, statistical material must not be taken for 'hard facts'.

The contemporary financial press also contains reports on the banking operations and links with certain companies and is therefore useful as a source of banking history. Individual bankers, including Jacques Laffitte, Carl Fürstenberg, Max von Schinckel, Arthur von Gwinner, Emile Moreau, Felix Somary, James P. Warburg, Hermann Wallich, Paul Wallich, Hjalmar Schacht, Hans Luther, Wilhelm Vocke and Hans Fürstenberg, have written their memoirs. Of course, they are useful as sources to clarify certain events only, if other sources are incomplete or unobtainable. At the same time, these books are important sources for learning about the personality of their author.

The intensive study of the history of banking did not begin until after the Second World War when the trail was blazed by the works of Bertrand Gille and Rondo Cameron. Because this research was begun so late, the few comprehensive surveys of the history of banking which have been published (by Dauphin-Meunier, Easton and Dunbar) are out of date, with the last one appearing in 1937. With a few exceptions, there is still a lack of comprehensive histories of banks in individual countries. Such national histories of banks as are available generally only cover the 19th century or even shorter periods of time, although good monographs on the development of different types of banks, important events and problems in the history of banking do exist. The *Institut für bankhistorische Forschung* at Frankfurt is working on a German Banking History in three volumes. Vol. 1 (until 1800) was published in 1982; vols. 2 and 3 are to appear in 1983. The systematic analysis of the older literature on the theory and practice of banking also yields plenty of material. The number of monographs on the history of individual banks is large, most of them having been written to mark a firm's anniversary, usually on behalf of the respective banking firm itself. This means that the quality of their material is often problematical. Nevertheless, however little they conform to the requirements of scientific research, these jubilee publications are useful and often even indispensable aids to the discovery of historical detail.

2. Bibliography

(N.B. This bibliography provides no more than a selection of the relevant literature available in English. Some titles in French and German are also mentioned. A fuller list which contains further foreign language titles may be found in the German original of this book).

General Histories and Economic Histories of the 19th and 20th Centuries: G.N. Clark et al., eds., *The New Cambridge Modern History*, vols. 9ff., Cambridge 1960ff; H.J. Habakkuk and M. Postan, eds., *The Cambridge Economic History of Europe*, vols. 6/1-2, Cambridge 1965ff.; C.M. Cipolla, ed., *The Fontana Economic History of Europe*, vols. 3f., London 1973.; D.S. Landes, *The Unbound Prometheus*, London 1969; W.W. Rostow, *The Stages of Economic Growth*, London 1960; W.W. Rostow, ed., *The Economics of Take-off into Sustained Growth*, London 1963; J. Schumpeter, *Business Cycles*, 2 vols., New York-London 1939.

General and National Histories of Banking: W. Dodsworth, ed., *A History of Banking in all the Leading Nations*, 4 vols., New York 1896f.; C.F. Dunbar, *Theory and History of Banking*, New York 1917; Fuji Bank, ed., *Banking in Modern Japan*, Tokyo 1967; H. Krooss, *Documentary History of Banking and Currency in the United States*, 4 vols., New York 1969.

Currency and Money in the 19th Century: A. Feavearyear, *The Pound Sterling*, Oxford ^{2}1963; M. Friedman and A.J. Schwartz, *A Monetary History of the United States, 1867-1960*, New York 1963; R. Sedillot, *Le franc*, Paris 1953.

The Rise of Central Banks: C.A. Conant, *A History of Modern Banks of Issue*, New York-London 1927; A. Andréades, *History of the Bank of England, 1640-1903*, London ^{4}1966; J. Clapham, *The Bank of England. A History*, 2 vols., Cambridge ^{3}1966; R. Bigo, *La Caisse d'Escompte (1776-1793) et les origines de la Banque de France*, Paris 1927; J. Dauphin-Meunier, *La Banque de France*, Paris 1936; C. Lebeau, *La Banque de France*, Paris 1930; C. Schauer, *Die Preussische Bank*, Halle 1912; M. Seeger, *Die Politik der Reichsbank im Lichte der Spielregeln der Goldwährung*, Berlin 1968; P. Warburg, *The Federal Reserve System*, 2 vols., New York 1930.

Banks and Banking to the Middle of the 19th Century

Private Bankers and Public Banks: H. D. MacLeod, *History of Banking in Great Britain*, New York 1898; R. D. Richards, 'The Pioneers of Banking in England', *Economic History*, 1/1929; R.W. Hidy, *The House of Baring in American Trade and Finance, 1763-1861*, New York ^{2}1970; H. Lüthy, *La*

Banque protestante en France de la révocation de l'Edit de Nantes à la Révolution, 2 vols., Paris 1961; C. Helbing, Die Bethmanns, Frankfurt 1948; H. Schnee, Die Hoffinanz und der moderne Staat, 4 vols., Berlin 1955ff. J.G. Van Dillen, ed., History of the Principal Public Banks, The Hague 1934; H. Hellwig, Die Preussische Staatsbank-Seehandlung, 1772-1922, Berlin 1922.

Private Bankers and the State Loan Business: R.W. Hidy, The House of Baring in American Trade and Finance, New York ^{2}1970; B. Gille, La banque et le crédit en France, 1815-1848, Paris 1959; B. Gille, Histoire de la maison de Rothschild, 2 vols., Geneva 1965/67; M. Schwann, Ludolf Camphausen, 3 vols., Essen 1915.

Railway Finance: R. Fulford, Glyn's 1753-1963, London 1953; B. Gille, Histoire de la maison de Rothschild, Geneva 1965/67; W. Kumpmann, Die Entstehung der Rheinischen Eisenbahngesellschaft, Essen 1910; K. Grunwald, Türkenhirsch. A Study of Baron Maurice Hirsch, Entrepreneur and Philanthropist, Jerusalem 1966; A.M. Johnson and B.E. Supple, Boston Capitalists and Western Railroads, Cambridge (Mass.) 1967.

The Financing of Early Industrialization: F. Crouzet, ed., Capital Formation in the Industrial Revolution, London 1972; B. Gille, 'Banking and Industrialization in Europe, 1730-1914', in: C. Cipolla, ed., The Fontana Economic History of Europe, Vol. 3, London 1973; M. Lévy-Leboyer, Les banques européennes et l'industrialisation internationale dans la première moitié du XIXe siècle, Paris 1964; R. Cameron, France and the Economic Development of Europe, 1800-1914, Princeton 1961; L.S. Pressnell, Country Banking in the Industrial Revolution, Oxford 1956; W.O. Henderson, The State and the Industrial Revolution in Prussia, 1740-1870, Liverpool 1958; R. Tilly, Financial Institutions and Industrialization in the German Rhineland, 1815-1870, Madison 1966; R. Cameron, ed., Banking in the Early Stages of Industrialization, New York 1967; L. E. Davis, 'Capital Mobility and American Growth', in: R.W. Fogel and S.L. Engerman, eds., The Reinterpretation of American Economic History, New York 1971.

Joint-Stock Banks, Big Banks and the Concentration Movement up to the First World War

General Developments: W.F. Crick and J.E. Wadsworth, A Hundred Years of Joint Stock Banking, London 1935; J.H. Lenfant, 'Great Britain's Capital Formation 1864-1914', Economica, 18/1951; S.G. Thomas, The Rise and Growth of Joint Stock Banking, London 1934.

The Big Five in England: T.E. Gregory, The Westminster Bank through a Century, 2 vols., London 1936; P.W. Matthews, History of Barclays Bank Ltd., London 1926; R.S. Sayers, Lloyds Bank in the History of British Banking, Oxford 1957.

Crédit Mobilier Banks in France and Central Europe: R. Bigo, *Les banques françaises au cours du XIXe siècle*, Paris 1947; J. Bouvier, *Le Crédit Lyonnais de 1863 à 1882*, 2 vols., Paris 1961; B. Gille, *La banque en France au XIXe siècle*, Geneva 1970; H. Böhme, 'Preussische Bankpolitik, 1848-1853', in: H. Böhme, ed., *Probleme der Reichsgründungszeit*, Cologne 1968; W. Däbritz, *David Hansemann und Adolph von Hansemann*, Dusseldorf 1954; R.E. Lüke, *Die Berliner Handels-Gesellschaft in einem Jahrhundert deutscher Wirtschaft, 1856-1956*, Berlin 1956; M. Wolff, *Die Disconto-Gesellschaft*, Berlin 1930.

Major Banks in the United States: F.L. Allen, *The Great Pierpont Morgan*, New York 1930;, V.P. Carosso, *Investment Banking in America*, Cambridge (Mass.) 1970; G.F. Redmond, *Financial Giants of America*, 2 vols., Boston 1922; R. Sylla, 'The United States, 1863-1913', in: R. Cameron, ed., *Banking and Economic Development*, New York-London 1972; J.K. Winkler, *Morgan the Magnificent*, New York 1930.

The Japanese zaibatsu Banks: Fuji Bank, ed., *Banking in Modern Japan*, Tokyo ²1967; O.D. Russell, *The House of Mitsui*, New York 1939; K. Yamamura, 'The Founding of Mitsubishi', *Business History Review*, 41/1967; K. Yamamura, 'Japan, 1868-1930. A Revised View', in: R. Cameron, ed., *Banking and Economic Development*, New York-London 1972.

Agricultural Credit, Savings Banks and Credit Co-operatives: S. Rosenblum-Farzani, *Le Crédit Foncier*, Lausanne 1938; F. Hecht, *Die Organisation des Bodenkredits in Deutschland*, 2 vols., Leipzig 1901; H.O. Horne, *A History of Savings Banks*, London 1947; F. Lepelletier, *Les Caisses d'Epargne*, Paris 1911; H. Faust, *Geschichte der Genossenschaftsbewegung*, Frankfurt 1965.

Capital Export and Foreign Policy in the Age of Imperialism

Capital Exports of Indiviudal Countries: H. Feis, *Europe – the World's Banker, New York* ²1961; A.R. Hall, ed., *The Export of Capital from Britain, 1870-1914*, London 1968; L.H. Jenks, *The Migration of British Capital to 1875*, New York ³1963; J.F. Rippy, *British Investments in Latin America, 1822-1949*, Minneapolis 1959; R.E. Cameron, *France and the Economic Development of Europe, 1800-1914*, Princeton 1961; J.E. Favre, *Le capital français au service de l'étranger*, Paris 1917; F. Lenz, 'Wesen und Struktur des deutschen Kapitalexports vor 1914', *Weltwirtschaftliches Archiv*, 18/1922; J. Mai, *Das deutsche Kapital in Russland, 1850-1894*, Berlin 1974; A. Confalonieri, *Banca e Industria in Italia, 1894-1906*, 3 vols., Milan 1974ff.

The Baghdad Railway: H.S.W. Corrigan, *British, French and German Interests in Asiatic Turkey, 1881-1914*, London 1954; J.G. Williamson, *Karl Helfferich*, Princeton 1971.

Capital Exports and Foreign Policy: K.F. Helleiner, *The Imperial Loans*, Oxford 1965; A. H. Imlah, *Economic Elements in the Pax Britannica*, New

York [2]1969; D.C.M. Platt, *Trade and Politics in British Foreign Policy,
1815-1914*, Oxford 1968; R. Girault, *Emprunts russes et investissement
français en Russie, 1887-1914*, Paris 1973; R. Poidevin, *Les relations
économiques et financières entre la France et l'Allemagne, 1898-1914*, Paris
1969; F. Stern, *Gold and Iron. Bismarck, Bleichröder and the Building of
the German Empire*, New York 1977; P. Guillen, *L'Allemagne et le Maroc
de 1870 à 1905*, Paris 1967; J.G. Butler, *Life of McKinley*, Youngstown
(Ohio) 1924; H.F. Pringle, *The Life and Time of William H. Taft*, 2 vols.,
New York 1943; D.S. Landes, *Bankers and Pashas*, London 1958.

Banking Systems before the First World War: W. Bagehot, *Lombardstreet*,
London 1873; J. Clapham, *The Bank of England*, 2 vols., Cambridge [3]1966;
C.A.E. Goodhart, *The Business of Banking, 1880-1914*, London 1972; R.
Hawtrey, *A Century of Bank Rate*, London 1962; E. Nevin and E.W. Davis,
The London Clearing Banks, London 1970; R. Bigo, *Les banques françaises
au cours du XIXe siècle*, Paris 1947; J. Bouvier, *Un siècle de banque
française*, Paris 1973; B. Gille, *La banque en France au XIXe siècle*, Geneva
1970; C.A. Michalet, *Les placements des épargnants français de 1815 à
nos jours*, Paris 1968; E. Achterberg, *Kleine Hamburger Bankgeschichte*,
Hamburg 1964; E. Achterberg, *Der Bankplatz Frankfurt a.M.*, Frankfurt
1955; G.v. Schulze-Gävernitz, *Die deutsche Kreditbank*, Tübingen
1915; E. Rosenbaum, 'M.M. Warburg & Co., Merchant Bankers of Hamburg'.
Year-Book VII of the Leo Baeck Institute, London 1962; C. Adler,
Jacob H. Schiff, 2 vols., New York 1929; F.L. Allen, *The Great Pierpont
Morgan*, New York 1949; P. Cagan, 'The First Fifty Years of the National
Banking System', in: D. Carson, ed., *Banking and Monetary Studies*, Homewood 1963; R. Cameron, ed., *Banking and Economic Development*,
London-New York 1972; V.P. Carosso, *Investment Banking in America*,
Cambridge (Mass.) 1970; C.A.E. Goodhart, *The New York Money Market
and the Finance of Trade, 1900-1913*, Cambridge (Mass.) 1969; N.F.
Hoggson, *Epochs in American Banking*, New York 1929; F.C. James, *The
Growth of the Chicago Banks*, 2 vols., New York 1938; F. Redlich, *The
Molding of American Banking: Men and Ideas*, 2 vols., New York 1947ff.;
P. Studenski and H.E. Kroos, *Financial History of the United States*, New
York [2]1963; E.R. Taus, *Central Banking Functions of the United States
Treasury, 1789-1941*, New York 1943; P.B. Trescott, *Financing American
Enterprise: The Story of Commercial Banking*, New York 1963; Fuji Bank,
ed., *Banking in Modern Japan*, Tokyo [2]1967.

The First World War and its Consequences

Financing the War: A. J. Bloomfield, *Monetary Policy under the International Gold Standard, 1880-1914*, New York [2]1964; P. Einzig, *The History
of Foreign Exchange*, London 1962; T.J. Kiernan, *British War Finance and
the Consequences*, London 1920; E.V. Morgan, *Studies in British Financial
Policy, 1914-1925*, Cambridge 1952; E.L. Dulles, *The French Franc, 1914-
1918*, New York 1929; V.P. Carosso, *Investment Banking in America*,

Cambridge (Mass.) 1970; J.M. Clark, *The Cost of the World War to the American People*, New Haven 1931; C. Gilbert, *American Financing of World War I*, Westport (Conn.) 1970; K. Rössler, *Die Finanzpolitik des Deutschen Reiches im Ersten Weltkrieg*, Berlin 1967.

Inter-Allied Debts and Reparations: J.T. Gerould and L.S. Turnbull, *Selected Articles of Interallied Debts and Revision of the Debt Settlement*, New York 1928; A. Philips Jr., *Economic Aspects of Reparations and Interallied Debts*, The Hague 1930; C.M. Frasure, *The British Policy on War Debts and Reparations*, Philadelphia 1940; J.M. Keynes, *The Economic Consequences of the Peace*, London 1920; E. Wandel, *Die Bedeutung der Vereinigten Staaten von Amerika für das deutsche Reparationsproblem, 1924-1929*, Tübingen 1971; E. Weill-Raynal, *Les réparations allemandes et la France*, 3 vols., Paris 1947.

The Inflation in Germany and France: C. Bresciani-Turroni, *The Economics of Inflation*, London 1937; C.-L. Holtfrerich, *Die deutsche Inflation, 1914-1923*, Berlin 1980; K. Laursen and J. Pedersen, *The German Inflation, 1918-1923*, Amsterdam 1964; H.G. Moulton, *The French Debt Problem*, New York 1926; R. Philippe, *Le drame financier de 1924 à 1928*, Paris 1931.

International Financial Relations, 1918-1929: S.O. Clarke, *Central Bank Co-operation, 1924-1931*, New York 1967; P. Einzig, *World Finance Since 1914*, New York 1935; H. Feis, *The Diplomacy of the Dollar, 1919-1939*, Baltimore 1950; M.F. Jolliffe, *The United States as a Financial Centre, 1919-1933*, Cardiff 1935; R.H. Meyer, *Banker's Diplomacy*, New York 1970; H.G. Moulton and L. Pasvolsky, *War Debts and World Prosperity*, Washinton 1932; B.H. Williams, *Foreign Loan Policy of the United States*, New York 1938.

The Banking System after the First World War in Various Countries: H. Clay, *Lord Norman*, London 1957; A.T.K. Grant, *A Study of the Capital Market in Post-war Britain*, London 1937; E. Nevin and E.W. Davis, *The London Clearing Banks*, London 1970; J. Sykes, *The Amalgamation Movement in English Banking*, London 1926; S.E. Thomas, *British Banks and the Finance of Industry*, London 1930; R. J. Truptil, *British Banks and the London Money Market*, London 1936; J. Lescure, *L'épargne en France, 1914-1934*, Paris [3]1936; M. Myers, *Paris as a Financial Center*, New York 1936; Deutsche Bundesbank, ed., *Deutsches Geld- und Bankwesen 1876-1975 in Zahlen*, Frankfurt 1976; K. Gossweiler, *Grossbanken, Industriemonopole, Staat*, Berlin 1971; Fuji Bank, ed., *Banking in Modern Japan*, Tokyo 1967; V.P. Carosso, *Investment Banking in America*, Cambridge (Mass.) 1970; L. Corey, *The House of Morgan*, New York 1930; J.S. Lawrence, *Banking concentration in the United States*, New York 1930; R. Sobel, *The Great Bull Market, Wall Street in the 1920s*, New York 1968; W.H. Steiner, *Investment Trusts: American Experience*, New York 1929.

Money and Credit during the 1930s and 1940s

The Banking Crises: C. Kindleberger, *The World in Depression*, London 1973; M. Nadler and J.J. Bogen, *The Banking Crisis*, New York 1933; F. Pecora, *Wall Street under Oath*, New York 1939; M.N. Rothbard, *America's Great Depression*, Princeton 1963; E.J. Bennett, *Germany and the Diplomacy of the Financial Crisis*, Cambridge 1962; K.E. Born, *Die deutsche Bankenkrise 1931*, München 1967; G. Helbich, *Die Reparationen in der Ära Brüning*, Berlin 1962; C.L. Mowat, *Britain between the Wars*, London 1956; A.E. Kahn, *Britain in the World Economy*, London-New York 1946; W.A. Morton, *British Finance*, 1930-1940, Madison 1943; E. Nevin, *The Mechanism of Cheap Money*, 1931-1939, Cardiff 1955; M. Perrot, *La monnaie et l'opinion en France et en Angleterre, 1926-1936*, Paris 1955; A. Sauvy, *Histoire économique de la France entre les deux guerres*, 2 vols., Paris 1965ff.

Devaluation of Currencies: H. Clay, *Lord Norman*, London 1957; A. Feavearyear, *The Pound Sterling*, Oxford ²1963; M. Friedman and A.J. Schwartz, *A Monetary History of the United States, 1867-1960*, New York 1963; A.J. Schwartz, *1933: Roosevelt's Decision. The United States Leaves the Gold Standard*, New York 1969; R. Sédillot, *Le franc*, Paris 1953.

Financing the Second World War: R.S. Sayers, 'Financial Policy, 1939-1945', in: *History of the Second World War*, (United Kingdom Civil Series) London 1956; W.H. McNeill, *America, Britain and Russia: Their Co-operation and Conflict, 1941-1946*, Oxford 1953; G.T. White, 'Financing Industrial Expansion for War', *Journal of Economic History*, 9/1949; A. Milward, *The German Economy at War*, London 1965; H. Schacht, *76 Jahre meines Lebens*, Bad Wörishofen 1953; A. Speer, *Inside the Third Reich*, London 1970; R. Sédillot, *Le franc enchaîné*, Paris 1945.

Money and Banking after the Second World War

The International Currency System: J.H. Adler, *Capital Movement and Economic Development*, London 1967; H. Aufricht, *The International Monetary Fund*, Washington 1964; G. Bell, *The Euro-Dollar Market and the International Financial System*, New York 1973; C. Coombes, *The Arena of International Finance*, New York 1976; P. Einzig, *Foreign Dollar Loans in Europe*, New York 1965; G.N. Halm, ed., *International Monetary Cooperation*, Chapel Hill 1945; R. Harrod, *The Life of John Maynard Keynes*, London 1951; J.M. Keynes, *Collected Works*, Vol. 25, London 1980; E.S. Mason and R.E. Asher, *The World Bank since Bretton Woods*, Washington 1973; J. Morris, *The World Bank*, London 1963; R.W. Oliver, *International Economic Co-operation and the World Bank*, London 1975; R.S. Sayers, *Modern Banking*, Oxford 1964; R.S. Sayers, *Banking in Western Europe*, Oxford 1962.

National Currency Systems: R. Hawtrey, *The Pound at Home and Abroad*, London 1961; S. Strange, *Sterling and British Policy*, London 1971; J.M. Jeanneney, *Forces et faiblesses de l'économie française, 1945-1959*, Paris 1959; E. Wandel, *Die Entstehung der Bank deutscher Länder und die deutsche Währungsreform 1948*, Frankfurt 1981; M. Friedman and A.J. Schwartz, *A Monetary History of the United States, 1867-1960*, Princeton 1963; N.H. Jacoby, ed., *United States Monetary Policy*, London-New York 1964.

National Banking Systems: E. Nevin and E.W. Davis, *The London Clearing Banks*, London 1970; J. Revell, *Changes in British Banking*, London 1968; P.C. Dupont, *Le contrôle des banques et la direction du crédit en France*, Paris 1952; E. Brehmer, *Struktur und Funktionsweise des Geldmarktes der Bundesrepublik Deutschland seit 1948*, Tübingen ²1964; R. Fry, *A Banker's World*, London 1970; D. Horowitz and P. Colliers, *The Rockefellers*, New York 1975; J.R. Longstreet et al., *Investment Banking and the New Issues Market*, Cleveland 1967; M. Mayer, *The Bankers*, New York 1976; M.S. Mendelsohn, *Money on the Move*, New York 1980; A. Sampson, *The Money Lenders*, London 1981; Federation of Bankers Association of Japan, ed., *Banking System in Japan*, Tokyo 1972; L.S. Pressnell, *Money and Banking in Japan*, London 1973.

Index of Banks

Akzept- und Garantiebank, Berlin (1931-1936), 265
Alexander & Co., London (f. 1810; since 1911: Alexanders Discount Co. Ltd.), 69
Algemeene Bank Nederland, Amsterdam (f. 1964 through merger of De Twentsche Bank and the Nederlandsche Handel Maatschappij), 308
Allgemeine Deutsche Credit-Anstalt, Leipzig (ADCA; f. 1856), 86f., 91, 171
Allgemeine Österreichische Boden-Credit-Anstalt, Vienna (f. 1864; merged with Österreichische Creditanstalt in 1929), 130
Allgemeine Versorgungsanstalt, Hamburg (1778-1811/23), 107
American Foreign Securities Co., New York (f. 1915), 202
Amsterdam-Rotterdam Bank, Amsterdam and Rotterdam (f. 1964 through merger of the Amsterdamsche Bank and the Rotterdamsche Bank), 308
Amsterdamsche Wisselbank (1609-1819/20), 27
André & Cottier, Paris (f. 1800; 1843-1896: Marcuard & Cie.: since 1896 de Neuflize & Cie.; later de Neuflize, Schlumberger & Cie.; since 1966 de Neuflize, Schlumberger, Mal-

let & Cie), 51, 82, 121, 123, 167
Anglo-Egyptian Bank, London and Alexandria (f. 1862; from 1925 Barclays Bank [Dominion, Colonial, Overseas] after merger with National Bank of South Africa and Colonial Bank), 127, 137
Anglo-Österreichische Bank, Vienna (f. 1863; renamed Anglo-Austrian Bank in 1922; merged with British Trade Corporation in 1926 to become Anglo-International Bank), 125

Badische Bank, Karlsruhe (f. 1870), 13f.
Baguenault & Co., Paris, 37
Banca Commerciale Italiana, Milan (f. 1894), 125, 142
Banca di Genova (f. 1870; 1895: transformed into Credito Italiano), 125
Banca Generala Romana, Bucharest (1897-1948), 129
Banca Nazionale del Lavoro, Rome (f. 1913 as Istituto Nazionale di Credito per la Cooperazione; since 1929 under its present name), 308
Banco di Roma, Rome (f. 1880), 308
Banco di San Giorgio, Genoa (1408-1797), 27

Index of Names

Abbas I. (1848-1854), Governor of Egypt, 136

Abd el Krim (1880-1963), Leader of the Rif-Kabyles, 223, 225

Abdul Hamid II (1842-1918), Sultan (1876-1909), 138, 140f., 156

Aehrenthal, Baron Alois (1854-1912), Austrian diplomat, 157

Aldrich, Nelson W. (1841-1915), U.S. Senator, 18

Alexander I (1777-1825), Russian Tsar (1801-1825), 38

André, David (?-1709), French merchant, 22

—, Dominique (1766-1844), French banker, 22f., 60

Anne (1664-1714), Queen of England (1702-1714), 21

Arabi Pasha, Achmed (1839-1911), Egyptian politician, 138, 148

Asquith, Herbert Henry (1852-1928), British politician, 194

Auriol, Vincent (b. 1884), French politician, 238

Baker, George F. (1840-1931), President of the First National Bank of New York, 98, 177, 181

—. -jr. (1874-1937), American banker, 272

Baldwin, Stanley, Earl of Bewdley (1867-1947), British politician, 205, 281

Balfour, Arthur James, Earl of (1848-1930), British politician, 143, 151, 105f.

Ballin, Albert (1857-1918), Director of HAPAG, 158

Bamberger, Ludwig (1823-1899), banker and Liberal German politician, 4, 13f., 88

Baring, Alexander, First Lord Ashburton (1774-1848), partner in Baring Brothers & Co., 39

Baring, Edward Charles, 1. Lord Revelstoke (1828-1897), English banker, 118

—, Evelyn, I. Earl of Cromer (1841-1917), British Consul General in Cairo, 32

—, Sir Francis (1740-1810), British merchant and banker, 21

—, Francis Thornhill, I. Lord Northbrooke (1796-1866), British politician, 32

—, Johann (d. 1748), German-English merchant, 21

—, John (1730-1816), British merchant and banker, 21

—, Thomas jr. (1800-1873), partner in Baring Brothers & Co., 7f.

—, Thomas George, Second Lord Northbrooke (1826-1904), British politician, 32

Barrère, Camille (1851-1940), French Ambassador to Rome, 147, 156